Prais

MACHINE | PLATFORM | CROWD

"Such is the speed of development in these emergent technologies that it is refreshing to take a step back and a look at some of the ways in which our lives and careers are changing—and will continue to change—at a fundamental level. Happily this volume by Andrew McAfee and Erik Brynjolfsson offers exactly this opportunity, using their deep knowledge of the business and technology sectors to build a detailed, cogent and conversational guide to where we are and where we are going. The story is warmly and richly told, using footnotes approaching a third of a page in length when things get really exciting, and amply supported by notes, references and links. This book is in many senses a primer, a thorough grounding for the digital warrior in the driving forces of the 21st-century economy."

—*Times Higher Education*

"Even Silicon Valley is surprised by the speed and scope of change today. The best way to stay on top of it is to understand the principles that will endure even as so much gets disrupted. This book is the best explanation of those principles out there."

—Eric Schmidt, former CEO of Google and former executive chairman of Alphabet Inc.

"The digital revolution we're entering can be unsettling, but McAfee and Brynjolfsson show how these incredibly powerful technologies will make our choices more important than ever. *Machine | Platform | Crowd* is a road map for leaders to make wise choices as they navigate this new world." —Arianna Huffington, former president and editor-in-chief of the Huffington Post Media Group, author of *Thrive* and *The Sleep Revolution*

"On their own, AI, platforms, and crowds are all transformative forces. That they're evolving in parallel means we're beginning to experience a new era of networked disruption, where productive but disorienting change becomes the status quo. For citizens, entrepreneurs, companies, and governments who want to successfully navigate this new world, the first step lies in finding reliable and prescient guides. Andrew and Erik are two of the best."

—Reid Hoffman, partner at Greylock Partners, cofounder of LinkedIn, and coauthor of the *New York Times* bestsellers *The Start-Up of You* and *The Alliance*

"The authors aptly illustrate how the extraordinary progress of technology is reshaping our lives, and they share powerful ideas relevant to world leaders. Nobody knows exactly how this future will unfold. What we do know is that the disruptive power of technology must be seized as an opportunity to design our future. The book compels us to ponder: Will we apply technology to help accelerate development, improve living standards, and foster inclusive growth? Will we take advantage of its power to cut red tape, invest in education, unleash entrepreneurial energy, and create new kinds of jobs? The book is a must-read for policymakers who seek a road map for how to combine the strengths of humanity and technology to build a better future for their citizens." —Christine Lagarde, managing director of the International Monetary Fund

"The authors explain the whys and hows soberly, answering just about every question on AI you could ask: which channels it will colonise next, whether we'll still need physical products in a virtual world and how Bitcoin will change commerce, among others. Throughout, they are eloquent and informed. They don't think humans will be obsolete, but they also don't pretend the solutions are simple."

—*People Management*

"Written . . . with real human intelligence, concern, feeling, and values. [*Machine | Platform | Crowd*] is a big, intense, always interesting, and almost intimidating book—and well worth the effort."
—Dylan Schleicher, 800-CEO-READ

"[McAfee and Brynjolfsson] have done us all a great service in explaining some of the powerful trends that will shape our future."
—Mark Cliffe, chief economist of the ING Group

"McAfee and Brynjolfsson are thoughtful observers of the emerging technological revolution which they described in their earlier *The Second Machine Age*. . . . They write clearly and are at their most devastating in analyzing how the various elements of the new age combine, wiping out large sectors of media, retail and music industries as they have gone."
—Roger Smith, *New Law Journal*

Also by Andrew McAfee and Erik Brynjolfsson

The Second Machine Age:
Work, Progress, and Prosperity in a Time of Brilliant Technologies

Race against the Machine:
How the Digital Revolution Is Accelerating Innovation,
Driving Productivity, and Irreversibly Transforming
Employment and the Economy

Also by Erik Brynjolfsson

Wired for Innovation

Also by Andrew McAfee

Enterprise 2.0: New Collaborative Tools for Your
Organization's Toughest Challenges

MACHINE

PLATFORM

CROWD

Harnessing Our Digital Future

Andrew McAfee & Erik Brynjolfsson

W. W. NORTON & COMPANY

Independent Publishers Since 1923

New York | London

For information about permission to reproduce selections from this book,
write to Permissions, W. W. Norton & Company, Inc., 500 Fifth Avenue,
New York, NY 10110

For information about special discounts for bulk purchases, please contact
W. W. Norton Special Sales at specialsales@wwnorton.com or 800-233-4830

Manufacturing by LSC Communications Harrisonburg
Book design by Lovedog Studio
Production manager: Julia Druskin

Library of Congress Cataloging-in-Publication Data

Names: McAfee, Andrew, author. | Brynjolfsson, Erik, author.
Title: Machine, platform, crowd : harnessing our digital future / Andrew
McAfee & Erik Brynjolfsson.
Description: First edition. | New York : W. W. Norton & Company, [2017] |
Includes bibliographical references and index.
Identifiers: LCCN 2017016682 | ISBN 9780393254297 (hardcover)
Subjects: LCSH: Information technology—Economic aspects. | Information
technology—Social aspects. | Economic development—Technological
innovations.
Classification: LCC HC79.I55 M3668 2017 | DDC 303.48/33—dc23
LC record available at https://lccn.loc.gov/2017016682

ISBN 978-0-393-35606-9 pbk.

W. W. Norton & Company, Inc.,
500 Fifth Avenue, New York, N.Y. 10110
www.wwnorton.com

W. W. Norton & Company Ltd.,
15 Carlisle Street, London W1D 3BS

1 2 3 4 5 6 7 8 9 0

To the McAfees of Bethesda, Maryland:
David, Shannon, Amelia, Aurora, and Avery Mae.
Thanks for letting me keep some of my money
some of the time at the poker table.

— *Andy*

To my mother, Marguerite,
whose smiles, love, and unshakable faith keep me going.

— *Erik*

CONTENTS

Part 1
MIND AND MACHINE

Part 2
PRODUCT AND PLATFORM

Part 3
CORE AND CROWD

MACHINE | PLATFORM | CROWD

CHAPTER 1

THE TRIPLE REVOLUTION

These parallels are close and striking enough to make it almost certain that, as in the earlier industrial revolutions, the main effects of the information revolution on the next society still lie ahead.

— *Peter Drucker, 2001*

Computers on the Go (Board)

Learning to play Go well has always been difficult for humans, but programming computers to play it well has seemed nearly impossible.

Go is a pure strategy game—no luck involved*—developed at least 2,500 years ago in China. One player uses white stones; the other, black. They take turns placing stones on the intersections of a 19×19 grid. If a stone or group of stones has all of its freedoms removed—if it's completely surrounded by opposing stones, essentially—it's "captured" and taken off the board. At the end of the game† the player with more captured territory wins.

People who love strategy love Go. Confucius advised that "gentlemen should not waste their time on trivial games—they should study Go." In many quarters, it's held in higher regard even than chess,

---

* A game theorist would call Go a "deterministic perfect information game."

† The game ends when both players agree that they can no longer make beneficial moves.

another difficult two-person, luck-free strategy game. As the chess grand master Edward Lasker says, "While the Baroque rules of chess could only have been created by humans, the rules of Go are so elegant, organic, and rigorously logical that if intelligent life forms exist elsewhere in the universe, they almost certainly play Go."

The game's apparent simplicity belies a complexity that's difficult to even conceptualize. Because of the large board and the great freedom that players have in placing their stones, it is estimated that there are about 2×10^{170} (that is, 2 followed by 170 zeros) possible positions on a standard Go board. How big is this number? It's larger than the number of atoms in the observable universe. In fact, that's a completely inadequate benchmark. The observable universe contains about 10^{82} atoms. So, if every atom in the universe were itself an entire universe full of atoms, there would still be more possible Go games than atoms.

The Game Nobody Can Explain

How do the top human Go players navigate this absurd complexity and make smart moves? Nobody knows—not even the players themselves.

Go players learn a group of heuristics and tend to follow them.* Beyond these rules of thumb, however, top players are often at a loss to explain their own strategies. As Michael Redmond, one of few Westerners to reach the game's highest rank, explains, "I'll see a move and be sure it's the right one, but won't be able to tell you exactly how I know. I just see it."

It's not that Go players are an unusually tongue-tied lot. It turns out the rest of us can't access all of our own knowledge either. When we recognize a face or ride a bike, on reflection we can't fully explain

---

* Many Go heuristics are somewhat vague—for example, "Don't use thickness to make territory."

how or why we're doing what we're doing. It is hard to make such tacit knowledge explicit—a state of affairs beautifully summarized by the twentieth-century Hungarian-British polymath Michael Polanyi's observation "We know more than we can tell."

"Polanyi's Paradox," as it came to be called, presented serious obstacles to anyone attempting to build a Go-playing computer. How do you write a program that includes the best strategies for playing the game when no human can articulate these strategies? It's possible to program at least some of the heuristics, but doing so won't lead to a victory over good players, who are able to go beyond rules of thumb in a way that even they can't explain.

Programmers often rely on simulations to help navigate complex environments like all the possible universes of Go games. They write programs that make a move that looks good, then explore all the opponent's plausible responses to that move, all the plausible responses to each response, and so on. The move that's eventually chosen is essentially the one that has the most good futures ahead of it, and the fewest bad ones. But because there are so many potential Go games—so many universes full of them—it's not possible to simulate more than an unhelpfully tiny fraction of them, even with a hangar full of supercomputers.

With critical knowledge unavailable and simulation ineffective, Go programmers made slow progress. Surveying the current state and likely trajectory of computer Go in a May 2014 article in *Wired* magazine, philosophy professor Alan Levinovitz concluded that "another ten years until a computer Go champion may prove too optimistic." A December 2015 *Wall Street Journal* article by Chris Chabris, a professor of psychology and the newspaper's game columnist, was titled "Why Go Still Foils the Computers."

Past Polanyi's Paradox
A scientific paper published the very next month—January 2016— unveiled a Go-playing computer that wasn't being foiled anymore.

A team at Google DeepMind, a London-based company special-izing in machine learning (a branch of artificial intelligence we'll discuss more in Chapter 3), published "Mastering the Game of Go with Deep Neural Networks and Tree Search," and the presti-gious journal *Nature* made it the cover story. The article described AlphaGo, a Go-playing application that had found a way around Polanyi's Paradox.

The humans who built AlphaGo didn't try to program it with superior Go strategies and heuristics. Instead, they created a system that could learn them on its own. It did this by studying lots of board positions in lots of games. AlphaGo was built to discern the subtle patterns present in large amounts of data, and to link actions (like playing a stone in a particular spot on the board) to outcomes (like winning a game of Go).*

The software was given access to 30 million board positions from an online repository of games and essentially told, "Use these to figure out how to win." AlphaGo also played many games against itself, generating another 30 million positions, which it then ana-lyzed. The system did conduct simulations during games, but only highly focused ones; it used the learning accumulated from studying millions of positions to simulate only those moves it thought most likely to lead to victory.

Work on AlphaGo began in 2014. By October of 2015, it was ready for a test. In secret, AlphaGo played a five-game match against Fan Hui, who was then the European Go champion. The machine won 5–0.

---

* Throughout this book we'll characterize technologies as doing humanlike things such as discerning, learning, seeing, and so on. We do this because we believe it's the right way to convey what's going on, even though it's true that computers don't rea-son like people do. We realize this convention is unpopular in some quarters; the old admonition is "Don't anthropomorphize computers—they hate it."

A computer Go victory at this level of competition was completely unanticipated and shook the artificial intelligence community. Virtually all analysts and commentators called AlphaGo's achievement a breakthrough. Debates did spring up, however, about its magnitude. As the neuroscientist Gary Marcus pointed out, "Go is scarcely a sport in Europe; and the champion in question is ranked only #633 in the world. A robot that beat the 633rd-ranked tennis pro would be impressive, but it still wouldn't be fair to say that it had 'mastered' the game."

The DeepMind team evidently thought this was a fair point, because they challenged Lee Sedol to a five-game match to be played in Seoul, South Korea, in March of 2016. Sedol was regarded by many as the best human Go player on the planet,* and one of the best in living memory. His style was described as "intuitive, unpredictable, creative, intensive, wild, complicated, deep, quick, chaotic"— characteristics that he felt would give him a definitive advantage over any computer. As he put it, "There is a beauty to the game of Go and I don't think machines understand that beauty. . . . I believe human intuition is too advanced for AI to have caught up yet." He predicted he would win at least four games out of five, saying, "Looking at the match in October, I think (AlphaGo's) level doesn't match mine."

The games between Sedol and AlphaGo attracted intense interest throughout Korea and other East Asian countries. AlphaGo won the first three games, ensuring itself of victory overall in the best-of-five match. Sedol came back to win the fourth game. His victory gave some observers hope that human cleverness had discerned flaws in a digital opponent, ones that Sedol could continue to exploit. If so, they

---

* By August of 2016, the thirty-three-year-old Sedol had already collected eighteen international titles, second only to the twenty-one held by his countryman Lee Chang-ho, who was more than eight years older.

were not big enough to make a difference in the next game. AlphaGo won again, completing a convincing 4–1 victory in the match.

Sedol found the competition grueling, and after his defeat he said, "I kind of felt powerless. . . . I do have extensive experience in terms of playing the game of Go, but there was never a case as this as such that I felt this amount of pressure."

Something new had passed Go.

What Happened to the Assets?

In March of 2015, strategist Tom Goodwin pointed out a pattern. "Uber, the world's largest taxi company, owns no vehicles," he wrote. "Facebook, the world's most popular media owner, creates no content. Alibaba, the most valuable retailer, has no inventory. And Airbnb, the world's largest accommodation provider, owns no real estate."

A skeptical reader might respond that some of these developments were less revolutionary than they at first appeared. Many companies in the taxi industry, for example, don't themselves own cars. They instead own medallions that confer the right to operate a taxi in a city, and they rent the medallions to vehicle owners and drivers. Similarly, many of the largest hotel companies don't actually own all the properties that bear their names, opting instead to sign licensing or management agreements with real estate holders.

But in all of these cases, the companies in question held long-lived assets, like licenses and contracts, that are important to the industry and thus valuable. Uber and Airbnb have none of these. Uber has no claim on any vehicle or medallion in any city in the world, and Airbnb has no long-term contract with any lodging owners anywhere. Yet both companies quickly reached millions of customers and billions in valuation, making the success that Goodwin observed all the more remarkable. At the time of his column, over a million people each day "took an Uber" to get somewhere in one of 300 cities in 60 countries, and Airbnb offered 640,000 different lodging options in 191 countries, ranging from a yurt in Mongolia to James Joyce's childhood home in Ireland.

China's Alibaba brought an asset-light approach to retailing, an industry where large reach had historically meant ownership of a great many things. Walmart, for example, owned by the end of 2016 more than 150 distribution centers and a private fleet of 6,000 trucks that drove 700 million annual miles to get products on the shelves of 4,500 shops across the United States. By October 31 of that year, the company's balance sheet included $180 billion of property and equipment assets. Yet on the same day, Walmart's total market value was less than that of Alibaba, which enabled sales of over half a trillion dollars in 2016.

Alibaba, founded in 1999 by former schoolteacher Jack Ma and seventeen colleagues, acted as an online middleman connecting buyers and sellers. Its most popular sites were the Taobao Marketplace, where individuals and small businesses sold goods to consumers, and Tmall, where larger companies did the same. By the end of 2016, the number of Chinese people using Alibaba's apps every month was greater than the entire US population.

In 2009, Tmall began promoting "Singles Day" in China. This was originally a celebration, apparently begun in the mid-1990s at Nanjing University, of not being in a relationship. It was held on the eleventh day of the eleventh month because that's the date with the maximum number of ones, or "bare sticks" that symbolize being alone. Tmall's "Singles Day" effort started out with just twenty-seven participating merchants, but it quickly became the most important shopping event in the country, with participants buying presents not only for their single selves, but also for people they're interested in.

On November 11, 2016, Alibaba's marketplaces enabled sales of $17.8 billion, three times the combined total of Black Friday and Cyber Monday in the United States.*

Of the four companies mentioned by Goodwin, though, Facebook might have the most extraordinary story. From its start in Mark Zuckerberg's Harvard dorm room eleven years earlier, it had grown from a social networking site at a few elite US universities into a global utility of communication, connection, and content, visited daily by 936 million people. As Goodwin pointed out, Facebook drew all these people in and kept them engaged for an average of fifty minutes per day without generating any of the information that appeared on the site. Its members' status updates, opinions, photos, videos, pointers, and other contributions were presented to other visitors in an ever-increasing flood that kept people coming back.

As it presented all this content to its users, Facebook also showed them ads, and eventually a lot of them. Facebook's revenues in the second quarter of 2016, virtually all of which came from advertising, were $6.4 billion. Profits were $2 billion.

News organizations and others online that develop their content the old-fashioned way—by spending money on salaries, travel, and so on—were alarmed not only because Facebook's costs were lower, but because in the eyes of advertisers, its quality was higher in important ways. The social networking giant knew so much about its members (they were, after all, telling the site a great deal about themselves with the information they provided and the contributions they made) that it could often target ads more precisely to them.

Every advertiser is haunted by some version of the rueful remark often attributed to the American department store pioneer John

---

* Black Friday (the day after Thanksgiving) is historically the busiest in-person shopping day of the year in the United States. Cyber Monday, three days later, is the day when many online merchants offer holiday deals to their customers.

Wanamaker: "Half the money I spend on advertising is wasted. The trouble is I don't know which half." Advertising has always been a hugely inexact science, in large part, it is commonly believed, because it can't be targeted to just the people most likely to respond. Facebook offered many advertisers a level of specificity in targeting that no mainstream media site could match, and it could do it continuously, globally, and at scale.

A Thin Layer, Spreading Quickly

Goodwin described the companies he was talking about as an "indescribably thin layer" and said "there is no better business to be in." Because they're so thin—because they own mainly applications and code and not physical assets and infrastructure—they could grow rapidly. Airbnb, for example, doubled the number of nights booked through the site in the twelve months after Goodwin's article appeared, and it became so popular that the governments of cities including Paris, Barcelona, Lisbon, Berlin, and San Francisco began to worry that it was negatively affecting the character of historic residential neighborhoods. The company's growth was so fast and so contentious that in July of 2016, technology writer Tom Slee blogged on *Harvard Business Review*'s site that "Airbnb is facing an existential expansion problem" as more cities and regions fought against its expansion.

Uber also continued experiencing both rapid growth and frequent controversies, and testing out new offerings. Its UberPool carpooling service, introduced in 2014, quickly proved popular in many cities, including New York. In May of 2016 the company announced that all weekly rush-hour UberPool rides in Manhattan below 125th Street would cost a flat $5, and in July of that year a special offer allowed New Yorkers to buy four weeks' worth of such rides for $79. At this price, the service would be cheaper than the subway for many commuters.

And Facebook, already a huge and profitable company when Goodwin wrote about it in March of 2015, continued to grow in size and influence, to greatly affect mainstream content producers, and to make sizable investments in innovation. In August of 2015 the web traffic analysis company Parse.ly released a report showing that across the major news and media sites it tracked, more viewers came via Facebook than from Google and other search engines. In March of 2016, Mark Zuckerberg unveiled the company's ten-year road map, which included major initiatives in artificial intelligence, virtual reality and augmented reality, and even solar-powered airplanes to bring Internet access to millions of people who live far from any telecommunications infrastructure.

How could companies that consisted of only an "indescribably thin layer" be having such an impact, and such success?

As Goodwin observed, "Something interesting is happening."

A Giant Reaches Out

By any standard, General Electric is one of the most successful US companies. Tracing its roots back to the iconic inventor Thomas Edison and his Edison Electric Light Company, GE was selected in 1896 as one of the twelve companies to be listed on the original Dow Jones Industrial Average. It's the only one of the group that remains on the index today. It has entered (and sometimes left) many industrial businesses, including power generation, aerospace and defense, plastics, health care, and finance, but throughout its long history, GE has always also developed products for consumers, from Edison's electric lamps to radios and TVs to household appliances.

GE also pioneered and excelled at running a large, diversified, global corporation. It invested heavily in research and development, often in partnership with universities. It was also one of the first large companies to devote substantial time and effort to advancing not only its technologies, but also the skills of its managers. The first dedicated corporate university was established by GE in 1956 in Crotonville, New York, a place name that has become synonymous with the professionalization of the practice of management.

The twenty-first century saw a major initiative in Crotonville, and throughout the company, to deepen capabilities in marketing, defined as understanding and then satisfying customers' needs across all lines of business. A 2013 review of GE's efforts in this area found that the company's most sought-after capability was to "create marketing innovation internally."

Then why did General Electric, a company that has an annual budget of $5.2 billion for R&D and that spends $393 million on marketing in the United States alone, opt in 2015 to work with a group of strangers across the Internet to help the company think up and design a new consumer product? And why was a company with a market cap of $280 billion and $90 billion cash on hand asking potential customers to commit to a several-hundred-dollar preorder well in advance of the product's availability?

Nuggets of Wisdom about Nuggets of Ice

In 2014, GE and the University of Louisville had launched a joint initiative called FirstBuild, a "co-creation community that is changing the way products come to market." It consisted of both an online presence and a "microfactory" equipped with the tools and materials needed to prototype products.

Alan Mitchell, an advanced development engineer at GE Appliances in Louisville, decided to use FirstBuild as a test-bed. He wondered whether it would be possible to more easily satisfy the craving many people have for . . . a particular kind of ice.

Most ice cubes are just frozen blocks of water of various sizes and shapes. Nugget ice is something different. Its small, barrel-shaped chunks are porous and only semifrozen. These qualities allow the ice to absorb flavors well and make it easier to chew, which is apparently what some people want—very much. A 2008 *Wall Street Journal* story by Ilan Brat had found that "munchable ice sells like hotcakes." The Sonic fast-food chain, which used nugget ice in its drinks, found that many of its customers just wanted the ice. So the company started selling the chilled nuggets in everything from cups to 10-pound bags.

Because making nugget ice is more complex than simply freezing water,[*] the machines that produce it cost several thousand dollars—too expensive for most households.[†] Mitchell wanted to see whether the FirstBuild community could design and prototype a viable nugget ice maker for the home, and an online competition was launched in 2015.

The winner was Ismael Ramos, a designer from Guadalajara, Mexico, whose "Stone Cold" design entry envisioned a cubical machine well suited to kitchen countertops, with a removable clear-plastic ice bucket. Ramos was awarded $2,000 and one of the first working versions of his brainchild. (Two runners-up in the contest were also awarded cash prizes and ice makers.)

People at the FirstBuild microfactory began making and refining prototypes of the nugget maker. All along, they interacted frequently with the online community that had formed around the project, asking questions about how the removable ice bucket should look, how

[*] To make the chewable nuggets, ice must be shaved off a surface while it's still being formed, then encouraged into chunks of the right size and shape.

[†] Some more affluent households indulged their passion for nugget ice (Ilan Brat, "Chew This Over: Munchable Ice Sells like Hot Cakes," *Wall Street Journal*, January 30, 2008). Amy Grant gave her husband, country music star Vince Gill, a restaurant-grade Scotsman ice machine for Christmas one year.

to sense when it was full, whether the machine should include an ice scoop, and so on.

If You Like It, Buy It—
Even Though It Doesn't Exist Yet

While this work was going on, GE also engaged in a newly available and nontraditional combination of marketing and market research. In July of 2015 it launched an Indiegogo campaign for the ice maker, which it had named the Opal. Indiegogo is an online "crowdfunding" community; it describes itself as a "launchpad for creative and entrepreneurial ideas of every shape and size." People providing financial support to these ideas are not investors; they do not receive an ownership stake or share of revenues or profits in exchange for their money. Very often, though, supporters are promised rewards. If they back a film, for example, they could be invited to an early screening, and if they support a product, they could be among the first to receive it. In essence, they preorder a product that doesn't exist yet, and might never exist without their votes of confidence.

Indiegogo was originally intended as a site for people and small companies without access to the financing required to realize their visions, but by mid-2015 large companies were using the site to test demand for potential products. With their campaign for the Opal, GE and FirstBuild asked people to contribute $399 (later increased to $499) and set a goal of raising $150,000. Within a few hours the campaign raised more than twice that, and within a week it attracted in excess of $1.3 million. By the time it closed in late August of 2015, the Opal campaign had attracted more than $2.7 million on Indiegogo, making it one of the site's ten most popular campaigns. The finished product was shipped to more than 5,000 preorder customers across the last three months of 2016 before going on sale to the general public. GE didn't need the money from the preorders, but it desperately wanted the market intelligence.

GE had found a new way to tap into the many minds that weren't on its payroll, as well as a market for its ice machine.

Machine | Platform | Crowd

The three examples we've just described—AlphaGo's triumph over the best human Go players, the success of new companies like Facebook and Airbnb that have none of the traditional assets of their industries, and GE's use of an online crowd to help it design and market a product that was well within its expertise—illustrate three great trends that are reshaping the business world.

The first trend consists of the rapidly increasing and expanding capabilities of *machines*, as exemplified by AlphaGo's unexpected emergence as the world's best Go player.

The second is captured by Goodwin's observations about the recent appearance of large and influential young companies that bear little resemblance to the established incumbents in their industries, yet are deeply disrupting them. These upstarts are *platforms*, and they are fearsome competitors.

The third trend, epitomized by GE's unconventional development process for its Opal ice maker, is the emergence of the *crowd*, our term for the startlingly large amount of human knowledge, expertise, and enthusiasm distributed all over the world and now available, and able to be focused, online.

From the rise of billion-dollar, Silicon Valley unicorns to the demise or transformation of Fortune 500 stalwarts, the turbulence and transformation in the economy can seem chaotic and random. But the three lenses of machine, platform, and crowd are based on sound principles of economics and other disciplines. The application of these principles isn't always easy, but with the right lenses, chaos gives way to order, and complexity becomes simpler. Our goal in this book is to provide these lenses.

The Work Ahead: Three Rebalancings

In all companies and industries, machine, platform, and crowd have counterparts. For machine intelligence, the counterpart is the human *mind*. Accountants with spreadsheets, engineers with computer-aided design software, and assembly line workers next to robots are all examples of mind-and-machine combinations.

The counterparts of platforms are *products*—in other words, goods and services. A ride across town is a product, while Uber is the platform people use to access it. The same is true with accommodations and Airbnb, or news stories and Facebook.

For the crowd, the counterpart is the *core*: the knowledge, processes, expertise, and capabilities that companies have built up internally and across their supply chains. The core of GE Appliances designs, manufactures, and markets refrigerators and ovens; NASA's core builds spaceships and tries to better understand our universe; Microsoft's core capabilities include developing personal computer operating systems and applications.

We're not going to tell you that minds, products, and the core are obsolete, or headed that way. Such a claim would be absurd. As we'll show repeatedly, human abilities, excellent goods and services, and strong organizational capabilities remain essential to business success.

We *will* try to convince you that because of recent technological changes, companies need to rethink the balance between minds and machines, between products and platforms, and between the core and the crowd. The second element in each pair has become much more capable and more powerful just within the past few years, so it needs to be considered with fresh eyes. Understanding when, where, how, and why these machines, platforms, and crowds can be effective is the key to success in the economy today. Our goal with this book is to help you with this important work. We'll try to convince you, in fact, that it's more than just important; it's essential.

Why Now?

We documented fast technological progress and discussed some of its economic consequences in our previous book *The Second Machine Age: Work, Progress, and Prosperity in a Time of Brilliant Technologies.* Since its publication, one of the most common questions we've been asked about it is, *When did this age start?* It's a great question, and a surprisingly difficult one to answer. We've had digital computers for well over half a century, after all, yet just about all of the advances we described in our earlier book were quite recent. So when did this important new, second machine age start?

We've arrived at a two-phase answer to this question. Phase one of the second machine age describes a time when digital technologies demonstrably had an impact on the business world by taking over large amounts of routine work—tasks like processing payroll, welding car body parts together, and sending invoices to customers. In July of 1987 the MIT economist Robert Solow, who later that year would win a Nobel prize for his work on the sources of economic growth, wrote, "You can see the computer age everywhere but in the productivity statistics." By the mid-1990s, that was no longer true; productivity started to grow much faster, and a large amount of research (some of it conducted by Erik* and his colleagues) revealed that computers and other digital technologies were a main reason why. So, we can date the start of phase one of the second machine age to the middle of the 1990s.

---

* Where we mention ourselves in this book, we use first names only: Andy and Erik.

Phase two, which we believe we're in now, has a start date that's harder to pin down. It's the time when science fiction technologies—the stuff of movies, books, and the controlled environments of elite research labs—started to appear in the real world. In 2010, Google unexpectedly announced that a fleet of completely autonomous cars had been driving on US roads without mishap. In 2011, IBM's Watson supercomputer beat two human champions at the TV quiz show *Jeopardy!* By the third quarter of 2012, there were more than a billion users of smartphones, devices that combined the communication and sensor capabilities of countless sci-fi films. And of course, the three advances described at the start of this chapter happened in the past few years. As we'll see, so did many other breakthroughs. They are not flukes or random blips in technological progress. Instead, they are harbingers of a more fundamental transformation in the economy—a transformation that's rooted in both significant technological advances and sound economic principles.

Phase two of the second machine age differs markedly from phase one. First, it's a time when technologies are demonstrating that they can do work that we've never thought of as preprogrammed or "routine." They're winning at Go, diagnosing disease accurately, interacting naturally with people, and engaging in creative work like composing music and designing useful objects. Within the past few years, they've clearly blown past Polanyi's Paradox and other limitations on their way to new territory. Machines aren't simply following carefully codified instructions provided by human programmers;* they're learning how to solve problems on their own. This development vastly enlarges the scope of applications and tasks that machines can now address.

Second, hundreds of millions of people started to have powerful,

---

* There's a reason we often call programmers "coders"; after all, they have historically codified knowledge, making the tacit explicit.

flexible, and connected computers with them at all times. These are smartphones and other similar devices, which have spread around the world with astonishing speed. By 2015, only eight years after the iPhone was introduced, more than 40% of the adults in twenty-one emerging and developing countries surveyed by the Pew Research Center reported owning a smartphone. In 2016, approximately 1.5 billion more were sold.

For the first time in human history a near-majority of the world's adults are now connected with each other digitally, and with a large chunk of the world's accumulated knowledge. What's more, they can contribute to this knowledge themselves, creating a virtuous cycle. They can also engage in many kinds of exchanges and transactions, bringing billions more participants into the modern global economy.

We find it difficult to overstate how important this is. Until quite recently, access to large knowledge repositories (like good libraries) and advanced communication and information-processing technologies was limited to the world's wealthy—those of us fortunate enough to be born into nonpoor families in nonpoor countries. That is no longer the case. And more and more powerful technologies will spread around the world in the years to come.

Computers that can excel at nonroutine work and the digital interconnection of humanity are both phenomena of the past few years. So we think a decent starting point for the second phase of the second machine age is the second decade of the new millennium. It's when minds and machines, products and platforms, and the core and the crowd came together quickly, and started throwing off sparks. As a result, many long-standing assumptions have been overturned and well-established practices made obsolete.

What Happened the Last Time?

A century ago, electricity was in the process of taking over from steam power in manufacturing. We bring up this period because it offers a critical caution: many successful incumbent companies—in fact, most of them—did not survive the transition from one power source to the other. Businesses that want to thrive in the coming era of digital transformation need to understand why this happened and to heed some critical lessons from the past.

By the 1910s, the United States had surpassed the United Kingdom as the world's largest economy. The reason was largely the strength of US manufacturing companies, which accounted for approximately 50% of the country's GDP at the time.

American factories were powered first by flowing water that turned waterwheels, then by steam. Around the start of the twentieth century, electricity appeared as another viable option. It first gained traction as a more efficient replacement for the single big steam engine that sat in the basements of factories and supplied power to all of their machines. But as companies gained experience with the new technology, they came to realize that it provided other benefits. F. B. Crocker, a professor at Columbia, wrote the following in 1901:

> There were many factories which introduced electric power because we engaged to save from 20 to 60 percent of their coal bills; but such savings as these are not what has caused the tremendous activity in electric power equipment that is today spreading all over this country. . . . those who first introduced electric power on this basis found that they were making other savings than those that had been promised, which might be called indirect savings.

Adopters of the new technology eventually came to realize that some long-standing constraints no longer applied. Once they were made electric, power sources could spread throughout a building (after all, they no longer needed to be next to smokestacks and piles of coal). There could also be several power sources instead of one huge one that drove every machine in the factory via an elaborate (and temperamental) system of shafts, gears, pulleys, and belts.

Most manufacturers eventually adopted some form of this "group drive"—a configuration in which a factory had several large electric motors, each providing power to a group of machines.* Some wanted to push this decentralization of power much farther and begin talking about "unit drive," or giving every individual machine in the building its own electric motor. After all, unlike steam engines, electric motors can be made quite small without any significant loss in efficiency.

Today, of course, it's completely ridiculous to imagine doing anything *other* than this; indeed, many machines now go even further and have multiple electric motors built into their design. But the concept of unit drive was met with deep skepticism when it first arose, and for a surprisingly long time afterward. The economic historian Warren Devine Jr. found that

> the merits of driving machines in groups or driving them individually were discussed in the technical literature throughout the first quarter of the twentieth century. Between 1895 and 1904, this subject was vigorously debated in meetings of technical societies; neither technique could be said to be best in all cases. . . . And, over 20 years later, group drive was still being strongly recommended for many applications. . . . Two textbooks printed in 1928 . . . make it clear that there were many situations in which group drive was justified.

---

* These motors were themselves powered by an electric generator located close to the factory, or by the then-new electric grid.

It's So Obvious in Hindsight;
Why Was It So Hard to See at the Time?

Why are technology progressions that are so obvious in retrospect so hard to see accurately while they're unfolding? And why are so many of the smartest and most experienced people and companies, and the ones most affected by the change, the least able to see it?

Research in many different fields points to the same conclusion: it's exactly *because* incumbents are so proficient, knowledgeable, and caught up in the status quo that they are unable to see what's coming, and the unrealized potential and likely evolution of the new technology. This phenomenon has been described as the "curse of knowledge" and "status quo bias," and it can affect even successful and well-managed companies. Existing processes, customers and suppliers, pools of expertise, and more general mind-sets can all blind incumbents to things that should be obvious, such as the possibilities of new technologies that depart greatly from the status quo.

This certainly appears to have been the case with factory electrification. A great deal of research has been done on this period, and much of it reaches the same conclusion. As economists Andrew Atkeson and Patrick J. Kehoe summarize, "At the beginning of the transition [to electric power], manufacturers [were] reluctant to abandon [their] large stock of knowledge to adopt what, initially, [was] only a marginally superior technology."* Another duo of economic historians, Paul David and Gavin Wright, found that a big reason it took so long to fully realize electricity's transformation potential was "the need for organizational and above all for conceptual changes in the ways tasks and products are defined and structured." Assembly lines, conveyor belts, and over-

---

* From the start, electric power was more consistent and cheaper than steam. But since those were its only immediate advantages in a factory powered by steam, electricity was considered only "marginally superior."

head cranes were examples of such conceptual changes. They were essential to unlocking electricity's full potential, yet unimaginable to many incumbents that had become large and successful during the steam era.

Electricity's Shocks

Clay Christensen built his career as a rock-star business academic by highlighting how often disruptive technologies have brought down high-flying companies. Electrification was one of the most disruptive technologies ever; in the first decades of the twentieth century, it caused something close to a mass extinction in US manufacturing industries.

At the start of that century, manufacturing industries in the United States were dominated by firms called "industrial trusts." These were large companies born of mergers; their owners aimed to take advantage of scale economies in production, purchasing, distribution, marketing, and so on. Certain trust builders also hoped to create companies so large that they would become monopolies, thereby gaining more power to set prices. A survey published in 1904 tallied more than 300 such trusts.

At the time, US industrial trusts seemed positioned to reign for a long time. They were well capitalized, staffed by the first generation of professional managers, and far from hostile to new technologies. They had easily learned to communicate by telegraph and ship goods via railroad, and they were willing to switch from steam to electric power in their factories. But all their resources and capabilities were not enough to keep them on top—or in many cases, in business—as electrification spread.

A survey conducted by the economist Shaw Livermore and published in 1935 found that over 40% of the industrial trusts formed between 1888 and 1905 had failed by the early 1930s. Another 11% were " 'limping' units, whose records were . . . a mixture of good and bad. . . . In general, the bad results have been witnessed in the more recent years of the period under review." Of the trusts that survived, most became much smaller. A study by economist Richard Caves and his colleagues of forty-two manufacturing firms that were dominant in 1905 and still in existence in 1929 found that their average market share declined by over one-third, from 69% to 45%.

These studies and others suggest that the competitive environment in US manufacturing industries turned nasty in the twentieth century, and that by the end of the 1920s many companies had been knocked from their previously strong positions. Was this at least in part because of electrification?

We believe it was. It's clear that intelligent electrification made a factory much more productive than it could otherwise be. The big gains came not from simple substitution of electric motors for steam engines, but from the redesign of the production process itself. Intelligently electrified factories—those with motors attached to every machine, with assembly lines and conveyor belts, with overhead cranes, and so on—were formidable weapons in any competitive battle. They could do more with less and enabled their owners to undercut their rivals on price and flexibility and to saturate the market with their goods. We also know that not all factories were able to electrify intelligently. Some companies and their leaders saw the potential of unit drive and embraced it, while others debated the matter for decades. For all these reasons, it seems likely that early-adopting factories contributed directly to the deaths of many of the old industrial trusts.

The great shake-up in early-twentieth-century American manufacturing had multiple causes, including the upheavals of World War I and President Teddy Roosevelt's trust-busting crusade, but the many shocks of electrification were one of the fundamental reasons why so many top companies failed or floundered.

Factory owners who considered electrification simply a better power source missed the point entirely, and over time they found themselves falling behind their electrified rivals. These laggards might have been making wonderful products, marketed brilliantly and sold through efficient distribution networks to loyal customers. But if their factories didn't electrify intelligently, they eventually went out of business. They couldn't compete on price, couldn't get their goods to market as quickly, and couldn't switch as easily from one set of products to another. They simply became uncompetitive, even though—or more accurately, because—they were doing exactly the same things that had previously led to success.

The Universal Machine

Today we're in the early stages of another industrial shake-up, but an even bigger and broader one. We struggle to think of any significant company in any market anywhere in the world that won't be affected by the technology surge under way now. The successful companies of the second machine age will be those that bring together minds and machines, products and platforms, and the core and crowd very differently than most do today. Those that don't undertake this work, and that stick closely to today's technological and organizational status quo, will be making essentially the same choice as those that stuck with steam power or group drive. And eventually, they'll meet the same fate.

Our goal for this book is to help you see where you might have the early-twenty-first-century equivalent of steam engines or group-drive configurations in your company, and to help you think about how to replace them with something that takes better advantage of the amazing technologies of today and tomorrow.

What's Ahead

This book is a guide to the world being created by the new machines, platforms, and crowds. It is, by necessity, an incomplete work. The business world is always changing, and during transitions as profound as this one, things are even more unsettled than usual. So we would never claim to have discovered the final and complete answers to business success as our economies and societies move deeper into the second machine age. The three rebalancings we describe here will take years, and their end points and exact trajectories are far from clear.

But in chaos lies opportunity. We know enough—from history, from previous research, from recent examples and developments, and from our own investigations—to say some things that we believe are both accurate and of value. As you'll see, a lot of these insights are rooted in economics, the field we draw on most heavily in our work.

Why is this? The Austrian economist Carl Menger gave a good answer in 1870: "Economic theory is concerned . . . with the conditions under which men engage in provident activity directed to the satisfaction of their needs."* Economics is the study of how organizations and people understand and shape their environments and futures, and of what happens as they come together and exchange goods, services, and information in order to achieve their goals. The discipline has developed a large and solid body of insight and theories on these topics, making it the right base for a book about how machines, platforms, and the crowd are shaking things up.

But we can't rely on economics alone. The phenomena we're interested in here are far too rich for one discipline and cut across many

---

* Nineteenth-century writers frequently used the term "men" when they meant "people."

other fields of study. So, we'll also bring in engineering, computer science, psychology, sociology, history, management science, and lots of others. The technology surge under way now is recent, but it has a long, rich, and fascinating heritage. We'll draw on it as we describe what's happening today and what might happen tomorrow.

We divide the discussion into three parts. Part 1 is about bringing together minds and machines. Part 2 does the same for products and platforms, and Part 3 for the core and the crowd. The broad theme of each part is the same: since the second element of the pair has become so much more powerful and capable in recent years, it's now critical to reexamine how best to bring the two together.

Part 1 shows how new combinations of minds and machines are rapidly changing the way businesses execute their most important *processes*. Part 2 reveals how pioneering companies are bringing together products and platforms to transform their *offerings*. Part 3 shows that the core and the crowd are altering what *organizations* themselves look like, and how they work.

The opening chapter in each part reaches back into the first phase of the second machine age and describes both the status quo that existed and the early indications that things were about to change. These chapters show that, about twenty years ago, a "standard partnership" was forged between minds and machines, products and platforms, and the core and the crowd. They also show the ways that this partnership came under stress as technology advanced and experience accumulated.

The remaining chapters in each part explore what we've seen and learned in recent years around each of the three rebalancings. They show the power of machines, platforms, and the crowd today, and tomorrow. Within each part the chapters are arranged on a "science fiction gradient," or ascending order of weirdness. We'll describe increasingly far-out developments, innovations, and business models. The final chapter of each part will consider topics like whether computers can ever be "creative," whether the entire economy will soon become an on-demand economy, and whether companies themselves are an endangered species.*

Throughout the book, each chapter will end with a short section summarizing its main insights and giving practical guidance. This is not a how-to book, or one that lays out a detailed playbook for business success with machines, platforms, and the crowd. We suspect that people who offer such a playbook are kidding either themselves or their readers. There's simply too much change and too much uncertainty at present. Indeed, if such a formulaic cookbook could be written, there would be little opportunity to gain competitive advantage by understanding the deeper forces and principles at work. So instead, we'll end with brief distillations of each chapter's main ideas, along with questions intended to help you think about applying these ideas in your organization.

* Very briefly, the answers to these questions are yes, kind of, and no.

MIND AND MACHINE

CHAPTER 2

THE HARDEST THING TO ACCEPT ABOUT OURSELVES

The tendency of these new machines is to replace human judgment on all levels but a fairly high one, rather than to replace human energy and power by machine energy and power.

— *Norbert Wiener, 1949*

ABOUT TWENTY YEARS AGO, BUSINESSES AROUND THE WORLD settled on a division of work between people and computers that seemed very sensible. The machines would take care of basic math, record keeping, and data transmission. This would free up people to make decisions, exercise judgment, use their creativity and intuition, and interact with each other to solve problems and take care of customers.

From Paperwork Mine to the Standard Partnership

This approach is so widespread now that it's hard to remember the era of nonstop paperwork that preceded it, when carts full of file folders traveled between people and departments. A disturbing window back to this time exists today at the "Paperwork Mine," an underground nightmare of inefficiency operated by the US government's Office of Personnel Management. The site exists to handle the necessary administrative steps when a federal employee retires. Because these steps have not been computerized, however, the routine tasks require 600 people, who work in a supermarket-sized room full of tall file cabinets; for baroque reasons, this room is located more than 200 feet underground in a former limestone mine. Back in 1977, completing the (quite literal) paperwork for a federal retirement took, on average, sixty-one days. Today, using essentially the same processes, it still takes sixty-one days. The state of Texas, which has digitized its process, currently does it in two.

The intellectual blueprint for an attack on the world's paperwork mines was *Reengineering the Corporation*, written by Michael Hammer and James Champy and published in 1993. The book was an enormous success; it sold more than 2 million copies around the world and was named by *Time* magazine one of the twenty-five most influential business books of all time.

Hammer and Champy's basic message was that companies should think of themselves not as conducting tasks within departments (for example, buying raw material within a purchasing department), but instead as executing business processes—such as taking, assembling, and shipping a customer's order—that inherently cut across departments. This sounds obvious now, but at the time it was considered both novel and important. Peter Drucker, the preeminent business guru of the twentieth century, said at the time, "Reengineering is new, and it has to be done." The process lens typically revealed many tasks that were unnecessary and could be eliminated, or as Hammer and Champy put it, obliterated.

The business process reengineering movement was accelerated in the mid-1990s by two advances: enterprise-wide information systems and the World Wide Web. Prior to the arrival of enterprise systems,* companies typically had a jumble of separate pieces of software, many of which were not linked. The larger the company, the worse the jumble was. Enterprise systems held out the promise of replacing the jumble with a single, large piece of software† explicitly designed to execute a particular set of cross-functional business processes. This software could be bought "off the shelf" from vendors like SAP and Oracle, then configured and customized to a degree.

Enterprise systems quickly took off; by one estimate, over 60% of the Fortune 1000 had adopted at least one of them by 1999. And while they could be quite expensive and time-consuming to install and maintain, they largely delivered on their promise. A study by Erik and his colleagues Sinan Aral and D. J. Wu, for example, found that adopting companies experienced significant improvements in labor productivity, inventory turnover, and asset utilization once they started using their new enterprise systems.

The advent of the World Wide Web extended the reach and power of enterprise systems to individual consumers via their computers (and later their tablets and phones). The web was born in 1989 when Tim Berners-Lee developed a set of protocols that allowed pieces of online content like text and pictures to link to each other, putting in practice the visions of hypertext first described by science and engineering polymath Vannevar Bush in 1945 (theoretically using microfilm) and computer visionary Ted Nelson, whose Project Xanadu never quite took off.

The web rapidly turned the Internet from a text-only network into

---

* Enterprise systems soon became known by their TLAs (three-letter acronyms)— ERP (enterprise resource planning), SCM (supply chain management), CRM (customer relationship management), HRM (human resource management), and so on.

† Or, to be more accurate, a few pieces of software. Not even the most confident vendors of enterprise software proposed that one single system would suffice for everything a company needed to do.

one that could handle pictures, sounds, and other media. This multimedia wonder, so much richer and easier to navigate than anything before, entered the mainstream in 1994 when Netscape released the first commercial web browser, named Navigator. (One of Netscape's cofounders was Marc Andreessen, a then twenty-two-year-old programmer who had worked on earlier web browsers. We'll hear more from Andreessen in Chapter 11.)* It coincided with the commercialization of the Internet, which had previously been primarily the domain of academics.

The web enabled companies to extend their business processes beyond the four walls of the company and all the way to the consumer—a trend that became known as e-commerce. People started to use the web not only to search for and learn about a company's products, but also to order and pay for them. This combination of efficiency and convenience has proved irresistible. Just ten years after the launch of Netscape, e-commerce accounted for approximately 10% of nonfood, nonautomotive retail sales in the United States.

For two decades, then, web-enabled enterprise systems have been facilitating more and more business processes by doing the routine things: keeping track of account balances and transactions, calculating the right quantity and timing for raw-material deliveries, sending paychecks to employees, letting customers select and pay for products, and so on.

People Should Use Their Judgment . . .

What should employees do once technologies like enterprise software and the World Wide Web free them from the "paperwork mine"? Hammer and Champy offered a clear answer in *Reengineering the*

---

* In recognition of his work literally inventing the web, Berners-Lee was dubbed Knight Commander, Order of the British Empire (KBE) by Great Britain's Queen Elizabeth in 2004. Andreessen was one of the winners of the inaugural Queen Elizabeth Prize for Engineering in 2013.

Corporation: with the computers handling the routine, people should be empowered to exercise their judgment. "Most of the checking, reconciling, waiting, monitoring, tracking—the unproductive work . . .—is eliminated by reengineering. . . . People working in a reengineered process are, of necessity, empowered. As process team workers they are both permitted and required to think, interact, use judgment, and make decisions."

This is a clear statement of a common belief: that even in a world pervaded by hardware, software, and networks, people remain valuable because of their judgment—their ability to reason in a way that goes beyond executing rote calculations on available data. Most of us accept that if all we could complete were routine tasks, we'd be out of a job by now because computers are so much better at them. But almost all of us also believe that we're capable of delivering a great deal more than digital technologies can, even as they continue to profit from Moore's law—the remarkably steady, remarkably fast growth over time in the amount of computing hardware available for the same dollar of spending—and become exponentially more powerful.

Decades of research confirm the idea that we do, in fact, reason in two different ways. This groundbreaking work resulted in a Nobel prize for Daniel Kahneman who, alongside collaborator Amos Tversky, pioneered the field that has come to be called behavioral economics.* The work of Kahneman and his colleagues showed that we all have two modes of thinking, which he labeled System 1 and System 2.† System 1 is fast, automatic, evolutionarily ancient, and requires little effort; it's closely associated with what we call intuition. System

---

* In recognition of his work, Kahneman was the first noneconomist to be awarded the Nobel Memorial Prize in Economics.

† The labels "System 1" and "System 2" were deliberately neutral and bland, so as not to activate the long-standing disagreements and debates around other terms.

2 is the opposite: slow, conscious, evolutionarily recent, and a lot of work. As Kahneman writes in his book *Thinking, Fast and Slow*,

> System 1 operates automatically and quickly, with little or no effort and no sense of voluntary control. System 2 allocates attention to the effortful mental activities that demand it, including complex computations. The operations of System 2 are often associated with the subjective experience of agency, choice, and concentration.

Both systems can be improved over time. System 2 is refined by taking a math or logic course, while System 1 gets better more naturally and broadly, just by living life and seeing lots of examples. Firefighters develop a sense over time of how fire spreads through a building, personnel managers hone their sense of who will be a good fit for the company by interviewing many candidates, and Go players become masters by mindfully playing the game. Of course, the two systems can and should be improved simultaneously. Pathologists, the medical specialists who diagnose disease, refine their skills both by studying biochemistry and by seeing many, many examples of both diseased and healthy tissue. Learning is often deeper and faster when we both understand the underlying principles and instantiate them with compelling examples.

The dominant style of business training has been to combine the two systems. Business school students sharpen their System 2 skills via accounting, finance, and microeconomics courses. They also discuss a great many case studies in entrepreneurship, leadership, ethics, and other areas to refine their intuition and judgment—System 1 skills. And many classes combine both approaches. Medical schools and law schools follow similar tacks.

A final well-established finding about people's abilities with System 1 and System 2 is that they vary widely. Some of us are brilliant at solving equations and brain teasers but lack intuition and "real-world" smarts. Others can't do arithmetic reliably but have great intuitive abilities.

As technology spreads, the people in this latter category aren't at any disadvantage. In fact, they thrive; with the computer doing all the logical, rule-based work, they are liberated to do what Hammer and Champy advocate: exercise their judgment, make decisions, and interact with other people to solve problems, seize opportunities, and take care of customers.

It seems to us, in fact, that in much of the business world today, System 1 is ascendant. Former CEOs write books with titles like *Straight from the Gut* and *Tough Choices*. "Technocrat" has become a pejorative term for a leader too focused on data and insufficiently attuned to the complexities of the real world. The 2010 book *Rethinking the MBA: Business Education at a Crossroads* identified "building judgment and intuition into messy, unstructured situations" as one of the major unmet needs of MBA programs. The consistent argument accords with *Reengineering the Corporation*: let people develop and exercise their intuition and judgment in order to make smart decisions, while the computers take care of the math and record keeping. We've heard about and seen this division of labor between minds and machines so often that we call it the "standard partnership."

. . . Except They're Often Lousy at It

The standard partnership is compelling, but sometimes it doesn't work very well at all. Getting rid of human judgments altogether—even those from highly experienced and credentialed people—and relying solely on numbers plugged into formulas, often yields better results.

This is a counterintuitive finding. It's also an unpopular one, for obvious reasons. So we need to support it thoroughly. Before we do that, though, we should emphasize that System 1 is not worthless in business. Far from it, in fact. We will see that human intuition, judgment, and fast thinking still have critical roles to play, and that leading companies are making use of them in novel and brilliant ways—ways that point to a new and improved partnership between minds and machines.

But first we have to demonstrate some of the weaknesses of System 1. Consider these pathbreaking studies that highlighted the often severe limitations of even expert human judgment and intuition.

▶ Sociology professor Chris Snijders used 5,200 computer equipment purchases by Dutch companies to build a mathematical model predicting adherence to budget, timeliness of delivery, and buyer satisfaction with each transaction. He then used this model to predict these outcomes for a different set of transactions taking place across several different industries, and also asked a group of purchasing managers in these sectors to do the same. Snijders's model beat the managers, even the above-average ones. He also found that veteran managers did no better than newbies, and that, in general, managers did no better looking at transactions within their own industry than at distant ones.

▶ Economics professor Orley Ashenfelter built a simple model—one using only four publicly accessible variables about the weather—to successfully predict the quality and price of Bordeaux wines long before they were ready to drink. Prices of these young wines had historically been strongly influenced by the opinion of acknowledged wine experts, but Ashenfelter wrote that "one of the most interesting issues raised by [research like this] is the role it implies for expert opinion in the determination of wine prices. . . . there is evidence that expert opinion is unrelated (that is, orthogonal) to the fundamental determinants of wine quality. . . . This naturally raises the unresolved question of just what determines the demand for expert opinion."

▶ Erik worked with Lynn Wu, now a professor at the Wharton School, to develop a simple model that predicted housing sales and prices. They used data from Google Trends, which reports how often words like "real estate agent," "home loan," "home prices," and the like were searched for each month in each of the fifty US states. They used their model to predict future housing sales and compared their forecasts to the published predictions made by experts at the National Association of Realtors. When the results came in, their model beat the experts by a whopping 23.6%, reflecting the power of incorporating Google search data into a prediction model.

▶ A separate project by Erik hit closer to home, developing a *Moneyball*-style model for academia. He worked with Dimitris Bertsimas, John Silberholz and Shachar Reichman, all at MIT, to predict who would get tenure at top universities. They looked at historical data on the early publication records and citation patterns of young scholars and used some concepts from network theory to see which ones had been writing the most influential and impactful work. They calibrated their model to predict which scholars would ultimately get tenure in the field of operations research. Their model agreed with tenure committees 70% of the time, but where they disagreed, the model's predictions yielded a set of scholars who, in the future, produced more papers published in the top journals and research that was cited more often than did the scholars who were actually selected by tenure committees.

▶ A study by Shai Danzinger and colleagues showed that Israeli judges were more likely to grant parole at the start of the day and after food breaks. And right before the judges took a break—when they were presumably tired or had low blood sugar—they were more likely to recommend continued imprisonment. Other research supports the idea that judicial decisions are often affected by factors well outside the case at hand. Economists Ozkan Eren and Naci Mocan found that in one US state, judges who were graduates of a prominent regional university handed down significantly harsher sentences immediately after their alma mater experienced an unexpected loss in a football game, and that these sentences were "asymmetrically borne by black defendants."

▶ In the Broward County, Florida, school district, the first step in having children identified as gifted used to be a nomination by their parents or teachers. Most students in Broward were minorities, but 56% of the children in gifted programs were white. In the first decade of the twenty-first century, the district decided to move away from the subjective method, and to try instead to be as systematic and objective as possible. They gave every child in the district a nonverbal IQ test. The results of this one change, as documented by economists David Card and Laura Giuliano, were striking: 80% more African American and 130% more Hispanic students were identified as gifted.

▶ Law professors Ted Ruger and Pauline Kim, along with political scientists Andrew Martin and Kevin Quinn, conducted a test to see whether a simple, six-variable model developed by Martin and Quinn could predict the rulings of the US Supreme Court during its 2002 term better than a team of eighty-three prominent legal experts could. Thirty-eight of these jurists had clerked for a Supreme Court judge, thirty-three were chaired law professors, and six were current or former law school deans. This team's predictions, when averaged, were consistent with slightly less than 60% of the court's rulings. The algorithm got 75% of them right.

Is the preceding list representative and fair? Or are we deliberately, or maybe even unconsciously, highlighting the cases when human judgment lost out to a purely data-driven approach, and ignoring examples of human superiority? An impressive body of research indicates that we're not.

A team led by psychologist William Grove went through 50 years of literature looking for published, peer-reviewed examples of head-to-head comparisons of clinical and statistical prediction (that is, between the judgment of experienced, "expert" humans and a 100% data-driven approach) in the areas of psychology and medicine. They found 136 such studies, covering everything from prediction of IQ to diagnosis of heart disease. In 48% of them, there was no significant difference between the two; the experts, in other words, were on average no better than the formulas.

A much bigger blow to the notion of human superiority in judgment came from the finding that in 46% of the studies considered, the human experts actually performed significantly *worse* than the numbers and formulas alone. This means that people were clearly superior in only 6% of cases. And the authors concluded that in almost all of the studies where humans did better, "the clinicians received more data than the mechanical prediction." As Paul Meehl, the legendary psychologist who began in the early 1950s to document and describe the poor track record of human expert judgment, summarized,

There is no controversy in social science that shows such a large body of qualitatively diverse studies coming out so uniformly in the same direction as this one [the relative validity of statistical versus clinical prediction]. When you are pushing over 100 investigations, predicting everything from the outcome of football games to the diagnosis of liver disease and when you can hardly come up with a half dozen studies showing even a weak tendency in favor of the clinician, it is time to draw a practical conclusion.

That practical conclusion, we believe, is that we need to rely less on expert judgments and predictions.

More and more American companies have come to the same conclusion. Working with the US Census Bureau, Erik and Kristina McElheren, now a professor at the University of Toronto, surveyed a representative sample 18,000 manufacturing plants and found that the adoption of data-driven decision making was increasing rapidly, catalyzed by increased use of IT and significantly better performance by firms that adopted this approach.

Despite these compelling examples, we must temper our litany of algorithmic successes with some important qualifications. In order to compare human judgment to a mathematical model, obviously a model needs to exist in the first place. That's not always possible, as Polanyi's Paradox suggests. Such models have to be tested and refined on data sets with multiple similar examples—a situation that characterizes only a subset of the decisions that humans must make. But the overall pattern is clear: in case after case, when a model can be created and tested, it tends to perform as well as, or better than, human experts making similar decisions. Too often, we continue to rely on human judgment when machines can do better.

Human Minds: Brilliant But Buggy

How can an approach that relies on System 2 only—on purely rational and logical calculations performed on numeric data—possibly be better than an approach that makes use of System 2 *and* System 1, the deep, innate, instinctual thinking facilities that all people have? System 1, after all, has worked well enough to help us survive and thrive through all of evolution's ruthless Darwinian challenges (we're still here, all 7.5 billion of us). So how could it be letting us down so badly?

These questions are too big to be tackled in a single book, let alone in one chapter. But in *Thinking, Fast and Slow*, Kahneman provides a short summary of a great deal of research (much of which he conducted):

> Because System 1 operates automatically and cannot be turned off at will, errors of intuitive thought are often difficult to prevent. Biases cannot always be avoided, because System 2 may have no clue to the error.

System 1 is amazing, in short, but it's also really buggy. It often takes shortcuts instead of reasoning something through thoroughly. It also contains a surprisingly large set of biases. Researchers working within psychology and behavioral economics, the discipline Kahneman helped to found, have identified and named a great many System 1 glitches.

A complete list of them would both bore and depress you; there are 99 chapters in Rolf Dobelli's book on the subject, *The Art of Thinking Clearly*, and 175 entries (at last count) in Wikipedia's "list of cognitive biases." Buster Benson, a product manager at the software company Slack, came up with what we think is a great way to group these biases and keep in mind the problems they pose for us:*

---

* Benson came up with this categorization after studying Wikipedia's list of cognitive biases while on paternity leave, and he published them on the "life hacking" blog *Better Humans* (http://betterhumans.net). It's a great example of insight coming from the online crowd, a phenomenon we'll discuss at greater length later in the third section of this book.

1. Information overload sucks, so we aggressively filter. . . . [But] some of the information we filter out is actually useful and important.

2. Lack of meaning is confusing, so we fill in the gaps. . . . [But] our search for meaning can conjure illusions. We sometimes imagine details that were filled in by our assumptions, and construct meaning and stories that aren't really there.*

3. [We] need to act fast lest we lose our chance, so we jump to conclusions. . . . [But] quick decisions can be seriously flawed. Some of the quick reactions and decisions we jump to are unfair, self-serving, and counter-productive.

4. This isn't getting easier, so we try to remember the important bits. . . . [But] our memory reinforces errors. Some of the stuff we remember for later just makes all of the above systems more biased, and more damaging to our thought processes.

We want to call attention to another serious problem with our cognitive abilities: we have no way of knowing when System 1 is working well, and when it isn't. In other words, we have lousy insight about our own intuition. We don't know whether the quick judgment or decision we reached is accurate or has been polluted by one or more of our many biases. So, in a strange twist on Polanyi's Paradox, we also know *less* than we can tell—less about System 1's products. The rational calculations of System 2 can often be double-checked, but as Kahneman points out, System 1 really can't—least of all by ourselves.

Recent research has revealed a particularly devilish bias related to

---

* There's a fancy name for this: "apophenia." Models in statistics and machine learning can make the same mistake, where it's typically called "overfitting" the data.

this aspect of Polanyi's Paradox: often, System 1 reaches a conclusion, then drafts System 2 to explain it. As the psychologist Jonathan Haidt argues, "Judgment and justification are two separate processes." The judging, powered by System 1, happens almost instantaneously. It's then justified in rational and plausible language supplied by System 2.* This subterfuge often fools not only other minds, but also even the one that came up with it. We are often "telling more than we can know," as the psychologists Richard Nesbitt and Timothy DeCamp Wilson put it. The behaviors we label rationalization and self-justification, then, are not always exercises in excuse making. They're also something much more fundamental: they're System 1 at work.

In 2006, Avinash Kaushik and Ronny Kohavi, two data analysis professionals who were then working at Intuit and Microsoft, respectively, came up with the acronym HiPPO to summarize the dominant decision-making style at most companies. It stands for "highest-paid person's opinion." We love this shorthand and use it a lot, because it vividly illustrates the standard partnership. Even when the decisions are not made by the highest-paid people, they're often—too often—based on opinions, judgments, intuition, gut, and System 1. The evidence is clear that this approach frequently doesn't work well, and that HiPPOs too often destroy value.

---

* As Jonathan Haidt explains in his book *The Happiness Hypothesis*, "This finding, that people will readily fabricate reasons to explain their own behavior, is called 'confabulation.' Confabulation is so frequent in work with split-brain patients and other people suffering brain damage that [psychologist Michael] Gazzaniga refers to the language centers on the left side of the brain as the interpreter module, whose job is to give a running commentary on whatever the self is doing, even though the interpreter module has no access to the real causes or motives of the self's behavior. For example, if the word 'walk' is flashed to the right hemisphere, the patient might stand up and walk away. When asked why he is getting up, he might say, 'I'm going to get a Coke.' The interpreter module is good at making up explanations, but not at knowing that it has done so." Jonathan Haidt, *The Happiness Hypothesis: Finding Modern Truth in Ancient Wisdom* (New York: Basic Books, 2006), 8.

Toward a New Mind-Machine Partnership

How can we make use of all this knowledge about biases and glitches in System 1 and System 2? How can it lead us to be smarter about making decisions, and to make better ones? The most obvious approach is to consider letting the machines make the decisions when and where they can—to let pure digital instances of System 2, turbocharged by Moore's law and fed from a fire hose of data, come up with their answers without input from System 1. Over time, this is exactly what more and more companies are doing.

An Automatic "Second Economy"

One of the earliest examples of fully automated decision making that we know of, which arrived right as the era of corporate computing dawned, was the development of a numeric score that reflected people's creditworthiness: the likelihood that they would repay a loan of a given size. This obviously critical decision had traditionally been made by local loan officers at bank branches who evaluated applications on the basis of their own experience, sometimes in conjunction with rules or guidelines. But Bill Fair and Earl Isaac thought data could do a better job. They founded the Fair Isaac Corporation in 1956 and began calculating FICO scores of creditworthiness.

Automatic credit assessment soon became the norm. By 1999, *American Banker* reported that "no [human being] even looks at any [credit request] for $50,000 or less—the computer does it all." FICO and its peers have proved to be highly reliable predictors of loan repayment, and as the amount and variety of digital information about a person has expanded in recent years, this "big data" has been used to enhance and extended credit scores.

The developers of these scores have to be careful that they're not engaging in digital redlining—the illegal practice of refusing or reducing credit to certain geographic areas on the basis of their racial or ethnic populations—but in general, they're providing a valuable service by opening up the opportunities of credit to more people and letting lenders extend their business with confidence. And there's evidence that redlining actually decreases as credit decisions become more automated. In 2007 the US Federal Reserve reported that a credit scoring model "reduces the opportunities for engaging in illegal discriminatory behavior . . . [and] may help diminish the possibility that credit decisions will be influenced by personal characteristics or other factors prohibited by law, including race or ethnicity."

Today, examples of valuable, high-quality, 100% automatic decisions are all around us. Amazon and other e-commerce sites generate recommendations for each shopper on each visit, and while many of them miss the mark, others are pretty compelling. Amazon, for example, estimates that 35% of its sales are from cross-selling activities such as recommending items. Prices for plane flights and hotel rooms change all the time in response to how supply and demand are projected to evolve, and how they actually change minute by minute. This approach to pricing, known as revenue management, is vitally important to countless companies (we'll come back to this theme in Chapter 8), yet few if any prices generated by revenue management algorithms are double-checked by a person before they're offered to customers. Physical goods, too, are now subject to automatic price changes. Amazon and Walmart altered the prices of 16% and 13%, respectively, of their entire US inventory on the day after Thanksgiving in 2015.

So many completely automatic decisions are taking place all around us, in fact, that the economist Brian Arthur uses the image of a "second economy," in which the transactions happen with no human involvement in a "vast, silent, connected, unseen, and autonomous" fashion. Over time, this automatic second economy is encroaching into the familiar human-mediated one, with algorithms taking over from experts and HiPPOs. As more and more of the world's information becomes digitized, it provides a plethora of data for improving decision making, converting intuition into data-driven decision making.

Advertising agencies have long helped their clients not only with the creative work of coming up with new television commercials, but also with the task of figuring out exactly when and where to show them: identifying which TV shows, geographic markets, and times were the best match for the advertisers' goals and budget. Data and technology have long been used for this work—the agency at the center of the hit TV drama *Mad Men* gets its first computer, an IBM System/360, in 1969 to help it better place commercials (and impress clients)—but it has remained driven largely by the judgments and decisions of people.

While working in a senior analytics role within Barack Obama's 2012 successful reelection campaign, Dan Wagner saw how much more precision was possible, and how beneficial it could be. Wagner and his colleagues had built up a roster of every voter in the United States. Using machine learning (a technique we'll discuss more in the next chapter), the Obama analytics team created three individual "scores" for everyone on the roster: a "support score" that predicted how likely each person was to support Obama (versus his opponent Mitt Romney), a "turnout score" that predicted how likely each was to actually go to the polls and vote in November, and a "persuasion score" that predicted how likely each would be to feel more favorably toward Obama after receiving his campaign's messaging.

For many years, demographic data has been available for each TV episode—how many eighteen- to twenty-four-year-old men in the Denver area, for example, watch reruns of the animated show *Family Guy* at 10:00 p.m. on Tuesday nights—and media buyers and strategists traditionally have relied heavily on this information when making decisions. If the Obama 2012 campaign wanted to get its message in front of lots of eighteen- to twenty-four-year-old men in Colorado, plenty of companies and people were available to advise them on whether to air ads during Tuesday night *Family Guy* reruns.

But, like most other advertising buyers, the Obama team knew that relying on demographics was terribly imprecise. They might be showing their ads mainly to hard-core Romney supporters. Or they might be showing them primarily to people who had already made up their minds to vote for Obama, which could also be wasteful. Relying on demographics meant relying on judgments and estimates so coarse that they were really little more than guesses: that eighteen- to twenty-four-year-old men were particularly up for grabs as a group during the election, or that viewers of *Family Guy*, or perhaps of cartoons in general, were more receptive to the Obama campaign's messages.

Wagner and his colleagues realized that their comprehensive voter roster had brought them halfway to a much better approach to media buying. With it, the campaign could identify which people were in the two groups it most wanted to reach: Obama supporters who needed to be convinced to actually go to the polls and vote on Election Day, and voters who were on the fence about Obama and could be persuaded to support him. The former were the "Get out the vote" (GOTV) group; the latter were the "Persuadables." The analytics team saw that members of both groups spanned a wide range of demographic categories, so selecting shows solely on the basis of demographics would miss people they wanted to reach. The team also learned from early experiments that the two groups responded well to very different types of ads, so they needed to differentiate the groups when buying time on TV shows.

By 2012, some ratings companies had gone far beyond capturing demographic data on TV shows and were instead able to specify which *individuals* were watching them.* This was exactly the second type of data that Wagner and his colleagues needed. They gave such companies the campaign's GOTV and Persuadables lists, and got back information about how many people in each group watched each show.† This let them readily identify the best buys—the shows that would give them the most GOTV individuals or Persuadables per dollar of advertising spending. As Wagner told us, "We ended up buying late-night programming like on TV Land, which is really weird. It just kind of popped out, and the reason it popped out was it was just so cheap. And those shows had a lot of persuadable voters, so we went and bought that."

After the election, Wagner founded a company called Civis Analytics to transform this highly data-driven approach to media buying into a product, and to make it available to companies and other organizations. He believes that now is the right time for an offering like Civis's, in large part because so many companies have extensive lists of individuals: prospective customers, current customers who might be amenable to further purchases, and so on. "If you're selling expensive tires," he told us, "there's a subset of the population that's willing to spend a lot of money on expensive tires and 90% that really couldn't care less because they don't drive or they're never going to buy expensive tires. You have a pretty good idea who your target people are, but you've never been able to know with the same precision and confidence what TV shows they're watching. Well, now you can." For advertisers, placing TV commercials is an

---

* This information came from "set-top boxes" that people agreed to have installed in their homes.

† To preserve privacy, a third party handled the matching process so that neither the Obama campaign nor the ratings company ever saw each other's lists.

important decision that has been made with some data, but also a lot of judgment. Civis is working to change this, and to make media buying something much closer to an exercise in optimization than intuition.

Of course, even a highly tuned data-driven system is far from perfect, especially if the quality of the data inputs is flawed. In 2016, Hillary Clinton's campaign used many similar methods but narrowly lost the election, in part because polling data inaccurately suggested she had big leads in three midwestern states that she ended up narrowly losing.

Another common risk is that decision makers don't always optimize the right end goal, or what Ronny Kohavi (cocreator of the term "HiPPO") calls the "overall evaluation criterion." Even if Wagner's team could successfully maximize Clinton's lead in national polls, that would not be the right goal. US presidential elections are determined by the electoral college, not the national popular vote, and that calls for a more nuanced, state-by-state strategy. Similarly, it's easy to measure page views or click-through generated by an online advertising campaign, but most companies care more about long-term sales, which are usually maximized by a different kind of campaign. Careful selection of the right data inputs and the right performance metrics, especially the overall evaluation criterion, is a key characteristic of successful data-driven decision makers.

Algorithms Behaving Badly

A real risk of turning over decisions to machines is that bias in algorithmic systems can perpetuate or even amplify some of the pernicious biases that exist in our society. For instance, Latanya Sweeney, a widely cited professor at Harvard, had a disturbing experience when she entered her own name into the Google search engine. Alongside the results appeared an ad that read,

Latanya Sweeney, Arrested? 1) Enter name and state 2) Access full background. Checks instantly. www.instantcheckmate.com

The ad suggested that she had a criminal record, but in fact she had never been arrested.

With further research, Sweeney found that searches for names more common among African Americans, like Trevon or Lakisha or, yes, Latanya were much more likely to show the "Arrested?" ad than were searches for names more often associated with whites, like Laurie or Brendan. While we don't know for sure why this pattern emerged, Sweeney suggested a disturbing explanation: Google's automated ad-serving algorithm might have noticed that click-throughs were more likely when the ads were associated with black-sounding names. Thus, rather than reflecting conscious discrimination by anyone placing the ad or at Google, this racial bias may reflect and amplify the society-wide pattern of discriminatory decisions by the millions of people who click on ads. Similarly, in January of 2017, typing the word "scientist" or "grandmother" into Google's image search yielded an overwhelming number of images of white people.

In an article in *Nature*, Kate Crawford and Ryan Calo noted the danger "that in some current contexts, the downsides of AI systems disproportionately affect groups that are already disadvantaged by factors such as race, gender and socio-economic background" and highlighted the importance of considering the social impacts of these systems, both intended and unintended.

We share these concerns and see both a challenge and opportunity in the growing reliance on algorithmic decision making. The challenge is that this approach can embed and perpetuate unfair, harmful, and unwanted biases. What's worse, these biases may emerge despite the best intentions of the designers to create unbiased systems, and they may be difficult to identify without extensive testing. All system design must confront this challenge.

The opportunity is that machine-based systems typically can be tested and improved. And once corrected, they are unlikely to make the same mistake again. In contrast, it is a lot harder to get humans to acknowledge their biases (how many avowed racists or sexists do you know?), let alone do the hard work required to overcome them. The ultimate standard for adopting a decision-making system—whether based on machines, on humans, or on some combination of the two—cannot realistically be perfection. Any system is likely to make mistakes and have biases. Instead, the goal should be to choose an approach that minimizes biases and errors, and that allows them to be easily and quickly corrected.

Putting Human Intelligence in the Loop, Intelligently

What role, if any, should people play in making decisions? With all that we know about the biases and bugs of System 1, and with oceans of data and computing power available, it can seem as if the second economy is just going to take over the first one, and that our digital System 2's will be making most of the decisions soon. There's an old joke that the factory of the future will have two employees: a human and a dog. The human's job will be to feed the dog, and the dog's job will be to keep the human from touching any of the machines. Is that actually what the company of tomorrow will look like?

We don't think so. While it's true that we have biases that computers don't, we also have strengths that they don't. For one thing, we take in an absolutely huge amount of data all the time from our senses, and we don't preselect it; we just take it all in as it comes. We have difficulty trying to hear only certain sounds or see certain things, even for a short time. Computers are exactly the opposite; they have great difficulty gathering more or different data from what their builders and programmers allowed.

This difference gives rise to an important job for people that Meehl called the "broken leg role." Consider his example of a professor who has gone to the movies every Tuesday night for several years. It would be reasonable for a computer model to predict that she will go again next week. Unfortunately, the professor breaks her leg on Tuesday morning and will be in a hip cast that won't allow her to fit into a theater seat (this example was concocted in 1954). Any human will instantly know that the professor's movie night will be canceled, but this "special power" is not easily duplicated by a computer algorithm. There simply exist too many "distinct, unanticipated factors" affecting the professor's behavior. Whoever designed the computer system cannot gather good data on all of these factors so that the program can take them into account. The only way to do that is to have a much more comprehensive model of the world than any computer system has.

Another huge advantage that humans have is good old common sense. Some of us have more than others, but all of us have infinitely more than even the most advanced computers. As soon as we're born, we start learning important things about how the world works, and we learn them reliably and quickly. Despite decades of research, however, we still don't understand very much about how we acquire our common sense, and our attempts to instill it in computers have so far been impressive failures, as we'll discuss more in the next chapter.

In many cases, therefore, it's a good idea to have a person check the computer's decisions to make sure they make sense. Thomas Davenport, a longtime scholar of analytics and technology, calls this taking a "look out of the window." The phrase is not simply an evocative metaphor. It was inspired by an airline pilot he met who described how he relied heavily on the plane's instrumentation but found it essential to occasionally visually scan the skyline himself. This approach can be highly beneficial, not only for preventing errors, but also for managing a company's reputation.

The car-hailing service Uber learned this the hard way in late 2014.

At that time the company was well known for its surge pricing (temporary increases in fares during busy periods), a tactic that many users found unpalatable. Uber maintained (and we agree) that surge pricing was helpful to balance supply and demand during these times. The company's algorithms bumped prices up in order to encourage more drivers to participate when actual or anticipated car supply was not keeping pace with consumer demand.

This practice earned the company some bad press when an Iranian cleric took eighteen people hostage at a café in Sydney, Australia, in December of 2014. Many people fled the area of the incident, and some tried to use Uber to do so. Uber's computer systems reacted to this sudden spike in demand by initiating surge pricing. To many, this was a wildly inappropriate response to a crisis, and the company faced intense criticism.

Uber issued this statement: "We didn't stop surge pricing immediately [during the Sydney siege]. This was the wrong decision." The company also apparently put in place the ability to override automatic surge pricing in some circumstances. Beginning on the evening of November 13, 2015, Islamic terrorists carried out a series of attacks across Paris. Within thirty minutes of the first one, Uber canceled surge pricing in the city and alerted all of its users to the emergency.*

Examples like this one show the wisdom of having human judgment and algorithms work together. As companies adopt this approach, though, they will need to be careful. Because we humans are so fond of our judgment, and so overconfident in it, many of us, if not most, will be too quick to override the computers, even when their answer is better. But Chris Snijders, who conducted the research on purchasing managers' predictions highlighted earlier in the chapter, found that "what you usually see is [that] the judgment of the aided experts is somewhere in between the model and the unaided

* Still, rumors spread widely that Uber's surge pricing continued during the Paris attacks.

expert. So the experts get better if you give them the model. But still the model by itself performs better."

We support having humans in the loop for exactly the reasons that Meehl and Davenport described, but we also advocate that companies "keep score" whenever possible—that they track the accuracy of algorithmic decisions versus human decisions over time. If the human overrides do better than the baseline algorithm, things are working as they should. If not, things need to change, and the first step is to make people aware of their true success rate.

This feedback is critically important because it's how System 1 learns and improves. As Kahneman and psychologist Gary Klein write, "You should never trust your gut. You need to take your gut feeling as an important data point, but then you have to consciously and deliberately evaluate it, to see if it makes sense in this context." The best way to improve the accuracy and decrease the biases of System 1 is to show it lots of examples and give it frequent and rapid feedback about its accuracy.

An Inverted Partnership Leads to a Clear Line

A final valuable technique, and one that some companies are starting to use, is to turn the standard arrangement on its head: instead of having machines provide data as an input to human judgment, they're having judgment serve as an input to an algorithm. Google is pioneering this approach in hiring, a critical area for the company, but one where analysis showed that the standard arrangement was working poorly.

While Laszlo Bock was head of People Operations at Google, he came to realize that most of the techniques then being used to select new employees were close to useless. When his team looked at what actually explained differences in on-the-job performance at the company, they found that prehire reference checks explained only about

7% of the difference, years of prior experience explained 3%, and unstructured job interviews—the kind that are still most common and start with questions like "What are your greatest strengths?" or "Walk me through your resume"—explained just 14%. The problem with these interviews, Bock said, is that

> they create a situation where an interview is spent trying to confirm what we think of someone, rather than truly assessing them.
>
> Psychologists call this confirmation bias. Based on the slightest interaction, we make a snap, unconscious judgment heavily influenced by our existing biases and beliefs. Without realizing it, we then shift from assessing a candidate to hunting for evidence that confirms our initial impression.

Here, once again, is System 1 in action, bringing its biases and glitches to an important decision.

So what's a better approach to hiring? Google came to rely heavily on structured interviews, which explain more than 25% of on-the-job performance. Structured interviews consist of a set of predefined questions designed to assess, for example, a person's general cognitive ability. Google adopted a hiring process in which all interviewers used structured interviews and asked largely the same questions, and, as Bock explained, "We then score the interview with a consistent rubric. . . . The interviewer has to indicate how the candidate did, and each performance level is clearly defined. . . . A concise hiring rubric . . . distills messy, vague, and complicated work situations down to measurable, comparable results."

In this approach individual interviewers' judgments are still valued, but they're quantified and used to assign a numeric score to job applicants. Bock believes that instead of trivializing and dehumanizing the interview process, this approach does just the opposite. The job candidates themselves appreciate being treated objectively and fairly (80% of rejected candidates who went through the redesigned interview process said they would recommend to friends that they apply to Google), and hiring decisions become easier. As Bock puts it, "You'll see a clear line between the great and the average."

Decisions Too Important to Be Left to the Decision Makers

The idea of significant changes to the standard arrangement of minds and machines—in some cases even the reversal of that arrangement—makes many people uncomfortable. Most of us have a lot of faith in human intuition, judgment, and decision-making ability, especially our own (we've discussed this topic with a lot of audiences and have almost never heard anyone admit to having below-average intuition or judgment). But the evidence on this subject is so clear as to be overwhelming: data-driven, System 2 decisions are better than those that arise out of our brains' blend of System 1 and System 2 in the majority of cases where both options exist. It's not that our decisions and judgment are worthless; it's that that they can be improved on. The broad approaches we've seen here—letting algorithms and computer systems make the decisions, sometimes with human judgment as an input, and letting the people override them when appropriate—are ways to do this.

We've heard this approach described as dehumanizing. Some people feel that letting computers take the lead on making decisions pushes people to the margins and diminishes them. We appreciate that losing decision-making authority you once had is uncomfortable,* and that no one likes feeling like a servant to a computer. But

---

* In fact, in one experiment, psychologist Sebastian Bobadilla-Suarez and his colleagues found that people were willing to pay in order to retain the ability to make a decision about allocating money, even though they knew they would receive more money overall if they let the decision be made automatically. People like having the

does this mean that the wrong inmates should be let out of or kept in prison, just so that judges and parole boards can continue to work as they used to? Or that medical misdiagnosis rates should be higher than they could be, just to let doctors and psychologists keep doing their usual work? That companies should hire the wrong people, just to let interviewers keep feeling smart?

For us, the answer to these questions is no. Good decisions are critical to well-functioning societies: they help the right resources, from rides to jobs to health care, get to the right people in the right place at the right time. The standard partnership advocated by Hammer and Champy, in which computers do the record keeping while HiPPOs exercise their judgment and make decisions, is often not the best way to accomplish this.

At this point it might not surprise you much to learn that we humans are also pretty lousy at predicting the future. Predicting and deciding, after all, are almost inseparable activities (to make a good decision, we usually need an accurate prediction about some aspect of the future—namely, what will likely happen if we decide one way or another). So if we're bad at one, we're likely to also be bad at the other. And sure enough, System 1's many shortcuts and bugs keep us from making good predictions.

Beginning in 1984, the political scientist Philip Tetlock and his colleagues undertook a decades-long project to assess the accuracy of predictions in many areas, such as politics, economics, and international affairs. Here again, the conclusions are both clear and striking. In a test involving more than 82,000 forecasts, Tetlock found that "humanity barely bests [a] chimp" throwing darts at the possible outcomes.

This should be cause for concern because the business world is full

---

power to decide. Sebastian Bobadilla-Suarez, Cass R. Sunstein, and Tali Sharot, "The Intrinsic Value of Control: The Propensity to Under-delegate in the Face of Potential Gains and Losses," SSRN, February 17, 2016, https://papers.ssrn.com/sol3/papers2 .cfm?abstract_id=2733142.

of predictions about the future. Many of them are clearly presented as what they are: forecasts about how well a particular stock will do, or the direction and magnitude of future interest rate moves, or the number of smartphones that will be sold in a given country in the coming year. In many other cases, forecasts are implicit within a proposed plan of action. A website redesign, for example, contains the implicit prediction that visitors will like it better, as does the redesign of a bank's branch offices. A splashy product launch is built on a high-stakes prediction that customers will prefer it, and the accompanying marketing campaign contains a prediction about how their preferences can be shaped.

How to Be Good

Of course, not all of these predictions are wrong. Tetlock found that some people, whom he calls "superforecasters," really are able to consistently generate forecasts more accurately than chance would predict. They tend to take in information from many sources and, perhaps more important, show an ability to adopt multiple viewpoints when looking at a situation. Less accurate forecasters, meanwhile, tend to have one fixed perspective that they always use in their analyses (both ardent conservatives and diehard liberals, for example, tend to make lousy political predictions). Tetlock calls the former group (the more successful, multiperspective predictors) "foxes," and the latter "hedgehogs"; he takes these labels from the ancient Greek poet Archilochus's aphorism "A fox knows many things, but a hedgehog one important thing."*

---

* "The Fox and the Hedgehog" was also the title of an essay by the philosopher Isaiah Berlin that divided thinkers throughout history into two categories: those who pursue a single big idea throughout their careers, and those who pursue many different ones.

A piece of guidance, then, is to rely on foxes instead of hedgehogs wherever possible. Foxes can be spotted by the multidimensional, multiperspective reasoning and analyses they present. They can also be spotted by their track records. People with verifiable histories of accurate prediction are likely to be foxes.

Predict Less, Experiment More

The existence of superforecasters aside, our most fundamental advice about predictions is to rely on them less. Our world is increasingly complex, often chaotic, and always fast-flowing. This makes forecasting something between tremendously difficult and actually impossible, with a strong shift toward the latter as timescales get longer.

Among excellent companies a fundamental shift is taking place: away from long-range forecast, long-term plans, and big bets, and toward constant short-term iteration, experimentation, and testing. These organizations follow the computer scientist Alan Kay's great advice that the best way to predict the future is to invent it. They do this in many small steps, getting feedback and making adjustments as necessary, instead of working in private toward a distant event with a confidently predicted outcome.

It's relatively straightforward to put this vision into practice with a website. Because websites gather such rich data on user activities, it's easy to see whether a given change was for the better. Some e-commerce sites are absolutely rigorous about changing themselves over time and testing all the changes. The Priceline travel site shot to prominence in the first wave of great excitement about the web in the late 1990s. Like many of the other high fliers of that time, it crashed hard after the turn of the century, in large part because users grew disenchanted with its original name-your-own-price approach.

The company reinvented itself as a collection of more conventional travel sites in the middle years of the last decade. What allowed it to flourish, though, was constant data-driven experimentation. As *VentureBeat* reporter Matt Marshall puts it, "It's often small ideas that lead to growth spurts, like improving the existing experience through tiny wins—tweaking things like colors, wording, and arrangements of data on the web page just to get incremental lifts. . . . Priceline .com found that changing the wording in a description of one of its properties to 'free parking' from just 'parking' created a 2 percent improvement in conversion—even though it was on an obscure portion of the page and was hardly noticeable by the average reader." Such gains are found all over. Through rigorous A/B testing—a common online experimentation protocol in which half the visitors see option A when they visit a site while the other half see option B— lingerie company Adore Me found that having models pose with a hand in their hair instead of on their hip could double sales for some items. Instead of spending weeks, days, or even hours having experts analyze and debate a proposed change, it's usually faster and more accurate to simply test the options online. Often the results will be surprising.

And experimentation is not confined to the online universe. It can also be productive when applied in physical environments. Many large companies are what business school professor David Garvin calls "multiunit enterprises" (MUEs). These organizations have many customer-facing locations, all of which look and operate largely the same. Many commercial banks, chain restaurants, retailers, and service businesses are MUEs. By one estimate of the Fortune 100 companies, 20% are, to some degree, multiunit enterprises.

The many locations of an MUE provide an excellent opportunity to experiment. According to innovation scholar Stefan Thomke and corporate experimentalist Jim Manzi, the department store Kohl's ran an experiment involving a hundred stores to learn whether opening an hour later on weekdays would harm sales. The shorter open hours didn't significantly decrease sales, which was good news for the retailer. Less welcome news came from the results of another experiment, this one involving seventy Kohl's stores, on the impact of selling furniture for the first time. It found that because furniture took so much floor space away from other products, overall store sales and customer traffic actually decreased. Although many executives had been optimistic about the new offering, the company decided to follow the evidence and not offer furniture. It's often infeasible to roll out a new way of doing things to every location in an MUE simultaneously, so a phased rollout creates a natural opportunity for an experiment. With a little bit of planning, a great deal can be learned from such phased implementations, comparing locations operating under the new policy with carefully matched locations still doing things the old way.

Predictions and experiments cannot be automated as readily as decisions. But they are still highly amenable to data and analytical rigor. These are the prime tools of System 2, and also of the second machine age. System 1 and its components of intuition, judgment, and accumulated personal experience, meanwhile, need to recede from the craft of making accurate predictions at least as much as from that of making good decisions. HiPPOs, in short, need to become an endangered species within organizations.

Chapter Summary

▶ The twenty-year-old "standard partnership" of minds and machines more often than not places too much emphasis on human judgment, intuition, and "gut."

▶ Why is human judgment so often so bad? Because our fast, effortless "System 1" style of reasoning is subject to many different kinds of bias. Even worse, it is unaware when it's making an error, and it hijacks our rational System 2 to provide a convincing justification for what is actually a snap judgment.

▶ The evidence is overwhelming that, whenever the option is available, relying on data and algorithms alone usually leads to better decisions and forecasts than relying on the judgment of even experienced and "expert" humans.

▶ Many decisions, judgments, and forecasts now made by humans should be turned over to algorithms. In some cases, people should remain in the loop to provide commonsense checks. In others, they should be taken out of the loop entirely.

▶ In other cases, subjective human judgments should still be used, but in an inversion of the standard partnership: the judgments should be quantified and included in quantitative analyses.

▶ Decision-making processes should not be set up so that decision makers feel good about themselves. They should be set up to produce the best decisions, based on the right goals and clear metrics.

▶ Algorithms are far from perfect. If they are based on inaccurate or biased data, they will make inaccurate or biased decisions. These biases can be subtle and unintended. The criterion to apply is not whether the algorithms are flawless, but whether they outperform the available alternatives on the relevant metrics, and whether they can be improved over time.

▶ As technology has spread, so have opportunities to move past the standard partnership and its overreliance on human HiPPOs, and to move toward more data-driven decision making. The data show that companies that do this usually have an important advantage over those that do not.

▶ People who can look at an issue from multiple perspectives and companies that can iterate and experiment effectively are better performers.

Questions

1. Are you systematically and rigorously tracking the performance over time of your decisions, judgments, and forecasts made by people *and* algorithms in your organization? Do you know which are doing a good job?'

2. Where is decision making by HiPPOs most common in your organization? Why is this?

3. Where do you have opportunities to flip the standard partnership on its head, so that people's subjective assessments are incorporated into data-driven analyses, rather than the reverse?

4. Which do you think are generally more biased: algorithms or humans?

5. Which do you find more persuasive: foxes or hedgehogs?

6. Does your organization tend to carry out a small number of long-term, high-stakes projects, or a large number of shorter-term, more iterative projects?

CHAPTER 3

OUR MOST MIND-LIKE MACHINES

I believe that at the end of the century the use of
words and general educated opinion will have altered
so much that one will be able to speak of machines
thinking without expecting to be contradicted.

— *Alan Turing, 1950*

AS SOON AS WE DEVELOPED DIGITAL COMPUTERS, WE TRIED
to get them to think the way we do. It was obvious from the start that
they'd be highly useful for performing routine mathematical calculations, but this was not novel. Humans, after all, had been building
calculating machines—from abacuses in Japan and Babylon to the
mysterious Greek Antikythera mechanism*—since before the time
of Christ.

What *was* novel was the ability to program the new digital

---

* This clock-sized mechanism was used to predict the motion of the sun, moon,
and planets. It is puzzling largely because it was so advanced for its time. As a 2015
article by Jo Marchant put it, "Nothing else like this has ever been discovered from
antiquity. Nothing as sophisticated, or even close, appears again for more than a
thousand years." Jo Marchant, "Decoding the Antikythera Mechanism, the First
Computer," *Smithsonian*, February 2015, http://www.smithsonianmag.com/history/
decoding-antikythera-mechanism-first-computer-180953979.

computers—to give them arbitrarily complicated instructions.* As we saw in the previous chapter, computer programs are ideal for executing algorithms: precise, step-by-step instructions for accomplishing a task. But brilliant thinkers in many disciplines soon started trying to get the new machines to do more than just stepping through predefined orders. These pioneers wanted to create combinations of hardware and software that could be smart on their own—that could, in other words, accomplish humanlike feats of reasoning and thus be artificially intelligent.

Two Roads Diverged on the Way to Artificial Intelligence

John McCarthy, a math professor at Dartmouth, defined artificial intelligence as the "science and engineering of making intelligent machines." He organized the first conference on the topic, held in 1956 on his school's campus. Just a few years later, the field's biggest and most enduring controversy began. To understand it, and to understand why it's so important, consider the difference between the way a young child learns a language and the way most adults learn a second one.

Children essentially learn a language by listening. They hear the people around them speaking, absorb some of the words and rules that make up language, and at some point start saying things themselves. They get feedback and corrections on the mistakes they make, and eventually they become quite good at the difficult work of speaking a human tongue.

---

* Alan Turing proved that a basic computer that stores a program could be thought of as a universal computing machine that, in principle, could be instructed to solve any problem solvable by an algorithm.

Adult learners know how difficult this is. When they set out to master a second language, they are immediately confronted by a thicket of rules: where to put the pronouns in a sentence; which preposition to use; how to conjugate verbs; whether nouns have genders and, if so, how many; how to distinguish between the subject and object (so that we know if the dog bit the man or vice versa); and so on. Memorizing vocabulary words is hard enough, but the tooth-grinding difficulty for most adult language learners is the sheer mass of cumulative, complicated, occasionally inconsistent rules.

Young children don't need explicit lessons on rules in order to learn to speak well.* Most adults can't learn without them. There's some overlap in the two approaches, of course—many kids eventually take language classes, and adults pick up some things by ear—but they are starkly different. The brains of young children are specialized for language learning: they operate on statistical principles to discern the patterns in language† (for example, When Mom talks about herself as the subject, she uses the word "I" and puts it at the start of the sentence. When she's the object, she uses "me" and places

---

* As the linguist Steven Pinker points out in his 1994 book *The Language Instinct*, a child who is upset with her parent's choice for bedtime reading could construct a complex sentence like "Daddy, what did you bring that book that I don't want to be read to out of up for?" Steven Pinker, *The Language Instinct* (New York: HarperCollins, 1994), 23.

† A tragic case study provided strong evidence that after a certain age, children can no longer acquire language. In 1970, authorities in southern California became aware of a thirteen-year-old girl, given the pseudonym "Genie," who had been the victim of horrific abuse and neglect. Since she was a toddler, she had been kept by her father in constant and almost complete physical and social isolation. She was bound and left alone in a silent room, and no one spoke to her. Many researchers and therapists who worked with Genie after she was rescued believed that she was not congenitally retarded, but despite all their efforts, she never learned to speak in anything but extremely simple sentences. The more complex rules of grammar eluded her. She now lives in a facility for mentally underdeveloped adults somewhere in California.

it later). Because adults' brains are different, they usually learn the rules explicitly when acquiring a new language.

Early on, the AI community split into two similarly differentiated camps. One pursued so-called rule-based, or "symbolic," artificial intelligence,* while the other built statistical pattern recognition systems. The former tried to bring about artificial intelligence the way an adult tries to learn a second language; the latter tried to make it happen in much the same way that children learn their first language.

At first, it looked as though the symbolic approach would dominate. At the 1956 Dartmouth conference, for example, Allen Newell, J. C. Shaw, and future Nobel prize winner Herbert Simon demonstrated their "Logic Theorist" program, which used the rules of formal logic to automatically prove mathematical theorems. It was able to prove thirty-eight of the theorems in the second chapter of *Principia Mathematica*, a landmark book on the foundations of math by Alfred North Whitehead and Bertrand Russell. One of Logic Theorist's proofs, in fact, was so much more elegant than the one in the book that Russell himself "responded with delight" to it. Simon announced that he and his colleagues had "invented a thinking machine."

Other challenges, however, proved much less amenable to a rule-based approach. Decades of research in speech recognition, image classification, language translation, and other domains yielded unimpressive results. The best of these systems achieved much worse than human-level performance, and the worst were memorably bad. According to a 1979 collection of anecdotes, for example, researchers gave their English-to-Russian translation utility the phrase "The spirit is willing, but the flesh is weak." The program responded with the Russian equivalent of "The whisky is agreeable, but the meat has

---

* Rule-based AI was called "symbolic" because it was expressed in words, numbers, and other symbols that humans could understand.

gone bad." This story is probably apocryphal, but it's not an exaggeration. As a group, symbolic AI systems generated deeply underwhelming results, so much so that by the late 1980s, an "AI winter" had descended over the field as major corporate and governmental sources of research funding dried up.

Over-ruled

What explains the broad failure of symbolic approaches to AI? There are two main obstacles. One poses serious challenges for the field, and the other is apparently insurmountable. First, to put it simply, there are a lot of rules in the world, as adult language learners well know, and it's generally not enough to know and follow most of them. Instead, you have to get virtually all of them right in order to perform well. A sentence that gets 80% of its grammar right is likely to be laughable, or even completely unintelligible.

And there are rules within rules. Knowing that the adjective is typically placed before the noun in an English sentence, for example, is not enough. As Mark Forsyth writes in his book *The Elements of Eloquence*, "adjectives in English absolutely have to be in this order: opinion-size-age-shape-color-origin-material-purpose Noun. So you can have a lovely little old rectangular green French silver whittling knife. But if you mess with that word order in the slightest you'll sound like a maniac. It's an odd thing that every English speaker uses that list, but almost none of us could write it out."

Furthermore, the worlds we inhabit, both the one populated by physical objects and the one of ideas and concepts, are lousy at sticking to one set of rules. Chairs have legs, except when they have pedestals or upholstered bases, or are suspended from the ceiling. In 2002 two men could not be married in the United States, but in 2015 they could. Squirrels don't fly, except for the ones that kind of do by gliding. In English, two negatives can make a positive ("she is never not cheerful"), but two positives can never make a negative. Yeah, right.

Attempts to codify all relevant rules for complex things like languages or furniture into computer systems, and to get the systems to do anything useful, have been largely unsuccessful. As the computer scientist Ernest Davis and neuroscientist Gary Marcus write, "As of 2014, few commercial systems make any significant use of automated commonsense reasoning . . . nobody has yet come close to producing a satisfactory commonsense reasoner." For the great majority of humans, our common sense does an admirable job of carrying us through the world's barrage of complexity and inconsistency, even though, as discussed in the previous chapter, it's biased and buggy. We have not yet designed symbolic digital systems that understand how the world actually works as well as our own biological System 1 does. Our systems are increasingly effective at "narrow" artificial intelligence, for particular domains like Go or image recognition, but we are far from achieving what Shane Legg, a cofounder of Deep-Mind, has dubbed artificial general intelligence (AGI), which can apply intelligence to a variety of unanticipated types of problems.

Polanyi's Pervasive Paradox

Davis and Marcus describe what is perhaps the most instrumental barrier to building such systems: "In doing commonsense reasoning, people . . . are drawing on . . . reasoning processes largely unavailable to introspection." In other words, the cognitive work that we humans do to navigate so easily through so many thickets of rules is an ongoing demonstration of Polanyi's Paradox, the strange phenomenon that we know more than we can tell. As we described in Chapter 1, it's this paradox that has, until recently, kept anyone from creating software that could play the game Go as well as the top human practitioners can. Keep in mind that this paradox is found all over. In many important cases, we simply don't and can't know what rules we ourselves are using to get something right.

This seems like an absolute roadblock to any kind of automation or artificial intelligence. If no entity on Earth knows the rules by which humans accomplish something, including the humans themselves, then how can we ever create a rule-based system, or indeed any computer system, to emulate these accomplishments? Polanyi's Paradox seems to place a hard limit on the types of human tasks that can be automated. As our MIT colleague economist David Autor writes, "The scope for this kind of substitution (of computers for people) is bounded because there are many tasks that people understand tacitly and accomplish effortlessly but for which neither computer programmers nor anyone else can enunciate the explicit 'rules' or procedures."

Can We Make Machines That Can Learn for Themselves?

The other main camp of artificial intelligence researchers—one that eschewed a symbolic approach—has been trying since the late 1950s to overcome Polanyi's Paradox by building systems that learn tasks the way a young child learns language: by experience and repetition, and through feedback. They've created the field of "machine learning," which is exactly what it sounds like.

One of the first digital machines that learned in this way was the Perceptron, a US Navy–funded attempt at building a thinking, learning machine led by Frank Rosenblatt, a scientist at the Cornell Aeronautical Laboratory. The goal with the Perceptron, which debuted in 1957, was to be able to classify things that it saw—dogs versus cats, for example. To this end, it was configured a bit like a tiny version of a brain.

The 100 billion or so neurons in our brain aren't arranged in any tidy pattern. Instead they're deeply interconnected: the typical human neuron takes inputs or messages from as many as 10,000 of its neighbors and then sends outputs to a roughly equal number. Every time enough inputs send a strong enough electric signal, the neuron sends its own signal to all of its outputs. The definitions of "enough" and "strong enough" here change over time, depending on feedback, as does the importance, called the "weight," that a neuron gives to each of its inputs. Out of this strange, complex, constantly unfolding process come memories, skills, System 1 and System 2, flashes of insight and cognitive biases, and all the other work of the mind.

The Perceptron didn't try to do much of this work. It was built just to do simple image classification. It had 400 light-detecting photocells randomly connected (to stimulate the brain's messiness) to a single layer of artificial neurons. An early demonstration of this "neural network," together with Rosenblatt's confident predictions, led the *New York Times* to write in 1958 that it was "the embryo of an electronic computer that [the Navy] expects will be able to walk, talk, see, write, reproduce itself and be conscious of its existence."

The promised breakthroughs did not come quickly, however, and in 1969 Marvin Minsky and Seymour Papert published a devastating critique titled *Perceptrons: An Introduction to Computational Geometry*. They showed mathematically that Rosenblatt's design was incapable of accomplishing some basic classification tasks. For most in the field of artificial intelligence, this was enough to get them to turn away not only from Perceptrons, but from the broader concepts of neural networks and machine learning in general. The AI winter descended on both camps of researchers.

Persistence with Perceptrons Pays Off

A few teams carried on with machine learning because they remained convinced that the right way to get computers to think in humanlike ways was to build brain-inspired neural networks that could learn by example. These researchers came to understand and overcome the limitations of the Perceptron. They did this with a combination of sophisticated math, ever-more-powerful computer hardware, and a pragmatic approach that allowed them to take inspiration from how the brain works but not to be constrained by it. Electric signals flow in only one direction through the brain's neurons, for example, but the successful machine learning systems built in the eighties by Paul Werbos, Geoff Hinton, Yann LeCun, and others allowed information to travel both forward and backward through the network.

This "back-propagation" led to much better performance, but progress remained frustratingly slow. By the 1990s, a machine learning system developed by LeCun to recognize numbers was reading as many as 20% of all handwritten checks in the United States, but there were few other real-world applications.

As AlphaGo's recent victory shows, the situation is very different now. While AlphaGo did incorporate efficient searches through large numbers of possibilities—a classic element of rule-based AI systems—it was, at its core, a machine learning system. As its creators write, it's "a new approach to computer Go that uses . . . deep neural networks . . . trained by a novel combination of supervised learning from human expert games, and reinforcement learning from games of self-play."

AlphaGo is far from an isolated example. The past few years have seen a great flourishing of neural networks. They're now the dominant type of artificial intelligence by far, and they seem likely to stay on top for some time. For this reason, the field of AI is finally fulfilling at least some of its early promise.

Why Do We Finally Have Artificial Intelligence Now ?

How did this flourishing come about, and why was it so fast and unexpected? As is often the case with such advances, a number of factors came together, and tenacity and serendipity both played a role. Many insiders believe that the single most important factor has been Moore's law. Neural networks become much more powerful and capable as their size increases, and it's only recently that sufficiently large ones have become cheap enough that they are available to many researchers.

Cloud computing has helped open up AI research to these smaller budgets. Technology entrepreneur Elliot Turner estimates that the computing power required to execute a cutting-edge machine learning project could be rented from a cloud computing provider like Amazon Web Services for approximately $13,000 by the fall of 2016. Oddly enough, the popularity of modern video games has also been a great boost to machine learning. The specialized graphics processing units (GPUs) that drive popular gaming consoles turn out to be extremely well suited to the kinds of calculations required for neural networks, so they've been drafted in large numbers for this task. AI researcher Andrew Ng told us that "the teams at the leading edge do crazy complicated things in the GPUs that I could never imagine two or three years ago."

The phenomenon of "big data"—the recent explosion of digital text, pictures, sounds, videos, sensor readings, and so on—has been almost as important to machine learning as Moore's law. Just as a young child needs to hear a lot of words and sentences in order to learn language, machine learning systems need to be exposed to many examples in order to improve in speech recognition, image classification, and other tasks.[*] We now have an effectively endless supply of such data, with more generated all the time. The kinds of systems built by Hinton, LeCun, Ng, and others have the highly desirable property that their performance improves as they see more and more examples. This happy phenomenon led Hinton to say, a bit

---

[*] Big data and analytics have also transformed human decision making, as we discuss in our article for *Harvard Business Review*: Andrew McAfee and Erik Brynjolfsson, "Big Data: The Management Revolution," *Harvard Business Review* 90, no. 10 (2012): 61–67.

modestly, "Retrospectively, [success with machine learning] was just a question of the amount of data and the amount of computations."

Hinton might not be giving himself enough credit. He's been responsible for multiple advances in neural networks, one of which essentially renamed the field. His 2006 paper "A Fast Learning Algorithm for Deep Belief Nets," coauthored with Simon Osindero and Yee-Whye Teh, demonstrated that sufficiently powerful and properly configured neural networks could essentially learn on their own, with no human training or supervision. If shown a large group of handwritten numbers, for example, they would correctly conclude that there were ten distinct patterns in the data (corresponding to the numerals 0 through 9), then also be able to accurately classify any new handwritten numbers they were shown into the ten categories they had identified.

This type of "unsupervised learning" remains relatively rare within the field of machine learning. Most successful systems rely instead on "supervised learning," where they're essentially given a paired set of questions and correct answers before they are asked to answer any new questions on their own. For example, a machine learning system might be given a large set of sound files of human speech and text files of the corresponding written words. The system uses this set of matched pairs to build up the associations within its neural network that enable it to transcribe new instances of recorded speech. Because both supervised and unsupervised machine learning approaches use the algorithms described by Hinton and his colleagues in their 2006 paper, they're now commonly called "deep learning" systems.

Demonstrations and Deployments

Except for a very small number of cases, such as the system LeCun built for recognizing handwritten numbers on checks, the business application of deep learning is only a few years old. But the technique is spreading with extraordinary speed. The software engineer Jeff Dean,* who heads Google's efforts to use the technology, notes that as recently as 2012 the company was not using it at all to improve products like Search, Gmail, YouTube, or Maps. By the third quarter of 2015, however, deep learning was being used in approximately 1,200 projects across the company, having surpassed the performance of other methods.

DeepMind, which has been particularly effective in combining deep learning with another technique called reinforcement learning,† has turned its attention and its technologies not only to the information products that the company delivers to its customers, but also to critical processes in the physical world. Google runs some of the world's largest data centers, which are extremely energy-intensive facilities. These buildings must supply power to as many as 100,000 servers while also keeping them cool. The cooling challenge is compounded by the fact that the facility's computing load—the total of

---

* Dean's many contributions have made him something of a legend at Google. His colleagues have collected a set of exaggerated "Jeff Dean facts" to convey his abilities. "The speed of light in a vacuum used to be about 35 mph. Then Jeff Dean spent a weekend optimizing physics" is a representative example. Kenton Varda, Google+ post, January 28, 2012, https://plus.google.com/+KentonVarda/posts/TSDhe5CvaFe.

† Reinforcement learning is concerned with building software agents that can take effective actions within an environment in order to maximize a reward. DeepMind's first public demonstration of its abilities in this area was the "deep Q-network" (DQN) system, which was built to play classic Atari 2600 video games like Space Invaders, Pong, Breakout, and Battlezone. The DQN system was not told by its programmers which game it was playing, what the rules were, which strategies might be effective, or which controls and actions were available to it. It was not even told, in fact, that it was playing a game at all. It was simply shown the screen of each game and told to maximize the score by moving the controller. The DQN was quickly able to beat the scores of expert human players in more than half of the forty-nine games presented to it. Volodymyr Mnih et al., "Human-Level Control through Deep Reinforcement Learning," *Nature* 518 (February 28, 2015): 529–33, https://storage.googleapis.com/deepmind-data/assets/papers/DeepMindNature14236Paper.pdf.

everything the servers are being asked to do—varies unpredictably over time. So does the weather outside, which obviously affects how the building needs to be cooled, and by how much.

Humans typically control the pumps, coolers, cooling towers, and other equipment that keep data centers at the right temperature. These people monitor thermometers, pressure gauges, and many other sensors and make decisions over time about how best to cool the facility. DeepMind wanted to see whether machine learning could be used instead. They took years of historical data on data centers' computing load, sensor readings, and environmental factors like temperature and humidity and used all of this information to train a set of neural networks to control all of the available cooling equipment. In a sense, they treated the data center like a giant video game and instructed their algorithms to try to get a higher score, which in this case meant better energy efficiency.

When control of an actual data center was turned over to these systems, the results were immediate and dramatic. The total amount of energy used for cooling fell by as much as 40%, and the facility's overhead—the energy not used directly for IT equipment, which includes ancillary loads and electrical losses—improved by about 15%. DeepMind cofounder Mustafa Suleyman told us these were among the largest improvements the Google data center team had ever seen.

Suleyman also stressed to us that DeepMind's approach is highly generalizable. The neural networks used by the team do not need to be completely reconfigured for each new data center. They simply need to be trained with as much detailed historical data as possible. This training is subtle and difficult work,* but it clearly pays off.

---

* Setting up a properly functioning neural network may sound easy—just pour in the data and let the system make its associations—but it's actually time-consuming and subtle work at present, vexing even to people with a strong background in computer science.

In fact, the best-performing machine learning systems in use today for applications as dissimilar as data center energy management, speech recognition, image classification, and automatic translation are remarkably similar. Instead of varying greatly by domain, they're all variants of deep learning. This is important because it suggests that this approach to artificial intelligence could diffuse throughout a variety of industries and economies with great speed. New neural networks can be duplicated and scaled up almost instantly, trained with new data, and then put to work.

Tech giants including Microsoft, Amazon, Google, and IBM have made their internally developed machine learning technologies available to other companies via a combination of the cloud and application programming interfaces, or APIs, which are essentially clear, consistent, published rules about how pieces of software will interact with each other. APIs make it much easier to combine code from different sources into a single application, and the cloud makes this code available on demand, all around the world.

With this infrastructure in place, there is an opportunity for machine learning deployments to spread quickly and deeply throughout the world. However, for reasons discussed in Chapter 1, we also expect it to spread unevenly, as business processes are reinvented at leading companies and new business models emerge. This is already happening in some unexpected places.

When Makoto Koike returned in 2015 to his parents' cucumber farm in Japan, he saw an opportunity to put machine learning to use. He had previously worked as a hardware and software engineer in the auto industry, so he was comfortable building equipment that combined code and machinery. He found an application for his talents in the work of cucumber sorting, which was done exclusively by Makoto Masaka, his mother. She used her years of experience to manually sort all the farm's produce into nine grades of quality. She was able to do this herself because the farm was small (nonrice farms in Japan average only 1.5 hectares, which is about one and a half baseball fields, or two soccer fields), but it was demanding work, requiring up to eight hours a day during peak harvesting season.

Makoto was impressed by AlphaGo's pattern-matching abilities and intrigued by TensorFlow, a suite of machine learning technologies made available by Google in November of 2016. He decided to use them to see whether he could automate the work of cucumber sorting on his family's farm. Even though he had no prior experience with machine learning, he trained himself on how to use TensorFlow, then trained the system on 7,000 images of the different grades of cucumbers. Using inexpensive, off-the-shelf cameras, computers, and hardware controllers, he built a fully automatic grader that achieved 70% accuracy in its first year of operation. Greater accuracy will almost certainly be possible with higher-resolution images and the next generation of cloud-based machine learning software, about which Makoto says, "I can't wait to try it." Efforts like his lead us to agree with Google's Kaz Sato, who says, "It's not hyperbole to say that use cases for machine learning and deep learning are only limited by our imaginations."

As we write this book, almost all commercial successes in the field so far have used supervised learning techniques, and a few have used reinforcement learning (for instance, the data center optimized by DeepMind). However, the main way humans learn is through unsupervised learning. A toddler learns everyday physics by playing with blocks, pouring water out of a glass, throwing a ball, and falling off a chair—not by being taught Newton's laws of motion or memorizing equations like $F = ma$. Yann LeCun has memorably highlighted the vast, largely untapped importance of unsupervised learning with a cake metaphor. He says, "If intelligence was a cake, unsupervised learning would be the cake, supervised learning would be the icing on the cake, and reinforcement learning would be the cherry on the cake. We know how to make the icing and the cherry, but we don't know how to make the cake." He thinks that developing better algorithms for unsupervised learning will be essential if we are ever to achieve AGI.

Minds and Learning Machines

More than once, we've heard builders of the current generation of neural networks refer dismissively to previous rule-based approaches as outdated "feature engineering." Many now believe that the approach of trying to amass all the relevant rules for a task and then program them into a computer is misguided. It's demonstrably much more productive, they believe, to build systems that can learn the rules on their own. The statistical camp of AI researchers is ascendant now and is delivering on at least some of the promises made by the discipline more than half a century ago.

As this happens, how are minds and machines being brought together? In a few different ways. One way combines them along the lines advocated by Paul Meehl and Tom Davenport in the previous chapter: have humans endowed with common sense watch over the decisions and actions of the artificial intelligence, and intervene if they see anything amiss. This is what DeepMind did when its neural networks took over optimization of a data center. The human controllers were always present and in the loop, able to take over control at any time.

So far, automakers that have introduced self-driving technologies have also taken this approach. They stress that the human is both literally and figuratively in the driver's seat, and is responsible for the safe operation of the car even when self-piloting technologies are operating. Always having a human in the loop seems prudent to many, since inattention can be fatal. In the summer of 2016, Joshua Brown's Tesla crashed into the side of a truck's trailer, killing him. The truck, which had a white trailer, was in the process of making a left turn off a highway onto a surface road. Brown was traveling toward the truck on the opposite side of the highway. Since the Tesla's brakes were not applied prior to the crash, it appears that neither Brown nor the car's camera noticed the white trailer against the bright Florida sky. Perhaps Brown had become overconfident in the abilities of the self-driving system after seeing it operate effectively in many previous instances and had begun to pay less and less attention to the road.

Google believes that because human inattention is a perennial problem, we need to be taken entirely out of the loop in driving. As Chris Urmson, the former head of the company's self-driving car project, put it, "Conventional wisdom would say that we'll just take these driver assistance systems and we'll kind of push them and incrementally improve them, and over time, they'll turn into self-driving cars. Well, I'm here to tell you that's like me saying that if I work really hard at jumping, one day I'll be able to fly. We actually need to do something a little different." So the company is working to build 100% self-driving cars that require no contributions from humans—known in the industry as "level 5 autonomy."

Their capabilities are impressive. As Urmson recounted at the 2015 TED conference, "Our vehicles were driving through Mountain View, and this is what we encountered. This is a woman in an electric wheelchair chasing a duck in circles on the road. Now it turns out, there is nowhere in the DMV handbook that tells you how to deal with that, but our vehicles were able to encounter that, slow down, and drive safely." Autonomous cars that can drive safely in *all* circumstances and conditions are not here yet. But we think they're coming quickly.

The ability of machine language to overcome Polanyi's Paradox is starting to be put to use in white-collar back-office work that has, to date, proved surprisingly resistant to complete automation. "Back office" is a catchall term for knowledge work that takes place out of sight of the customer, including purchasing, accounting, and IT.

As we discussed earlier, the highest-volume and most standardized elements of the back office were automated long ago by enterprise systems, but a great deal of manual work remains in most companies.

One way to automate at least some of this work would be to ask the people doing it what rules they're using, what the exceptions to these rules are, when they switch to a different set of rules or guidelines, and so on. However, the process of eliciting knowledge in interviews would consume a lot of time, would take people away from their job, and probably wouldn't work very well. The people doing the less routine back-office work are, in all likelihood, not able to accurately and completely tell someone else how to do their job.

The Japanese insurer Fukoku Mutual Life is taking a different approach. In December of 2016, it announced an effort to use IBM's Watson AI technology to at least partially automate the work of human health insurance claim processors. The system will begin by extracting relevant information from documents supplied by hospitals and other health providers, using it to fill in the proper codes for insurance reimbursement, then presenting this information to people. But over time, the intent is for the system to "learn the history of past payment assessment to inherit the experience and expertise of assessor workers." The technology, in other words, will learn as it goes and, over time, be able to take over more of the work from humans.

We expect for there to be more efforts like this in the future, and for deep learning and other machine learning approaches to spread rapidly. Much of the work of customer service, for example, consists of listening to people to understand what they want, then providing an answer or service to them. Modern technologies can take over the latter of these activities once they learn the rules of an interaction.

But the hardest part of customer service to automate has not been finding an answer, but rather the initial step: listening and understanding. Speech recognition and other aspects of natural language processing have been tremendously difficult problems in artificial intelligence since the dawn of the field, for all of the reasons described earlier in this chapter. The previously dominant symbolic approaches have not worked well at all, but newer ones based on deep learning are making progress so quickly that it has surprised even the experts.

In October of 2016, a team from Microsoft Research announced that a neural network they had built had achieved "human parity in conversational speech recognition," as the title of their paper put it. Their system was more accurate than professional human transcriptionists both for discussions on an assigned topic and for open-ended conversations among friends and family members. Commenting on this result, the linguistics professor Geoffrey Pullum wrote, "I must confess that I never thought I would see this day. In the 1980s, I judged fully automated recognition of connected speech (listening to connected conversational speech and writing down accurately what was said) to be too difficult for machines. . . . The speech engineers have accomplished it without even relying on any syntactic* analysis: pure engineering, aided by statistical modeling based on gigantic amounts of raw data. . . . I not only didn't think I would see this come about, I would have confidently bet against it."

A remark attributed to the legendary computer scientist Frederick Jelinek captures the reason behind the broad transition within the artificial intelligence community from rule-based to statistical approaches. He observed in the mid-1980s, "Every time I fire a linguist, the performance of the speech recognizer goes up." By the mid-2010s, the most successful group working on problems related to speech transcriptions had zero linguists, and their results surprised the world. We are very confident that more such surprises are in store.

We agree with Salesforce CEO and technology industry pioneer Marc Benioff that we're moving into what he calls an "AI-first world." Like us, he sees countless opportunities to replace decision making

---

* Rule-based, in other words.

by HiPPOs with something that will work much better. As he writes, "Many businesses still make important decisions based on instinct instead of information. . . . This will change in the next few years, as AI becomes more pervasive, potentially making every company and every employee smarter, faster, and more productive." A few years ago, such a prediction would have sounded like wild hyperbole. Now it seems like a safe bet.

Chapter Summary

▶ The rule-based or symbolic approach to AI is now dormant. It seems unlikely to be revived outside a few narrow domains, and perhaps not even there.

▶ Machine learning—the art and science of building software systems that can detect patterns and formulate winning strategies after being shown many examples—is finally fulfilling its early promise and accomplishing useful work.

▶ Machine learning systems get better as they get bigger, run on faster and more specialized hardware, gain access to more data, and contain improved algorithms. All of these improvements are taking place now, so machine learning is advancing rapidly.

▶ Neural networks have had their best successes with supervised learning, where the learning examples are tagged. But they have made little progress with unsupervised learning, which is the main way humans learn about the world.

▶ Supervised learning is ideally suited for automating many tasks that are currently done by people, especially in areas of pattern matching, diagnosis, classification, prediction, and recommendation. Vision, speech recognition, and other capabilities that once were impossible for machines are now performed at levels comparable to humans in many domains.

▶ We're still in the early phases of the spread of machine learning. It will become pervasive in our economies and societies, especially since it is now available in the cloud and on demand.

▶ Machine learning systems (and all other forms of AI) still lack common sense.

Questions

1. What are your most important pattern-matching, diagnosis, classification, prediction, and recommendation activities? Are you exploring machine learning solutions for any of them?

2. Which key decisions or operations, if any, would you consider turning over entirely to artificial intelligence systems? Which would you do while keeping a human in the loop?

3. Would you be comfortable riding in a self-driving vehicle for your daily commute tomorrow morning? Do you think you would be comfortable doing it in five years? Why or why not?

4. Fill in the blank: If our competitors implemented a successful machine learning system for _____, we'd be in serious trouble.

5. What is your machine learning strategy? How far along are you at bringing machine learning into your organization?

CHAPTER 4

HI, ROBOT

> Glistening-footed Thetis reached Hephaestus' house. . . .
> There she found him, sweating, wheeling round his bel-
> lows, pressing the work on twenty three-legged caul-
> drons, an array to ring the walls inside his mansion. He'd
> bolted golden wheels to the legs of each so all on their
> own speed, at a nod from him, they could roll to halls
> where the gods convene then roll right home again—a
> marvel to behold.
>
> — Homer, The Iliad, 8th century BCE
> (translated by Robert Fagles)

IT'S RARE FOR A MEAL TO BE SIMULTANEOUSLY NUTRITIOUS,
tasty, and affordable. It's even more uncommon for it to also provide
a glimpse of the future of automation.

The first Eatsa restaurant opened in San Francisco's SoMa neighborhood in 2015. It offered a selection of vegetarian dishes with a
main ingredient of quinoa, a grain of South American origin with
excellent nutritional properties.* At Eatsa, quinoa was accompa-
nied by ingredients like corn, beans, eggplant, and guacamole and
served in bowls with names like "Southwestern Scramble" and "No
Worry Curry."

---

* Quinoa is efficient to produce, requiring one-thirtieth the amount of energy compared to animal protein production. It's also cholesterol- and gluten-free.

Processes without People

Before Eatsa diners even tasted the food, however, they encountered something unusual: they ordered, paid for, and received their meals without encountering any employees. Upon entering the restaurant, customers saw a row of tablet computers. They used one of them to place their order and pay via credit card. (Eatsa had no ability to accept cash.) As their bowls were being prepared, customers' first names and last initials (taken from their credit cards) appeared on a large flat-screen display. As a name neared the top of the list, a number appeared next to it, corresponding to one of approximately twenty cubby holes—small openings in a wall—covered with panels. These panels were actually transparent liquid crystal displays; they showed the customer's name in the middle of the screen and a small bull's-eye symbol in the upper right-hand corner. When the customer double-tapped the bull's-eye, the panel opened to reveal the meal, packaged to go (the restaurant offered little indoor seating).

A small staff of concierges was available to guide newcomers through the ordering process and answer questions, but most customers didn't need them. Eatsa's early reviews were excellent; one Yelper said, "It's a restaurant where you don't have to speak to or interact with a single human being and in mere minutes get a delicious, nutritional, affordable meal through a computer screen. Marry me."

Eatsa's popularity illustrated an important phenomenon of the second machine age: many transactions and interactions that used to take place between people in the physical world are now completed via digital interfaces. And lots of business processes, it turns out, do not really require atoms to be transformed or moved from one place to another; instead, they are about moving and transforming bits, or pieces of information. Ordering an Eatsa meal, paying for it, and learning where to pick it up are examples of such processes. It's not quite correct to say that they've been automated; there's still a person involved—namely, the customer. It's more precise to say that they've been "virtualized."

Virtualization Is Reality

Virtualization is spreading. When we fly without checking a bag, we rarely talk to an airline employee until we arrive at the gate, since we download boarding passes to our phones or print them at the airport using a self-service kiosk. When we land in the United States after traveling abroad, we use Global Entry kiosks to supply customs and immigration information and be cleared to reenter the country. And it looks like we'll soon have fully automated security lanes when we fly within the country; the Transportation Security Administration announced in July of 2016 a plan to install and evaluate them at five domestic airports.*

Virtualization accelerates when networks and convenient digital devices are almost everywhere. As ATMs proliferated, many people no longer went to bank tellers to withdraw cash from their accounts. PC-based online banking enabled customers to review their statements, transfer funds, pay bills, and accomplish many other tasks from home, and smartphones and apps enabled these same tasks to be done from anywhere. Many banking apps eventually added another convenience: they enabled customers to deposit checks by taking a picture of them using their phone's camera. The ever-growing power,

---

* There's disturbing evidence that our current, labor-intensive methods of ensuring air travel safety don't work very well. In 2015 the Department of Homeland Security published a summary of attempts by its "Red Teams" to sneak weapons, explosives, and other forbidden materials through security screening at US airports. The Red Teams had a success rate of greater than 95%, getting the contraband through screening 67 of 70 times.

reach, and convenience of virtualized banking is probably a major reason why the total number of bank tellers in the United States is now falling year after year, and has dropped nearly 20% from its peak of 608,000 in 2007.

Will some transactions and processes remain largely unvirtualized? Many people and companies think so. Virginia Postrel, an insightful analyst of business and cultural shifts, believes that automated self-checkout kiosks at drugstores, supermarkets, and other retailers will never catch on, "because of technical problems. Nobody wants to listen to an endless loop of electronic reprimands while watching other shoppers move smoothly through the human-staffed queue."

We see Postrel's point. Most self-checkout technologies are confusing and hence slow to use, and they seem to seize up frequently. We probably keep using them more because of our research interests than because of their actual convenience. But we've noticed that they have gotten better over time, as we should expect. As the developers of self-checkout systems gain more experience, they'll improve the technology and the user experience, and figure out how to reduce error rates and frustrations.

This might mean future self-checkout machines and processes that look very different, but we predict that large-scale virtualization will arrive, despite unimpressive progress so far. When it does, it might look like Amazon Go, an 1,800-square-foot convenience store unveiled in Seattle by the online giant in December of 2016. It's a retailer with neither cashiers nor self-checkout kiosks. Instead, in-store sensors and cameras combine with machine learning technologies and a smartphone app to keep track of everything customers put in their shopping baskets, then bill them for whatever they leave the store with. Journalist Lloyd Alter observed that "Amazon Go is not a grocery store upgraded with online-style technology; it's an online experience surrounded by brick walls." In this experience, the shopping cart is real but the checkout counter becomes virtual.

Another argument against very widespread virtualization is the idea that some interactions require a human touch to put the focal person—the customer, patient, sales prospect, and so on—at ease and in the right frame of mind. We think there's truth to this, but we've also seen that at least some groups of people are willing—and maybe even eager—to virtualize exactly those transactions where the human touch has long been considered crucial.

The conventional wisdom within financial services has been that at least one face-to-face meeting is necessary to convince a person or family to turn over a large portion of their wealth to an investment adviser. Yet Wealthfront has taken more than $3 billion from over 35,000 households since it was founded in December of 2011, and all of this money was transferred to the company virtually, with no human investment adviser across the desk or in the loop. Wealthfront is a wealth management company that has not only turned away from using human judgment when making investment decisions, but also completely eliminated the classic staging and cast of characters of the wealth transfer transaction—the well-appointed office, the glossy brochures, the receptionist, the professional-looking adviser—and replaced it with an online form.

Self-Selection or Secular Trend?

Wealthfront's clients tend to be younger and more tech-savvy than the clients of other investment advisory companies. Economists use the term "self-selection" to refer to phenomena like this: cases in which people sort themselves into different groups based on their preferences. Self-selection is likely to be a powerful force shaping virtualization. Some people will give their money to Wealthfront to invest, use self-checkout machines at supermarkets, and lunch at

Eatsa. Others will want to meet a human investment adviser, have a cashier ring up their purchases, and order lunch from a person.

At present, we see companies explicitly appealing to one side or the other of this self-selection. The fast-food chain McDonald's is, like Eatsa, increasing virtualization. By November 2016 it had installed digital self-service ordering and payment stations in 500 locations across New York, Florida, and southern California and announced plans to expand the touchscreen technology to all 14,000 of its American restaurants. The Discover credit card, in contrast, is stressing the human touch. A series of ads, first aired in 2013, featured phone conversations between customers and employees played by actors who look very similar. The idea, of course, was to convey that the company provided deeply personal and hence more authentic customer service. One of the ads even suggested that the company was more concerned about interpersonal connection than about making more money. Its narrator said that "with Discover Card you can talk to a real person in the US day or night, plus we're not going to waste your time trying to sell you a bunch of other products you don't really need."

Eatsa, Wealthfront, McDonald's, Discover, and many other companies are chasing market segments defined by customer preferences for or against virtualization. This is a natural and appropriate thing to do, but we wonder how long the antivirtualization market will be a large one. The recent decline in the number of bank tellers in the United States indicates to us that once virtualization that is robust enough becomes available for a given process, many people will take advantage of it, especially as time passes and more and more of the population consists of "digital natives." This is especially true if the human option takes longer or is otherwise less efficient and pleasant. If completely automated and equally safe and private airport security suddenly became available, how many of us would choose to stand in line and be screened by a human TSA agent?

After enough technical progress, enough experimentation, and enough iteration, we believe that automated and digitally mediated processes will become quite widespread and will take the place of many that are now mediated by people. We believe, in short, that virtualization is a secular trend, where "secular" is used in the way the finance industry uses it: to denote a long-term development that will unfold over several years, rather than a short-term fluctuation.

Automatons Explode

Eatsa wants to do more than virtualize the task of ordering meals; it also wants to automate how they're prepared. Food preparation in its kitchens is highly optimized and standardized, and the main reason the company uses human cooks instead of robots is that the objects being processed—avocados, tomatoes, eggplants, and so on—are both irregularly shaped and not completely rigid. These traits present no real problems for humans, who have always lived in a world full of softish blobs. Most of the robots created so far, however, are much better at handling things that are completely rigid and do not vary from one to the next.

This is because robots' senses of vision and touch have historically been quite primitive—far inferior to ours—and proper handling of a tomato generally entails seeing and feeling it with a lot of precision. It's also because it's been surprisingly hard to program robots to handle squishiness—here again, we know more than we can tell—so robot brains have lagged far behind ours, just as their senses have.

But they're catching up—fast—and a few robot chefs have already appeared. At one restaurant in China's Heilongjiang Province, stir-fries and other wok dishes are cooked over a flame by an anthropomorphic purple robot, while humans still do the prep work. At the Hannover Messe Industrial Trade Fair in April 2015, the UK company Moley Robotics introduced a highly automated kitchen, the centerpiece of which was a pair of multijointed robotic arms that descended from the ceiling. These arms emulated movements made by master chefs as they prepared their signature dishes. At the fair, the arms whipped up a crab bisque developed by Tim Anderson, a winner of the UK's televised *MasterChef* competition. One online reviewer said of the dish, "It's good. If I was served it at a restaurant I wouldn't bat an eye." Here again, though, food preparation had to be done by a human, and the robot arms had no eyes, so they would fail if any ingredients or utensils were not exactly where they were expected to be.

The most advanced robot cook the two of us have seen is the hamburger maker developed by Momentum Machines, a startup funded by venture capitalist Vinod Khosla. It takes in raw meat, buns, condiments, sauces, and seasonings, and converts these into finished, bagged burgers at rates as high as 400 per hour. The machine does much of its own food preparation, and to preserve freshness it does not start grinding, mixing, and cooking until each order is placed. It also allows diners to greatly customize their burgers, specifying not only how they'd like them cooked, but also the mix of meats in the patty. We can attest to their deliciousness.

DANCE of the Robots

These automatic chefs are early examples of what Gill Pratt, the CEO of the Toyota Research Institute (and our former MIT colleague) calls an unfolding "Cambrian Explosion" in robotics. The original Cambrian Explosion, which began more than 500 million years ago, was a relatively brief period of time during which most of the major forms of life on Earth—the phyla—appeared. Almost all the body types present on our planet today can trace their origins back to this burst of intense evolutionary innovation.

Pratt believes we're about to experience something similarly transformative with robotic innovation. As he wrote in 2015, "Today, technological developments on several fronts are fomenting a similar explosion in the diversification and applicability of robotics. Many of the base hardware technologies on which robots depend— particularly computing, data storage, and communications—have been improving at exponential growth rates." One of the most important enablers of the Cambrian Explosion was vision—the moment when biological species first developed the ability to see the world. This opened up a massive new set of capabilities for our ancestors. Pratt makes the point that we are now at a similar threshold for machines. For the first time in history, machines are learning to see, and thereby gain the many benefits that come with vision.

Our conversations and investigations point to recent major developments in five parallel, interdependent, and overlapping areas: data, algorithms, networks, the cloud, and exponentially improving hardware. We remember them by using the acronym "DANCE."

Data. Music CDs, movie DVDs, and web pages have been adding to the world's stock of digitally encoded information for decades, but in the past few years the rate of creation has exploded. IBM estimates, in fact, that 90% of all the digital data in the world was created within the last twenty-four months. Signals from sensors in smartphones and industrial equipment, digital photos and videos, a nonstop global torrent of social media, and many other sources combine to put us in an era of "big data" that is without precedent.

Algorithms. The data deluge is important because it supports and accelerates the developments in artificial intelligence and machine learning described in the previous chapter. The algorithms and approaches that are now dominating the discipline—ones like deep learning and reinforcement learning—share the basic property that their results get better as the amount of data they're given increases.

The performance of most algorithms usually levels off, or "asymptotes," at some point, after which feeding it more data improves results very little or not at all. But this does not yet appear to be the case for many of the machine learning approaches in wide use today. Andrew Ng told us that with modern algorithms, "Moore's law and some very clever technical work keep pushing the asymptote out."

Networks. Technologies and protocols for communicating wirelessly over both short and long distances are improving rapidly. Both AT&T and Verizon, for example, announced 2016 trials of wireless 5G technology with download speeds as high as 10 gigabits per second. This is fifty times faster than the average speed of LTE networks (the fastest networks currently in wide deployment), and LTE is itself ten times faster than the previous generation, 3G technology. Such speed improvements mean better and faster data accumulation, and they also mean that robots and flying drones can be in constant communication and thus coordinate their work and react together on the fly to quickly-changing circumstances.

The cloud. An unprecedented amount of computing power is now available to organizations and individuals. Applications, blank or preconfigured servers, and storage space can all be leased for a long time or rented for a few minutes over the Internet. This cloud computing infrastructure, largely less than a decade old, accelerates the robotic Cambrian Explosion in three ways.

First, it greatly lowers barriers to entry, since the kinds of computing resources that were formerly found only in great research universities and multinationals' R&D labs are now available to startups and lone inventors.

Second, it allows robot and drone designers to explore the important trade-off of local versus central computation: which information-processing tasks should be done in each robot's local brain, and which should be done by the great global brain in the cloud? It seems likely that the most resource-intensive work, such as replaying previous experiences to gain new insights from them, will be done in the cloud for some time to come.

Third, and perhaps most important, the cloud means that every member of a robot or drone tribe can quickly know what every other member does. As Pratt puts it, "Human beings take decades to learn enough to add meaningfully to the compendium of common knowledge. However, robots not only stand on the shoulders of each other's learning, but can start adding to the compendium of robot knowledge almost immediately after their creation." An early example of this kind of universal "hive mind" is Tesla's fleet of cars, which share data about the roadside objects they pass. This information sharing helps the company build over time an understanding of which objects are permanent (they're the ones passed in the same spot by many different cars) and thus very unlikely to run out into the middle of the road.

Exponential improvements in digital hardware. Moore's law—the steady doubling in integrated circuit capability every eighteen to twenty-four months—celebrated its fiftieth anniversary in 2015, at which time it was still going strong. Some have suggested recently that the law is running up against the limits of physics and thus the doubling will increasingly slow down in the years to come. This may be true, but even if the tech industry's scientists and engineers can't figure out how to etch silicon ever more finely in future decades, we are confident that we'll continue to enjoy simultaneously lower prices and higher performance from our digital gear—processors, memory, sensors, storage, communications, and so on—for a long time to come.

How can this be? Chris Anderson, CEO of drone maker 3D Robotics, gave us a vivid illustration of what's going on in the drone industry and, by extension, in many others. He showed us a metal cylinder about 1 inch in diameter and 3 inches long and said, "This is a gyro sensor. It is mechanical, it cost $10,000, it was made in the nineties by some very talented ladies in an aerospace factory and hand-wound, et cetera. And it takes care of one axis of motion. On our drones we have twenty-four sensors like this. That would have been $10,000 each. That would have been $240,000 of sensors, and by the way, it would be the size of a refrigerator. Instead, we have a tiny little chip or a few tiny little chips that cost three dollars and are almost invisible."

Anderson's point is that the combination of cheap raw materials, mass global markets, intense competition, and large manufacturing scale economies is essentially a guarantee of sustained steep price declines and performance improvements. He calls personal drones the "peace dividend of the smartphone wars, which is to say that the components in a smartphone—the sensors, the GPS, the camera, the ARM core processors, the wireless, the memory, the battery—all that stuff, which is being driven by the incredible economies of scale and innovation machines at Apple, Google, and others, is available for a few dollars. They were essentially 'unobtainium' 10 years ago. This is stuff that used to be military industrial technology; you can buy it at RadioShack now."

Together, the elements of DANCE are causing the Cambrian Explosion in robots, drones, autonomous cars and trucks, and many other machines that are deeply digital. Exponentially cheaper gear enables higher rates of innovation and experimentation, which generate a flood of data. This information is used to test and refine algorithms, and to help systems learn. The algorithms are put into the cloud and distributed to machines via robust networks. The innovators do their next round of tests and experiments, and the cycle continues.

Where the Work Is Dull, Dirty,
Dangerous, and Dear

How, then, will robots, drones, and all the other digital machines that move in the physical world spread throughout the economy? What roles will they assume in the coming years? The standard view is that robots are best suited for work that is dull, dirty, and dangerous. We would add to this list one more "D"—namely, "dear," or expensive. The more of these attributes a given task has, the more likely it is to be turned over to digital machines.

Visiting construction sites to check on progress is an excellent example. These sites are usually dirty and sometimes dangerous, and the work of ensuring that the job is being done according to plan, dimensions are correct, lines are plumb, and so on can be dull. It's worth it, however, to regularly send a person to the site to perform these checks because small mistakes can amplify over time and become very expensive. It seems, though, that this work could soon be automated.

In the fall of 2015 the ninety-five-year-old Japanese firm Komatsu, the second largest construction equipment company in the world, announced a partnership with the US drone startup Skycatch. The American company's small aerial vehicles would fly over a site, precisely mapping it in three dimensions. They would continuously send this information to the cloud, where software would match it against the plans for a site and use the resulting information to direct an autonomous fleet of bulldozers, dump trucks, and other earth-moving equipment.

Agriculture, too, could soon be transformed by drones. Chris Anderson asked us to imagine a farm where drones fly over the fields every day, scanning them in the near-infrared wavelengths of light. These wavelengths provide a great deal of information about crop health, and current drone sensors are accurate enough to assess each square foot of land separately (and, given exponential improvement in the sensors, soon it will probably be possible to look at each plant individually). Flying a plane over the fields every day would be both dull and dear, but both of these barriers vanish with the arrival of small, cheap drones. Information gained from these daily flyovers enables a much deeper understanding of change over time with a given crop, and also enables much more precise targeting of water, fertilizer, and pesticides. Modern agricultural equipment often has the capability to deliver varying amounts of these critical ingredients foot by foot, rather than laying down a uniform amount. Drone data helps make the most of this capability, enabling farmers to move deeper into the era of precision agriculture.

It's likely that drones will soon also be used by insurance companies to assess how badly a roof was damaged after a tornado, to help guard herds of endangered animals against poaching and remote forests against illegal logging, and for many other tasks. They're already being used to inspect equipment that would be dull, dirty, dangerous, or dear to get to. Sky Futures, a UK company, specializes in flying its drones around oil rigs in the North Sea, where metal and cement are no match over time for salt water and harsh weather. Sky Futures' drones fly around and through structures in all conditions so that human roughnecks don't have to climb and dangle from them in order to see what's going on.

We see this pattern—machines assuming the dull, dirty, dangerous, or dear tasks—over and over at present:

▶ In 2015, Rio Tinto became the first company to utilize a fleet of fully remote-controlled trucks to move all the iron ore at its mine in Western Australia's Pilbara region. The driverless vehicles run twenty-four hours a day, 365 days a year and are supervised from a control center a thousand miles away. The savings from breaks, absenteeism, and shift changes enable the robotic fleet to be 12% more efficient than the human-driven one.

▶ Automated milking systems milk about one-quarter of the cows in leading dairy countries such as Denmark and the Netherlands today. Within ten years, this figure is expected to rise to 50%.

▶ Ninety percent of all crop spraying in Japan is currently done by unmanned helicopters.

Of course, this pattern of machines taking over tasks has been unfolding for many decades inside factories, where engineers can achieve high levels of what our MIT colleague David Autor calls "environmental control," or "radically simplify[ing] the environment in which machines work to enable autonomous operation, as in the familiar example of a factory assembly line." Environmental control is necessary when pieces of automation have primitive brains and no ability to sense their environments. As all the elements of DANCE improve together, however, pieces of automation can leave the tightly controlled environment of the factory and head out into the wide world. This is exactly what robots, drones, autonomous vehicles, and many other forms of digital machines are doing at present. They'll do much more of it in the near future.

What Humans Do in a World Full of Robots

How will our minds and bodies work in tandem with these machines? There are two main ways. First, as the machines are able to do more work in the physical world, we'll do less and less of it, and instead use our brains in the ways described in earlier chapters, and in the next one. This is clearly what's happening in agriculture, humanity's oldest industry.

Working the land to bring forth a crop has long been some of the most labor-intensive work done by people. It's now some of the most knowledge-intensive. As Brian Scott, an Indiana farmer who writes the blog *The Farmer's Life*, puts it, "Do you think when my grandfather was running . . . harvesters and combines . . . he could've imagined how . . . today's machines would be . . . driving themselves via invisible GPS signals while creating printable maps of things like yield and grain moisture? Amazing!" Similarly, workers in the most modern factories no longer need to be physically strong and hardy. Instead, they need to be comfortable with both words and numbers, adept at troubleshooting problems, and able to work as part of a team.

The second way people will work with robots and their kin is, quite literally, side by side with them. Again, this is nothing new; factory workers have long been surrounded by machines, often working in close quarters with them. Our combination of sharp minds, acute senses, dexterous hands, and sure feet have not yet been matched by any machine, and it remains a hugely valuable combination. Andy's favorite demonstration of it came on a tour of the storied Ducati motorcycle factory in Bologna, Italy. Ducati engines are particularly complex,[*] and he was interested to see how much automation was involved in assembling them. The answer, it turned out, was almost none.

Each engine was put together by a single person, who walked alongside a slow-moving conveyor belt. As the belt passed by the engine parts that were needed at each stage of assembly, the worker picked them up and put them where they belonged, fastening them in place and adjusting as necessary. Ducati engine assembly required locomotion, the ability to manipulate objects in a variety of tight spaces, good eyesight, and a highly refined sense of touch. Ducati's assessment was that no automation possessed all of these capabilities, so engine assembly remained a human job.

Similar capabilities are required in the warehouses of many retail-

---

[*] Much of this complexity comes from the way the parts that open and close valves are configured on a Ducati engine.

ers, especially those like Amazon that sell products of all shapes, sizes, and consistencies. Amazon has not yet* found or developed a digitally driven hand or other "grabber" that can reliably pick all products off the shelf and put them in a box. So the company has hit on a clever solution: it brings the shelves to a human, who grabs the right products and boxes them for shipment. Racks of shelves are whisked around the company's huge distribution centers by knee-high orange robots originally made by Boston-based Kiva Systems (Kiva was bought by Amazon in 2012). These robots scoot underneath a rack, lift it up, and bring it to a stationary human. When this person has taken the items needed, the rack-and-robot unit scoots away, and another one takes its place. This arrangement allows the people to use their skills of vision and dexterity, where they have an advantage over machines, and avoid the physical exertion and lost time that comes from walking from one shelf to another.

How much longer will we maintain our advantages over robots and drones? It's a hard question to answer with any confidence, especially since the elements of DANCE continue to advance individually and together. It seems, though, that our senses, hands, and feet will be a hard combination for machines to beat, at least for a few more years. Robots are making impressive progress, but they're still a lot slower than we are when they try to do humanlike things. After all, our brains and bodies draw on millions of years of evolution, rewarding the designs that solved well the problems posed by the physical world. When Gill Pratt was a program manager at DARPA, the US Defense Department's R&D lab, he oversaw its 2015 robotics challenge. Its automaton contestants moved at such a careful pace that he compared being a spectator at the competition to watching a golf match. Still, this represented a big improvement over the original

---

* At least as of when we are writing this book. We know they've made several attempts, but none have yet lived up to their requirements.

2012 competition. Watching that one, according to Pratt, was more like watching grass grow.

The Shapes of Things to Come

As the examples in this chapter show, progress with all things digital is enabling us to build machines that go beyond the universe of bits and interact with people and things in the world of atoms. The same progress is also taking this one big step further: it's enabling us to arrange atoms—to build things—in ways that were never before possible. We can see this happening with what are almost certainly the most common human-made objects in the world: plastic parts.

Global plastics production in 2015 was 250 million tons, and a single modern car has over 2,000 plastic parts of all shapes and sizes. To manufacture most of these parts, it is first necessary to make a mold—a metal part that the hot plastic will be injected, pressed, or otherwise forced into. The contours and hollow spaces of the mold determine the final shape of the part.

The need for a mold has three important implications. First, it's extremely important to get the mold right, since it will be the template for the thousands or millions of parts that come out of it. Molds thus tend to be durable, heavy, and very precisely engineered—a combination that also makes them expensive. Second, the need for a mold imposes limitations on the kinds of parts that can be made. It's easy to make a simple plastic gear with a mold, for example, but impossible to have a set of interlocking gears on a base pop out of a single mold, ready to turn. More complex parts generally require more complex molds—with some of the greatest complexity arising from the engineering required to get all the plastic into the mold, and to make sure that the hot material fills the space evenly and fully. Third, the thermodynamics of molds—the way they heat up and cool down with each part—are critically important. It's clearly a bad idea to remove parts while they're still hot enough to deform, but it's also inefficient to have the full mold cooling down longer than necessary. Yet different parts of the mold may cool at different rates. So designers and engineers have to balance a range of factors to ensure both high-quality parts and high-productivity molds.

About thirty years ago, a diverse group of technologists began asking, essentially, why have a mold at all? They took inspiration from laser printers, which work by using the laser to fuse a very thin layer of ink onto a piece of paper in the desired pattern of text and images.

But why stop at one layer? Why not repeat this process over and over, thereby gradually building up not just a two-dimensional pattern, but instead a three-dimensional structure? It would take a while, since each layer was so thin, but making things this way would open up a huge range of possibilities. For one thing, complexity would be free, as 3D printing researcher Luana Iorio puts it. In other words, it would cost no more to make an extraordinarily complex part than a very simple one, since both are, at base, simply a bunch of very thin layers. An assembly of interlocking gears, for example, would be as easy to create as a single 3D-printed component.

Innovators have also brought the techniques of 3D printing to making metal parts, which are built up by having a laser melt successive thin layers of powdered metal onto the structure below (which is itself made up previous layers). This process gives rise to another highly desirable property: hardness becomes free. Extremely hard metals like titanium can be difficult and expensive to machine, but they're just about as easy as softer ones like aluminum to build up one layer at a time; all that's required is an adjustment of the power setting on the laser.

When both complexity and hardness become free, many long-standing constraints are eased. It becomes easy, for example, to make molds for plastic parts that can be cooled down much more quickly. DTM Corporation of Austin, Texas, accomplished this by 3D-printing metal alloy molds that have many small, thin channels running through them in complex paths that could not have been created by conventional means. Hot plastic doesn't flow through these channels; cold liquids do, in order to quickly cool things down after each new part is formed. As a result, parts can be produced 20%–35% faster and with greater quality.

A skeptic might ask at this point whether we want to generate innovations that keep flooding the world with more and more cheap plastic parts, stuffing our landfills and fouling our oceans with them. We see things differently. While we agree that overconsumption and inappropriate disposal of plastics are bad, we think that the advances in 3D printing are profoundly beneficial.

Consider the case of the 3D-printed tumor model. Prior to the advent of 3D printing, surgeons simply had no realistic way to make an accurate representation of the mass of malignant tissue they were going after. They could not have afforded the dollars and time required to create a conventional mold, which makes economic sense only when you know you're going to make many copies of a part.

But what if you want to make only a single model or prototype? Or a part fails and you want a single spare, quickly? Or you want to make a small set of parts, each one a bit different from the others? Conventional fabrication methods have been largely useless in these cases. 3D printing is ideal for them.

The most profound benefit of 3D printing is probably that it makes experimentation and customization inexpensive. The path from idea or need to finished, useful part no longer has to include the time-consuming and expensive steps like mold making and other conventional manufacturing practices.

Carl Bass, the former CEO of design and engineering software company Autodesk, sees 3D printing as only one part of a much larger story. As he told us, "I think additive manufacturing is a sub-set of what has really transformed manufacturing, which is the use of low-cost microprocessors to precisely control machinery." Bass's point is that sensors and code are not just being used now to pre-cisely place very thin layers of material on top of each other; they're also being applied to just about every other fabrication technique, from cutting glass sheets and ceramic tiles to bending and milling all kinds of metals.

The machines that do this work—that transform atoms into the final shapes we want—are improving these days, thanks to Moore's law. They might not be getting simultaneously better and less expen-sive as fast as CPUs and memory chips are, but their progress is still impressive. Compared to their equivalents of twenty years ago, they're cheaper, yet able to do more things at higher levels of qual-ity. These advancements put them within reach of innovators of all kinds—more hobbyists, backyard inventors, students, engineers, and entrepreneurs—and gives people the ability to explore more possibil-ities. We're confident that the innovations that democratized high-quality tools will lead to a cascade of even more innovations in the near future.

Chapter Summary

▶ Many business processes that today involve people are virtualiz-ing: they're moving to digital channels and including fewer peo-ple. Often, the only person involved is the customer.

▶ Some people will continue to self-select human-to-human inter-actions, but we believe virtualization is a long-term trend that will generally increase over time as machines gain more capabilities.

▶ Robotics is undergoing a "Cambrian Explosion" as machines learn to see, as well as by many other kinds of digital progress. Automatons of all kinds—robots, drones, self-driving cars, and so on—are becoming cheaper, more widely available, more capable, and more diverse all at the same time.

▶ Drivers of the robotic Cambrian Explosion include data, algorithms, networks, the cloud, and exponential improvements in hardware: DANCE.

▶ Robots and their kin will be increasingly used wherever work is dull, dirty, dangerous, and dear.

▶ People are still more agile and dexterous than even the most advanced robots, and they probably will be for some time to come. These abilities, combined with our senses and problem-solving skills, mean that we'll be working side by side with robots in many settings.

▶ 3D printing is important in its own right and also an example of a broader trend: the spread of digital tools into traditional manufacturing processes. This is an example of an innovation that itself leads to higher rates of innovation.

Questions

1. If you have business processes that require a lot of person-to-person interaction, is this because your customers (or employees, suppliers, or other partners) value it, or because they don't have an equally efficient digital alternative?

2. Which aspects of work in your industry are most likely to be virtualized in the next three to five years? If given the choice, which of your customers would prefer more virtualized interactions?

3. What aspects of your organization's work are most dull, dirty, dangerous, or dear? Have you looked recently at robots or other automation that can help with this task?

4. How is physical work (if any) in your organization divided up between people and machines? How about primarily cognitive or information-processing tasks? How about tasks that are primarily interpersonal?

5. In your innovation and prototyping work, how are you taking advantage of the new technologies for making things?

CHAPTER 5

WHERE TECHNOLOGY AND INDUSTRY STILL NEED HUMANITY

> There are three rules for writing a novel. Unfortunately, no one knows what they are.
>
> — *attributed to Somerset Maugham (1874–1965)*

"WHICH ABILITIES WILL CONTINUE TO BE UNIQUELY HUMAN as technology races ahead?" That's the most common question we hear about minds and machines. As the digital toolkit challenges human superiority in routine information processing, pattern recognition, language, intuition, judgment, prediction, physical dexterity, and so many other things, are there *any* areas where we should *not* expect to be outstripped?

Do Androids Dream Up Creative Leaps?

The most common answer we hear to the question posed in the preceding paragraph is "creativity." Many people we've spoken with, if not most, argue that there's something irreducible or ineffable about the human ability to come up with a new idea. We think there's a lot of truth to that; in fact, we said something very similar in *The Second Machine Age*. But recent demonstrations within the creativity-heavy field of industrial design indicate to us that machines are getting quite good at coming up with powerful new ideas on their own.

It's probably safe to say that most people never think about heat exchangers. But people who design refrigerators, furnaces, engines, and other pieces of equipment think about them a lot. An exchanger's job is to let heat move from one fluid (in other words, a liquid or gas) to another while preventing either fluid from coming into contact with the other. A bedroom radiator is a heat exchanger—it passes heat from the steam flowing through it to the air around it—and so is the room's air conditioner.

Creating a good heat exchanger is tough. It has to accomplish its primary goal of transferring the right amount of energy, and it has to be efficient, safe, durable, and cheap. To satisfy all of these requirements, the designer has to understand required performance levels, thermo- and fluid dynamics, material properties, manufacturing methods and costs, and so on. In practice, of course, many designers draw on the huge amount of useful knowledge already embedded in previous successful heat exchangers; they tweak an existing design to satisfy the requirements of a new use case.

But what would a heat exchanger designer who had all the required knowledge but none of the accumulated experience come up with? What if, in other words, the designer knew exactly what the required performance "envelope" was—dimensions, cost, life span, energy transfer, and so on—and was a world-class expert in all the relevant scientific and engineering disciplines, but had never worked on a heat exchanger before, or even recognized that such a thing might be valuable? What would a designer like this come up with?

Figure 1 shows one example. And as you probably guessed by now, it was designed by a computer.

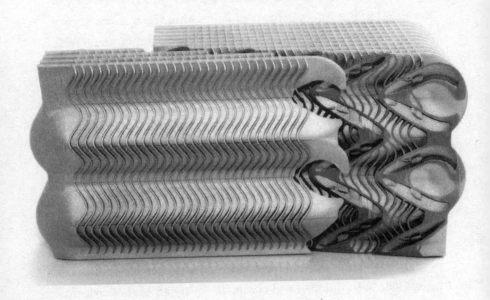

Figure 1

A heat exchanger designed using generative design software. (© Autodesk)

Natural Artificial Designs

The heat exchanger shown in Figure 1 is an example of "generative design," a process in which software is used not to help a human designer create drawings, perform calculations, and explore trade-offs, but instead to do all that work itself, 100% automatically, and to come up with one or more complete designs that satisfy all requirements.

This part was manufactured by 3D printing. In fact, it would have been impossible to make using traditional manufacturing processes. But now that 3D printing is a reality, generative-design software is no longer constrained by older production methods and is free to imagine and propose a vastly wider range of shapes. And unlike most, if not all, human designers, the software isn't consciously or subconsciously biased toward existing methods, so it really does explore more freely.

Is generative-design software really "creative?" It's a hard question because creativity is a prime example of what AI pioneer Marvin Minsky called a "suitcase word." As he put it, "Most words we use to describe our minds (like 'consciousness,' 'learning,' or 'memory') are suitcase-like jumbles of different ideas." We see just such a jumble in different definitions of creativity. The *Oxford English Dictionary*, for example, states that creativity is "the use of imagination or original ideas, especially in the production of an artistic work."

A heat exchanger made by generative-design software doesn't really meet this definition, since it's not intended to be an artistic work and it didn't result from anyone's imagination. Merriam-Webster, however, has a quite different definition of creativity: "the ability to make new things or think of new ideas." By this definition, we think generative-design software is clearly creative.

Humans played no role in designing the part shown in Figure 1, but they were essential for telling the generative-design software what kind of part to design. People specified the inputs to the software in that they defined what the part had to be able to do. To do this work well, they had to understand where the part needed to fit, the environment it had to be able to survive and operate in, and the energy it needed to be able to transfer, and so on. In short, these human specifiers had a great deal of relevant domain knowledge and skill—maybe almost as much as human heat exchange designers themselves would need to propose a design.

Drive Hard, Design Weird

What if at least some of that relevant knowledge could also be generated automatically? What if additional tools could be added to the combination of generative-design software and 3D printing to advance even further the state of creative digital technologies? Starting in 2013, Autodesk teamed up with a group of car designers and stunt drivers in Los Angeles to find out. Their goal was an automated system that could design a race car chassis from scratch and determine for itself how well the chassis needed to be able to perform—in other words, its specifications.

To do this, the team first built a stripped-down traditional race car—essentially just the chassis, transmission, engine, seat, and wheels. The team then blanketed the chassis with sensors that measured quantities of interest—stresses, strains, temperatures, displacements, and all the other things that the chassis had to be able to accommodate. As we discussed in the previous chapter, digital sensors are now simultaneously small, cheap, and capable, so the team could inexpensively obtain huge amounts of accurate data from this "instrumented" chassis.

They took this sensored-up car to the Mojave Desert, where a test driver pushed the envelope with it—accelerating, braking, and steering as hard as he could without crashing, while the car's sensors collected data. By the end of this breakneck session, the team had some 20 million data points about the car's structure and the forces acting on it, which were then plugged into Project Dreamcatcher—a generative-design technology from Autodesk—and applied to a 3D model of the existing chassis. Figure 2 shows what the software came up with. To us, it's only vaguely recognizable as a race car chassis. It looks much more like the skull of a mammoth or whale, or perhaps the microscopic silicon dioxide skeleton of a diatom.[*]

This is not a coincidence. Bones, exoskeletons, and other structures in nature are the winning entries in evolution's ancient, relentless competition, the outcomes of which are literally life and death. Evolution has resulted in marvelous designs—designs that are simultaneously resilient, durable, energy efficient, intricate, strong, and slim.

---

[*] Diatoms are a type of algae found throughout the world's waters.

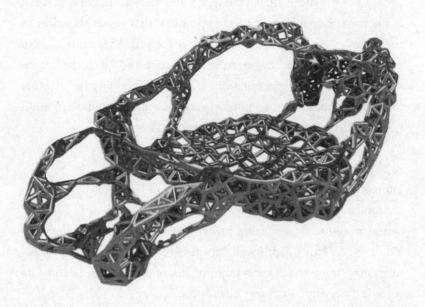

Figure 2
Race car chassis model. (© Autodesk)

So perhaps we shouldn't be too surprised that when generative-design software is given the task of designing an optimal structure to satisfy a set of performance requirements, it comes up with something that looks as if it came from nature.

Do you notice another unusual characteristic? This chassis is also asymmetric; its right and left sides are not mirror images of each other. This makes sense. Because a race car turns more often in one direction than the other as it does laps, the two sides of its chassis are subject to quite different forces. Human designers have been aware of this fact for a long time, but their creations have rarely, if ever, been as deeply asymmetric as the ones that emerge from generative-design software.

Examples like this race car chassis convince us that digital creativity is more than mimicry and incrementalism. Computers can come up with more than extensions and recombinations of what humans have already done. We're optimistic that something close to the opposite can happen: that when they're primed with our accumulated scientific and engineering knowledge and given the performance requirements of a situation, or enough data to figure out what those requirements are, computers can and will come up with novel solutions that never would have occurred to us.

Computer Says, "Eureka!"

Digital designers do not have the biases and blinders that humans accumulate, probably inevitably, as they build experience. The staggering amount of computing power now available means that digital designers can quickly and inexpensively explore many possible solutions—more than even a building full of humans could come up with. In fact, digital creators already are.

In the sciences, coming up with a new theory, one eventually supported by experimental results, is the stereotypical example of "Eureka!"-style creativity. A clever study by computational biologists at Baylor College of Medicine and analytics experts at IBM demonstrated that IBM's Watson artificial intelligence technology could be used to come up with useful scientific hypotheses. The team was hunting for kinases* that activate protein p53, which is sought after because it curbs the growth of cancers. They had Watson "read"† 70,000 scientific papers published on the topic, then asked the technology to predict kinases that would turn on or off p53's activity. Watson predicted seven candidates.

How do we know whether these were good or bad candidates? We know because the researchers only gave Watson papers that were

---

* Kinases are enzymes that regulate much activity within cells.

† Watson doesn't (yet) understand language the way humans do, but it does find patterns and associations in written text that it can use to populate its knowledge base.

published prior to 2003. This meant that they could use the ten years of scientific progress between 2003 and 2013 to determine which of Watson's hypotheses, if any, had been scrutinized and supported. All seven of the candidate kinases proposed by Watson did, in fact, activate p53. These results are particularly impressive when we consider that over the last thirty years, science in this area discovered about one p53-activating kinase per year. This is not a toy problem.

But the Arts Are Different—Aren't They?

Digital creativity has also reached the arts. Simon Colton's program The Painting Fool paints scenes without any human input, Patrick Tresset has built a number of robotic arms that draw portraits of live models in different "hands," and Emily Howell, a program developed by music professor David Cope, composes music in many different styles.

We often hear that digital painters, composers, and other artists are not as talented as their human counterparts—that the creations of machines are still clearly more shallow than those of minds. But Cope says he's noticed an interesting phenomenon. As a 2010 story about his work by Ryan Blitstein in *Pacific Standard* magazine tells it, "At one Santa Cruz concert, the program notes neglected to mention that Emily Howell wasn't a human being, and a chemistry professor and music aficionado in the audience described the performance of a Howell composition as one of the most moving experiences of his musical life. Six months later, when the same professor attended a lecture by Cope on Emily Howell and heard the same concert played from a recording, Cope remembers him saying, 'You know, that's pretty music, but I could tell absolutely, immediately that it was computer-composed. There's no heart or soul or depth to the piece.'"

We probably shouldn't be too surprised that a digital composer can make music that people find haunting or lovely. Human aesthetics— the things we find beautiful, or that appeal to our taste and senses—

are complex, and understanding them is difficult (especially since they change over time and across groups and cultures), but it's not impossible. We've discovered at least some of the rules and principles—like frequently using the "golden ratio" of about 1.618 to 1 when arranging the elements of a painting or other visual composition—and we are learning more all the time (even though some may elude us for quite a while).

This knowledge is being embedded in technology and put to use in a wide range of industries. The Grid is a startup offering people and companies highly customized websites that reflect their taste and follow leading principles for web design but don't involve any human web designers. IBM has deployed its Watson technology in the kitchen, where it has come up with full cookbooks' worth of recipes presenting novel combinations of ingredients and flavors that people are known to enjoy.* The Shanghai Tower is a 128-story modern skyscraper in the heart of the city's Pudong neighborhood. It's highly energy efficient, using technology that reduces its carbon footprint by 34,000 metric tons per year, and sparing enough in its use of materials to save $58 million in construction costs. What's more, we find its twisting, gleaming form quite beautiful. Both the building's initial shape and structure were computer-generated. They were then advanced and refined by teams of human architects in a highly iterative process, but the starting point for these human teams was a computer-designed building, which is about as far from a blank sheet of paper as you can get.

---

* *Fast Company* journalist Mark Wilson loved the "Bengali Butternut" barbecue sauce that Watson came up with (Mark Wilson, "I Tasted BBQ Sauce Made by IBM's Watson, and Loved It," *Fast Company*, May 23, 2014, https://www.fastcodesign .com/3027687/i-tasted-bbq-sauce-made-by-ibms-watson-and-loved-it), but called its "Austrian Chocolate Burrito" the worst he'd ever had (Mark Wilson, "IBM's Watson Designed the Worst Burrito I've Ever Had," *Fast Company*, April 20, 2015, https://www .fastcodesign.com/3045147/ibms-watson-designed-the-worst-burrito-ive-ever-had).

What We Are That Computers Aren't

Autogenerated-music pioneer David Cope says, "Most of what I've heard [and read] is the same old crap. It's all about machines versus humans, and 'aren't you taking away the last little thing we have left that we can call unique to human beings—creativity?' I just find this so laborious and uncreative." We know how he feels. The debate over whether computers are, or ever can be, truly creative might be of interest to some people, but we are much more excited by questions about how to maximize the total amount of creativity in the world. The right way to do this, we believe, is to push ahead on two fronts: continuing to work on making computers that can come up with good new ideas, and figuring out the best ways to bring them together with human creators. The best solutions here will come from minds and machines working together.

Far too often, when we bring them together, we ask the minds to do boring and routine tasks that should be handled by the machines. As we described in Chapter 2, the whole point of the long-standing "standard partnership" established twenty years ago was to free up people to do higher-level thinking by giving the rote work to the computers. But designers and other creative professionals today spend too much of their time doing mind-numbingly dull things. As former Autodesk CEO Carl Bass explained to us,

> Using [computer-aided design] tools, it's like eleventh-grade geometry. You're sitting there, you draw a line, you find the midpoint, you do this, you draw another thing, you extrude it, you put a fillet* on it. What's interesting about it is, you do it prematurely to actually knowing whether your thing solves the problem. You

---

* A mechanical fillet is a smooth transition from one area of a part to another—for example, a rounded corner between two surfaces that meet at a right angle.

can work on all these details for weeks and only then find out that the mechanism you're building is really not going to work. We've trained a whole generation of people to work this way. I think we've given people bad tools.

Autodesk and other companies are working on better tools to support creativity. These next-generation products will do a few things differently.

First, they'll let people test out the overall feasibility or appropriateness of their ideas before asking them to do lots of "eleventh-grade geometry." The archetypal first design is a sketch on the back of a napkin. The digital tools of the near future will be able to take something like this sketch—something produced quickly, in a moment of inspiration—and give quick and accurate feedback about whether it'll work: whether the building will stand in an earthquake, or the engine will be able to put out enough power.

Second, the new tools will, at every stage of the design process, do more of the routine work automatically. We're lousy at this work— we take too long and make too many mistakes—so we really should hand it off to technology and finally update the standard partnership for creative endeavors.

For a long, long time to come, people will still have a large role to play in creative work, even as technology races ahead. Earlier in this book we advocated a relatively minor role for people in a lot of situations that call for a decision, judgment, diagnosis, or forecast. Why is creativity different? It's different because in many domains, creating something new and good in the world probably requires that the creator be living in that world, and computers are not "living" in ours in any real sense of the word. This is not the place to have a discussion of what "consciousness" is—many lives and libraries have been devoted to *that* suitcase word—except to say that computers are not conscious at the moment. Knowing what people want next usually requires a deep understanding of what it means to be a person, and what it's like to experience the world with all our senses and emotions. As far as we can tell and for a long time to come, we humans are the only ones with that knowledge.

The lyricist Andrew Bird was onto something when he observed in 2008 that "the only thing that separates a mess of seemingly disparate observations and a song is a moment of excessive confidence." We like his insight but think he's being too modest. Computers never lack confidence, and they can generate endless lists of disparate or linked observations about love and loss. We'll be very surprised, though, when a digital lyricist comes along that can generate great lyrics as reliably as Cole Porter, Joni Mitchell, or Jay Z. Their creativity springs, in large part, from understanding the human condition. We see nothing to indicate that we're getting close to digitizing this understanding. AI pioneer Yann LeCun thinks that we'll get there someday but that, at present, "there are major conceptual advances that we still don't know how to make." Andrew Ng, another great researcher, agrees. He told us, "We have no idea how the brain works, and our algorithms do not work anything like the brain works."

Until they do, we'll have the kind of AI-generated poetry and prose collected at *CuratedAI*, "a literary magazine written by machines, for people." A representative entry is "The Music Is Satisfied with Mr. Bertram's Mind," which the neural network Deep Thunder came up with in August of 2016 after being "fed on Jane Austen novels." It begins like this:

Chilly, and no recollection of such going at Grief. To your eldest say when I tried to be at the first of the praise, and all this has been so careless in riding to Mr. Crawford; but have you deserved far to scarcely be before, and I am sure I have no high word, ma'am, I am sure we did not know that the music is satisfied with Mr. Bertram's mind.

We have no idea what that means, and will be sticking with human-generated fiction and lyrics for the foreseeable future.

Human Connections in a Digitized World

The human condition is inherently interpersonal. We are deeply social beings who have been living in ever-larger groups—families, bands, tribes, cities—throughout modern evolutionary history. An inevitable consequence of this trend is that we are acutely attuned to each other, both as individuals and as group members. Virtually all of us care constantly and deeply about how we are relating to others, and about what others think of us (true sociopaths and people with extreme cases of autism spectrum disorder are among the few exceptions). Our MIT colleague and prodigiously talented researcher Deb Roy has pointed out that this social nature gives us a powerful way to predict what jobs and tasks will remain least affected by technological progress: very simply, they're the ones that tap into our social drives.

Roy's list of these drives includes compassion, pride, embarrassment, envy, justice, and solidarity. To see how they apply in the world of work, take the example of a high school girls' soccer coach. It would be great if she had a deep strategic understanding of the sport and an ability to observe the flow of a game and shift tactics appropriately, but since there aren't large financial consequences associated with wins versus losses, the ability to deliver wins isn't what's most important for this job. Instead, what matters is the ability to get the girls to work well together in pursuit of a goal, to teach them to be good and supportive teammates for each other, and to develop their characters through athletics. The coach accomplishes this in large part by tapping into her own compassion and the girls' pride. She also makes use of the girls' desire for approval from her, a role model and authority figure.

Most of us appreciate that good soccer coaches are rare, but we forget that nonhuman ones don't exist. Try to imagine an all-digital, artificially intelligent girls' soccer coach. Could it pick out the natural leaders and difficult personalities on the team and know what to do if some girls were both? Would it be able to bond the team together over the course of a season, navigating the highs and lows? Would it be able to motivate a girl to push past fatigue and self-doubt, and accomplish things she didn't think possible? We've learned never to say never with technology, but here we'll say "almost certainly not."

Computers are getting good at tasks like determining people's emotional states by observing their facial expressions and vocal patterns, but this is a long, long way from doing the things we just listed. We're confident that the ability to work effectively with people's emotional states and social drives will remain a deeply human skill for some time to come. This implies a novel way to combine minds and machines as we move deeper into the second machine age: let the computers take the lead on making decisions (or judgments, predictions, diagnoses, and so on), then let people take the lead if others need to be convinced or persuaded to go along with these decisions.

Health care provides many examples of how this world can be put into practice. Medical diagnosis is a pattern-matching exercise, and thanks to the digitization of health care information and advances in machine learning and other fields, computers are achieving superhuman levels of performance at this exercise. If the world's best diagnostician in most specialties—radiology, pathology, oncology, and so on—is not already digital, it soon will be. It might still be a good idea to have a human expert review this diagnosis,* but the computer should take the lead.

Most patients, however, don't want to get their diagnosis from a machine. They want to get it from a compassionate person who can

---

* Or it might not be a good idea. Only time and research will tell.

help them understand and accept often difficult news. And after a diagnosis is made, medical professionals who can form interpersonal connections and tap into social drives are highly valuable because they stand a better chance of getting patients to comply with the prescribed course of treatment. Noncompliance is a major problem in health care, negatively affecting the health of millions of people and costing as much as $289 billion a year in the United States for prescriptions alone, according to one estimate.

Iora Health, a company based in Cambridge, Massachusetts, that by mid-2015 was running thirteen health care practices in six states, attempts to keep people well by pairing them with "health coaches." These professionals provide medical advice but also take pains to listen, spend time with patients, and make the whole experience of health care seem deeply interpersonal instead of highly impersonal. This approach seems to be working. As a *Boston Globe* story reported, "At one Iora site, hospitalizations are 37 percent lower and health care spending 12 percent lower than with a control group using a more conventional health care system, according to the company. . . . At two other sites, emergency room visits were down at least 30 percent."

People will continue to be critically important in the improved health care delivery systems of the future, but not always in the same roles as today. Emotionally and socially astute care coordinators, rather than brilliant diagnosticians and other HiPPOs, might move to center stage. Earlier, we told the old joke about the two employees—person and dog—in the factory of the future. We suggest a slight tweak for health care: the medical office of the future might employ an artificial intelligence, a person, and a dog. The AI's job will be to diagnose the patient, the person's job will be to understand and communicate the diagnosis, and to coach the patient through treatment, and the dog's job will be to bite the person if the person tries to second-guess the artificial intelligence.

Chapter Summary

▶ Computers can now do more and more things that meet most definitions of "creativity"—designing functional and beautiful objects, composing music, advancing useful scientific hypotheses, and so on.

▶ Computers' creative abilities are expanding rapidly. They're now able, for example, not only to design a part that meets requirements, but also to figure out from a mass of data what those requirements should be.

▶ Digital creators often come up with very different solutions than human ones do. This is a good thing, since diversity of viewpoints often leads to better results.

▶ But computers still don't really understand the human condition, since they don't experience the world the way we do. We don't expect a decent novel to be written by a machine anytime soon.

▶ Creative endeavors are one of the most fruitful areas for new combinations of minds and machines. One promising approach is to have the machines take care of the "busywork," and to generate initial proposals that people can extend and improve.

▶ Digital technologies do a poor job of satisfying most of our social drives. So, work that taps into these drives will likely continue to be done by people for some time to come. Such work includes tasks that require empathy, leadership, teamwork, and coaching.

▶ As technology advances, high-level social skills could become even more valuable than advanced quantitative ones. And the ability to combine social with quantitative skills will often have the highest payoff of all.

Questions

1. How much boring, routine work do the most creative and innovative people in your organization have to do?

2. Are you confident that you could reliably tell the difference between a human-generated painting, melody, web page design, or scientific hypothesis and a machine-generated one? Are you confident that the human-generated one would be better?

3. Where would better human connections most help your performance and that of your organization?

4. Of the tasks currently being done by humans in your organization, which will be the hardest for computers to take over? Why do you believe this?

5. Looking at the existing tasks and processes in your job or organization, what do you see as the ideal division of work between humans and machines?

6. What new products or services could be created by combining the emerging capabilities of machines with a human touch?

PART 2

PRODUCT AND PLATFORM

CHAPTER 6

THE TOLL OF A NEW MACHINE

Economic progress, in capitalist society, means turmoil.

— *Joseph Schumpeter, 1942*

WITHIN ONE GENERATION, SEVERAL LONG-STANDING INDUS-tries were transformed permanently and deeply by a single computer network. The business world has rarely, if ever, seen disruption at this speed and scale before.

The first sentence in the previous paragraph exaggerates—the Internet had some help from other technologies as it remade sector after sector—but we don't think the second sentence does. As we described in Chapter 1, there have been technology-driven industrial revolutions before, based around advances like the steam engine and electrification, but they took longer to unfold and arguably didn't affect as many parts of the global economy.

The Calm before the Storm

Perhaps the best way to grasp the impact of the Internet is to consider where things stood about twenty years ago. Mobile telephones were an expensive novelty in the United States; in 1995 they cost roughly

$1,000 and only 13% of people had bought one. The great majority of American households had a landline phone (though the term did not yet exist) connected to the national network by copper wires. The AT&T monopoly that had built that network had been broken up by court decree in 1982, but the company still existed as one of a handful of long-distance providers. In the 1990s, calls between more distant phones cost more, and most households received two monthly bills: a fixed one for unlimited local calling, and a separate one that varied depending on how many long-distance calls had been made.

In the mid-1990s, almost every American community was served by at least one daily newspaper, and a few, like the *New York Times*, *Wall Street Journal*, and *USA Today*, had national reach. Together, the country's 2,400 papers generated $46 billion in annual revenue. Weekly and monthly magazines were a further $19 billion business. These businesses made money from a combination of subscriptions and ad sales. In 1995, US newspapers made 30% of their revenue from classifieds, 49% from nonclassified advertising, and 21% from circulation sales. For many newspapers, classified ads were particularly important sources of revenue and profit, since they cost little to create or print and could run for a long time (until those who posted the ad had accomplished their goals or were tired of paying for the ad).

Radio stations also flourished. In the year 2000, there were well over 10,000 AM and FM stations operating in the United States, collectively generating revenues of $20 billion. The majority of these played music at least some of the time and existed in a happy relationship with the recorded-music industry; when listeners heard a song they liked on the radio, they often bought the album on which it appeared. In 2000, recorded music was a $14.3 billion industry, growing at 7% annually over the previous decade.

Demand for recorded music, especially from the pop era's most iconic performers, seemed robust enough to engender creative financing. In 1997, David Bowie and investment banker David Pullman teamed up to offer "Bowie bonds," a novel security backed by sales from the artist's extensive catalog of music, which spanned twenty-one years and twenty-five albums at that point. The bonds quickly sold out, raising $55 million, and inspired other artists, from Iron Maiden to Rod Stewart and James Brown, to try something similar.

People could get their hands on this music by joining mail-order album-of-the-month clubs such as Columbia, or by going to music stores like HMV and Tower Records. Fans would line up outside the stores to secure copies of anticipated albums like 1996's *HIStory*, a collection of Michael Jackson's hits.

A substantial number of music stores were in enclosed malls, an American innovation that spread rapidly as suburban living did. America's love affair with shopping malls began in 1956, when the nation's first fully enclosed, climate-controlled mall, Southdale, opened its doors outside Minneapolis. In the 1960s, car culture spawned the suburbs and launched a half-century indoor-mall boom; 1,500 were built from 1956 to 2005.

In the mid-1990s, many Americans used a trip to the shopping mall as an occasion to drop off film or pick up developed photos. Film photography was a $10 billion industry in 1997, comprising camera and film purchases and developing fees. The first mainstream consumer digital camera, the Casio QV-10, was introduced in 1995, but it was not a breakout success. Its $900 price tag was high, and it could store only ninety-six low-resolution photos (0.07 megapixels) in its nonremovable memory. Investors in Kodak, the iconic, century-old American film manufacturer, didn't seem too worried by Casio and other early digital cameras. Kodak's market capitalization reached a new record high of $31 billion in the first quarter of 1997.

The Shatterer of Worlds

We're sure you're not surprised to learn that it never went higher. The value of Kodak as a corporation collapsed in the fifteen years between 1997 and 2012, when it declared bankruptcy.* Kodak's example is not isolated or exceptional. Throughout the industries in the economic snapshot just described, waves of painful changes have arrived since the mid-1990s.

▶ By 2013, total US newspaper print ad revenue had declined by 70% over the previous decade, and online ads had contributed back only $3.4 billion of the $40 billion lost in annual sales. A saying emerged in the newspaper industry that "print dollars were being replaced by digital dimes." From 2007 to 2011, 13,400 newspaper newsroom jobs were cut in the United States. Help-wanted classified ad revenue dropped by more than 90% in the decade after 2000, from $8.7 billion to $723 million. Newspaper companies including the *Tucson Citizen* (Arizona's oldest continuously published daily newspaper) and the *Rocky Mountain News* went bankrupt. Others, like the McClatchy Company, lost more than 90% of their value. On August 5, 2013, the *Washington Post* made a surprise announcement that it had been acquired by Amazon founder Jeff Bezos for $250 million.

▶ Similar patterns held in magazine publishing, with total circulation and advertising revenue in precipitous decline. The parent companies of magazines as diverse as *Penthouse* (General Media) and the *National Enquirer* and *Men's Fitness* (American Media)

---

* Kodak's bankruptcy proceedings were not the end of the company's fortunes. Since 2013, they have focused on commercial printing and imaging. By the end of 2015 the company's 6,400 employees had helped it generate annual revenues of $1.7 billion. We discuss the Kodak story in more detail in *The Second Machine Age*.

declared bankruptcy. *Newsweek*, which had been in print since 1933 and at one point had a circulation of 3.3 million, saw its total circulation dropped by more than 50% between 2007 and 2011 and ceased publishing a print edition altogether in 2012. The *New Republic*, a once influential political magazine (in the mid-1990s it had a reputation for being "required reading on Air Force One") was bought by Facebook cofounder Chris Hughes in 2012 for an estimated $2 million.* Perhaps the clearest sign of deep shifts in the industry was *Playboy*'s announcement in October of 2015 that after sixty-two years, it would no longer feature nude photos. Founder Hugh Hefner, who in 2006 was named by the *Atlantic* as one of the most influential living Americans in large part because of photos of unclothed women, agreed with the move. One of the reasons for this change was that, like other publications, *Playboy* depended increasingly on traffic from social media, but sites like Facebook and Instagram did not allow nudity.† (In February of 2017, Cooper Hefner, the magazine's chief creative officer and son of its founder, announced that partial female nudity would return to *Playboy*.)

---

* Hughes invested a reported $20 million in the *New Republic* over the next four years (Ravi Somaiya, "The New Republic Is Sold," *New York Times*, February 26, 2016, https://www.nytimes.com/2016/02/27/business/media/the-new-republic-is-sold.html). However, the attempt to rebrand the organization as a digital media company did not succeed, and he subsequently sold the business in February 2016.

† According to Cory Jones, *Playboy*'s chief content officer, Playboy.com's traffic shot up 400% after it became a "safe-for-work" site in 2014 (David Segal, "Playboy Puts On [Some] Clothes for Newly Redesigned Issue," *New York Times*, February 4, 2016, https://www.nytimes.com/2016/02/04/business/media/playboy-puts-on-some-clothes-for-newly-redesigned-issue.html). "Don't get me wrong," he said soon after the decision to stop publishing nudes was announced, "12-year-old me is very disappointed in current me. But it's the right thing to do" (Ravi Somaiya, "Nudes Are Old News at Playboy," *New York Times*, October 12, 2015, https://www.nytimes.com/2015/10/13/business/media/nudes-are-old-news-at-playboy.html).

▶ Worldwide sales of recorded music declined by 45%, from $27 billion to $15 billion, between 1999 and 2014. The year 2014 was also the first that the global music industry generated the same proportion of revenue from digital channels as from physical formats such as CDs. In 2002, five major labels controlled 75% of the world market for recorded music. The consolidation in the industry has left standing just three major content providers: Universal Music Group, Sony Music Entertainment, and Warner Music Group. These three now account for 85% of music distributed in the United States. Tower Records went bankrupt in 2006, and HMV "called in the administrators" (equivalently bad news for an English company) early in 2013. In 2004 the rating agency Moody's downgraded David Bowie's bonds from investment grade to junk status. The Bowie bonds did make all of their payments as scheduled, but securitization of other recording artists' portfolios never took off. In 2011, Goldman Sachs tried to issue bonds for artists such as Bob Dylan and Neil Diamond, but it did not find a sufficient market for them.

▶ Two thousand seven was the first year in half a century that a new indoor mall didn't open somewhere in the United States. Between 2005 and 2015, 20% of US shopping malls closed, and companies that specialize in building and maintaining them faced financial distress. When General Growth Properties, one of the largest mall operators in the nation, filed for bankruptcy in 2009, it became the biggest commercial real estate collapse in US history.

▶ Both local and long-distance landline telecommunication proved to be difficult businesses. In 2000, US households spent $77 billion on their long-distance voice calls; by 2013, the number had dropped to $16 billion. As mobile telephony spread, many

US households gave up tethered ones altogether. By 2015, 44% of American adults lived in households with cell phones but no landline connection. Among millennials (born between 1977 and 1994), the percentage was closer to two-thirds.

▶ Total nationwide radio station revenue declined by almost 30%, from $20 billion in 2000 to $14 billion in 2010, forcing many independent stations to sell themselves to consolidators. The largest radio station operator, Clear Channel, grew from 196 stations in 1997 to 1,183 stations in 2005.

As these examples show, a large amount of turbulence, encompassing many apparently dissimilar industries, has occurred in the past twenty years. And this list is far from complete; in the chapters ahead we'll see many other examples of business disruption, memorably defined by Thomas Friedman in his book *Thank You for Being Late* as "what happens when someone does something clever that makes you or your company look obsolete." Digital technologies are perhaps the most powerful tools ever wielded by clever disruptors.

The Economics of Free, Perfect, and Instant

To see why we say this, and to get an intellectual foundation for seeing and predicting the destructive power of the second machine age, it's necessary to understand two unusual kinds of economics: those of information goods that are made of bits rather than atoms, and those of networks.

The first two important attributes of information goods are *free* and *perfect*. Once something has been digitized, it's essentially free to make an additional copy of it. This new copy will, it's true, take up space on a hard drive or other storage medium, and storage isn't literally free, but it's incredibly cheap by historical standards. A gigabyte of storage in 2016 cost $0.02, compared with $11 in 2000, and it's getting cheaper all the time. As an economist would say, the marginal cost is approaching zero. So, free is a fair approximation.

And perfect is, well, perfect. Once a digital original is created, copies are every bit as good as their digital originals. In fact, a digital copy is exactly identical to the original digital version.* If you've ever made a photocopy of a photocopy, you know this isn't true for analog copies. But with digital copies, no bits are lost or degraded from original to copy,† regardless of whether one, a hundred, or a billion copies are made.

Free and perfect are two desirable properties, but a hard drive full of millions of copies of the same photo, file, or song is not valuable. The economic power of information goods increases once a network is available because networks add a critical third attribute: *instant*. Networks allow distribution of a free, perfect copy of information goods from one place to another, or from one place to many, virtually immediately.

The Internet is a particularly powerful network because it expands the concept of free in two important ways. First, it's typically free to transmit an additional copy of a song or picture over this network, since flat-rate Internet pricing plans are common. Once people pay for Internet access, they don't pay per bit of traffic they send or

---

* It's true that the digital representations of a song or movie are in some sense inferior to their analog counterparts because some information is lost during the translation to bits, and some people don't want to settle for digital. Director Quentin Tarantino resurrected the 70mm film format in late 2015 when he released his film *The Hateful Eight* (Peter Suderman, "There's One Great Reason to See Quentin Tarantino's *The Hateful Eight* in Theaters," *Vox*, January 4, 2016, http://www.vox.com/2016/1/4/10707828/hateful-eight-70mm-roadshow), and many of us know at least one audiophile who prefers vinyl albums to digitally encoded music. But digital versions are good enough for the great majority of us the great majority of the time.

† Unless an error or modification occurs—and, unlike with analog copies, errors or changes of even a single bit can be digitally detected using authentication techniques based on public key cryptography.

receive.* Second, it's free to send that bit next door or halfway around the world. The Internet's architecture is, in fundamental ways, indifferent to physical separation, leading to what the journalist Francis Cairncross has called "the death of distance" as a factor limiting the spread of information.

Free, perfect, and instant make a powerful combination, worth more than each of these characteristics separately. Thus it is very difficult to compete with. Imagine trying to run a physical newspaper or music retailer against a rival that could replicate and distribute the same products freely, perfectly, and instantly. Even if that rival faced the same *fixed* cost of reporting and writing the news stories, or of producing the music, the overall cost advantage would be significant because the marginal cost of making and distributing additional, identical copies was so low. For most of history, few, if any, goods and services have been free, perfect, and instant. But with digital, networked goods, these three properties are automatic.

As Platforms Combine, Incumbents Contract

Platforms are online environments that take advantage of the economics of free, perfect, and instant. To be more precise, a platform can be defined as a digital environment characterized by near-zero marginal cost† of access, reproduction, and distribution.

The Internet, of course, is the platform most familiar to most of us, and the one responsible for the industrial disruptions we described earlier. In a sense, it is a platform of platforms. These examples highlight an important feature of platforms: they can often be

---

* As long as they stay within the total usage limits set by their Internet service provider.

† The marginal cost is the cost of producing or distributing one more item. For most Internet access plans, the marginal cost of a bit is zero.

built on top of each other. The World Wide Web, for example, is a multimedia, easy-to-navigate platform built on top of the original Internet information transfer protocols. Those protocols have been around for decades, but before Sir Tim Berners-Lee invented the web,[*] the Internet was primarily a platform for geeks. One platform (the Internet), was a foundation or building block for another (the web). As we wrote in our previous book, *The Second Machine Age*, this building-block feature is valuable because it enables combinatorial innovation—the work of coming up with something new and valuable not by starting from scratch, but instead by putting together in new ways things that were already there (perhaps with a few generally novel ingredients).

Combinatorial innovation can be fast and cheap, and when it's leveraged by the power of the free, perfect, and instant characteristics of platforms, the results are often transformative. In 1995, computer programmer Craig Newmark expanded a simple e-mail distribution list into a public website to let people list local events in the San Francisco area. Craigslist grew very rapidly, reaching 700 local sites in seventy countries by 2014, and soon became the dominant online destination for real estate listings, help-wanted ads, and other classified ads in the cities where it operated. Because of the favorable economics of platforms, Newmark was able to run and grow a healthy business with estimated profits of $25 million in 2008 while charging fees for only a few categories of ads, such as job ads or brokered apartment rentals in New York. All other listings were free. Craigslist

---

[*] By October 1990, Berners-Lee had created three of the most important building blocks of what would become the World Wide Web: HTML (the formatting language), URL (an address system for identifying and retrieving information), and HTTP (enabling links across the web). He also wrote the first web browser and web server. World Wide Web Foundation, "History of the Web," accessed February 7, 2017, http://webfoundation.org/about/vision/history-of-the-web.

pricing was highly attractive to the people and businesses that used the site, but deadly to many newspapers. One study concluded that Craigslist cost the print industry over $5 billion between 2000 and 2007. In this case, print dollars became digital pennies.

Newspapers and magazines saw their revenues decline further as two other types of platforms appeared. The first were platforms for disseminating content freely, perfectly, and instantly. A huge number of content platforms, spanning every medium, topic, industry, and contributor type, from professional journalists to freelancers to unpaid enthusiasts, emerged as alternatives to mainstream print media. The second were platforms to serve targeted ads across all these types of content. Services like DoubleClick, AppNexus, and Google AdSense developed fast and automated processes for matching advertisers with content providers. This technology made the transactions more efficient for both parties, but also provided more transparent measurement of the effectiveness of the activities when compared to nondigital media. These matching platforms quickly became the dominant originator of online display advertising, accounting for an estimated $22 billion of US marketers' budgets in 2016. And their scale is enormous, AppNexus alone has over 8,000 servers that, at peak times, can process 45 billion ad buys per day on every continent, even including Antarctica.

The speed and severity with which these new content and advertising platforms disrupted print media were dismaying to the industry's incumbents, who sometimes offered confused responses to the threats they faced. Beginning in 2007, groups representing Belgian, German, and Spanish newspaper publishers won court cases against Google News, a service that aggregates news and displays headlines, photos, and short excerpts from newspapers' stories. In each case, aggregators were forced to shut down in the country unless they shared revenues with the publishers. In each case, Google pointed out that since its

News product did not include any advertising, there was no revenue to share. Nonetheless, it shut down its News product. As a result, traffic to newspapers' websites decreased substantially, and in each case the publishing groups asked for the court decision to be reversed, restoring the flow of traffic.

We see the same pattern time and time again: the free, perfect, and instant economics of platforms offer stiff competition. In 2009, Jan Koum and Brian Acton released WhatsApp, a smartphone application that let users send text messages to each other via their phones' data networks, rather than as SMS messages. This difference was important because many users, especially those outside the world's richest countries, paid their mobile phone company for each SMS they sent or received. Data networks typically have flat-rate pricing, and if the phone was connected to a Wi-Fi network, data transfers were completely free. Price-sensitive users opted for WhatsApp in large numbers, and by 2016 it had over a billion active users sending each other more than 40 billion messages per day. The world's mobile carriers were not happy about this—SMS traffic was highly profitable for them—but there was little they could do to combat the free, perfect, and instant popularity of WhatsApp.

The Irresistible Effect of Networks

Over time, even mobile phone users with generous SMS plans switched to WhatsApp for most of their messages. Why? For the simple reason that many of the people with whom they wanted to exchange messages already used WhatsApp, so they too had to adopt it.

This is a clear example of what economists call a "network effect": the fact that some goods, like WhatsApp, become more valuable to each user as more people use them. The economics of network effects are central to understanding business success in the digital world and were worked out in a series of papers in the 1980s,[*] which is, not coincidentally, when modern computer networks and digital software started becoming especially important economically.

Network effects are also called demand-side economies of scale,[†] and as the WhatsApp example shows, they can be extremely compelling—so compelling that in 2014, Facebook paid $22 billion to acquire the company. At the time, the messaging service had 600 million monthly active users but just 70 employees and was handling 50% more messages every day than the entire global SMS network. To see the importance of network effects, imagine an app, call it "WhatsWrong," that was identical in all its functionality and user experience design to WhatsApp, except it had zero users. How much do you think Facebook, or anyone else, would pay for WhatsWrong?

WhatsApp shows that network effects arise in part because of the choices made by platform creators. If the app's developers had decided to make their creation easily interoperable with established SMS networks, users of these networks would have switched over to WhatsApp for cost reasons only, if at all. As the app grew in popularity, however, SMS users increasingly felt left out, so they became more likely to turn their backs on the old messaging technology in favor of the new one. And as more and more of them did this, the network

---

[*] Key contributions were made by Joe Farrell and Garth Saloner (for example, Joseph Farrell and Garth Saloner, "Standardization, Compatibility, and Innovation," *Rand Journal of Economics* 16, no. 1 [Spring 1985], 70–83, http://www.stern.nyu.edu/networks/phdcourse/Farrell_Saloner_Standardiization_compatibility_and_innovation.pdf), and independently by Michael Katz and Carl Shapiro ("Network Externalities, Competition, and Compatibility," *American Economic Review* 75, no. 3 [June 1985]: 424–40, https://www.jstor.org/stable/1814809?seq=1#page_scan_tab_contents).

[†] Meaning that the benefits to users (the source of demand) grow as the scale increases. Demand-side economies of scale parallel supply-side economies of scale, where the average costs to suppliers fall as scale increases.

effects grew stronger. Computer pioneer Mitch Kapor observed that "architecture is politics." With platforms, it's also economics.

From Servers to Songs, Platforms Proliferate

Platform economics, Moore's law, and combinatorial innovation continue to produce developments that take industries and their incumbents by surprise. As the e-commerce giant Amazon grew, it found that each systems integration project—each effort, for example, to connect a database of customers to an application that let them track the shipment status of their order—was a lot of work, even though the company had undertaken similar projects before. It seemed like Amazon was reinventing the wheel with each integration effort, and this duplication of effort was an expensive and time-consuming waste. So, CEO Jeff Bezos assigned Rick Dalzell the task of "hardening the interfaces" between systems—making sure, in other words, that all the main databases and applications had the same set of ways that they could be accessed, and that no one took a shortcut around these standards in the name of expediency. This was not technologically groundbreaking work—standard interfaces have been around for a long time—but it was organizationally demanding. Dalzell was described as a bulldog as he went through the company ensuring that interfaces were hardened and shortcuts eliminated.

The project was highly successful, and Amazon soon realized that it possessed a powerful new resource: a modular set of digital resources (like storage space, databases, and processing power) that could be combined and recombined almost at will—all accessible all over the world via the company's existing high-speed Internet connections. Might these resources be valuable to people who wanted to build a database, application, website, or other digital resource but didn't want to go through the trouble of maintaining all required hardware and software themselves?

Amazon decided to find out and launched Amazon Web Services in 2006. It originally offered storage (Amazon S3) and computing (Amazon EC2) services on the platform. Within eighteen months, Amazon claimed to have more than 290,000 developers using the platform. Amazon Web Services added more tools and resources over time, maintained hardened interfaces, and kept growing dramatically. By April 2016, it was contributing 9% of Amazon's total revenue and, remarkably, over half of the company's total operating income. In early 2016, AWS was called the fastest-growing enterprise technology company in history by Deutsche Bank analyst Karl Keirstead. This description certainly pleased Amazon shareholders, who experienced share price rises of 2,114% (from $35.66 to $753.78), in the ten years after the launch of AWS on July 11, 2006. But it was probably not as warmly received elsewhere in the enterprise IT industry.

The recorded-music industry provides an excellent final example of the disruptive power of platforms because it's been repeatedly transformed over time by three generations of them. Worldwide revenue from recorded music dropped by over half between 2000 and 2015, from $37 billion to $15 billion, even though people aren't listening to less music now than before the turn of the century.* Clever research

---

* Tracking music sales was straightforward in the era of CDs and vinyls. As digital formats emerged, the industry agreed that ten downloads (called a TEA) and 1,500 streams (called a SEA) were equivalent to the sale of a traditional physical album. This standardization enables approximate comparisons over time. Across 2015, Americans purchased or legally consumed the equivalent of 560 million albums (Keith Caulfield, "Drake's 'Views' Is Nielsen Music's Top Album of 2016 in the U.S.," *Billboard*, January 5, 2017, http://www.billboard.com/biz/articles/7647021/drakes-views-is-nielsen-musics-top-album-of-2016-in-the-us). In 2000, they bought 785 million albums (Jake Brown, "2016 Soundscan Data: Total Music Sales and Consumption," *Glorious Noise*, January 6, 2017, http://gloriousnoise.com/2017/2016-soundscan-data-total-music-sales-and-consumption). The difference, of course, is that there is substantially more illegal (therefore untraceable) music consumption today.

by economist Joel Waldfogel* indicates that the quality of recorded music available hasn't declined in recent years, which means music lovers have benefited greatly. We're listening to at least as much music that's at least as good as in the past, while paying less for it overall. The creators and owners of this music are probably happy about the first two of these trends, but not about the third.

Piracy was the music industry's first culprit for declining sales. If customers can get a free, perfect, and instant copy of a song or album, after all, many of them will take advantage of this opportunity and not feel a moral compulsion to compensate whoever holds the rights to the music. And soon after the web appeared, other Internet-based platforms emerged to facilitate ripping and sharing songs, which was in many cases a euphemism for acquiring music without paying for it.†

Napster, launched in 1999, was one of the first of these platforms; others included Kazaa, LimeWire, and Grokster. They quickly became popular with a wide variety of people except music rights holders, who reacted with indignation, a public relations blitz, and armies of lawyers. The Recording Industry Association of America sued Napster in 1999, as did the heavy metal band Metallica in 2000. Napster's fate as a free peer-to-peer file-sharing platform was sealed in 2001 when a federal judge in San Francisco ordered it shut down.

---

* Joel developed smart ways to measure music quality, including an index based on critics' retrospective lists (for example, *Rolling Stone*'s 500 best albums) and an analysis of each era's airplay and music sales long after it was initially released (if it's good quality, it will be in demand longer). Joel Waldfogel, *Copyright Protection, Technological Change, and the Quality of New Products: Evidence from Recorded Music since Napster*, NBER Working Paper 17503 (October 2011), http://www.nber.org/papers/w17503.pdf.

† As digital music proliferated in 2001, Apple introduced the memorable slogan "Rip, Mix, Burn," to the annoyance of music executives. Apple, "Apple Unveils New iMacs with CD-RW Drives & iTunes Software," February 22, 2001, https://www.apple.com/pr/library/2001/02/22Apple-Unveils-New-iMacs-With-CD-RW-Drives-iTunes-Software.html.

The shutdowns and lawsuits probably had some effect on reducing piracy, but they didn't stop the decline in revenue from recorded music. Nor did Apple's popular iTunes Music Store. In fact, this platform contributed to the decline because it allowed consumers to unbundle music purchases.

Prior to iTunes, albums (collections of songs) were the dominant form of recorded music. In 2002 (the year before the iTunes launch), CD albums outsold CD singles 179 to 1. But consumers often really wanted to listen to only one or two songs from the album—the hits they'd heard on the radio or elsewhere. So, a mismatch typically existed between musical artists, who wanted the listener to experience the entire album (and a music label, which wanted the greater revenue from the whole album), and the majority of consumers, who wanted only a song or two. iTunes flipped this mismatch in favor of consumers by allowing them to buy perfect and instant copies of individual songs whenever they liked. These songs were not free, but they were far cheaper than entire albums.

This is a common feature of digital platforms: they can unbundle resources that used to be tightly clustered together, and therefore difficult to consume one by one. Platforms like iTunes turn this form of unbundled consumption from difficult into the default. This makes them very popular with consumers, which in turn makes it difficult for incumbents like music rights holders to ignore. Unbundling music becomes much more attractive as networks proliferate. To see this, note that delivering to customers ten music CDs, each with a single song, costs about ten times as much as delivering one CD. Multiply that by millions of customers, and you can see the attraction of bundling the songs onto a single CD. That's the economics of atoms. But on a network the costs of delivery are virtually zero, so there's no real penalty for selling songs à la carte. That's the economics of networks.

Unbundling is not the end of the story. As Jim Barksdale, former CEO of Internet browser company Netscape, observed, "There's only two ways I know of to make money: bundling and unbundling." As it turns out, both halves of this advice apply to music. Those same rights holders who unbundled music also had trouble staying away from the third wave of music platforms, which are streaming services like Spotify and Pandora. Streaming services took advantage of advances like powerful smartphones with Wi-Fi capability and generous data plans to offer consumers an enticing proposition: a huge library of music, consumable as individual songs or in an infinity of combinations and playlists,* available all the time freely, perfectly, and instantly, no matter what device was being used. Essentially, they rebundled music into subscriptions: consumers would pay for a large—in some cases, virtually unlimited—stream of music with a flat fee each month. Instead of buying individual songs, they bought the right to listen to a massive bundle of music.

Another unexpected fact about the economics of free, perfect, and instant is that goods can be rebundled in new ways. In particular, massive bundles of information goods, like music subscriptions, are often more profitable than selling the same goods à la carte. Many consumers have an easier time paying a fixed monthly amount than deciding whether to make a payment each time they consume a lit-

---

* In Spotify's early years (after launching in 2008) it focused on negotiations with music rights holders and building the infrastructure required to deliver a vast library of songs, on demand, to many consumers. By 2013, these challenges had been broadly addressed (Erik Bernhardsson, "When Machine Learning Matters," *Erik Bernhardsson* [blog], August 5, 2016, https://erikbern.com/2016/08/05/when-machine-learning-matters.html), and the company shifted focus toward using machine learning to deliver highly personalized music recommendations (Jordan Novet, "Spotify Intern Dreams Up Better Music Recommendations through Deep Learning," *VentureBeat*, August 6, 2014, http://venturebeat.com/2014/08/06/spotify-intern-dreams-up-better-music-recommendations-through-deep-learning). Spotify launched its algorithm-powered Daily Mix option in September 2016 (Spotify, "Rediscover Your Favorite Music with Daily Mix," September 27, 2016, https://news.spotify.com/us/2016/09/27/rediscover-your-favorite-music-with-daily-mix). It creates a customized playlist every twenty-four hours for every user.

tle bit more music. This tendency reflects both psychology (making decisions, especially about spending money, is taxing) and economics (subscription models can reshape demand so that selling bundles is more profitable and more efficient than selling goods separately).* The same business models don't work as well when goods are not digital: a massive bundle inevitably includes many components that go unused. If the marginal cost of those components is close to zero (as with online music), then there's no real waste from making them available. But if the goods are made of atoms (as with vinyl records or plastic CDs), then sending the consumer lots of never-to-be-used components is costly, and ultimately unprofitable.

The subscription approach for music proved to be a compelling offer, and streaming services exploded in popularity. For the first six months of 2016, streaming accounted for 47% of total US music revenues. The revenue-sharing structure that Spotify set up with rights holders was intended to mimic terrestrial radio agreements, which work out to approximately $0.007 per person who hears the song each time it is played.† The difference, of course, was that while some radio listeners would presumably buy the song after hearing it, very few Spotify listeners would, since they could use the service to listen

---

* The surprising economics of bundling and sharing for information goods were worked out in a series of papers by Erik with Yannis Bakos, and other coauthors. See, for example, Yannis Bakos and Erik Brynjolfsson, "Bundling Information Goods: Pricing, Profits, and Efficiency," *Management Science* 45, no. 12 (1999): 1613–30; Yannis Bakos and Erik Brynjolfsson, "Bundling and Competition on the Internet," *Marketing Science* 19, no. 1 (2000): 63–82; and Yannis Bakos, Erik Brynjolfsson, and Douglas Lichtman, "Shared Information Goods," *Journal of Law and Economics* 42, no. 1 (1999): 117–56.

† The rates are periodically reassessed by a special set of judges on the congressional Copyright Arbitration Royalty Panel (CARP), where Erik had the pleasure of testifying in 2005 about the economics of the industry. US Copyright Royalty Judges, "In the Matter of Digital Performance Right in Sound Recordings and Ephemeral Recordings: Determination of Rates and Terms," Docket No. 2005-1 CRB DTRA, accessed March 1, 2017, https://www.loc.gov/crb/proceedings/2005-1/rates-terms2005-1.pdf.

to it again, when and wherever they liked. Radio station plays were, in a real sense, advertisements, and thus complements, for recorded music (we'll discuss complements more in the next chapter). Spotify plays were more like substitutes.

Streaming services, then, changed purchasing behavior: they turned many people from à la carte music buyers into buyers of subscriptions or bundles of music. In doing so, they helped fulfill, at least in part, David Bowie's 2002 prediction that "the absolute transformation of everything that we ever thought about music will take place within 10 years, and nothing is going to be able to stop it. . . . Music itself is going to become like running water or electricity."

Something like this did, in fact, come to pass, but not in a way that made most music rights holders happy. The singer-songwriter Taylor Swift withdrew her music from Spotify in November 2014, saying that "file sharing and streaming have shrunk the numbers of paid album sales drastically, and every artist has handled this blow differently," but most other artists and rights holders went along. The economic architecture of free, perfect, and instant platforms was too compelling to consumers to be ignored by incumbents.

It's a pattern we'll see more often in the future, we predict. We agree with the business scholars Geoffrey Parker, Marshall Van Alstyne, and Sangeet Choudary, who write in their book *Platform Revolution* that "as a result of the rise of the platform, almost all the traditional business management practices . . . are in a state of upheaval. We are in a disequilibrium time that affects every company and business leader."

Chapter Summary

▶ The Internet and related technologies disrupted diverse industries, from retailing to journalism to photography, over the past twenty years. Revenues fell even as consumers gained new options, and new entrants flourished.

▶ This disruption happened largely because of the free, perfect, and instant economics of digital information goods in a time of pervasive networks. The marginal cost of an additional digital copy is (almost) zero, each digital copy is a perfect replica of the original, and each digital copy can be transmitted across the planet virtually instantly.

▶ Most traditional goods and services are not free, perfect, or instant, putting them at a competitive disadvantage.

▶ Networked goods become more valuable as more people use them. The result is "demand-side economies of scale," giving an advantage to bigger networks.

▶ A platform can be described as a digital environment characterized by near-zero marginal cost of access, reproduction, and distribution.

▶ Platform economics, Moore's law, and combinatorial innovation continue to reshape industries as dissimilar as computer hardware and recorded music.

Questions

1. Where are the next places that the free, perfect, and instant economics of bits will be put to use in your organization?

2. What are the most important digital platforms in your industry today? What do you think they will be in three years?

3. How many of your current offerings could conceivably be delivered via the cloud? Are you taking action fast enough to move them there?

4. Put yourself in the shoes of some of your archetypal customers. Compared to the status quo, what to them might be a more attractive bundling, unbundling, or rebundling of your offerings together with others?

5. What are the most realistic scenarios for how network effects could become stronger or more common in your industry?

CHAPTER 7

PAYING COMPLEMENTS, AND OTHER SMART STRATEGIES

> The curious task of economics is to demonstrate to men how little they really know about what they imagine they can design.
>
> — *Friedrich von Hayek, 1988*

IN 2007, STEVE JOBS WAS IN THE MIDDLE OF WHAT WAS PER-haps the greatest tenure as a CEO in US corporate history. But throughout that year, his failure to fully appreciate a basic insight from economics threatened to stall his company's momentum.

How Steve Jobs Nearly Blew It

Early in 2007, Apple introduced the iPhone, a product that deserves the label "iconic." Its groundbreaking design and novel features, including multitouch screen, powerful mobile Internet browser, accelerometer, and GPS made it an instant hit, with rapturous reviews and sales of over 6 million handsets in its first year. The iPhone had plenty of doubters prior to its release. These included Microsoft cofounder Steve Ballmer, who said, "$500? Fully subsidized? With a plan? I said that is the most expensive phone in the world. And it doesn't appeal to business customers because it doesn't have a keyboard. Which makes it not a very good email machine." Two thousand seven and later years proved the skeptics very wrong.

But Jobs himself spent the first year of the iPhone's existence on the wrong side of a critically important debate. From the beginning, the iPhone was intended to be as much a computer as a phone; it had a processor, memory, storage, an operating system, a user interface, and many other familiar attributes of computers. So of course it also had applications, which came to be called "apps," in part to distinguish them from the software found on full-sized desktops and laptops.

Jobs had become legendary for maintaining tight control over his company's products. He believed that this was the only way to guarantee an excellent and consistent user experience, so he wanted Apple to develop all of the iPhone apps. As Walter Isaacson writes in his biography *Steve Jobs*, "When [the iPhone] first came out in early 2007, there were no apps you could buy from outside developers, and Jobs initially resisted allowing them. He didn't want outsiders to create applications for the iPhone that could mess it up, infect it with viruses, or pollute its integrity." Jobs told the *New York Times* in January of 2007, "You don't want your phone to be like a PC. The last thing you want is to have loaded three apps on your phone and then you go to make a call and it doesn't work anymore."

Highly placed people inside and outside of Apple—including senior vice president of marketing Phil Schiller, board member Art Levinson, and venture capitalist John Doerr—argued in favor of letting external developers make iPhone apps. Jobs brushed them off until after the product launched, then entertained the idea of outside apps, discussing it at four of the company's board meetings.

The Real Power of Digital Platforms

We know, of course, that Jobs eventually changed his mind and allowed outside apps onto the iPhone (and later the iPad). And that this was the right decision. It's hard to imagine a successful smartphone today without a large constellation of apps from independent developers. But *why* was it such a good decision? Is it simply that more is better?

Having a large set of apps available for a smartphone is certainly good, but it's not the whole story. To see why not, imagine that the iPhone has tons of great free apps available, but they're all games. The device would be highly attractive to gamers, but other consumers wouldn't be too interested in it. Now imagine that there are lots of apps of all kinds available, but each one costs $100 or more. Such an iPhone would be the must-have gadget for plutocrats, but the rest of us wouldn't have much use for it.

These two hypotheticals highlight the intuition that there's something about the variety of apps, combined with a range of prices, that help make the iPhone popular. To sharpen this intuition, and to get a deeper understanding of the power of platforms, we need to introduce two topics covered in every intro to microeconomics course: supply and demand curves, and the idea of complements. These concepts can sound arcane (a perception reinforced by the way they're presented in too many economics textbooks and classes), but they're really not, and exploring them a bit yields valuable insights.

Getting the Picture of Supply and Demand

Demand curves capture the simple notion that for most products, overall demand goes up as price goes down. We buy more flour, timber, computers, and airplane flights as the cost of each goes down, all other things being equal. To represent this simple reality graphically,

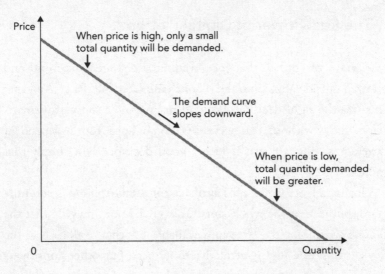

Figure 3
The "demand curve" for most things

economists draw demand curves for such products that look roughly like the curve shown in Figure 3.

The vertical axis represents the price of the good or service, and the horizontal axis, the total quantity demanded at that price. If the price is very high, the total quantity demanded will be quite low, while if the price drops to zero, demand will be much higher (although probably not infinitely so, since not everyone wants flour, timber, a computer, or a ride in an airplane, even if they are free). For normal products, plotting all the combinations of price and quantity demanded yields a picture like the one in Figure 3, which, for obvious reasons, is called a "downward-sloping demand curve."

Supply, of course, has a very different relationship with price. The more timber merchants and computer makers can get for their products, the more they will produce. So a typical supply curve, drawn on the same axes, looks something like Figure 4.

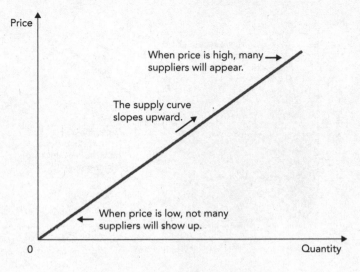

Price

When price is high, many →
suppliers will appear.

The supply curve
slopes upward. ↙

← When price is low, not many
suppliers will show up.

0

Quantity

Figure 4
The "supply curve" for most things

The obvious next step is to draw the two curves on the same graph and see where they intersect, as we've done in Figure 5. Curves like this are drawn in every Econ 101 textbook because they provide a great deal of information. They show the price and quantity where demand just matches supply. That price multiplied by that quantity—in other words, the area of the shaded rectangle in the graph—is the total revenue that the producer will receive from the product.

Now look at the triangle-shaped area above the revenue rectangle. In this region are the consumers who got a great deal. They were willing to pay more than P^* for the product, but they had to pay only P^*. The triangle captures all the money left in the pockets of all such consumers; it's known as "consumer surplus." Producers aren't necessarily thrilled with consumer surplus. They'd rather get all the money each customer is willing to pay (and sometimes they find a way to do that by charging them different prices). But more often they can't. In

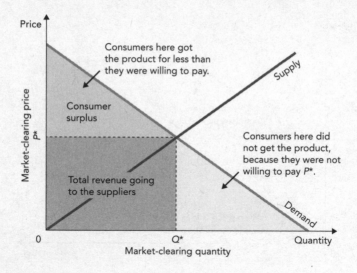

Figure 5
The supply and demand graph that appears
in every microeconomics textbook

competitive markets with well-informed consumers, the same products sell for the same single price everywhere. It's a phenomenon so
consistent that it's known in economics as the "law of one price." The
triangle to the right of the revenue rectangle represents consumers
who didn't get the product because they weren't willing or able to
pay P^* for it. They are the segment of the market that is unserved at
what's called the "market equilibrium price."

An iPhone has a demand curve that looks something like the one
in Figure 3, and so does each available app for the phone. But it
doesn't make sense to think about the iPhone curve and the app
curve separately, because iPhones and apps aren't independent of each
other. Instead, they're what economists call complementary goods, or
more simply, "complements." And the essential property of complements is that their demand curves interact as closely and predictably
as ballroom dance partners.

Complements Shift Curves

Ground beef and hamburger buns are the classic example of comple-ments. If a supermarket puts ground beef on sale during a summer weekend, it had better have plenty of buns in stock because demand for them is going to go up. In general, complements are pairs of goods with the following property: when the price of good A goes down, the demand curve of good B shifts out (meaning that demand goes up).* As Figure 6 shows, this means that a higher quantity of good B will be in demand, even though its price doesn't change at all.

Complements are all over the place (for example, bottles and bottle caps, crop seeds and fertilizer, steel and cement, cars and tires, and so on). And companies have known for some time how to use them to maximize demand and profit; makers of disposable razor blades, for example, commonly spur demand for them by discounting or giving away the complement of the razor handle itself. Steve Jobs surely understood that apps would be complementary to the iPhone—so much so that its home screen was essentially a grid of them. But by initially not allowing outside apps onto the phone, he cut off Apple from two beneficial phenomena: that different consumers have very different notions of complements, and that many people and compa-nies are willing to make their apps available for free.

Consumer preferences vary widely; vegetarians are not going to buy more hamburger buns no matter how cheap the ground beef. For them, the complement to buns might be a package of ingredi-ents for delicious veggie burgers. In the same way, the "killer app" varies across potential iPhone customers. Some want games, some want business tools, some want to stream music while others want to make music, some want to use social media, some want to use their phones as small scientific instruments, and so on. The best way

* More formally, the cross-price elasticity is negative when goods are complements.

Figure 6a   *When the price of hamburger meat goes down . . .*

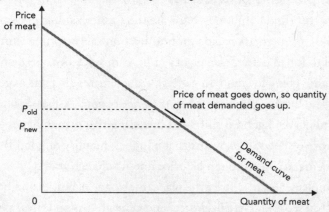

Figure 6b   *. . . the demand curve for hamburger buns shifts outward.*

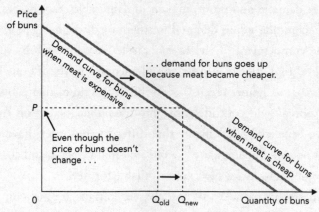

Figure 6

to discover these preferences, let alone to satisfy them, is to turn the App Store into something closer to an open marketplace than a store with a single owner. No single company, even one as innovative as Apple, could have come up with both Shazam—an app that listens to the music in the room you're in and then tells you the name of the song that's playing—and Angry Birds, a game in which you help the justifiably angry birds get their eggs back from the pigs that have stolen them.

Angry Birds was released in late 2009 and became one of the most downloaded games of all time. It was also free,* which is a very interesting property for one member of a pair of complementary goods to have. Let's go back to demand curves, and this time we'll draw two of them: one for the Angry Birds app, and one for the iPhone. For simplicity's sake we'll draw them the same size (even though this is inaccurate, it won't hurt the points we're trying to make).

If we price Angry Birds at $10, its demand curve tells us the total quantity that will be demanded—in other words, how many downloads it will get (Figure 7). This downward-sloping curve also tells us that if we price the game instead at $5, it will obviously have greater total demand. And if we price it at zero—if it's free—the curve tells us that there will be even more demand for it, but the curve also tells us something more interesting: that a huge amount of consumer surplus will be generated. The total triangle area under the demand curve, in fact, will be all consumer surplus, as Figure 7 illustrates, since everyone who is willing to pay *any* amount of money for the game will be getting what is, in their eyes, a bargain.

---

* Rovio, the Finnish company behind Angry Birds, generated $142 million in revenues in 2015 (Rovio Entertainment, "First Quarter of 2016 Shows Successful Turnaround for Rovio after Expected Difficult 2015," April 6, 2016, http://www.rovio .com/first-quarter-2016-shows-successful-turnaround-rovio-entertainment-after-expected-difficult-2015). In addition to in-app purchases, merchandising and licensing activities for products such as toys generate significant income (Alvaris Falcon, "85 Cool Angry Birds Merchandise You Can Buy," Hongkiat, accessed February 4, 2017, http://www.hongkiat.com/blog/cool-angry-birds-merchandise), smartphone covers, and the 2016 *Angry Birds Movie*, the country's most internationally successful film of all time (Rovio Entertainment, "The Angry Birds Movie Is the Most Internationally Successful Finnish Movie of All Time!" January 4, 2017, http://www.rovio.com/ angry-birds-movie-most-internationally-successful-finnish-movie-all-time).

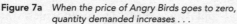

Figure 7a *When the price of Angry Birds goes to zero, quantity demanded increases . . .*

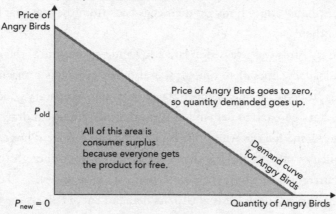

Price of Angry Birds

Price of Angry Birds goes to zero, so quantity demanded goes up.

P_{old}

All of this area is consumer surplus because everyone gets the product for free.

Demand curve for Angry Birds

$P_{new} = 0$

Quantity of Angry Birds

Figure 7b *. . . and the demand curve for iPhones shifts outward.*

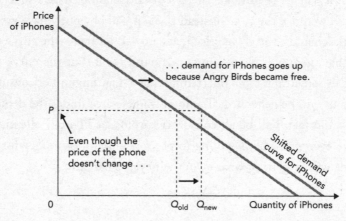

Price of iPhones

. . . demand for iPhones goes up because Angry Birds became free.

P

Even though the price of the phone doesn't change . . .

Shifted demand curve for iPhones

0   Q_{old} Q_{new} Quantity of iPhones

Figure 7

The Big Nudge: When Complements
Are Free, Perfect, and Instant

Keep in mind that we've already said that the app and the phone are complements. This means that the notional price drop of Angry Birds—from any potential consumers' previous expectations to the actual price of zero—has the effect of shifting the iPhone's demand curve outward, increasing the number of people who are willing to pay the iPhone's price. So, the existence of free apps like Shazam and Angry Birds has two effects: it generates consumer surplus (which is great because you always want your customers to feel like they're getting a bargain), and it nudges the iPhone's demand curve outward, which is exactly what Apple wants—more people who are willing to pay the iPhone's price.

Each of these apps probably shifts the phone's demand curve outward only a small amount; after all, how many more people are going to be willing to pay $599 (the original 2007 iPhone price) for an iPhone just because they can play a game on it? But the effects of these complements are cumulative. Each free app adds one dollop of consumer surplus to the total bundle offered by the iPhone, and also pushes its demand curve that much farther out in the direction desired by Apple. An expensive phone doesn't become that much more attractive a purchase because there's one desirable and free app available for it. But what about when there are hundreds of thousands of free apps, some large subset of which are going to be desirable to almost any imaginable customer? Such a huge collection of apps would yield a lot of consumer surplus, and would push the demand curve out a long, long way. Expectations play a role as well: all those apps and app developers give consumers more confidence that their phone will continue to be valuable, or perhaps become even more valuable, as time passes and new apps are introduced.

Who's writing all these free apps? Pure altruists, or people who just want the world to see what they can do? There are people like that among developers of free apps, but there are a lot of others too. Unless you thought a lot about the economics of free goods, the proliferation of free apps would have been hard to foresee in 2007, but it turns out that there are a lot of people and organizations willing to make their apps available for free, and for a variety of reasons.

"Freemium" businesses. Companies like cloud-based storage provider Dropbox and clipping manager Evernote settled on a business model in which they offered customers a basic level of service for free, then charged for extras (extra functions or capacity) on top of this base. This approach proved quite popular (Steve Jobs made a "nine-digit" acquisition offer for Dropbox in 2009, when the company was only two years old) and was supported by useful free apps from these and other companies. Smart companies realize that the free goods can be a complement, not a substitute, for more expensive versions: free goods increase demand for paid versions, rather than cannibalizing them.

Ad revenue. Many free apps make money for their creator by showing ads to users. Google's iPhone-specific search engine, the driving-direction app Waze, and many others include ads, and the revenue generated from them can be impressive. Facebook's app on the iPhone is free to consumers, but mobile advertising represented 84% of total revenue for Facebook in the third quarter of 2016.

Customer service. Many companies in banking, insurance, investing, and other industries develop free apps for their customers. In October 2010, Amazon rolled out a feature that let iPhone owners take a picture of the bar code of a product they had found in a store; the app would immediately tell them if they could get it more cheaply from Amazon. In August 2010, Chase's free consumer-banking app let users deposit checks simply by taking pictures of them. This great leap forward in consumer surplus was soon copied by other banks.

Public service. Many government agencies and not-for-profits make apps available as part of their mission. Because we live in the Boston area, we like Street Bump, which uses the iPhone's sensors to determine when we've driven over a pothole, then transmits its location back to the city. And because we're obsessed with economic data, we like the FRED app from the Federal Reserve Bank of St. Louis, which makes a wide range of economic data public and easily accessible. Code for America, founded by Jennifer Pahlka, is an innovative nonprofit that lets geeks take sabbaticals from their jobs at leading technology firms in order to work with city governments to develop apps and other public-facing software.

Pairing with products. As digital products pervade our lives, apps that go along with these products proliferate on our phones. Health and fitness devices like the Fitbit and Nike+ FuelBand, smart door locks like the August, the Drop kitchen weighing scales, Sonos music speakers, and a lot of other gear can be controlled via apps. After installing gear from Viper and other companies, you can even unlock and start your car via smartphone.

These are just some of the motivations for developing a free app. Only after Jobs was convinced of the advantages of opening up the app store to outside developers was Apple able to tap into all of them and reap their benefits of consumer surplus and demand curve shifting. In July of 2008, Apple announced that about 800 externally developed apps were available at the company's app store. Within three days they had been downloaded more than 10 million times—an accomplishment that Jobs described as a "grand slam."

The Importance of Being Open

Recall that our definition of a platform is a digital environment with near-zero marginal cost of access, duplication, and distribution. The iPhone certainly meets this definition. But it was originally a closed platform when it came to apps, since only Apple could add them.

After the company opened up its platform, tremendous innovation and growth ensued.

As the example of Apple shows, opening up popular platforms provides benefits. Most fundamentally, it brings to the platform owner a greater volume and variety of contributions, motivations, and ideas than the owner alone ever could have mustered. These contributions deliver two powerful economic benefits: they increase consumer surplus and they push out the demand curve for complementary products, which means that more of them will be sold at any given price point.

Two other benefits also accrue to platform owners when they open up their creations. First, they get data: about what kinds of apps (or other aspects of the platform) are popular, how this popularity changes over time, the preferences and behaviors of platform members, and so on. This data is critical for troubleshooting, making personalized recommendations to platform members, deciding which initiatives to pursue, and many other purposes (some of which we'll explore in the next chapter) Second, open platforms create new revenue opportunities. Many iOS apps are not free, and Apple keeps 30% of the cost of paid ones. In 2015, this revenue source yielded $6 billion for the company.

If your goal is to maximize revenue, it is also possible for a platform to be *too* open. Aside from revenues, there are other trade-offs to consider. The web is the world's largest digital platform, and its infrastructure and architecture reflect its original intent: to allow anyone to join and start participating. This openness has led to great benefits for the world, but it has also led directly to malware, cybercrime and cyberwarfare, distributed denial-of-service attacks, phishing and identity theft, darknets for exchanging child pornography, doxxing, fake news, and other developments that can make one despair for humanity.

Curation Counters the Corruptors

The solution to all this bad behavior and bad content is to build better platforms—ones that use curation, reputation systems, and other tools to keep out the bad and encourage the good, however the platform owner defines these terms. Steve Jobs realized how important curation would be when he finally agreed to let Apple open up the iOS iPhone platform to applications from outside developers. As Walter Isaacson relates in his biography of Jobs, "Jobs soon figured out that there was a way to have the best of both worlds. He would permit outsiders to write apps, but they would have to meet strict standards, be tested and approved by Apple, and be sold only through the iTunes Store. It was a way to reap the advantage of having thousands of software developers while retaining enough control to protect the integrity of the iPhone and the simplicity of the customer experience."

Apple's application approval process has faced criticism for being too slow, opaque, and restrictive. Whatever the merits of this argument, it highlights an important fact: platform owners have a great deal of discretion in deciding how to configure and curate their creations. Platforms are the property of their owners, and property rights are strong.

This means that popular platforms—the ones that best harness the economics of network effects, consumer surplus, and complements—become very influential because of the choices they make about curating content, membership, traffic, and so on. As we write this in late 2016, many media companies are trying to figure out how to respond to Facebook's offer to publish their articles directly on the social network, instead of or in addition to on their own sites, and split any associated advertising revenue. The lesson is clear: powerful platforms can force hard choices on companies within their sphere of influence.

The Art of Platform War: Be Different, and Be Early

The runaway success of Apple's App Store led others within the telecom and technology industries to build and create their own platforms. Taken together, the results of these efforts offer a few more insights.

In 2005 Google bought Android, a startup about which little was known, for approximately $50 million. The technology blog *Engadget* commented at the time that "we only have the faintest idea why Google just bought Android, a stealthy startup that specializes in making 'software for mobile phones.'" Within a few years, though, the value of a robust alternative to Apple's platform for apps became quite clear. In 2010, David Lawee, a vice president of corporate development at Google, said it was the search giant's "best deal ever." And one that almost didn't happen: Android founder Andy Rubin had actually flown to South Korea and offered his company to Samsung weeks before selling to Google.

From the start, Google's app platform and the mobile phone operating system that underpinned it were different from Apple's. First, Android was released as open-source software and made available for free to device manufacturers, while Apple's iOS remained available only on Apple phones (and later, tablets). Google saw Android not as a revenue source itself, or a way to spur sales of its own devices, but instead as a vehicle for continuing to spread its products, services, and, crucially, its mighty advertising revenue engine.[*] The company also realized that to counter Apple's head start and strong

---

[*] In the fourth quarter of 2016, Google received 96% of all search ad clicks on mobile devices. More mobile users mean more mobile searches and ad revenues. Jack Nicas, "Alphabet's Earnings Rise but Falls Short of Views—Update," Morningstar, January 26, 2017, https://www.morningstar.com/news/dow-jones/TDJNDN_2017012614626/alphabets-earnings-rise-but-falls-short-of-viewsupdate.html.

momentum, it had to distribute its own platform widely and quickly. Releasing Android as open-source software helped because it assured potential adopters that Google could not at a later time unilaterally change the rules for using Android by, for example, imposing a licensing fee. This strategy worked well. By 2011, Android had become the world's most popular mobile operating system and went on to power 88% of all smartphones sold in the third quarter of 2016.

The second difference was that apps were less heavily curated on Android than on iOS. Google has an official store that offers free and paid apps that have been vetted by the company, but Android phone owners can easily install and use apps that are not part of the store. Here again, Google decided to make its platform less centralized and tightly curated than its rival's, and here again it's hard to argue with the results to date.

Other attempts to build a platform for mobile phones have not been as successful. Microsoft, which had ambitions both to sell its own devices (like Apple) and to generate revenue from search engine advertising (like Google) began working on its Windows Phone effort in 2008. It was considered so important to the company that in 2013 Microsoft bought the mobile phone business of the Finnish manufacturer Nokia, a company that at one time had dominated the global phone industry itself but had been too slow to recognize and respond to the threat posed by app-centric smartphones. Nokia found itself squeezed between smartphones on one side and much cheaper basic phones from Asian manufacturers on the other.

The purchase by Microsoft didn't help much, unfortunately. The combined company's efforts to build a vibrant platform to rival iOS and Android never achieved significant traction, and many popular apps, including Snapchat, declined to offer a Microsoft version. By the first quarter of 2016, Microsoft phones represented less than 1% of worldwide smartphone sales. By the end of that year, commentators had declared, "Microsoft's Nokia experiment is over." The failure resulted in more than 20,000 layoffs and almost $8 billion in write-downs, the largest in Microsoft history.

Other efforts fared even worse. BlackBerry was an early leader in the mobile device market, especially among busy executives who became addicted to their e-mail-enabled "CrackBerries." By 2009, the BlackBerry operating system powered 20% of new smartphones, and parent company Research In Motion (RIM) was worth over $77 billion. Although BlackBerry's security features and long battery life were attractive to corporate customers, their handsets were not as appealing to consumers as iPhones and Android devices were. Developers responded by creating fewer consumer apps for the BlackBerry platform. The mobile phone networks wanted the company to succeed, in order to reduce the negotiating power of Apple and Google, but RIM lost momentum and never recovered. By the end of 2016 the company had announced it was stopping production of its own hardware, and it saw its market value drop below $4 billion, a 95% collapse from its peak.

The lesson from these examples is that there is often room for only a limited number of platforms in any particular domain or activity, especially when users don't feel comfortable using multiple platforms at a time, a practice called "multihoming." While consumers prefer to have more than one choice, in part to prevent any single platform provider from feeling or acting like a monopoly, they don't appear to value more than a handful of viable options—often no more than two. In the case of mobile phones, few use more than one platform at a time.

Habits of Successful Platforms

What are the characteristics of the winners in the platform battles we've observed, and those that will be waged in the future? While they are not all identical, we've already seen that winning platforms—those that grow quickly and deliver value to both their participants and their owners—tend to share a few characteristics.

1. They're early to the space. They don't have to be the first (Android certainly wasn't), but they had better not be so late that many potential participants have already chosen a platform and network effects have taken hold.

2. They take advantage of the economics of complementary goods whenever possible, realizing that low prices for one complement lead to increased demand for others.

3. They open up their platforms to a broad range of contributors and contributions. This variety increases total consumer surplus, especially if some of the contributions are offered to users for free, and it pushes the demand curve outward in a series of nudges.

4. While they maintain a broad rule of openness, they also curate their platforms to deliver a consistent and positive experience to participants, and to minimize unpleasant surprises.

As Apple and Google demonstrate, there is more than one way to strike a balance between completely closed systems that don't allow third parties to create complementary offerings, and completely open systems that aren't able to capture a significant share of value from the platform, but this tension must be managed.

Experience as Strategy

Just about all the successful platform builders also do one other thing: they work obsessively on the user interface and user experience that they deliver to their participants. The user interface is the set of ways in which a person interacts with a technology. For an iPhone, for example, the user interface includes the touchscreen, home button, volume controls, microphone, and speaker. Interfaces need to be appealing to users and as intuitive as possible. The best of them follow advice often attributed to Einstein: "Make things as simple as possible, but not simpler."

User experience is a broader concept, encompassing how effective and pleasant a product is to use. The difference between the two was wittily summarized by the designer Ed Lea with two pictures: a spoon representing the user interface, and a bowl of cereal representing the user experience.

Facebook shows two benefits from getting the user interface and user experience right. Many people have forgotten, or never knew, that Facebook was not the first social network, or even the first popular one. Friendster had been around since 2002, and MySpace, founded in 2003, seemed to have such devoted users and strong network effects that News Corp bought it for $580 million in 2005.

But over time, these platforms failed to deliver to their users in important ways. Friendster's site slowed down and performed poorly as it grew, and MySpace gave its members perhaps too much freedom in designing their spaces. As the interactive marketing agency Fame Foundry noted on its blog in 2009,

> Of the people you know, how many could lay plans for their own house, paint a beautiful portrait worthy of hanging in your living room or perform cosmetic surgery? Chances are, few . . . good web design is an exact art and science. MySpace disagrees, however, and allows their users to hack everything in the page until nothing is usable, legible or tolerable. . . . In contrast, Facebook has chosen to restrict at least the foundational framework of the site.

MySpace was sold by News Corp to the online marketing company Viant in 2011 for just $35 million.

The success of the payment company Stripe shows that if platform builders understand user experience needs well enough, they don't even need to be an early entrant. By 2010 there was certainly no shortage of intermediaries helping online merchants accept payments from their customers. Some, like PayPal, were aimed at individuals and small businesses, while others, like Chase Paymentech and Authorize.Net, served large-scale sellers.

But brothers Patrick and John Collison, who were at the time twenty-one and nineteen years old, respectively, felt that the user interfaces and user experiences these companies were offering weren't fast, simple, and good enough for developers at online merchants, especially as online commerce evolved. E-commerce was becoming a broad phenomenon—moving well beyond filling up a shopping cart at a retailer's website and clicking the "checkout" button—and one increasingly carried out on mobile devices. This trend presented novel user interface and user experience challenges. As Patrick Collison explained to us, "Getting redirected [from within an app] to PayPal to log in to your account could not possibly work on a phone." So the two brothers decided to build something like Amazon Web Services for payments: an easy-to-access, cloud-based service that would be appropriate for the needs of a particular group of users (namely, online and app-based merchants) and scale with their needs.

As the Collisons set to work, they quickly learned how numerous these needs were, and how many of them were left unsatisfied by existing payment offerings. Merchants' needs were simple: they just wanted to be able to accept payments from their customers. But these payments could come from many different sources—checking accounts, debit cards, corporate lines of credit, and so on—via different networks, and in different currencies. The mix of requirements varied for each merchant and also changed over time as merchants grew, worked with different customers, and internationalized. And hand in hand with these changes was a shifting mix of fraudsters, laws and regulations, taxes and reporting requirements, and other gadfly complications and distractions.

As Patrick Collison told us in the summer of 2015, "It's hard to convey to outsiders how screwed up so much of the payment stuff is. [For example,] it's almost impossibly difficult to be a Chinese business that sells to consumers outside of China. It's not so much because any agent—be it the Chinese government or US government or whatever—doesn't want it. It's more because it's so complex and no one has managed to navigate it yet. Conversely, you cannot be a US business that sells to Chinese consumers. A vast majority of Chinese consumers pay with Alipay . . . [but] you can't get a merchant account with Alipay in the US.* . . . there are a lot of business models that should be possible, should be pursued, but they can't literally because of these kinds of frictions."

So, Stripe set out to be something that did not yet exist: a payment platform with a user experience centered around shielding merchants from all of this complexity, and a user interface for developers that consisted of nothing more than adding a few simple lines of code.

This was a risky goal to pursue at the time, not only because it would be difficult to achieve, but also because it might not be what the market wanted. Many within the payments industry believed that merchants value low prices above all,† and Stripe's per-transaction fee was not particularly low (especially for purchases made with debit cards). The company gambled that many merchants would be willing to accept higher fees in exchange for quick onboarding, lower up-front costs, easy technical integration, freedom from the hassles and delays associated with other payment processors, and the ability

---

* Stripe began supporting Alipay payments in August of 2015.

† Many within the payments industry continue to believe this.

to scale easily. According to Collison, "We had the idea that there should be a unified payments platform that can go right from the lone developer with an idea they're not sure about right through to one of the largest companies in the world. There should be both of these, and every point in between."

The Collison brothers' gamble paid off. Within five years of its public launch, Stripe had processed at least one payment for half of all US Internet users, and by November 2016 the company was valued at $9 billion. One of the fundamental reasons for this growth, Patrick Collison told us, was that Stripe's approach allowed its customers, especially smaller and newer ones, to experiment until they found something that worked well. He used Postmates, which we'll hear about more in the next chapter, as an example: "Our customer Postmates is a logistics company. They've partnered with Apple to do delivery right from the Apple store. The reason I like them as an example is because they started out as a different company. They were a courier service that you needed to book in advance. This is the promise of Stripe; we hide the payments complexity and let them try out a bunch of things instead of constricting them to a particular path."

Stripe's approach lets merchants try new things easily, quickly, and without worrying at all about payment issues. It lets them, in other words, more easily iterate and experiment, and these capabilities are most valuable in times of rapid innovation and change. As Stripe's services grew, these customers very likely found value in more and more of them, like currency conversion, invoicing, fraud detection, tax collection, and compliance with money laundering statutes.

These services played much the same economic role for Stripe that iPhone apps did for Apple: they were complements that could increase overall demand. Fraud detection from Stripe increases consumer surplus and also nudges out the demand curve for the service as a whole, which is exactly what the company wants.

Both Sides Now

As is the case with many successful platforms, Stripe benefits from network effects. In Stripe's case these effects are particularly strong because they are "two-sided." Participants on the company's platform fall into two broad groups: merchants who want to get paid, and financial institutions like banks and credit card companies involved in delivering payments to merchants. Financial institutions like China's Alipay clearly want to be where there are many merchants, since a lot of business will be done there. For similar reasons, merchants want to be where there are a lot of financial services firms.

Throughout digital industries, two-sided platforms exist with strong network effects, and we'll see several more in the next chapter. For now we just need to note their power, and note that Stripe is one of them. Patrick Collison eloquently described his ambition to us: "We want to build the infrastructure required to grow the GDP of the Internet."* Stripe seems to be well on its way, thanks in no small part to its acuity in harnessing the power of platforms to provide an excellent user experience.

Chapter Summary

▶ Digital platforms are the drivers of many the world's most successful companies today. They are powerful aggregators of both supply and demand.

▶ Two products are complements if a drop in the price of one pushes out the demand curve for the other.

---

* In other words, the total amount of worldwide economic activity that happens over the Internet.

▶ When a platform is opened up to allow outside contributions, its owner realizes an important benefit: demand for the owner's product goes up as others contribute complementary goods. When these complements are digital, many of them will be free, perfect, and instant.

▶ After opening up a platform, platform owners typically have to curate contributions from outsiders to maintain standards. Chaotic, unsafe, or fraudulent contributions can diminish a platform's value.

▶ Platform owners compete on their ability to draw in contributions and curate them effectively. But it becomes much more difficult to build a vibrant platform if at least two are already in place, particularly when consumers are unwilling to multihome.

▶ The builders of successful platforms pay a great deal of attention to their user interfaces and user experience.

▶ Many platforms are two-sided, with one type of customer on one side and a different type on the other side.

Questions

1. What are the possible complements for your offerings? How can you best use them to increase total demand?

2. Does it make more sense for you to try to build your own platform, or to participate in someone else's?

3. If you're building a platform, what's your strategy for curating

contributions? How will you encourage broad participation while ensuring high enough quality?

4. If a successful platform already exists in your space, what will you do not to mimic it, but instead to substantially differentiate yourself from it? If more than one platform already exists, why should anyone pay attention to yours?

5. What are your guiding principles for delivering a compelling user experience? What value are you offering, or problem are you solving, for your intended users?

CHAPTER 8

THE MATCH GAME: WHY PLATFORMS EXCEL

> This is it! This is a shot across our bow! If we don't invent a way to deal with (revenue management), we're history!
>
> — Donald Burr, CEO of People Express Airlines, 1985

GROUP EXERCISE SEEMS LIKE ONE OF THE LEAST LIKELY human activities to be transformed by digital technology. Many of us, it turns out, like working out with a bunch of people all doing the same thing, and the feeling of being in the middle of a sweating and energized crowd will be hard to replicate even with the powerful virtual reality technologies now on the horizon.* It's easy to conclude, then, that running a group exercise studio might be immune

---

* But as always with technology, never say never. The indoor cycling company Peloton sells a $1,995 stationary bike that has a Wi-Fi-enabled twenty-two-inch screen enabling riders to remotely stream live spin classes (there are least ten every day) with real instructors, as well as a back catalog of on-demand sessions, from their own home. In February 2016, Peloton announced it was working with Oculus Rift on a virtual reality headset that could replace the need for the screen. Mark Prigg, "Now You Can Track Your Gym Sessions Too: Peloton Teams Up with Strava App to Monitor Spin Classes—and Says It Is Also Working on Oculus Rift VR Workouts," DailyMail .com, February 18, 2016, http://www.dailymail.co.uk/sciencetech/article-3452996/ Now-track-gym-sessions-Peleton-teams-Strava-app-monitor-spin-classes-says-working -Oculus-Rift-VR-workouts.html.

from digital disruption. The example of ClassPass, however, indicates otherwise, and shows that exactly the same attributes that have made platforms powerful in bit-based industries are also now allowing them to pervade atom-based industries—those that offer a good or service in the physical world. Within the past decade, many such platforms have sprung up. And they're just getting started.

When the World Isn't Free, Perfect, and Instant

In his novel *Ulysses*, James Joyce attributes to the German poet Goethe this guidance: "Be careful of what you wish for in youth because you will get it in middle life." It's advice that might resonate with ClassPass founder Payal Kadakia, who made a decision when her business was young that she would reverse later in its life. The change caused ire among ClassPass members and reveals much about running platform businesses for nondigital goods and services.

In a November 2016 post on the company's blog, Kadakia announced that her company's popular ClassPass Unlimited offering was ending. ClassPass Unlimited members had been able to take as many exercise classes as they wanted each month for a flat fee (but no more than three at any single studio). She explained that the company launched the Unlimited program in May 2014 to encourage new members to learn about flexible fitness plans and join ClassPass. "It worked," she wrote.

In fact, it worked too well. Said Kadakia, "Many of you began to work out every other day—some of you even every single day! I applauded you for that. . . . Yet, we realized the impact this had on our business was unsustainable."

ClassPass Unlimited members reacted quickly, and with dismay. Many took to social media to vent, including @NakesaKou, who tweeted "UGH. Hearing the news that #classpass is getting rid of their unlimited plan broke my heart. WHY?!" The negativity was so widespread that *Business Insider* published an article entitled "People Are Freaking Out about ClassPass Killing Its Unlimited Membership Plan."

The Unlimited membership seemed misguided from the start. As Kadakia admitted, "It can't be a long-term membership option because it doesn't align our business with our promise. What kind of business would we be if we wanted our members to work out less to reduce costs?" But a closer look at ClassPass's history shows how hard the company tried to make this option work, and it provides insights about what happens when the economics of bits meet those of atoms.

ClassPass Unlimited was a simple, enticing proposition to customers: for a flat monthly fee, they could take as many classes as they wanted at participating studios in their city, and in all other cities where ClassPass operated. The proposition to studio owners was about as simple: ClassPass would fill up otherwise empty spaces in their classes—the ones not taken up by the studio's regular members—and pay the owner a specified amount for each ClassPass member who showed up.

With these propositions, ClassPass was trying to build a two-sided platform with strong network effects: as more individuals joined, the offer to studios became more attractive, and as more studios participated, the offer looked better to individual members (both current and prospective ones). Dangers loomed, however, as the company grew. They stemmed from the basic fact that physical-world offerings like a space in a yoga class are not like digital ones; the economics of free, perfect, and instant don't apply to atoms the way they do to bits. Builders of platforms for physical products need to be keenly aware of these differences and clever about responding to them.

So, what were the dangers ClassPass faced as it grew? Essentially, it had to contend with the fact that studios might not use it enough, while individuals might use it too much. Let's look first at the challenges on the studio side, and how ClassPass addressed them.

The Perils of Perishing Inventory

ClassPass's value to studios was essentially that it enabled them to make revenue from class spaces that would otherwise be empty. To say the same thing a bit more formally, it enabled the studio to make incremental revenue from *inventory* (space in a class) that would otherwise *perish* (be empty during the class). This sounds great, but how can a studio know in advance which classes will have empty spaces, and how many? How can it know which of its inventory will perish and thus bring in no money for the business?

This question is critically important because the amount ClassPass would pay for studio inventory that would otherwise perish was a discounted rate. The platform essentially said to the studio, "Look, you've committed to put on the class, and you've incurred all the fixed costs associated with it: rent, utilities, instructor salaries, and so on. The marginal cost of adding one more student in the class is quite low—just hot water for the shower and the cost of washing towels—so as long as we're paying you more per person than that marginal cost, you should be willing to accept our members into the class."

A smart studio owner's reply to this was something like, "That makes a lot of sense, but I have to be careful. You're right that my marginal costs are low and my inventory is perishable, but I also have to keep in mind that my inventory isn't infinite: each class has room for only so many people. The spaces I let you reserve at a discount for your members aren't available for me to sell at full price, and they're not available to my members—the ones paying me a monthly fee. I really don't want them to start complaining that they can't get into classes because of all the ClassPassers that start showing up. So I have to be careful."

This hypothetical back-and-forth shows that the economic properties of physical space in an exercise class are different from the free, perfect, and instant attributes of digital offerings. Because class space is perishable, it's far from perfect, and because class size is limited, it's a good that can't be freely and infinitely expanded. The marginal cost of adding another customer is very low when there is unused inventory, but it skyrockets once capacity is reached. Finite capacity and perishable inventory are attributes shared by exercise classes, airplane flights, nights in hotels, and many other physical-world offerings. And like almost all offerings, these services have a downward-sloping demand curve: a few people would be willing to pay a lot for them, and a lot more people would be willing to pay substantially less for them.

Math, Data, and Apps: Revenue Management to the Rescue

"Revenue management" is the name given to the set of algorithms and technologies developed over the years to help service businesses deal with finite capacity and perishable inventory, and turn them to their best possible advantage. The fundamental goal of revenue management is to let service companies sell as much as possible of their finite and perishable inventory to those customers with the highest willingness to pay, then sell off the rest to customers further down the demand curve. Revenue management began with airlines,* spread to

---

* The US Civil Aeronautics Board was established in 1938 to regulate the airline industry. The board essentially ensured that fares stayed artificially high for decades. The passing of the Airline Deregulation Act in 1978 removed governmental control and allowed airlines to freely set prices. It also saw the entrance of low-cost players into the market, such as People Express. The new airline initially grew rapidly; within five years it was flying a million customers a month and was the fifth biggest in the United States (Markus Salge and Peter M. Milling, "The Pace or the Path? Resource Accumulation Strategies in the U.S. Airline Industry," paper presented at the Annual Conference of the Systems Dynamics Society, Oxford, England, 2004, http://www.systemdynamics.org/conferences/2004/SDS_2004/PAPERS/150SALGE.pdf). A key driver of People Express's success was its low fares, typically 40%–55% lower than its competition's prices.

This posed a major threat to incumbents such as American Airlines (AA). To

hotels, and transformed both. We know of no sizable and successful companies in these industries today that are not proficient at it.

To studios on its platform, ClassPass can offer not only revenue management software delivered through its app, but also a large supply of people farther down the demand curve to fill up available spaces—the spaces, in other words, that the studio could not fill on its own.

However, there's a problem with this happy arrangement, and it's a big one: *Why should studio owners trust ClassPass to use revenue management software to look after their interests rather than its own?* It's obvious that ClassPass's revenue management efforts, if executed competently, would benefit itself. It's a lot less obvious that they would benefit individual studios. Wouldn't the platform have a strong incentive to flood classes with its own members, even if that was not the best outcome for the studios?

Studios' reluctance to turn over to ClassPass decisions about who

---

compete more effectively, AA invested millions in one of the first examples of revenue management technology and introduced "Ultimate Super Saver fares" for tickets that were bought well in advance and included conditions like a minimum length of stay. At the same time, AA kept prices for seats purchased closer to takeoff as high as possible. This strategy enabled AA to segment the market between leisure and business travelers and profit from the fact that these two segments have different willingness to pay. In its 1987 annual report, AA described revenue management as "selling the right seats to the right customers at the right price." (ThinkWell Consulting, "Yield Management to the Rescue: The American (Airlines) Way," 3, accessed February 5, 2017, http://thinkwellconsulting.com/wp-content/uploads/2015/10/ThinkWell_WhitePaper_w_Graphics1.pdf.)

AA maximized the number of seats sold and grew the highly profitable business class segment. Overall, revenue management provided quantifiable benefits of $1.4 billion for a three-year period (Barry C. Smith, John F. Leimkuhler, and Ross M. Darrow, "Yield Management at American Airlines," *Interfaces* 22, no. 1 [1992]: 22, http://202.120.24.209/DBD/reading/AmericanAirlines.pdf). To put this in perspective, the holding company that owned AA delivered only $892 million net profit across the same period. People Express could not compete, and it started to lose market share. By 1987 the airline had gone out of business.

gets into each class is understandable. To address the problem, the platform proposed to studios that they run a simple, low-risk experiment: turn over these decisions for single classes, and for a short time.

These trials quickly showed the benefits of working with the platform. As vice president of pricing and inventory Zach Apter told us,

> We say, "Give us a couple weeks. Give us one class and let's see what we can do." Then they see that, "Wow, there are five empty spots an hour and a half before class. ClassPass isn't taking them, that's interesting." Then lo and behold, five people walked up five minutes before class. That happens enough times, and they say, "Wow, this is really amazing. We don't know how you guys are doing this. We wouldn't have had the confidence ourselves, to go right up to that threshold of what the right number of spots is for ClassPass."

ClassPass's big data, broad reach, and many members allowed it to bring the benefits of revenue management to individual exercise studios, and its user interface and user experience around experimentation convinced many studios that their interests were well served by adopting it.

Here again, we see the power of complements: the revenue management function that comes with ClassPass software is a zero-cost complement that pushes out the demand curve of studios for the entire ClassPass bundle.

Revenue management entices more studios to join ClassPass, and to make more space in their classes available to the platform's members. The increase in availability, in turn, entices more people to sign up and keeps the network effects going. But there's a problem for ClassPass with this virtuous cycle: its most workout-hungry members can use the platform too much and hurt the platform's profitability.

How to Get to Infinity

As Kadakia's post announcing the end of ClassPass Unlimited makes clear, this is exactly what happened. The problem was that the platform's revenues grew in proportion to its total number of members, but its costs (in the form of payments to studios) grew in proportion to the total number of classes they took. As its members used the platform to take more classes each month, this imbalance between revenues and costs grew and became hard to address, even with highly sophisticated revenue management techniques.

Postmates, another platform that bridges the online and offline worlds, found a clever way to keep revenues and costs in balance better, even after it unveiled an unlimited offering in a rapidly growing two-sided network.

Despite the scale and efficiency of large e-tailers like Amazon, it can be difficult for them to deliver with very short lead times.* So, Postmates was started by Bastian Lehman, Sean Plaice, and Sam Street in 2011 with the idea of providing a platform for consumers to receive deliveries within the hour from local restaurants and stores via a network of couriers. Instead of building a new warehouse on the outskirts of a city, Postmates took advantage of the stores and inventory already in place and dispatched couriers via a smartphone app. The platform originally charged buyers a 9% service charge, which Postmates kept, plus a delivery charge, most of which went to the couriers, that ranged between $5 and $20 depending on the complexity of the order and the amount of demand at the time the order was placed. The company soon expanded beyond San Francisco, and within three years it had made 1.5 million deliveries. The platform owners believed, though, that if they wanted it to grow even faster, they had to reduce costs to consumers.

In January of 2015, Postmates tried an experiment. It made deliv-

---

* At least until the delivery drones arrive.

eries from select merchants in San Francisco, New York, and Los Angeles for a flat fee of $4.99. As expected, lowering this price and eliminating the service charge boosted demand. Within ten weeks, 20% of all orders in these markets took advantage of the new offer. What's more, these orders were, on average, twice as large as others on the platform. Because participating merchants saw so much more revenue, they agreed to pay up to 20% of the retail cost of items ordered with the delivery platform. A smaller number paid up to 30% for prominent placement within the app. As still more orders came in, couriers were able to complete more than one delivery per trip, driving down cost per delivery and making the whole business more efficient.

Encouraged by the results of the flat-fee experiment, in March 2016 the company introduced Postmates Plus Unlimited, which offered free delivery on all orders over $30 for a flat fee of $10 per month. Because this offering, unlike ClassPass Unlimited, generates revenue for the platform with each transaction (by charging merchants a percentage of the price for each item delivered), it has the potential to remain viable no matter how quickly the company grows. What's more, to help it grow as quickly as possible, Postmates built an interface to its app so that partners like Apple, Starbucks, Chipotle, and Walgreens could easily connect their information systems to it. By September of 2016, the platform was completing 1.3 million deliveries a month across forty US markets.

Quenching Our Thirst for O2O

ClassPass and Postmates exemplify a trend that has been gaining force over the past decade: the rise of platforms not just for offerings that can be represented completely in bits (that is, digitally encoded information), such as software, music, and banking services, but also for goods and services that involve atoms and take place in the physical world. The first generation of large, influential, and often disruptive Internet platforms covered the information industries. We're now seeing a second generation spreading throughout the rest of the economy.

Our favorite label for such platforms, which we first heard from artificial intelligence rock star Andrew Ng, is "O2O," which means "online to offline." We like this shorthand because it captures the heart of the phenomenon: the spread from the online world to the offline world of network effects, bundles of complements, and at least some of the economics of free, perfect, and instant.

By the end of 2016, O2O platforms existed in a wide range of industries: Lyft and Uber for urban transportation, Airbnb for lodging, Grubhub and Caviar for food delivery, Honor for in-home health care, and many others. All of these companies are working to productively (and eventually profitably) bring together the economics of bits with those of atoms. Very often the physical inventory being offered on these platforms is perishable, as with spaces in exercise studios or nights of lodging, but sometimes it's not. Even then, as the example of Rent the Runway shows, data, math, and network effects can be combined in powerful ways.

Having the perfect designer dress for every special occasion can be expensive, especially if you don't want to be seen (in person or on social media) in the same one more than once. This dilemma helps explain why, according to one estimate, half of the items in the closet of an average American are worn fewer than three times. Jennifer Fleiss and Jennifer Hyman, the founders of the online company Rent the Runway, thought they could use the power of digital platforms to address this sartorial challenge. Their business enables women to rent clothing and accessories online, choose a delivery date, keep the items for four or eight days, and then return them in the included packaging. Members can even add a backup size of the same dress to their order at no extra charge. Rentals typically cost about 10% of the full retail value of the item, ranging from $5 for costume jewelry earrings to hundreds of dollars for couture evening gowns.

Rent the Runway owns all the garments available on its site. (Caring for them led the company to develop the largest dry-cleaning operation in America.) Because these assets were long-lived rather than perishable, owning them enabled Rent the Runway to take advantage of interesting opportunities that opened up as the service grew and spread around the country. Unlike spaces in an exercise class, designer dresses don't perish, but they do depreciate, becoming less valuable over time. However, this depreciation is not uniform: a new handbag, for example, might go out of style quite quickly in fashion-forward New York, but then become popular elsewhere in the country. Rent the Runway thus practices a type of revenue management that differs from ClassPass's approach—one aimed at preserving the value of durable inventory as long as possible by presenting it to the people around the country with the highest willingness to pay, as determined by the company's algorithms.

By the spring of 2016, Rent the Runway felt confident enough in its revenue and inventory management expertise to launch its own version of an unlimited service, one that treated articles of clothing much the way Netflix treated physical DVDs. For a flat $139 per month, a Rent the Runway member could keep three items with her at all times. As soon as she returned one, the next one on her wish list would be sent to her. With this approach, the company hoped to encourage constant use while preventing the kind of overuse that sank the ClassPass Unlimited offering.

Platforms Go Where Consumers Don't

All of the preceding examples, and most of today's better-known O2O platforms, are consumer-facing. To some, this fact indicates that the online-to-offline phenomenon will not soon spread to the rest of the economy—to the goods and services that companies exchange with each other, and not with individual consumers.

We don't agree. Most of the same economic fundamentals apply, whether the platform is consumer-facing or mainly business-to-business. We predict that O2O platforms will spread quickly throughout the world of atoms, whether or not they include or involve consumers. In fact we're already seeing examples of intriguing business-to-business platforms bridging the online and offline worlds—B2B O2O:

▶ The US trucking industry generates revenues of $700 billion per year, yet it remains a market full of inefficiencies. As much as 15% of all miles driven are by trucks with empty trailers, and the haulage brokers who match trucks with cargoes (and collect an estimated $80 billion in annual fees) still use phone, fax, and e-mail as the primary methods of connecting all parties involved. Transfix is building an online platform to update and move online the industry's outdated processes for matching supply and demand.

▶ Companies that make or deliver products often have excess warehouse space much of the time (because they need enough capacity for periods of peak demand). Flexe is a Seattle-based startup building a platform that connects partially or temporarily empty warehouses with companies that need short-term additional space.

▶ Elance and oDesk were two of the pioneering online resources for connecting freelancers and clients. In 2015 the companies combined to form a new company, called Upwork. Businesses use the site to post projects that independent freelancers or agencies then bid on. The tasks undertaken can range from web design and copywriting to accountancy and data entry. The Upwork platform matches experts from anywhere in the world—why not, if the deliverables are digital?—with the jobs they are best placed into and provides tools for, among other things, project management and payment. By 2016, Upwork was facilitating over 3 million projects annually, worth over $1 billion.

▶ Finding and booking a venue for business conferences has traditionally been a time-consuming activity. Event organizers spend days or weeks contacting venues directly to understand their facilities, capabilities, availability, and pricing. Human agents existed to help with this work, but their fees were often high. Cvent was started in 1999 to provide a platform to move this process online. Over the years the company has expanded its offering to include mobile invitations, tickets, and surveys. By 2015, the company was helping 15,000 customers annually manage events worth $9.2 billion.

▶ Sociologist Robert K. Merton (father of Robert C. Merton, our MIT colleague and winner of the 1997 Nobel Prize in economics) was commissioned to find out how Americans were responding to mass communication during World War II. This challenge led him to create what is now commonly known as the "focus group," a tool used by countless marketers over the years to test messages and better understand their current and prospective customers. Finding people to participate in a focus group or answer questions in a survey has long been handled by agencies and professional recruiters, many of whom simply approached, on the street or in malls, people who appeared to have the desired characteristics. Now there are numerous online platforms for convening focus groups and conducting surveys. These include UserTesting, Survata, dscout, and Google Consumer Surveys.

Planetary Proliferation

The ecosystem for technology entrepreneurship in the United States has been very effective at nurturing and scaling many high-tech businesses, so it sometimes looks as if all the good ideas of the second machine age originated there. But they didn't, and interesting O2O platforms are springing up around the world to reflect and take advantage of local environments and opportunities.

France's intercity train system is extensive but expensive, and was long protected from lower-cost competition by sharp restrictions on private buses.* Frédéric Mazzella, Nicolas Brusson, and Francis Nappez saw an opportunity and founded BlaBlaCar in 2006. This platform matches people driving their car from city to city with passengers who want to make the same trip. In exchange for the ride, passengers help cover the drivers' expenses. These passenger payments are set by BlaBlaCar; drivers can vary them but cannot raise them above a maximum amount determined by the company. BlaBlaCar's insistence that "BlaBlaCar drivers don't make a profit" has endeared the company to many people, kept its prices low, and eased negotiations with regulators in many regions. (It also helps that the platform is not directly competing with taxis; the average BlaBlaCar trip is 200 miles.) By September 2016, the company's ride-sharing platform was operating in twenty-one countries, and facilitating over 10 million rides every quarter.

Indonesia's most popular O2O transportation platform is very

---

* These restrictions eased in July 2015, when the French government effectively allowed buses to offer new routes across the country (Oxera, "En Route to French Transport Liberalisation: The Coach Market," August 2015, http://www.oxera.com/ Latest-Thinking/Agenda/2015/En-route-to-French-transport-liberalisation-the-co .aspx). Travelers soon took advantage of the new option. In 2013, only 100,000 passengers took an intercity bus trip. In 2016, an estimated 5 million did ("Liberalization of Intercity Bus Market in France," *Busradar.com* [blog], August 13, 2015, https:// www.busradar.com/blog/liberalisation-france).

different from France's. Jakarta's epic traffic jams convince many to hop on the back of a motorbike taxi, which can weave past plodding or motionless cars. In 2015 Go-Jek, a mobile app–based platform, launched to connect riders and bikes. It offered fixed prices, which proved popular because they eliminated the time and uncertainty associated with haggling. By the middle of 2016 the platform was averaging 20 million rides per month, and it had expanded into meal, grocery, and package delivery; car maintenance; and even housecleaning. In August 2016, Go-Jek raised $550 million in investor funding, making it Indonesia's first "unicorn," worth over $1.3 billion.

With its population of nearly 1.4 billion people, deep smartphone penetration, and strong track record of technology entrepreneurship, China is the world's most fertile territory for mobile O2O platforms. Representative examples include Edaixi, a service that uses a digital platform to make it easier for people to have a large bag of laundry collected, cleaned, ironed, and returned within seventy-two hours for $15. By August 2015, Edaixi was operating in sixteen cities and processing 100,000 orders per day; a year later it had expanded to twenty-eight cities with a combined 110 million residents.[*]

For less than $5, Guagua Xiche will send a professional technician to wash a car wherever it is parked in a city. Users specify the vehicle's location and license plate number, and they don't need to be present during the cleaning. The firm raised $58 million in 2015 and has expanded to twelve cities.

Hao Chushi will summon a private chef to cook an in-home meal, taking into account diners' preferences and dietary restrictions. Excluding ingredients, the cost for a family of four is approxi-

---

[*] American entrepreneurs have tried to mimic some of the Chinese O2O successes, but with mixed results. Washio, a similar laundry O2O service based in the United States, raised almost $17 million in funding before shutting down in 2016. Unlike Edaixi, Washio was generally perceived to be expensive. The delivery fee alone was $5.99.

mately $15. Despite its appeal, Hao Chushi is unlikely to significantly impact the popular Chinese food delivery business Ele.me, which raised over $1 billion in funding. In fact, very large investments in O2O businesses in China are not uncommon. 58 Daojia, an O2O platform for cleaning, babysitting, and beauty care, raised $300 million for its Series A* in October 2015, while Chinese search giant Baidu committed most of its $3.2 billion three-year investment in O2O to Nuomi, which handles everything from cinema tickets to hairdressers.

Engines of Liquidity

As business scholars, we're fascinated by O2O platforms. For one thing, they show again the power of complements, especially free ones, for pushing out demand curves. For example, the pricing optimization tools that Airbnb offers its hosts for free increase the number of property owners using that platform as opposed to one of its competitors, all other things being equal.

For another, O2O platforms represent the richest combination we've yet seen of the economics of bits and the economics of atoms. As they scale, these platforms handle huge volumes of information—about members and their choices and activities, the availability and pricing of goods and services, payments and problems, and so on. All of this information approaches the ideals of free, perfect, and instant. It's very cheap to store, process, and transmit, and it's getting cheaper. This means that all relevant and useful information can be everywhere on the platform, all the time. It also means that the demand-side economies of scale—the network effects, in other

---

* A Series A investment is typically the first round of formal investment in a startup. Usually the amount involved is much closer to $1 million than $300 million.

words—can eventually grow much faster than costs. Furthermore, when a complement is free, even a small effect for each person can add up quickly if millions of people use it.

This is important because information and algorithms—the stuff of bits—help meet the thorniest challenges posed by the economics of atom-based goods and services. Running an exercise studio, delivery service, or transportation network is tough in large part because capacity is finite and inventory must be carefully managed. These are facts of life in the atom-based world, and they make it easy to stumble at the central task of matching supply and demand over time.

The tools and techniques of revenue management, which have been refined by decades of research and real-world stress testing, can help greatly with this task but typically need lots of data to run well. They also benefit from being applied across lots of supply and lots of demand. In other words, they work better and better across bigger and bigger networks, and network effects are one of the defining characteristics of platforms. So, an exercise studio gains access to powerful yield management algorithms that let it maximize total revenue for each class. Airbnb hosts get pricing assistance so that their lodging is rented for the revenue-maximizing price during both busy and quiet periods. Uber drivers get "heat maps" showing them where to position themselves to maximize their chances of quickly getting a fare. Mathematically sophisticated, data-rich services like these used to be out of reach for many real-world businesses, especially small ones. Thanks to the free, perfect, and instant economies of bits, they're now available everywhere O2O platforms are.

As these platforms grow, they offer one of the most irresistible economic properties of them all: liquidity, or the assurance that a transaction will happen without huge price changes. A commuter in Jakarta, a budget traveler seeking to go from Bordeaux to Lyon, a trucker trying to make some money on what would otherwise be a trip back home with an empty rig—they all really want the same thing: to arrange a transaction quickly, advantageously, and with no unpleasant surprises. The best way to ensure this is to have a lot of potential participants on the other side of the transaction, and this is what popular O2O platforms offer.

Calling All Disciplines

In addition to those from economic theory, insights from several other disciplines are routinely incorporated into these platforms. The best routes for Uber drivers to take as they pick up and drop off overlapping fares, for example, is a variant of the classic "traveling salesman" problem in operations research, where the salesman has to figure out the shortest route that will take him through all the cities he's responsible for once and only once.

The huge amount of data that O2O businesses generate makes them fertile territory for machine learning, the information-heavy approaches to artificial intelligence that are now dominant, as we discussed in Chapter 3. User interface and user experience design, too, are experiencing a heyday, in large part because of the popularity of platforms. It's extremely hard to make websites flexible, powerful, and intuitive all at the same time, and even harder to do the same for apps (because they have to run on phones' small screens). All the platform builders we've talked to have stressed how hard they've worked on their user interfaces, and how much they continually iterate and experiment to refine them over time. It's also clear how hard they work on their broader user experience. Troubleshooting, customer support, and problem resolution are critical activities, not least because bad word of mouth spreads quickly.

A final reason we're professionally fascinated by O2O platforms is that they really weren't possible even a decade ago. Many of the businesses described in this chapter rely on powerful mobile computing devices, and as we've seen the smartphone era only started in 2007 with the iPhone (and apps from outside developers took another year to arrive). Smartphones were not only the first truly mobile computers; they were also the first location-aware ones, thanks to their GPS sensors. These are indispensable complements to almost every successful O2O system.

Cloud computing was also critical to the success of many platform businesses, because it freed them from having to correctly predict just how successful they would be. With cloud providers, essentially unlimited amounts of additional computing capacity are available very quickly, instead of having to be planned for and purchased well in advance. As Charlie Songhurst, the former head of strategy at Microsoft and an early investor in ClassPass and Flexe, told us, it's easier for startups and other online experiments to scale quickly because

they don't have to forecast their own success. [The cloud] removed a huge variable, which is having to predict your future demand. You just stop having to think about it, plan it, and spend money on it . . . you can try [something], and if it works, [the cloud] will cover it. You might end up with a big Amazon Web Services bill, but it's not authorized capital when your product's taking off. They don't have to buy service two months before their products are taking off, and hire a guy to run around making sure that they're working and that sort of stuff. That's the change in the industry.

Effectively, the cloud gave entrepreneurs the right, but not the obligation, to scale up if and when demand increased. The value of this sort of "real option" can be substantial, and it is often overlooked in conventional models that seek to assess the value of a business.[*]

To Tread Lightly, Leverage Assets

We also like O2O platforms for the simple reason that they bring a lot of benefits. They provide more opportunities for people who own assets—from cars and trucks to spare rooms and exercise studios to their own human capital—to make use of them. As they do this, platforms increase the efficiency and utilization of these assets. These sound like the kinds of benefits that only accountants, operations research geeks, and economists care about, but we should all welcome them. They improve our quality of life while simultaneously helping us tread more lightly on the planet.

The first of these two good outcomes is probably the easier to see. Varying a workout routine, finding a cheap ride across town or across the country, getting delivery from more restaurants, and having the perfect outfit to wear for a big event are all good things. But they're also all forms of consumption. And consumption uses up resources, and many resources are finite. So how can consumption-encouraging platforms be good news for the planet?

They can by increasing the utilization rate of many resources in the world of atoms. Fancy dresses and passenger cars alike sit idle most of the time. Rent the Runway and Uber, respectively, enable more productive use of them. The average passenger car sits idle 95% of the time. Ride sharing can reduce that to 50%. That means we can get the same amount of capital services with one-tenth as much cap-

---

[*] Avinash Dixit and Robert Pindyck worked out much of the economics of real-options pricing, building on earlier work by Bob Merton, Myron Scholes, and Fischer Black, among others. See, for example, Avinash K. Dixit and Robert S. Pindyck, *Investment under Uncertainty* (Princeton, NJ: Princeton University Press, 1994).

ital. It's therefore reasonable to expect that total new production of goods like these could drop in the future as platforms allow a smaller number of them to be used more heavily. This won't happen if total future demand for these goods increases enough to offset the utilization gains, but how many more occasions will call for an evening gown? There are already signs that car ownership is in decline among younger US city dwellers. By 2013, people born in the 1980s or 1990s owned 13% fewer cars than the generation before them when they were the same age. These people represent exactly the smartphone-having demographic we would expect to be using Uber and other O2O automobile platforms.

Resources don't have to be sitting completely idle to be underutilized. Empty seats on car trips and empty trucks heading back home are also forms of waste, and ones that are now being reduced by platforms like BlaBlaCar and Transfix. This waste reduction will continue as O2O platforms spread. We believe, in fact, that it will accelerate as powerful mobile computers spread around the world, as the cloud and other enabling technologies continue to advance, and as innovators and entrepreneurs continue to bring the economics and advantages of bits to the world of atoms.

Chapter Summary

▶ Digital platforms are rapidly spreading into industries like exercise, transportation, and lodging that deal in physical goods and services. These are sometimes called O2O, or online-to-offline, platforms.

▶ Perishable inventory in these industries may have low marginal costs, but it also has capacity constraints. This makes O2O different from the free, perfect, and instant economics of pure information goods. As a result, platform owners typically incorporate techniques from revenue management to improve matches between supply and demand

▶ Like their purely digital counterparts, online-to-offline platforms can include many complementary products that increase overall demand.

▶ O2O platforms are appearing around the world, and in industries that are not consumer-facing. In particular, China has been a hotbed of O2O innovation.

▶ Because they can add new members quickly, control the customer experience, leverage preexisting capital and labor resources, and use data and algorithms to improve matches, O2O platforms can scale rapidly and compete aggressively. Investors see the potential of O2O and have been willing to fund aggressive expansion plans.

Questions

1. What's your strategy for cooperating or competing with a platform that brings network effects and revenue management capabilities to your industry?

2. Customers value unlimited offerings. Can you find a way to economically provide them?

3. Compare the user interface and user experience of your online offerings to those of the dominant platform in your industry. How do they stack up?

4. How much of your inventory perishes? How much of your capacity sits idle? Have platforms appeared yet in your space to help lower these figures?

5. What would happen to your revenue, profits, and growth if the utilization of the key assets in your industry quickly and dramatically increased?

CHAPTER 9

DO PRODUCTS HAVE A PRAYER?

The wise learn many things from their enemies.

— *Aristophanes, 414 BCE*

UBER'S URBAN TRANSPORTATION PLATFORM WAS BORN IN Paris in 2008 when Travis Kalanick and Garrett Camp had difficulty hailing a cab. "So," the company's website explains, "they came up with a simple idea—tap a button, get a ride." Their original vision (initially called UberCab) focused only on limos. Early growth was steady but slow. When Camp first suggested that Kalanick should run Uber full-time, Kalanick said no because he felt the opportunity was "supercrazy freakin' small."

Incumbents Get Taken for a Ride

By late 2010, Kalanick had begun to see a bigger opportunity. He rejected the idea of simply building an app-based limo service and instead steered the then four-person company toward a larger vision: changing the transportation industry by tapping into the power of the two-sided network effects that the company had created. More cars on Uber's platform meant more riders, and more riders meant more cars. Eighteen months later they launched UberX, allowing standard cars and their drivers to join the platform. UberPool, launched in August of 2014, further expanded the capacity of the network by combining rides at a lower price.

The platform model and network effects created one of the fastest-growing companies in history. In 2016 the company reportedly generated $20 billion in annual gross bookings. By June 2016, Uber was valued at $68 billion and had raised $15 billion from investors, which it used to aggressively fund even more rapid expansion around the world.

In many cities, taxi companies and other incumbents in urban personal transportation have seen their business fall off as Uber has grown. Traditional taxis provided 8.4 million trips in Los Angeles in 2012, the year before the arrival of Uber and Lyft in the city. Within three years, taxi rides had declined by almost 30%, and prearranged taxi rides were down 42%. Further north, San Francisco's largest taxi company, Yellow Cab Cooperative, filed for bankruptcy in January of 2016.

Taxi medallions—transferable licenses to legally operate a cab and pick up street hails—had long been considered good investments. In New York City, for example, the price of a medallion rose steeply in the early years of the twenty-first century, reaching more than $1.3 million by 2013. Less than three years later, though, the value of the medallions had fallen from this peak by as much as half.

Medallion-holding incumbents found it difficult to reverse their losses, because Uber's two-sided network effects, smooth user interface and user experience, and ample capital were formidable advantages. Attempts to build competing platforms such as Lyft in the United States and Hailo in Europe did not slow down the fast-growing startup. The only thing that could, it sometimes seemed, was regulation.

Utility Players?

The legality of the Uber platform has been challenged around the world, and new rules and statutes about transportation services have been proposed and passed. It is sometimes hard to avoid the impression that they were written with Uber and its platform peers in mind, and with the intent of handicapping them. Lawmakers in France, for example, outlawed UberX's close relative UberPop in 2014 and imposed fines on Uber and key managers. And as of early 2017, Uber was prohibited altogether in Vancouver, Canada.

In finance, as in urban transportation, regulation was at times the incumbents' best defense against digital upstarts. In June 2015 the *Economist* published an article with the title "Why Fintech Won't Kill Banks." Many of the financial technology innovations it discussed were, in fact, platforms, including platforms for payments, foreign exchange, and peer-to-peer lending (a phenomenon we'll discuss in Chapter 11). The article pointed out that incumbent banks were much, much larger than these newcomers and also "able to create credit more or less at a whim," and that these were important advantages. But it also pointed out that the bank's strongest offerings were also its most protected ones, "notably the current account, which allows people to store money in a way that keeps it safe and permanently accessible. Few in Silicon Valley or Silicon Roundabout want to take on that heavily regulated bit of finance."

The Economist's article highlighted the biggest worry facing banks, even if their regulatory protections endured: "a future as a sort of financial utility—ubiquitous but heavily regulated, unglamorous and marginally profitable." We think this is a plausible future, perhaps even a likely one, for many industries beyond finance. In many sectors, nonplatform participants will see their margins shrink and their positions become less and less secure, no matter how excellent and sophisticated their products.

A Parade of Profitless Product Makers

These dynamics are clearly visible in the global wireless communication industry. As we described in the previous chapter, highly popular platforms opened in this sector starting in 2007, first with Apple's iPhone and iOS operating system, then with Google's Android. Since then, it's been difficult to thrive. Nokia and BlackBerry faded because they tried and failed to compete on the software side against iOS and Android. For those who build only products, things have often not gone much better.

In the years since Android appeared, a succession of Asian companies making phones for it have appeared, with some flying high, but most crashing in the face of stiff competition. In January 2015, Lei Jun, CEO of Chinese smartphone manufacturer Xiaomi, wrote an open letter to his employees, announcing that the company was worth $45 billion, making it the most valuable technology startup in the world at the time. In the previous twelve months, Xiaomi had sold 61 million smartphones and had become the Chinese market leader.* Xiaomi's smartphones were some of the cheapest in China, typically selling for $149 in 2015, less than half the market average. This price left very little room for profit on each device, but the company's backers were betting on plans to generate revenue from Internet services once the handsets (and other hardware the company made) became widespread.

They may have underestimated the size of this challenge. In the twelve months following its record-breaking valuation, Xiaomi twice missed its smartphone sales targets and had Internet services of less than 5% of revenue. By the second quarter of 2016, Xiaomi's sales had dropped by almost 40% compared to the same period in 2015, leading analyst Richard Windsor to suggest that Xiaomi's valuation was closer to $3.6 billion.

The Korean company Samsung had been a dominant force early

---

* Xiaomi broke the Guinness World Record for the most mobile phones sold in a twenty-four-hour period in April 2015. Kevin Lynch, "Mi.com Sells 2 Million Smartphones in a Day to Set Sales World Record," Guinness World Records, April 9, 2015, http://www.guinnessworldrecords.com/news/2015/4/mi-com-sells-2-million-smart phones-in-a-day-to-set-sales-world-record-376583.

in the smartphone era as it rolled out a series of popular phones and tablets, but it, too, eventually saw sales and earnings deteriorate. Total unit sales in 2016, after four consecutive years of decline, were lower than they had been since 2011. Modern smartphones are incredibly complicated devices that must be designed well and built reliably. The engineering expertise and global supply chain capabilities required to do this are so formidable that only a handful of companies in the world ever try. Yet, as expectations and specifications continually change, few of them make much money for any length of time, even though they serve an enormous global market that has emerged in less than a decade.

Instead, profits have gone to the platform providers. By one estimate, Apple captured 91% of global smartphone profits in 2015. How high can the profit share go for a dominant platform? Results became even more lopsided the next year, when analyst Tim Long of BMO Capital Markets estimated that Apple had made fully 103.9% of total operating profits across all mobile device manufacturers in the third quarter of 2016. Samsung made 0.9%, and all others lost money.

In its financial statements, Google, Apple's only real competition as a successful platform builder in the smartphone era, doesn't break out revenue and profits for Android and the myriad mobile services it supports. But they also appear to be quite large. In January of 2016 an attorney for the software company Oracle, which was suing Google over a payment dispute, revealed in court its estimate that Android had contributed $31 billion to the revenue of its parent company, and $22 billion in profits.*

---

* In January 2016, Oracle lawyers persuaded a federal court judge to release details about Google's revenue-sharing agreements for Android as part of a long-running lawsuit relating to a claimed copyright infringement of Oracle's Java technology. The lawyer who verbally disclosed the estimates in court did not say how they were arrived at or even what time period they covered. Google then urged the judge to redact and seal portions of the public transcript relating to the disclosure as the "non-public

The Many Advantages of Platforms

Are the trials of Xiaomi and Samsung examples of a pattern that will become more apparent as platforms continue to spread? Will platforms eventually take over every industry and strip away the profits of incumbents? Yes, and no.

The platform revolution is not nearly finished, and its impact will be profound. Recent examples like Stripe, ClassPass, Postmates, and Transfix are the vanguard of a large trend: the diffusion of platforms, especially those leveraging the world's rapidly improving digital infrastructure. This diffusion into other industries will continue because of the significant advantages that platforms have over their competitors, and because of the many advantages they bring to their participants.

Not all business activity, though, will happen on platforms in the future; their takeover will not be complete. Some industries will see a peaceful coexistence between product companies and platform companies; other industries will remain largely unchanged. Profitable strategies exist not only for platform owners, but also for the rest of their ecosystem.

Whether they are one-sided or two-sided, however, platforms will spread quite widely. The network effects they can tap into are powerful. They can also become self-reinforcing, especially if they're supported with a steady stream of refinements to both the visible

---

financial data is highly sensitive, and public disclosure could have significant negative effects on Google's business" (Joel Rosenblatt and Jack Clark, "Google's Android Generates $31 Billion Revenue, Oracle Says," Bloomberg, January 21, 2016, https://www.bloomberg.com/news/articles/2016-01-21/google-s-android-generates-31-billion-revenue-oracle-says-ijor8hvt). Estimating Android's profits is difficult and subjective. It's probably fair to include all of the revenues from the Play Store (Google keeps 30% and developers get 70%), as well as some of the revenues from mobile search ads and mobile display ads. Nicholas Iovino, "Oracle Wins Chance to See Google Contracts," Courthouse News Service, January 14, 2016, http://www.courthousenews.com/?s=Oracle+Wins+Chance+to+See+Google+Contracts.

user interface and the algorithms running behind the scenes. And such refinements themselves become easier to generate as platforms grow, since growth provides ever-larger test beds for iteration and experimentation.

As we've seen, larger networks bring with them the promise of greater liquidity, which is probably the characteristic of any marketplace most valued by its participants. Larger networks also generate ever more data, which smart platform operators exploit to great advantage. They use it to better understand their members, to predict and shape their members' behavior, and to give their members sophisticated tools for revenue management, pricing, and other critical activities.

Regardless of their size, platforms control the user experience and user interface for their members. They determine what information is seen by users and how processes and transactions are executed. When platform owners exercise control well, two important things happen: First, they can reduce or remove long-standing barriers that have kept people from transacting with each other. Second, they can influence the flow of transactions so that more benefits go to the platform owner.

Lemons into Lemonade: Reducing Asymmetries

It's bad for business when one party knows a lot more about a proposed transaction than the other one does. It's bad for both parties because the less informed party will often recognize that they are at an information disadvantage and therefore unable to properly evaluate the proposal. So, rather than take the chance of being ripped off, they won't do business at all. This is a shame, because at least some of the passed-up deals actually would have been advantageous for both parties. Knowledge differentials, unfortunately, kept these transactions from happening.

The idea that such "information asymmetries" are harmful not just for the less informed party but also for markets overall was formalized by economist George Akerlof in his classic 1970 paper "The Market for 'Lemons.'" Akerlof showed that the used-car market could suffer greatly because of the existence of "lemons"*—apparently fine cars that, in fact, had bad mechanical problems. Sellers know which cars are lemons but most buyers don't, and this information asymmetry will keep the used-car market small and inefficient unless it's addressed by, for example, having dealers offer money-back guarantees to customers who feel that they've been cheated.

Akerlof showed that in extreme cases, information asymmetry could lead to complete market breakdown and the end of trade. This insight was so counterintuitive and radical at the time that his paper was repeatedly rejected from the top journals in economics, with one referee explaining that the journal "did not publish papers on subjects of such triviality" while another took the opposite tack, writing "if this paper were correct, economics would be different," so it couldn't be correct. But Akerlof was right about the critical importance of information asymmetries—economics *was* different—and ultimately he was recognized with a Nobel prize for this work.

Few information asymmetries are deeper or more important than the one that exists between someone who wants a ride across town and a stranger offering to provide that ride in a private car. Even if most drivers are completely honest and safe, the financial and personal risk of getting a bad one appears unacceptably high. Unless this inherent information asymmetry was overcome, the market for person-to-person rides would never take off.

But by March of 2016, Uber was handling 50 million rides per month in the United States. The great majority of Uber's ride suppliers were not professional chauffeurs; they were simply people who wanted to make money with their labor and their cars.

---

* For a variety of reasons, car quality has improved tremendously since 1970, so it's not as common to hear the term "lemon" used in this way as it was back then.

So how did this huge market overcome severe information asymmetries? In 2013, California passed regulations mandating that transportation network companies (TNCs) such as Uber and Lyft conduct criminal background checks on their drivers. These checks certainly provided some reassurance, but they were not the whole story. After all, UberX and its competitor Lyft both grew rapidly before background checks were in place, and by August 2016, BlaBlaCar still did not require them for its drivers.

Instead, these companies used their platforms' user interfaces to overcome the information asymmetries that plagued their markets. In particular, they asked all parties to rate each other after each transaction, and they prominently displayed everyone's cumulative ratings.* In addition, TNCs typically keep detailed records of each trip, using data from phones' GPS sensors.

These simple steps replace ignorance with knowledge. Even though this knowledge is imperfect, it's still hugely valuable both for individuals and for the platform itself, since it provides much-needed symmetry. And the TNCs continue to experiment and innovate. Uber, for example, was by early 2017 conducting spot checks by asking drivers to periodically take "selfie" photos. The company compared them to the pictures on file to make sure that the approved person was, in fact, driving the car.

The economists Tyler Cowen and Alex Tabarrok highlight online user reviews of platforms and other products as examples of a broad reduction in information asymmetries. This reduction has come

---

* The French long-distance ride-sharing company BlaBlaCar incorporates particularly precise ratings. Its name comes from the ability of drivers and passengers to communicate their talking preferences in their profiles: "Bla" if they do not like to talk with the other people in the car, "BlaBla" if they like to talk a little, and "BlaBlaBla" if they're quite chatty. Rawn Shah, "Driving Ridesharing Success at BlaBlaCar with Online Community," *Forbes*, February 21, 2016, http://www.forbes.com/sites/rawnshah/2016/02/21/driving-ridesharing-success-at-blablacar-with-online-community/#73ea3e4679a6.

about because of the diffusion of powerful technologies like smartphones, sensors, and networks, and because of ever-growing amounts of data. As Cowen and Tabarrok write, "Many of the exchanges in the sharing economy . . . use two-way reputational systems. That is the customer rates the Uber driver, but in turn the Uber driver rates the customer. Dual reputation systems can support a remarkable amount of exchange even in the absence of law or regulation."

In the case of Uber and others, much of this "remarkable amount of exchange" comes from temporary and part-time drivers. Many of these people would not find it worthwhile to go through a burdensome and time-consuming traditional background check or government licensing process, let alone to invest in an expensive taxi medallion. But they are willing to participate if it's relatively fast and frictionless to get approved as a driver. Uber and its platform peers have found a way to do this.

Airbnb CEO and cofounder Joe Gebbia refers to this system of peer reviews and ratings as "design for trust" and highlights another of its benefits: it can help us overcome our personal biases. We're sure that most Airbnb hosts don't consider themselves racist, but the company's data show that, on average, hosts are slightly less willing to rent out to minority guests than to white ones.* However, this effect reverses itself for minority guests with a good overall rating and more than ten reviews. Prospective hosts are actually more likely to rent to such guests than to white ones without many ratings. "High reputation beats high similarity," as Gebbia puts it; his company has found that its platform's user interface and user experience "can actu-

---

* Benjamin Edelman, Michael Luca, and Dan Svirsky found in an experiment that Airbnb hosts were, on average, 16% less likely to rent to prospective guests whose newly created profiles included a distinctively African American name. Benjamin Edelman, Michael Luca, and Dan Svirsky, "Racial Discrimination in the Sharing Economy: Evidence from a Field Experiment," Ben Edelman.org, September 16, 2016, http://www.benedelman.org/publications/airbnb-guest-discrimination-2016-09-16.pdf.

ally help us overcome one of our most deeply rooted biases—the 'stranger-danger' bias."

Of course, platforms' rating systems and other mechanisms for reducing information asymmetries are not perfect. Crimes have been committed by drivers, passengers, hosts, and guests, and discrimination persists. But the explosive growth of these platforms strongly suggests that such problems are not severe or frequent enough to impair business in the ways identified by Akerlof. In part because of clever design and curation, these markets are not so full of lemons that they're driving people away.

Brands, New

A platform's ability to shape its members' interactions and experiences gives it many advantages. Consumers, for example, often form stronger associations with the platform than with the company on the other side of the two-sided network—a fact that helps greatly with brand building. For many of its members, ClassPass has become a sort of studio that has it all—yoga, Pilates, kickboxing, spinning, and so on—and exists in many different cities. The fact that the company has built this reputation without building any actual studios is impressive. And it's intimidating to anyone trying to build a fitness brand the traditional way. If the gyms and studios that have spent time and energy on building a physical presence and in-person experience come to be seen as somewhat interchangeable components under the ClassPass brand, they have a problem.

This problem for traditional companies is compounded if, over time, they lose pricing power to the platform. Owners of premium brands can charge more for their offerings, but the owners of two-sided networks want to pay to sellers as little as possible of the money they take in from buyers. The result is an obvious tension. Many platforms, especially when they're new and trying to build volume and network effects, want to have on board at least one prestigious brand.

But as platforms grow, they want to keep more of the consumer's share of both mind *and* wallet.

Toward this end, the best weapon that platforms have is control of the user interface and of the digital user experience. Excellence here is often beyond the reach or outside the expertise of a single fitness company, but it is in the sweet spot of a platform builder like ClassPass. The platform can also use the extensive tool kit of revenue management techniques to shape which suppliers each buyer sees, and how prominently. It's not too cynical to expect that a platform might use this power to feature lesser-known suppliers over more famous ones, all else being equal.

When combined, these capabilities add up to a formidable advantage for platforms as they build membership, volume, and brand awareness. Faced with this advantage, many well-known brands are so far electing to stay off platforms altogether. SoulCycle, for example, is a New York City–based chain of spinning studios with a devoted following and presence in eleven states. By early 2017, it had yet to put any of its classes on ClassPass. As platforms spread more widely, it will be interesting to see how many other brands make similar decisions.

Why Platform Prices Are Low Prices

These decisions will be informed by one other important consideration: platforms with two-sided networks typically prefer lower prices than their sellers do. It's not immediately clear why this should be the case. After all, aren't the interests of sellers and platform owners very well aligned? Don't they both want to maximize the total amount of revenue that flows through the platform? Because of differences between the economics of bits and the economics of atoms, the peculiarities of demand curves, and the power of network effects, they sometimes don't.

Big Elasticities; Long, Low Rectangles

Some products are barely affected by changes in prices: you're unlikely to haggle with an emergency room doctor when she recommends a lifesaving drug. In other markets, a small change in price can make a big difference: a seller trying to charge even a little more than the going spot price for oil would have no takers, but one charging a penny less would have no trouble finding buyers. The economic jargon for the difference between these two examples is "price elasticity": the percentage change in the quantity demanded following a 1% change in price. Of course, price elasticities are usually negative: higher prices lead to lower sales.

For many products, elasticities are different at different price points. The demand increase that would result from lowering the price of milk from $20 to $10, for example, is smaller than it would be if the price dropped from $2 to $1. The demand curves for such products have a particular shape: they flatten out as they move down and to the right, as shown in Figure 8.

Now suppose that you as a supplier could introduce only one product into this market, and that the cost of each additional unit sold was zero. What should its price be? The answer, as always, is that the product should be priced to maximize revenues. That means picking the place where the "$p{\times}q$" rectangle has the largest area.[*] After all, revenue is *price* times *quantity*. And for products with a demand curve that looks like the one in Figure 8, the biggest rectangle turns out to be a long, low one. The revenue-maximizing price, in other words, is surprisingly low.

This appears to be the case for rides in cars within cities. As Uber has lowered prices, first with UberX and then with UberPool (and perhaps eventually with self-driving cars), demand has expanded

---

[*] See Figure 5 in Chapter 7 (page 156) for an explanation of the $p{\times}q$ (price times quantity, or revenue) rectangle.

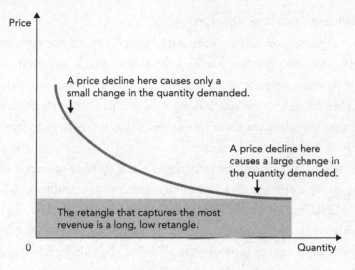

Figure 8
Most demand curves are not straight lines.
Sometimes, they have this shape.

greatly.* Uber very much wants to satisfy this demand by charging extremely low prices, since doing so will maximize its revenue.

But in two-sided markets, simply working its way down the demand curve is only a small part of the story.

To better understand Uber's pricing decisions, let's revisit some of the economics of networks first introduced in Chapter 6 when we discussed WhatsApp. Like WhatsApp, Uber benefits from network effects. But unlike WhatsApp, telephones, or faxes or many other networks, Uber is a two-sided network. Two-sidedness is at the core of many modern platforms. It has some counterintuitive economics.

---

* A 2016 study by economists at Uber, Oxford, and the University of Chicago used almost 50 million UberX rides across four US cities to estimate the actual demand curve for the service. The results indicate that this curve does, in fact, flatten out as prices decline. Peter Cohen et al., "Using Big Data to Estimate Consumer Surplus: The Case of Uber," August 30, 2016, https://cbpp.georgetown.edu/sites/cbpp.georgetown.edu/files/ConsumersurplusatUber_PR.PDF.

Whose Side Are You On?

Uber actually provides two separate apps, for two separate sets of users. The company has one app for riders, which lets them hail drivers, and a separate app for drivers, which lets them find riders. People who sign up for ride hailing via Uber don't directly benefit if other people adopt the same app, the way they do when their friends adopt WhatsApp.

Instead, what ride hailers care about is the number of *drivers* who sign up for a *different* app, the companion app that enables them to find riders. Having more drivers on the rider-finding app increases the likelihood that an available car will be nearby, and therefore makes the service more attractive to people using the ride-hailing app; it shifts out the app's demand curve. Without such a shift, there really wouldn't be much demand at all: a ride-hailing app that somehow managed to get millions of users but was connected to zero actual drivers would not be very attractive to these ride hailers. Similarly, drivers don't benefit when other drivers sign up for the rider-finding app, but they do benefit from more users of the ride-hailing app.

The two-sided network we see for Uber riders and drivers is far from unique: credit card users and merchants also constitute a two-sided network. If Visa is everywhere you want to be, but the Discover card is not as widely accepted by merchants, then many consumers will prefer to carry a Visa card, even if the Discover card has no annual fee. In turn, the larger consumer base makes it more attractive for merchants to accept Visa.

Airbnb is also a two-sided network. So, too, is a nightclub that attracts men and women hoping to find each other for dancing and romance. Android apps and their respective handsets, computer operating systems and the applications than run on them, and video games and gaming consoles are all examples of two-sided networks. In each case, users on one side of the market benefit when more users join the other side of the market. A wise intermediary, or platform owner, understands these linkages and manages the two sides accordingly. That often means focusing on recruiting one side of the network to attract more of the other side.

Pricing strategies for two-sided networks can be aggressive and seemingly nonsensical if you don't understand their peculiar economics. In particular, changes in the quantity demanded on one side of the network can affect demand on the other side of the network. Let's look back at the example of Uber lowering its prices to users. Of course, as we discussed, lowering prices increases the number of riders on the network, as Uber moves down the demand curve. But an important second effect of lowering prices is that it makes the platform more attractive to Uber drivers as well, who will see all the new riders and flock to them. Lowering the price on *one* side of the network increases demand on *both* sides of the network, creating an extra benefit for each price cut.

Companies that understand the economics of two-sided networks have prospered. For instance, credit cards provide a valuable service to both consumers and merchants. In theory, credit card issuers could charge both halves of this two-sided market. In practice, they sometimes do exactly that: charging annual fees to consumers and processing fees of 2% or more to merchants. In fact, in the early days, almost all card issuers charged their users for the privilege of using the cards. But increasingly, instead of charging the users, they give them away for free to maximize demand. That way, they make more money on merchant fees on the other half of the two-sided market. By lowering the annual fees and other user charges on their cards, credit card issuers can not only increase the market share of the cards, but also increase the attractiveness of their networks to merchants, as well as the associated processing fees.

If giving away the card for free boosts demand, why not go even further? Could it be profitable to charge consumers *less* than zero? Many credit card companies have concluded that the answer is yes.

These issuers pay users 1% or more cash back or give consumers frequent-flier miles when they make purchases. Some even give consumers direct cash bonuses for using a card. Charging negative prices for a product or service would make little sense for ordinary goods, but for a two-sided market it can be a sustainable and consistently profitable strategy.

Giving It Away and Locking Them In

A number of important tactical and strategic decisions remain. For instance, in credit card markets, why are consumers typically subsidized and merchants charged, rather than vice versa? A key consideration is the concept of elasticity of demand that we introduced earlier: How many extra users would you gain by lowering the price a little bit, and conversely, how many would you lose by increasing the price? The smart strategy is to lower the price on the side of the market with the greater elasticity and raise it on the side with less price elasticity. A second factor is, What is the "cross-elasticity"? That is, what happens to the *other* side of the market when you lower the price on the first side? The greater the cross-elasticity, the more you can influence the other side of the market.

In the case of credit cards, these factors work in favor of lower prices for consumers and higher prices for merchants. Lots of consumers sign up for cards with low, zero, or even negative prices. In turn, widespread consumer use drives merchants on the other side of the market to accept those cards, even if they have to pay a bit more in processing fees than they'd like. The net result can be higher market share and higher profits for the platform owner.

One other factor can make a big difference for pricing in both two-sided networks and their simpler, one-sided, cousins: switching costs. If it's easy to switch from one network to another, then there is much less incentive to invest heavily in getting users on board. They might pocket your incentive and then just switch to another network the next day. But if it's costly to switch, then once they join your network, a bandwagon effect is much more likely to take off. Other users will also join, and then, later, even if the initial incentive disappears, the users will still find it unattractive to go elsewhere, not only because of the switching costs, but also because of all the other users on the network. These users will be "locked in," as economists say.

By definition, when network effects are important, larger networks are more attractive to new users than smaller networks, so whichever network is largest will have the easiest time attracting even more users, extending its advantage. In other words, there's a tendency toward winner-take-all markets when network effects are strong. This phenomenon creates yet another incentive for lowering prices, at least initially, when building a networked business.

All of these effects can interact, so it can be a delicate balancing act to provide just the right incentives for both sides of the market. If a platform owner tries to extract too much value from one side of the market, the participants on that side might start to leave its network, which, of course, makes it less attractive to the other side of the network. The wonderful virtuous cycle of two-sided networks then becomes a vicious cycle of downward-spiraling market share.

Furthermore, platform owners can't just focus on pricing. They have a variety of other levers to manage, including the user interface and user experience, reputation systems, marketing budgets, and core network technology. The most successful platform owners carefully curate the value that each side of the market gets from participating and aren't too greedy.

Once you understand the logic of two-sided markets, the next step is to apply it to multisided markets. Two-sided markets often become multisided markets with dozens or even thousands of distinct subgroups interacting through the platform. For instance, iTunes is a great way to get music on an iPhone. The more artists who put their music on iTunes, the more attractive it is to buy an iPhone. That's a nice two-sided network. But the increase in iPhone sales not only makes iTunes more attractive to music artists; it also increases the value of the platform for developers Pandora, Waze, Uber, Lyft, Evernote, Clash of Clans, and every other mobile app. And the more apps there are on a platform, the more attractive that platform becomes to even more users. Each of the participants in a multisided network can benefit each time another participant joins, even if the new participants are selling a different product to a different set of consumers.

One of the reasons platforms have become so powerful is these interactions. The cross-elasticity from users of one product to another may be very small for any individual users, but in a world of free, perfect, and instant digital goods and services, even a small boost per user can be multiplied by millions of adopters to create an almost inexorable advantage for the platform and its participants. That's why effective curation of the whole ecosystem creates value not only for the platform owner, but for each of the participants.

Betting Billions on Platform Economics

Let's come back to our example of Uber and see how these factors interact and, in this case, reinforce each other. First, when Uber lowers prices, ridership goes up, just as demand would for any ordinary good when a company lowers the price. The relatively elastic demand for Uber rides makes it attractive to set prices where the revenue rectangle is long, low, and large. Second, because Uber is a two-sided network, the increase in demand doesn't just affect the consumers who use its ride-hailing app; it also increases demand for drivers who use rider-finding apps. In fact, as the number and thus density of riders increases, each driver will have less downtime and make more money per hour. Third, switching costs make it attractive to invest heavily in growing the network in the early stages of adoption, to bring on more users and riders.

Uber's investors are making the bet that the (two-sided) network effects and switching costs are large enough to make it worth investing billions of dollars to encourage adoption of the platform by both riders and drivers. Their strategy is complicated by the fact that geographically distinct markets each have their own local network effects. If you're hailing a ride in Beijing, it makes little difference if Uber has lots of drivers in New York or New Delhi. The battle isn't one big winner-take-all contest, but hundreds of separate ones, with only weak network effects across different geographies. They're winning some and losing others.

As it works to build its platform, Uber has two huge advantages. The first is a set of deep-pocketed and patient investors, who are willing to cover Uber's costs while it scales. These initial costs—for technology development, marketing, driver recruiting, staffing, and so on—are substantial, and Uber was estimated to have raised more than $15 billion in loans and investments by July 2016 to fund its global growth.

Investors have been willing to supply that money because they see the second advantage: if and when the company activates network effects and achieves scale, its marginal cost of arranging a ride somewhere in the world will be extraordinarily low. The free, perfect, and instant economics of bits will dominate, and these traits support charging very low prices. So Uber, the theory goes, will eventually be able to profitably charge the very low prices that maximize total revenue; owning a dominant platform will make the company valuable enough to reward the investors that supported its initial growth period.

The theory has worked for a host of platform companies, provid-

ing a potent illustration that digital platforms and the economics of
bits are perfectly suited for markets where the elasticity of demand
is high—where there's a lot of potential far down on the demand
curve. Of course, even platform economics doesn't provide immunity
to new competition, management mistakes, or technological shifts.
None of today's platform heroes can grow complacent.

The Atom Test: Can Product Makers Tolerate Platform Prices?

Successful platforms are great news for consumers—look at how
much consumer surplus there is on top of the revenue rectangle in
Figure 8—but they present challenges to incumbent companies dominated by the economics of atoms. For taxis and other cars, the marginal cost of taking someone across town is clearly not zero, or even
close, since gas and the driver both must be paid for. For this reason,
most companies prefer to operate higher on the demand curve, where
prices are greater, even if total demand will be lower.

Two forces push prices downward. The first is consumers, who
obviously want to pay as little as possible and thus side with platform builders that seek to rapidly grow their networks. The second
is that in most markets, many suppliers compete for business, and
many other potential suppliers are waiting in the wings. Platforms
usually enhance this competition by reducing barriers to entry, and
they often commoditize the suppliers, making them more interchangeable to the consumer. Competition and commoditization,
of course, tend to drive down prices, and to deliver the business
to the companies willing to supply products most cheaply (while
maintaining acceptable quality). In short, platform builders and
consumers both want low prices, and competition among suppliers
tends to result in them. And there's often potential for the platform
to increase utilization and efficiency, thereby driving down prices
even more.

Delimited Disruption: Where the Old Guard Endures

This chapter and the three before it have described the extraordinary disruptive power of online platforms. In industry after industry, online platforms have unseated incumbents, shifted profits and prices, and underpinned the rise of important new companies. Their ability to harness network effects and the economics of bits, their control of the user interface and user experience, and their frequent preference for prices that are painful to established suppliers combine to give platform companies formidable advantages.

Are these advantages insurmountable and universal? Are platforms, in other words, going to spread everywhere and take over everything, destroying old-line companies or reducing them to low-profit remnants of what they once were? As we've shown, this is what's happened time and time again over the past twenty years. And as we've hopefully made clear, there's more to come; the changes brought by platforms are not yet finished.

But they also won't be destructive to everything that existed before. The destructive potential of platforms is both real and large, but it's not unlimited. Many hotels, for example, have continued to do quite well even as Airbnb has spread widely and quickly. The lodging-industry benchmarking company STR, for example, found that 2015 and 2016 had the two highest overall occupancy rates on record for the US hotel industry. And these high occupancy rates are not always achieved through discounting. In Los Angeles the daily hotel rate rose 8% in 2015, even though Airbnb rentals represented 12% of all lodging.

Why Airbnb Won't Vacate Hotels

Why have platforms deeply disrupted the business of traveling around cities, but not the business of staying in them? The reason is that getting a ride across town is a largely undifferentiated experience, while staying overnight is definitely not. And platforms are particularly good at displacing incumbents when there's not a lot of perceived difference among their offerings.

Residents, tourists, and business travelers all have essentially the same goal when they want to go somewhere in a city: to get there quickly, safely, and cheaply. Sometimes the luxury level and amenities of the vehicle are important (as when a company wants to show clients how much it values their business), but most of the time they're not, and clean enough is good enough. For all these groups, hailing a ride with Uber will accomplish their goals, since their goals are so similar. Our personal experiences bear this out. In Boston where we live, and in cities all over the world where we've traveled for business and pleasure, we've used Uber countless times. If the car that shows up is a Mercedes S-Class instead of a Toyota Prius, that's a nice plus, but it doesn't fundamentally change the value proposition of getting efficiently from point A to point B.

Lodging for travelers, on the other hand, varies widely, and these differences matter. Tourists on a budget want a cheap place to stay in an interesting neighborhood, and often they also want a local's advice on what to do. The archetypal professional on a business trip, meanwhile, attends a conference downtown and wants laundry service, a gym, a place to take meetings, and coffee delivered to the room in the morning. Airbnb is an ideal platform to help the tourists find lodging, but it is much less useful to the business traveler who, let's face it, really wants a hotel and its bundle of services. And if a company wants to hold its own conference and thus needs ballrooms, meeting rooms, catering, and help organizing the whole thing, Airbnb is almost no use at all.

This contrast highlights the fact that while urban rides might be close to a single product market within each city, urban stays are clearly not. With its platform, Airbnb essentially introduced a second product in this market, one aimed at people who wanted something different, and often cheaper, than what hotels traditionally provided. This product—short-term lodging in a variety of residences, often including interactions with the host—has been quite popular and expands the market for lodging more than it cannibalizes it.

The disruptions that the platform has brought to the hotel industry have occurred exactly where we'd expect: at the boundary between the two products. Research from economists Georgios Zervas and Davide Proserpio found that Airbnb was responsible for a 10% decline in overall hotel revenues in Austin, Texas, over five years, but that its "impact is not uniformly distributed, with lower priced hotels and those not catering to business travelers being the most affected."

Durable Differentiation

Several factors keep hotel stays from becoming an undifferentiated single-product market, and hence more vulnerable to destruction by a platform. Business travelers often want to stay in a specific location, or with the chain that has their favorite rewards program. There are large and meaningful differences in room furnishings and amenities. Some cater more to families, or to extended stays. In the first wave of e-commerce, Priceline tried to build a platform that ignored many of these differences and instead matched travelers with rooms solely according to their willingness to pay for a given quality level. This approach was strenuously resisted by many hotel companies and eventually faded; Priceline now operates a more traditional travel site (with, as we saw in Chapter 2, a rigorous approach to improving the site via testing and experimentation). More recently, platforms like Hotel Tonight have appeared to match same-day travelers with hotels that have rooms available that night. This service has improved occupancy rates but does not yet seem to have greatly shaken up the industry.

When offerings are differentiated and customers can be locked into a specific company or brand, the destructive potential of platforms is probably more limited. What else might limit it? Well, it seems unlikely that the US Department of Defense would ever turn to a digital platform to source the military's next fighter plane or submarine. This is because the market contains very few possible participants (only one buyer and very few sellers). In addition, the transaction is incredibly complex and requires enormous amounts of communication. Markets in which players are few and offerings are complicated will probably be some of the least amenable to platforms. So, activities like designing and building a power plant, providing tax advice on a large merger, and coordinating all the details of bringing together art from around the world for a major museum exhibit will likely continue to be carried out as they have in the past, and will not be taken over by digital platforms.

Chapter Summary

► Platforms can capture much, most, or even all of the value as they spread throughout an industry.

► Platforms succeed at capturing and creating value in part because they reduce information asymmetries that previously kept some beneficial transactions from happening.

► The key to many platforms is the power of two-sided networks, where decisions with one set of customers and products can profoundly affect demand by a different set of customers for a different set of products.

▶ Platforms with two-sided networks can become multisided networks, amplifying the role of cross-elasticities.

▶ Switching costs can temporarily lock in customers, increasing incentives for networks to invest in growing their market share early, in order to reap benefits later.

▶ As platforms grow, incumbents can find themselves looking like utilities, with reduced opportunities for profits and growth.

▶ Popular platforms can quickly build powerful brands. This sometimes encourages them to try to reduce the value of incumbents' brands.

▶ When physical goods and services are differentiated and customers can be locked in, the disruptive potential of online-to-offline platforms is more limited.

Questions

1. What are a handful of scenarios for how products and platforms will come together in your industry over the next three to five years?

2. If information asymmetries in your industry were reduced, what new opportunities and businesses would open up?

3. What are your main strategies for avoiding the commoditization and price reductions that platforms can bring to incumbent product companies?

4. If you're building a network with two or more sides, which side(s) are you willing to let join and participate for free, or even to subsidize? Who has the greatest elasticity of demand?

5. Are you confident that you can continue to differentiate your offerings as platforms spread? If so, why? What are your sustainable sources of differentiation?

PART 3

CORE AND CROWD

CHAPTER 10

THAT ESCALATED QUICKLY: THE EMERGENCE OF THE CROWD

I hope, that in our archives and historical filings of the future, we do not allow the techie traditions of hierarchy and false regularity to be superimposed on the teeming, fantastic disorderliness of human life.

— *Theodore Nelson, 2008*

SHORTLY BEFORE THE WEB BURST INTO THE MAINSTREAM, the author Robert Wright predicted one of its most important consequences. In his essay "Voice of America," which appeared in the September 13, 1993, issue of the magazine the *New Republic*, Wright reported on his forays into Usenet, a set of online discussion groups organized by topic. Usenet software in the early 1990s was not very user-friendly, and getting online itself was difficult; permanent broadband connections were still far in the future. But despite these obstacles, the discussion groups Wright found were vibrant places. As he wrote, "Most newsgroup traffic is from serious people finding communication they need or, at least, really want. And the level of discourse, though uneven, is often very high."

Wright commented astutely on many aspects of online discourse and culture that would blossom in the years to come, from the ease of finding shared interests to emoticons. For those interested in the net's impact on the business world, his most important insight concerned how easy it was to get a question answered. His query was, "Why does the standard set of clubs no longer include a 2 iron?" Dozens of answers arrived within forty-eight hours.

Wright got a "plausible reply" to his question,* and an insight: even more important than the ability to get a question answered was the phenomenon of who was doing the answering. "The things [the net] changes are the arbitrary constraints on interaction. Distance is not an impediment. Race doesn't matter. Being a big strapping male or a nubile female won't affect the amount of deference you get. . . . This does lead to a freer, truly disembodied mingling of minds."

Early on, then, Wright realized something critically important about the online world that was only faintly visible to most people in 1993: it was an unprecedented means of gathering together diverse bits of knowledge from all over—from all over the world, and from all different kinds of people. And large collections of knowledge are valuable because people can consult them easily, and so become smarter.

Here's Everybody

This, after all, was the idea behind the library, one of civilization's oldest and most enduring institutions. Libraries are founded and funded by monarchs, churches, democratically elected governments, and philanthropists, and they are typically staffed by trained professionals who select, arrange, and maintain their collections. They're

---

* Ironically, Wright didn't include this answer in his article. Here's ours: 2 irons are not included mainly because they're really hard to use.

a great example of what we call the "core," which we define as the dominant organizations, institutions, groups, and processes of the pre-Internet era. To be clear up front, we don't think the core is bad or obsolete. Both of us have used and have benefited from libraries all our lives, and we take a geeky pride in MIT's excellent library system.

What Wright foresaw, even if he couldn't have anticipated its size and speed, was the emergence of an alternative to the core, which we call the "crowd" and define as the new participants and practices enabled by the net and its attendant technologies. The web today is a crowd-generated library—a huge, sprawling, constantly growing, and changing one. Like just about all the aspects of the crowd, it's enabled by the free, perfect, and instant economics of bits, and in fact is heavily dependent on them: today's web wouldn't exist if we had to pay every time we accessed or added to it.

The difference between the Web and the world's libraries highlights how dissimilar the crowd is from the core. For one thing, the web is bigger. An estimated 130 million books have been published throughout human history, of which about 30 million are available in the world's largest (physical) library, the Library of Congress in Washington, DC. In contrast, the portion of the web visible to modern search engines had by 2015 grown to approximately 45 billion pages, with far more accessible privately. The web also now includes digital representations of at least 25 million of those books, thanks to scanning efforts by Google and others.

The online world also generates information in many different forms. Libraries usually specialize to some degree—in books, maps, archival records, and so on—but the web has it all: text, music, pictures, podcasts, videos, virtual reality environments, and so on. And it has more of all of these, all the time. For instance, an estimated 80 million videos are on YouTube alone, with many more on Facebook and other sites. No one is "in charge of" this ocean of content; no person or board decided that one more photo-sharing utility was

needed, or green-lighted the cornucopia of media for blogging, tweet-
ing, or newsfeeds. The core is characterized by government bodies,
approval loops, and people and groups with the formal power to say
no. There's a great deal less of all of this with the crowd (although
there are certainly some very influential information brokers).

Dealing with a Sometimes Unruly Mob

An inevitable result of this lack of hierarchy is that the crowd is far
more unruly than the core. It's inherently and deliberately decentralized and uncontrolled. This structure enables freedom of expression
and innovation, which are great.

Except when they're not. The uncontrolled nature of the crowd
brings with it two difficult problems. The first is that it can be hard to
find what you're looking for in an ocean of uncontrolled information,
fed by countless free-flowing rivers of contribution.

The core solves this search problem by curating content—by controlling what gets in and applying human intelligence to the work
of organizing it. So, libraries have acquisitions departments and card
catalogs, magazines have editors and tables of contents, and so on.
In the early years of the web, numerous attempts were made to apply
some of these approaches to the content generated by the crowd.
Yahoo originally stood for "Yet Another Hierarchically Organized
Oracle," and it rose to prominence as a sort of card catalog for the
net; a human-created and -maintained set of website categories and
subcategories.*

Yahoo and its peers, however, had trouble keeping up as online
content continued to grow exponentially, and many observers felt

---

* After Yahoo's role as the web's curator faded, so did its reason for being. Verizon
agreed to buy the company in 2016 in what was called the "saddest $5B deal in tech his-
tory." Brian Solomon, "Yahoo Sells to Verizon in Saddest $5 Billion Deal in Tech His-
tory," *Forbes*, July 25, 2016, http://www.forbes.com/sites/briansolomon/2016/07/25/
yahoo-sells-to-verizon-for-5-billion-marissa-mayer/#7084344771b4.

that the web would soon become (or already was) a chronically disorganized mess. As the mathematician and author John Allen Paulos observed in the early days of the web, "The Internet is the world's largest library. It's just that all the books are on the floor."

The solution to this problem came, surprisingly enough, from the content itself. Larry Page and Sergey Brin, while still students in Stanford's computer science department, realized that many pieces of web content, if not most, pointed to other pieces by linking to them; after all, that's why Tim Berners-Lee had named it the "web." They surmised that these links could be used to build an index of all the content out there—one where the "best" page on a given topic was the one that had the most other pages linking to it. In a way, this is how academic reputations are built: by noting which papers have the most citations from other papers. Page and Brin added a clever twist by weighting the importance of each link by the number of pages that in turn linked to each of the pages that originated the links, and so on, and so on.

The algorithm that Page and Brin developed created a rank of every page and was called "PageRank." Their paper describing this approach, titled "The Anatomy of a Large-Scale Hypertextual Web Search Engine," was presented in April 1998 at the Seventh International World-Wide Web Conference in Brisbane, Australia. The company that the pair created to put this approach into practice—initially called BackRub, but later renamed Google—was founded in September 1998 in Silicon Valley.

Google changed the world with the realization that even though the crowd's online content was uncontrolled, it wasn't disorganized. It, in fact, had an extremely elaborate and fine-grained structure, but not one that was consciously decided on by any core group of humans. Instead, it was a structure that emerged from the content itself, once it was analyzed by the company's PageRank algorithm and all of its relatives. This emergent structure changes and grows as the content itself does, and lets us smoothly and easily navigate all the content that the crowd comes up with.

The second problem that inevitably comes with an uncontrolled crowd is that some of its members misbehave in hurtful ways. The core can evict bad actors—from the company, the library, or the payroll—but the web really can't; it's too easy to come in by employing another user name or IP address,* or to hide behind anonymity. So, as we discussed in Chapter 8, we get many types of hateful speech, bad behavior, and criminality.

This behavior is distressing, but it's not fatal to the idea of the crowd. For one thing, most of us who participate are not bad actors. We're creating and contributing in good faith, so the good content far outweighs the bad. In addition, powerful search tools like Google's help push the bad content farther from view. And the builders of the web's most popular platforms have largely adopted an enlightened approach: they follow the advice summarized as one of Wikipedia's pillars: "Act in good faith, and assume good faith on the part of others."

Instead of trying to assess potential members' proclivity for bad behavior, they monitor what people are doing over time and take action as necessary. This approach works well, by and large, and has allowed the crowd to grow enormously without being sabotaged by its worst members.

Not all versions of the crowd are equally successful at this gentle policing. The year 2016 saw challenges to this approach in the form of "fake news" on Facebook and other social media, and large amounts of racism, sexism, anti-Semitism and other despicable vitriol on Twitter. Jimmy Wales has argued that Wikipedia, the crowd-sourced encyclopedia that he cofounded, is relatively immune to fake news in part because of its governance methods. By adopting the

---

* IP addresses are numbers assigned to all the devices that access the Internet.

right principles, norms, institutions, and technologies, the crowd can do a great deal to maintain quality standards, though there may be other trade-offs, like how easily or quickly participants can post new items, how quickly they are shared, who gets to see them, and, yes, how much profit can be earned from the content. We discuss some of these principles later in this chapter.

As we write this in early 2017, it remains to be seen how the largest platforms that give the crowd a voice will respond to these challenges. We are confident that effective solutions will be possible by bringing together minds and machines. One promising approach here is to allow people to flag fake or offensive content while training machine learning systems to spot it automatically.

The Magic of Markets, the Purest Crowds of All

Large collections of information like libraries and the web are obviously valuable because we can consult and learn from them. Many crowd-created collections have another benefit: as they accumulate the contributions of many people, they spontaneously generate new kinds of knowledge. This is a kind of magic that actually happens, all the time.

The first person to clearly point out this benefit, and thus to become a kind of patron saint of the crowd, was the Austrian economist Friedrich Hayek in his 1945 article "The Uses of Knowledge in Society." At the time, a fierce debate was raging about whether centrally planned economies like that of the Soviet Union—in other words, economies where there was a single core responsible for creating and distributing goods and services—worked better than free market economies where planning and production were done by an undirected, decentralized crowd. Many felt that central planning would be, or at least could be, superior. With a single paper, Hayek showed how wrong they were.

What's the Problem with Central Planning? Ask Hayek and Polanyi

The reason central planning could never work, Hayek maintained, was that "the 'data' from which the economic calculus starts are never for the whole society 'given' to a single mind which could work out the implications." But why not, especially now that we have such powerful technologies for monitoring and analysis? Why not just slap sensors on all the gear, conduct surveys and listen to social media to understand everyone's preferences, and feed all this data into a "single mind"—a giant economic optimization algorithm that would run continuously to "work out the implications"? Because, Hayek explained, that algorithm would never get all the data it actually needed; it could never "secure the best use of resources known to any of the members of society, for ends whose relative importance only these individuals know."

Hayek argued that something like Polanyi's Paradox applies throughout the economy: we can't tell all of what we know, what we have, what we want, or what we value. As a result, the giant optimizing algorithm of any central planning core could never have the data it truly needed, so it would do bizarre and counterproductive things. It would be a society-wide version of the well-meaning but addled relative who drives all over town to find you the Christmas present you wanted last year but no longer care about. Even if the central planners were always trying to act only in the best interests of everyone else (and simply stating that assumption highlights its implausibility), overcentralization would create an economy that's simultaneously Orwellian and Kafkaesque.

How does a free market economy do better? By letting people freely transact with each other without much central control, and by using the prices of things not only to balance supply and demand, but also to transmit critical information throughout the economy in a remarkably parsimonious way. As Hayek wrote,

> The marvel [of prices] is that in a case like that of a scarcity of one raw material, without an order being issued, without more than perhaps a handful of people knowing the cause, tens of thousands of people whose identity could not be ascertained by months of investigation, are made to use the material or its products more sparingly; i.e., they move in the right direction. . . . I am convinced that if [the price system] were the result of deliberate human design, and if the people guided by the price changes understood that their decisions have significance far beyond their immediate aim, this mechanism would have been acclaimed as one of the greatest triumphs of the human mind.

Hayek's paper, which anticipated many of the ideas of what would coalesce into complexity theory later in the twentieth century, highlighted that the actions of individual members could generate information that was highly valuable to the entire crowd. What's more, this information often can't be gleaned from observing a small number of members: you'll never learn the price of tin by watching just a couple of miners or metalworkers. Markets are therefore called "emergent" systems: prices emerge from all members' interactions and can't be observed just by looking at a few.

Market-Based Solutions

Groups often behave in ways that are emergent and thus generate knowledge. As groups went online and became the crowd, innovators found different ways to detect and harvest this knowledge. Prediction markets were one of the earliest of these, and the ones that built most directly from Hayek's insights. These are markets not for goods and services, but for future events, such as a particular person being elected US president in 2020, an upcoming movie making between $50 million and $100 million in the box office in its first week, or the official US inflation rate averaging more than 3% over the next quarter.

Here's how prediction markets work. First, the market maker creates a set of securities that participants can buy and sell, just like they sell a company's shares on the New York Stock Exchange or Nasdaq. One way to do this is to create a security that pays $1 if inflation (for example) averages above 3% in a quarter, and $0 if it does not. Next, a group of participants—the more the better—are invited into the market and encouraged to start trading the securities with each other. Those who think that inflation will be greater than 3% will be willing to pay more for the security than those who think it will be less than that. If the price stabilizes at $0.70, a reasonable interpretation is that the market as a whole believes that there's a 70% chance that inflation will average more than 3% for the quarter (or that the movie will make between $50 million and $100 million, or that so-and-so will become president in 2020). Finally, when the event actually occurs—in this case, when the quarter ends and average inflation can be calculated—the market maker pays out to all of the people holding the right securities. If inflation did, in fact, average more than 3%, all the people holding the "above 3%" security would get $1 for every share they had.

Results from prediction markets confirm Hayek's insights about the knowledge-aggregating power of prices within markets. In markets like the ones just described, events with final share prices of about $0.70 tend to actually happen about 70% of the time, making these prices pretty accurate probability estimates.

There are active debates about whether prediction markets provide more accurate forecasts than other methods (such as properly weighted averages of polls, or reliance on the superforecasters identified by Philip Tetlock and discussed in Chapter 2), but few people anymore doubt that prediction markets can be very effective under the right conditions. As economist Robin Hanson, the scholar who has done the most to advance both the theory and practice of prediction markets, puts it, "Prediction markets reflect a fundamental principle underlying the value of market-based pricing: Because information is often widely dispersed among economic actors, it is highly desirable to find a mechanism to collect and aggregate that information. Free markets usually manage this process well because almost anyone can participate, and the potential for profit (and loss) creates strong incentives to search for better information."

How Can You Organize a Crowd?

The price system that Hayek highlighted and praised and that Hanson and others have put to innovative use is a marvelous by-product of the actions and interactions of market participants. In other words, most prices are not the result of any deliberate effort to create and communicate system-wide knowledge. So, what can happen when there *is* just such an effort—an attempt to convene an online crowd and get it to work together to create something?

It seems like a hopelessly naïve idea, and it's easy to generate a list of reasons why it would never work. Who would show up to work on such a project, especially if pay was not being offered? And how could anyone be sure that those who showed up were, in fact, the right people? How should the work be divided up, and who would do the dividing? What would constitute a good, or good enough, contribution, and who would set and enforce these criteria? Throughout millennia of human history, we've developed different variations of the core to settle these issues. How could the crowd ever do the same?

Developing an Operating System for Developing Operating Systems

If this question was troubling Linus Torvalds on August 25, 1991, it didn't stop him from posting the following message on the Usenet group devoted to a computer operating system called "Minix":

> Hello everybody out there using minix
>
> I'm doing a (free) operating system (just a hobby, won't be big and professional like gnu*) for 386(486) AT clones. This has been brewing since april, and is starting to get ready. . . . I'd like to know what features most people would want. Any suggestions are welcome, but I won't promise I'll implement them :)

Torvalds was asking for help with a computer operating system he had started writing. It was still quite new, but he'd made good progress on a *kernel*, the heart of an operating system and one of its most complicated elements. Rather than buying a complete commercial operating system like Microsoft Windows, Torvalds instead wanted to create a free one, where free meant "free to view, modify, and extend" even more than it meant "free of charge" (or, as the developer community likes to explain, free as in "free speech," not "free beer"). In contrast, Microsoft does not make public the Windows source code—the software underlying that operating system—so no one outside the company knows exactly how it works or has the ability to modify it. People within the "free and open source" software community believed this lack of transparency was a mistake for a number of reasons, and Torvalds shared their views.

The operating system that Torvalds first described in April of 1991 came to be called Linux, and his initial claim that it "won't be big

---

* GNU is also an open-source operating system. The initials stand for "GNU's Not Unix. " Hackers love recursion.

and professional" will surely go down as one of the most inaccurate statements ever made in the history of computing. In all of its forms and derivatives, Linux is without question the biggest and most professional operating system in the world, today found on everything from the servers in data centers bigger than a football field to over 1.5 billion Android phones and tablets.

Writing a New Playbook

Studying Linux's history reveals several principles that appear to be important, perhaps even essential, for bringing the crowd together to accomplish something significant. These include openness, noncredentialism, verifiable and reversible contributions, clear outcomes, self-organization, and geeky leadership.

Openness. When Torvalds made his initial request for contributions, he made it as broad as possible; he didn't limit it to firms, or to people with experience programming operating systems, or to any other specified group. This approach seems odd and misguided to many—after all, if you were building a house, it's unlikely you would issue an open call for people to just show up and start putting things together—but it has clearly worked. In the decade leading up to 2015, 11,800 individual developers contributed to the kernel, and major technology companies including Samsung, IBM, Google, and Intel had contributed both funding and talent. In Chapter 7 we noted that there are many motivations for writing smartphone apps; people and organizations also have many different motivations for contributing to an open-source operating system project. Because of its openness, Linux was able to tap into all of them.

Noncredentialism. One aspect of openness is so important, yet so counterintuitive, that it deserves special mention. This is noncredentialism, or abandoning the view that people should be allowed to contribute to an effort only if they have the right credentials: diplomas, job titles, letters of recommendation, years of experience, good grades, and so on. Torvalds required none of these, and didn't even ask for them. He just made the Linux source code available and asked for help improving it. This was an early example of what the writer, publisher, and technology guru Tim O'Reilly distilled in 2005 as a key principle of Web 2.0 (the second generation of the web, which was by then coming into view): trusting users as codevelopers. Torvalds didn't know this at the time, though. As he freely admitted in 2016, "There was no intention behind using the kind of open-source methodology that we think of today to improve it. It was more like, 'Look, I've been working on this for half a year, I'd love to have comments.'" The brilliance in not asking contributors for their credentials, though, is that he didn't turn away those without any—think of a high school student who loves coding but has none of the trappings of a "real" programmer—or those whose credentials might have struck him as inadequate or inappropriate.

Verifiable and reversible contributions. The reason openness and noncredentialism work well for software efforts (much better than for house-building projects) is that it's relatively easy to see whether a proposed a new piece of software works well, and also relatively easy to reject it if it doesn't. A printer driver, for example, has to make the printer print out pages correctly and reliably; if it doesn't, it shouldn't be included in the operating system. There are many ways to verify software quality, from visually examining the code to testing it once in place. This means that writing an operating system is very different from endeavors to generate other creative products, like novels or symphonies. It's not at all clear or externally verifiable whether someone's proposed contribution of a new chapter or character to a novel improves the work.

Objective and verifiable measures of quality help explain why crowd-written Linux is the world's most popular operating system, but to our knowledge, no successful novels have been written by a large group. And because it's standard practice to keep an archive of all previous versions of a piece of software (thanks to the free, perfect, and instant economics of information, this is cheap and easy to do), if a piece of code degrades performance, it's easy to just revert to the most recent version of the software that didn't include that code. It's much easier for Linux to remain open and noncredentialist when the contributors who show up can't irreversibly break or worsen the software through malice or cluelessness.

Clear outcomes. The people who showed up to contribute to Linux knew what the end result of their efforts would be, in two ways. First, they obviously knew they were working on a computer operating system. Second, and at least as important, they knew how their work could and couldn't be used in the future—who could own it, modify it, profit from it, restrict access to it, and so on.

Early in Linux's history, Torvalds decided to put it under the GNU General Public License, or GNU GPL, a software license developed by the free-software pioneer Richard Stallman in 1989. It specifies two important considerations. The first is that the software remains free for end users—whether individuals, organizations, or companies—to run, study, copy, and modify. The second is that all modifications, extensions, and future versions of Linux would remain equally free. The GPL gives everyone involved with Linux the assurance that the operating system can never be closed down or made proprietary, and that the rules under which they contribute to it won't change over time. For people who believed in the principles of the free-software movement, these assurances were critical. This is generally true: the crowd wants clarity not just on how contributions will be evaluated, but also on how they'll be used, and who will be able to benefit from them.

Self-organization. People and organizations decided for themselves which aspects of Linux to work on; they weren't assigned tasks by Torvalds or any other central authority. So, how can the effort as a whole ensure that the really important work gets done? By realizing that in this case, "important" actually means the work that's most relevant to the community of end users, by enabling these users to contribute, and by having some confidence that they will do so. As large tech companies like Samsung or Intel joined Linux, they of course directed their employees to work on specific areas, but the overall effort remained highly decentralized and unscripted. In fact, there was not even an attempt to stick to one version of Linux. Instead, the operating system could "fork" so that it had one version called Raspbian optimized for the Raspberry Pi, a credit card–sized programmable computer that costs less than $40, while other Linux variants were optimized for giant servers. Forking was seen as evidence of Linux's success, rather than as a loss of control, and it showed the benefits of letting contributors organize themselves and their work.

Geeky leadership. Torvalds has remained a highly influential figure as Linux has grown, and he has exemplified a leadership style that we label "geeky." We mean that not as an insult, but rather as a description of behaviors and practices that are found within technology development efforts, especially those that span many otherwise unaffiliated people and organizations. Geeky leadership is very often technically proficient leadership. Torvalds is a lifelong programmer and a very good one—a fact that gives his views great credibility within the Linux community. Geeky leaders also articulate a vision for what they're working toward. This vision does not have to be grandiose—as Torvalds once said, "I am not a visionary. I do not have a five-year plan. I'm an engineer. . . . I'm looking at the ground, and I want to fix the pothole that's right in front of me before I fall in"—but it does need to be clear, and it needs to be able to motivate people to devote their time and effort to achieving it.

Building a perennially free and open-source operating system for a wide range of computing devices has clearly been motivating to a lot of people. Geeky leaders, we've observed, often have strong opinions. Torvalds is passionate about what he calls tasteful code (which he says "is about really seeing the big patterns and kind of instinctively knowing what's the right way to do things") and is well known for periodically posting very strongly worded views.* These broadsides have probably alienated at least some contributors, but they show the community as a whole that its founder remains engaged and informed, two hallmarks of geeky leadership.

These principles help explain Linux's extraordinary success, and how it was able to bring the crowd together to build, maintain, and improve over time a world-class operating system, one of the most complicated pieces of software. Openness and noncredentialism made the work available to as many people as possible. Self-assignment meant that they worked on what they wanted, which typically turned out to be what Linux most needed. Verifiability ensured that only helpful contributions survived in the software, and clear outcomes kept people from feeling that they could be duped or their efforts hijacked. And dedicated geeky leadership from Torvalds and others maintained the ideals, culture, and momentum of Linux.

---

* In July of 2016, for example, Torvalds opined on the "right" way for programmers to add comments to their code. He told the Linux Kernel mailing list, "If the networking people cannot handle the pure awesomeness that is a balanced and symmetric traditional multi-line C style comments, then instead of the disgusting unbalanced crap that you guys use now, please just go all the way to the C++ mode. . . . I'm not even going to start talking about the people who prefer to 'box in' their comments, and line up both ends and have fancy boxes of stars around the whole thing. I'm sure that looks really nice if you are out of your mind on LSD." Linus Torvalds, Linux Kernel Mailing List post, July 8, 2016, 10:19:26, https://lkml.org/lkml/2016/7/8/625.

Some Is Not Enough: The Story of a Nearly Failed Experiment

What happens when a collaborative online effort follows only some of these principles? How successful will it be? A lot of research would be needed to answer this question definitively, of course, but a fascinating and illuminating experiment occurred in the early years of the web when Jimmy Wales and Larry Sanger started an effort to build a free and open, universally accessible online encyclopedia.

Encyclopedias have a long history—one of the first was Pliny the Elder's *Naturalis Historia*, published in the first century CE—and lofty goals. Ephraim Chambers said that his 1728 *Cyclopaedia: or, An Universal Dictionary of Arts and Sciences* contained the "sum of all human knowledge."* They tended to be very expensive, however, and thus reserved for society's elites.

With the emergence of the web, Wales saw an opportunity to bring the vast scope of encyclopedias to everyone by tapping into people's spirit of volunteerism. So, in 1999 he hired Sanger, who was then a graduate student working toward a PhD in philosophy, to help him launch Nupedia, which was to be the web's first free online encyclopedia. Wales and Sanger begin recruiting volunteer editors to help accomplish this goal. To ensure high quality, Nupedia had this policy: "We wish editors to be true experts in their fields and (with few

---

* More specifically, Chambers described the *Cyclopaedia* as "Containing the Definitions of the Terms, and Accounts of the Things Signify'd Thereby, in the Several Arts, both Liberal and Mechanical, and the Several Sciences, Human and Divine: the Figures, Kinds, Properties, Productions, Preparations, and Uses, of Things Natural and Artificial; the Rise, Progress, and State of Things Ecclesiastical, Civil, Military, and Commercial: with the Several Systems, Sects, Opinions, etc; among Philosophers, Divines, Mathematicians, Physicians, Antiquaries, Criticks, etc.: The Whole Intended as a Course of Ancient and Modern Learning." ARTFL Project, "Chambers' Cyclopaedia," accessed February 7, 2017, https://artfl-project.uchicago.edu/content/chambers-cyclopaedia.

exceptions) possess Ph.D.s." The encyclopedia also set up a seven-step process for writing and editing each of its articles.

1. Assignment

2. Finding a lead reviewer

3. Lead review

4. Open review

5. Lead copyediting

6. Open copyediting

7. Final approval and markup

Did this work? After eighteen months of effort and $250,000 of spending, Nupedia had twelve completed articles and 150 in draft stage.

Frustrated by the slow pace, Wales and Sanger begin looking around for other ways to create and refine encyclopedia articles. Early in 2001 they learned about wikis, an extremely egalitarian kind of digital whiteboard created by Ward Cunningham in which any user could make a contribution, edit someone else's contribution, or undo any previous edit. The Nupedia team set up a website based on this software, and on January 15, 2001, Sanger wrote the community a note: "Humor me. Go there and add a little article. It will take all of five or ten minutes."

The site was called "Wikipedia." By the end of January, it contained 617 articles. By the end of 2001 there were 19,000. By 2016 there were 36 million articles across 291 languages, and Wikipedia was the sixth-most-popular website in the world.

The transformation from Nupedia to Wikipedia clearly unlocked a tremendous amount of energy and let Wales and Sanger succeed far beyond any of their dreams of creating a free and open encyclopedia for the world's people. The example of Linux shows why the move to wikis was so important. Wikipedia, unlike Nupedia, was able to activate the crowd because it adopted the principles of openness, non-credentialism, and self-organization. It abandoned the notion of standardized, multistep work flows and the requirement that editors be experts or have PhDs. Instead, it threw open the work of building an encyclopedia to any and all to come together and work together in any ways they saw fit.

To keep these collaborations from descending into chaos, Wikipedia soon adopted the principle of verifiability, which meant that "other people using the encyclopedia can check that the information comes from a reliable source. Wikipedia does not publish original research."* Wikipedia also assured its contributors that their work could not be taken private by adopting a variant of the GPL, called the GFDL, intended for documents rather than software.

And Wales and other senior "Wikipedians" practice geeky leadership, contributing heavily to the encyclopedia and remaining actively involved in guiding its development.† A community has

---

* "Verifiable accuracy" became part of the "five pillars" intended to guide the Wikipedia community. Wikipedia, "Wikipedia:Five Pillars," last modified February 6, 2017, at 10:52, https://en.wikipedia.org/wiki/Wikipedia:Five_pillars.

† Larry Sanger left the Wikipedia community in the early years of the twenty-first century over differences about its governance. He came to feel that it was harmfully antiauthoritarian. Larry Sanger [timothy, pseud.], "The Early History of Nupedia and Wikipedia, Part II," Slashdot, April 19, 2005, https://slashdot.org/story/05/04/19/1746205/the-early-history-of-nupedia-and-wikipedia-part-ii.

emerged that enforces these norms, rewarding those who make useful contributions, and fostering a remarkable number of voluntary contributions.*

There are encouraging signs that even within older and more traditionally run organizations, geeky approaches to getting things done are gaining acceptance and momentum. Andy advocated such approaches in his 2009 book *Enterprise 2.0*, but at that time neither the tools nor the managerial mind-sets necessary for allowing open, noncredentialist, and self-organizing work within organizations were widely available. Now, it seems, they are.

Slack, a group-level tool that facilitates messaging and collaboration within and across organizations, was launched in August of 2013. It allowed many kinds of free-flowing and nonhierarchical communications, including chat, group document editing, polls, and so on. By October of 2016, Slack had more than 4 million active daily users and 1.25 million paying customers (nonpaying customers used a version of Slack that had fewer features). The style of work that led to Linux and Wikipedia is finally, it appears, finding acceptance in the mainstream business world.

Chapter Summary

▶ The crowd is, in many ways, the opposite of the core: it's huge, diverse, largely uncontrollable, and often messy.

---

* Wikipedians are not paid for their contributions and are mostly anonymous, so fame is of limited power as an incentive. As shown in a clever field experiment by Jana Gallus, they do seem to respond well to recognition, even if it's just from fellow Wikipedians. Jana Gallus, *Fostering Voluntary Contributions to a Public Good: A Large-Scale Natural Field Experiment at Wikipedia*, Natural Field Experiments 00552 (2016), https://ideas.repec.org/p/feb/natura/00552.html.

▶ The core remains relevant and useful, but in an era of global networks and robust platforms the crowd has become an increasingly powerful force.

▶ The crowd is not unstructured, however. Its structure is emergent, appearing over time as a result of the interactions of members. Stock markets, prediction markets, and modern search engines extract valuable information from this emergent structure.

▶ Overcentralization fails because of Hayek's insights and Polanyi's Paradox: people can't always articulate what they have, what they know, what they want, and what they can do.

▶ Large crowds can be brought together to build highly useful products like Linux. Such efforts require "geeky leadership" that follows principles of openness, noncredentialism, self-selection, verifiability, and clarity about goals and outcomes.

▶ Following only some of these principles seems not to work very well, as the example of Wikipedia's predecessor Nupedia shows. Getting the right balance can be unpredictable, often requiring trial, error, and luck.

Questions

1. How, and how much, are you using the crowd?

2. Where, if anywhere, are you allowing and encouraging work to be open, noncredentialist, verifiable, self-organizing, and led by geeks?

3. The internal decision-making and resource allocation processes of many organizations still look a lot like those of centrally planned economies. How can you incorporate more market-like mechanisms?

4. Are there new ways to use technology for decentralization in your industry that don't necessarily involve markets?

5. Is the core of your organization ready to give up some of its power and authority?

CHAPTER 11

WHY THE EXPERT YOU KNOW IS NOT THE EXPERT YOU NEED

I could not but smile to think in what out-of-the-way corners genius produces her bantlings! And the Muses, those capricious dames, who, forsooth, so often refuse to visit palaces, and deny a single smile to votaries in splendid studies, and gilded drawing-rooms—what holes and burrows will they frequent to lavish their favors on some ragged disciple!

— *Washington Irving, 1824*

WHEN THINGS GET REALLY COMPLEX, DON'T LOOK TO THE experts. Instead, call in the outsiders.

That's the conclusion from a fascinating study conducted by the innovation scholars Karim Lakhani, Kevin Boudreau, and their colleagues. They wanted to find a faster way to sequence the genomes of large numbers of human white blood cells, which are the body's main defense against bacteria, viruses, and other antigens.

Beginners Beat Benchmarks in Biology

This is clearly important work, since we want to better understand how the immune system functions. But it's also incredibly difficult, because white blood cells need to be able to generate a huge array of weapons to fight off the human body's many antigens, all of which are constantly evolving. The body's clever solution is to have its antibodies and other weapons encoded by genes within each white blood cell, but to have these genes themselves made up of a long set of gene segments strung together, sometimes with mutations. The precise sequence of active segments varies from cell to cell, which means that different cells produce different weapons. A lot of them. By one estimate, the 100 or so relevant segments in a human white blood cell can be combined and recombined to create 10^{30} possible molecular weapons. This is about a trillion times the number of grains of sand on Earth.

A common and important task for researchers is to annotate a white blood cell's gene—to correctly identify, in order, each of its component segments. As you might imagine, computers carry out this work. However, it can be approached in many different ways, and it's not clear in advance which method will yield the best— the fastest and most accurate—results. The popular MegaBLAST algorithm, developed by the US National Institutes of Health, could annotate 1 million sequences in about 4.5 hours with 72% accuracy. The idAb algorithm, created by Dr. Ramy Arnaout of Beth Israel Deaconess Medical Center, improved greatly on this performance, doing the same volume of annotation in less than forty-eight minutes with 77% accuracy.

To see how much more improvement was possible, Lakhani, Boudreau, and their colleagues devised a two-step process and invited in the crowd. First, they converted gene segment annotation from a specific immunogenetics problem into a general algorithmic one. Doing this removed the need for domain-specific knowledge about genetics, biology, and so on, and opened up the challenge to many more participants.

Second, the researchers posted this generalized challenge to Topcoder, an online platform for computationally intensive problems. At the time of the research in 2013, Topcoder had a community of approximately 400,000 software developers around the world who had come to the platform at least in part because they enjoyed working on tough challenges. The research team told the potential solvers how their submissions would be evaluated—using a score that was a combination of speed and accuracy—and gave them a bunch of data to work with. This data was divided into two sets: a public set made available to all solvers, and a private set that they could "plug into" on the Topcoder site; solvers could not see or download this data, but they could run their algorithms against it and get back a score. (A third data set, also private, was used to generate final scores for the competition.)

The Topcoder contest ran for fourteen days. During that time, 122 people or teams submitted algorithms at least once to obtain a score, and many did so multiple times; 654 total submissions were received. Participants formed a highly diverse group—they came from sixty-nine different countries and ranged from eighteen to forty-four years old—and also a largely inexperienced one, at least by conventional measures. Approximately half were still students and, as the research team put it, "None were academic or industrial computational biologists, and only five described themselves as coming from either R&D or life sciences in any capacity."

Were their solutions any good? Not all were, of course. The majority were less accurate than MegaBLAST or idAb (although almost all were faster than both of them). But thirty were more accurate than MegaBLAST, and sixteen were more accurate than idAb. Eight submissions from the crowd, in fact, reached 80% accuracy, which the researchers estimated was the theoretical maximum for this data set.* And the group of submissions that were at least as accurate as idAb ran at an average of eighty-nine seconds, which was more than thirty times as fast as that benchmark. The three fastest ran in just sixteen seconds, or almost 180 times as fast as the best precontest benchmark.

One more thing: The total prize money offered during the contest was $6,000.

What's Wrong with the Experts?

Are these results exceptional or typical? We went to Karim Lakhani with this question, since he is a pioneering researcher in competitions involving the crowd and has led many studies in addition to the one we just described. He told us,

> In the more than 700 challenges we have run on crowds for NASA, for the medical school, for companies—you name it— over the past five years, we've only had one failure [where] the crowd did not show up or did not work on the problem.† In all the other circumstances, we either met or vastly exceeded the internal solutions that existed.

This is a pretty unbelievable finding, isn't it? After all, companies and organizations like the National Institutes of Health and Beth

---

* As the authors explain, "The remaining error corresponds to sequences that cannot be correctly annotated." Karim Lakhani et al., "Prize-Based Contests Can Provide Solutions to Computational Biology Problems," *Nature Biotechnology* 31, no. 2 (2013): 108–11, http://www.nature.com/nbt/journal/v31/n2/full/nbt.2495.html.

† Lakhani believes that this failure happened because the organizers of the challenge either didn't specify the problem clearly enough or didn't offer sufficient rewards.

Israel spend a great deal of time, money, and effort building up their innovation and problem-solving resources: R&D labs, scientific and technical staff, engineering departments, and so on. These resources, in fact, are really at the core of the core. So why is it so easy for the crowd to outperform them at exactly the kinds of problems these resources were marshaled to tackle?

Is it that the experts of the core actually aren't that good? After all, we presented plenty of evidence in Chapter 2 that domain experts, like all humans, suffer from a range of biases that degrade the quality of their work. It could be that as people become more prominent and senior in their fields, these blind spots—such as the well-documented biases toward overconfidence and confirmation (that is, only really considering information that supports what you were already thinking)—become stronger and thus lead to worse outcomes.

It could even be that many "experts" actually aren't expert at all—that they've been kidding themselves and the rest of us about their abilities and the quality of their work. In today's complex, fast-changing, technologically sophisticated world, it can be quite hard to distinguish who actually knows what they're talking about.

There are definitely some less-than-expert established experts out there, but we don't think they're a big part of the reason that so often the crowd is so much better than the core. We're confident that the great majority of the scientists, engineers, technicians, and others working inside organizations today are actually qualified for their jobs and interested in doing them well. So why does the crowd beat them almost all the time?

Massive Mismatch

Organizations have a lot of virtues, but they often get in their own way; they do things that are counterproductive and that worsen their performance in innovation, R&D, and virtually every other area.

Organizational dysfunctions are real things—not only the subjects of countless *Dilbert* cartoons—and they do keep the core from working as well as it could.

The bigger reason, though, is more nuanced than mere dysfunction: the core is often mismatched for the kinds of challenges and opportunities it faces, while the crowd, because it's so big, almost never is. But why is the core so frequently misaligned and mismatched? Isn't the whole point of setting up an R&D lab or engineering department to bring together exactly the resources needed for the work at hand, and ahead? It's not like genetics labs hire a bunch of metallurgists by mistake and then are continually surprised when the team can't unravel the mysteries of DNA. Why the frequent misalignment?

A few things appear to be going on. One is that important new knowledge is being created constantly in almost all disciplines, and that knowledge can be slow to enter the core. The human genome, for example, was completely sequenced in 2003—an accomplishment with huge implications for medicine, biotechnology, pharmaceuticals, and other industries. As sequencing technology has spread while declining exponentially in cost,* farming, animal husbandry, and other sectors have also been affected. If the innovators, researchers, and problem solvers working within the core of organizations in all these fields have not worked hard to keep their skills up to date, the crowd—especially its younger and more recently educated members—will easily be able to beat them. Cutting-edge gene-editing tools, for example, are completely different from what they

---

* The estimated cost for generating that initial human genome sequence was $500 million or higher in 2000. The cost to generate a high-quality "draft" whole human genome sequence in mid-2015 was just above $4,000, and by late 2015 that figure had fallen below $1,500. National Human Genome Research Institute, "The Cost of Sequencing a Human Genome," last modified July 6, 2016, https://www.genome .gov/sequencingcosts.

were just five years ago. This is because of the development in 2012 of CRISPR, a tool kit derived from bacteria like *Streptococcus* that allows for unprecedented precision in finding, cutting out, and replacing any desired segment on the very long double helix of the DNA molecule.

We've also seen fast recent changes in artificial intelligence and machine learning (as we discussed in Chapter 3), energy production (thanks to both fracking of oil and gas and very steep declines in the cost of solar power*), and many other fields. When such rapid progress is occurring, the knowledge of the core in organizations within these industries can easily become out of date. Somewhere out there in the crowd, meanwhile, are, in all likelihood, at least some of the people who help come up with the latest advances, or their students, and thus are quite familiar with them. The core can become stale, in short, while the crowd really can't.

Marginal Utility

The other reason that the crowd often beats the core is probably more important. It's that many problems, opportunities, and projects, if not most, benefit from being exposed to different perspectives—to people and teams, in other words, with multiple dissimilar backgrounds, educations, problem-solving approaches, intellectual and technical tool kits, genders, and so on. This is absolutely the definition of the crowd, and it's very hard, probably even impossible, to replicate within the core. The R&D lab within a pharmaceutical company, for example, is unlikely to keep a couple of astrophysicists or cryptographers on the payroll on the off chance that they'll be exactly what's needed to crack a tough problem. This is completely rational as a business decision, but if the work remains within the

---

* Ramez Naam has shown that every doubling of solar capacity installed has been associated with about a 16% decline in costs. Ramez Naam, "How Cheap Can Solar Get? Very Cheap Indeed," *Ramez Naam* (blog), August 10, 2015, http://rameznaam .com/2015/08/10/how-cheap-can-solar-get-very-cheap-indeed.

core at this company, no astrophysicist or cryptographer will be able to help with it.

Shutting out potentially useful input from unlikely-seeming sources is a shame, because very often it's knowledge and expertise from an apparently faraway discipline that's needed. As the open-source software advocate Eric Raymond puts it, "Given enough eye-balls, all bugs are shallow." All problems get easier to solve, in other words, as both the volume and diversity of potential solvers go up. The genome-sequencing competition demonstrated this: of all the solutions submitted that were both faster and more accurate than the benchmarks, none came from computational biologists. Again, this superior performance from outsiders does not appear to be unusual. When Lakhani and Lars Bo Jeppesen studied 166 scientific chal-lenges posted on InnoCentive, another online clearinghouse, they found that the ones most likely to be successfully solved were those that attracted "marginal" eyeballs—people who were technically or socially "far away" from the organization that posted the challenge.[*]

The crowd is so valuable, in large part, because it's massively mar-ginal: it contains huge numbers of people who are some combination of smart, well trained, experienced, tenacious and motivated, and quite far away[†]—geographically, intellectually, and/or socially—from any organization's core. As interconnected computing power has spread around the world and useful platforms have been built on top of it, the crowd has become a demonstrably viable and valuable resource.

---

[*] We cited this study in our last book, and we're citing it again here because the point is fundamental.

[†] The importance of distant, or "weak," connections has been emphasized in several papers in the sociology literature, including the widely cited classic Mark S. Gran-ovetter, "The Strength of Weak Ties," *American Journal of Sociology* 78, no. 6 (1973): 1360–80; and the more recent Sinan Aral and Marshall Van Alstyne, "The Diversity-Bandwidth Trade-off 1," *American Journal of Sociology* 117, no. 1 (2011): 90–171.

The Core Wakes Up to the Crowd

Smart organizations are figuring out how to take advantage of the crowd to get their problems solved, and for many other purposes. This work is still in its early stages, but we've already seen many intriguing ways for the core and the crowd to come together.

Getting work done. As we've seen with Wikipedia and Linux, the crowd can come together to build things of great value, especially if a set of principles like openness and noncredentialism is followed. Some organizations are putting these principles into practice in order to offer what might be called crowd construction as a service to companies. One of the earliest examples was Amazon's Mechanical Turk, which started as an internal effort to find and eliminate duplicate product pages and was released for outside use in November 2005. Today, the crowd of "Turkers" is used for a wide variety of tasks, such as transcribing text from business cards into a spreadsheet, answering surveys for psychology research, and labeling images for input into AI programs. Refinements to the basic Mechanical Turk platform include find-fix-verify, a "programming design pattern" developed by MIT's Michael Bernstein and colleagues that lets Turkers self-select into either doing a task or spotting and fixing errors.

Topcoder, the company that ran the white blood cell genome-sequencing competition described at the start of this chapter, takes a similar approach. It runs competitions in order to find programming talent around the world, then acts as an intermediary and integrator between this talent and companies that want to outsource a large application development or systems integration project. The members of Topcoder's global community include not only programmers, but also people who identify as designers, students, data scientists, and physicists. Topcoder offers this crowd a series of corporate projects, lets them self-select into teams and into roles, stitches all their work together, and monitors quality. It uses monetary and competitive rewards, along with a bit of oversight, to create Linux-like efforts for its clients. Kaggle does the same thing for data science competitions.

Finding the right resource. Sometimes you don't want to bring together an entire crowd; you simply want to find, as quickly and efficiently as possible, the right person or team to help with something. The chances of finding a good fit increase with the number of people who see the request, which explains why platforms for task matching have become so popular. These include 99designs and Behance for graphic design and other creative work, Upwork for information technology and customer service tasks, Care.com for personal services, and TaskRabbit for a wide variety of odd jobs, like officiating at a wedding, delivering ice cream cake to someone's grandfather, or waiting in line at the Apple Store ahead of a new iPhone release. The insight common to these businesses is that the web and the smartphone brought unprecedented opportunities to better match supply and demand for business services, as we highlighted in this book's section on bringing together products and platforms (Part 2), and that one way to do this was to put a request in front of as many eyeballs as possible.

Conducting market research. As we described in Chapter 1, General Electric, one of the largest, oldest, and most successful industrial companies in the world, turned to the crowd to assess consumer demand for its nugget ice maker. It was not the first large organization to realize that crowd platforms might provide valuable signals about the level of interest and enthusiasm for some types of offerings, particularly those likely to appeal to a niche audience. The TV show *Veronica Mars*, for example, which was about a teenage detective played by Kristen Bell, had a devoted but relatively small following when it aired between 2004 and 2007. Its fans didn't go away when the show ended. They continued to talk about it online and at conventions.

This continued interest intrigued the movie studio Warner Brothers, Bell, and the show's creator, Rob Thomas. They wondered whether it meant that there would be sufficient demand for a *Veronica Mars* movie, even one that came out several years after the show had last aired. To find out, they launched a campaign on the popular crowdfunding site Kickstarter. The campaign included a short trailer for the proposed movie, videos from Bell and Thomas, and the offer of rewards for different levels of support.* The campaign's stated goal was to raise $2 million. It actually took in that amount within the first twelve hours and went on to generate $5.7 million in total. The movie premiered on March 14, 2014, both in theaters and on video on-demand services. It received generally positive reviews and was judged a financial success.

Marc Andreessen, who started his career as the main programmer of the most successful early web browser and has since become a prominent venture capitalist, thinks crowdfunding could become one of the main ways that new offerings are developed. He said to us, "One could argue that the way that products and services—including entertainment media, including shoes and food and everything—the way that everything comes to market for the last 2,000 years has been backwards. Which is that it's been supply driven. But by the time you discover whether the market likes it or not, you've already put a lot of money into it. Crowdfunding reverses the model. You don't come to market with something unless people have prebought it. Which also provides prefunding for it. . . . Crowdfunding is a way to preassemble financial capital against something with social capital. You try to

---

* For $350 a cast member would record an outgoing voicemail message for you, $1,000 got you two red-carpet tickets for the premiere, you could name a character in the movie for $6,500, and $10,000 got you a walk-on part.

create a movement around something, and you try to get people in advance to buy something."

In early 2016, Indiegogo introduced a dedicated section of its site and a set of tools for "Enterprise Crowdfunding," offering large companies the promise of receiving "real-time customer feedback before investing in manufacturing" and turning "research from a cost into an opportunity for pre-sales and customer acquisition."

Acquiring new customers. In addition to platforms for crowdfunding, crowd*lending* platforms have appeared and become popular in recent years. Many of these, if not most, were originally intended as peer-to-peer services, matching individuals looking to invest with those who needed a personal or business loan but were unable or unwilling to get one from a traditional lender. Over time, however, many institutional investors (including some of the world's largest hedge funds) realized that there were opportunities within these large pools of loan seekers. Default rates were at least somewhat predictable and interest rates were competitive, which meant that risk/reward profiles were often attractive. And as the platforms grew, they generated a lot of these good opportunities, enough to be attractive to big investors. In 2014, well over half of the total loan volume on both Prosper and Lending Club, two of the largest platforms in the United States, came from institutional investors, who often used specialized software to comb through available opportunities. In reality, it turned out, peer-to-peer lending often became something much less novel: personal and small business loans offered by big, established lenders to customers identified in a new way.

But it's not just large hedge funds that are finding new customers thanks to crowd-centric new businesses; it's also popular voices that emerge from the crowd itself. Marc Andreessen told us about the startup Teespring, founded in 2011 by Walter Williams and Evan Stites-Clayton. As Andreessen explained to us,

Teespring is the modern method to convert social capital into financial capital. It's one of these things where it first will strike you as absurd, and then if you swallow the red pill, you'll realize what's happening.* It's a way for a Facebook group or a YouTube star or Instagram star to be able to sell T-shirts. At first you're like, whatever, merchandise—big deal. But it actually turns out that what happens is that you have these Facebook groups or YouTube stars that have a million followers . . . [and] social capital is real. Your followers or your fans are people who value what you do, and they don't have a way to pay you. They love you and they want to support you. . . . Now what we would argue is that T-shirts are just the beginning. It could just be anything; it just has to be something. It's memorabilia, and you care about it and you're passionate and you're indicating something about yourself. . . . It's like a totem; it's a psychological anchor into something that you care about.

Acquiring innovation. It was thought for a long time that large, established companies would be the biggest innovators. They're the ones, after all, with the resources to afford large labs and R&D staff. The great Austrian economist Joseph Schumpeter challenged this view. He maintained that smaller, younger, more entrepreneurial firms—companies that had no interest in maintaining the status quo—were more likely to come up with truly novel goods and services. As he put it, "In general it is not the owner of stage coaches who builds railways." And indeed, Clay Christensen's landmark work on disruptive innovations showed that disruptions rarely came from

---

* Andreessen was referring to the popular 1999 science fiction film *The Matrix*. In it, the main character is offered a choice between a blue pill, which will return him to the comfortable illusion in which he has, until then, been living, and a red pill, which will enable him to see things as they really are.

successful industry incumbents and, in fact, often took them very much by surprise.

Another powerful line of research on innovation emerged from the work of our MIT colleague Eric von Hippel, who highlighted the large role that "lead users" play in coming up with innovations in many domains. These are users of existing products and services who come to find them deficient and start not only envisioning improvements, but building and using them. Von Hippel has documented extensively user innovation in areas ranging from surgical instruments to kitesurfing equipment, and we also see an explosion of examples in the modern high-tech industries. Many of the sector's prominent companies, it turns out, were founded by people frustrated with the status quo who said to themselves, "There *must* be a better way," and set to work.

The errand-running service TaskRabbit, for example, was conceived by Leah Busque, a then twenty-eight-year-old IBM engineer living in Massachusetts. On a wintry night in 2008, she needed food for her dog (a yellow lab named Kobe) and thought, "Wouldn't it be nice if there were a place online you could go. . . . A site where you could name the price you were willing to pay for any task. There had to be someone in my neighborhood who was willing to get that dog food for what I was willing to pay."

Many of today's technology giants have apparently heeded the lessons of Schumpeter, Christensen, and von Hippel, and constantly scan the crowd for innovations that could disrupt them. And when they find one, the instinct is often not to smash it or put it out of business, but instead to buy it and thus internalize the innovation. Between 2011 and 2016, Apple acquired 70 companies, Facebook more than 50, and Google nearly 200.

Often in these cases, the acquirer already had a competing offering. Facebook, for example, included both messaging and photo sharing when the company bought WhatsApp and Instagram. It would have been particularly easy in both cases for the incumbent to convince itself that the upstart posed no risk. But instead, some signal from the crowd—something about how the innovation was different and how quickly it was being adopted—convinced leaders at the larger, older firm to acquire what the lead users or other innovators had come up with. This is often expensive; Facebook paid $1 billion for Instagram and more than $20 billion for WhatsApp. But it's a lot cheaper than being disrupted.

Using the Crowd to Change the Trade of Trading

We predict that in the coming years, we'll see a lot of incumbent businesses, many of them quite successful, challenged by crowd-based rivals. An early example of such a challenge is visible in the arcane and highly geeky arena of automated investing.

Throughout the long human history of investing in assets— company stocks, government bonds, precious metals and other commodities, real estate, and so on—virtually all decisions about what to buy have been made by humans. Massive amounts of technology have been deployed to automate the work of actually buying the assets once the decisions have been made (and then keeping track of them over time), but these decisions were almost always made by minds, not machines.

This started to change in the 1980s when pioneers like Jim Simons (one of the most accomplished mathematicians of his generation) and David Shaw (a computer scientist) founded, respectively, Renaissance Technologies and D. E. Shaw to use machines to make investment decisions. These companies sifted through large amounts of data, built and tested quantitative models of how assets' prices behaved under different conditions, and worked to substitute code and math for individual judgment about what and when to buy.

The best of these "quant" firms built up spectacular track records.

D. E. Shaw had over $40 billion under management in October 2016, and its Composite Fund generated 12% annualized returns in the decade leading up to 2011. Two Sigma, a firm run by a former artificial intelligence academic and a mathematics Olympian, manages the $6 billion Compass Fund, which logged an annualized return of 15% over a decade. Almost every fund's returns are dwarfed by those of the Medallion Fund, which exists within Renaissance and is open almost exclusively to its employees. It averaged a greater than 70% annual return (before fees) for more than twenty years starting in the mid-1990s. After generating lifetime profits of more than $55 billion, it was described on the Bloomberg Markets website as "perhaps the world's greatest moneymaking machine."

John Fawcett, a programmer and entrepreneur who had worked within financial services, was impressed by the quants' performance but concerned that there weren't enough of them working within the core of the investment industry. Fawcett estimated that there was a worldwide total of 3,000–5,000 professional quantitative investors by 2010. As he told us, "That seemed way too low to me. It bothered me that [more investors] were not getting access to enough of what I considered state-of-the art investment practice. It's like, 'What field is there where you would bet on humans operating alone versus a human plus a machine?' Every single time, you're going to want the more automated version."

Fawcett became obsessed with the idea of opening up quantitative investing to the crowd, and he founded Quantopian with Jean Bredeche in 2011 to make it happen. The company faced the daunting task of building a technology platform for quants comparable to the ones within the industry's top companies. Such a platform had to be able to let investors upload their algorithms, then quickly test them under different market conditions—booms and recessions, periods of high and low interest rates, and so on. One way to do this is to "back-test" the algorithms with historical data. Fawcett and his colleagues worked to build a backtester as robust as those available within large institutional investors.

The startup also had to let investors accurately assess the market impact of their trades—the fact that if they bought or sold a large amount of an asset, that action would itself change the asset's price. Assessing market impact is a tricky exercise in estimation, one that consumed a lot of time at Quantopian. The company's platform also, of course, had to handle automatic execution of the trades generated by algorithms, record keeping, compliance with relevant regulations, and so on.

Fawcett knew that if Quantopian succeeded at building a robust platform, and at drawing prospective "algo traders" to it, the company would have an important advantage: it could use lots of the good ideas that its crowd generated, not just the top one. Many crowdsourcing efforts are attempts to find a single solution: the best design for a nugget ice maker, or the best algorithm for sequencing the genomes of white blood cells. The second or third best entries in these competitions might be almost as good as the winner, but this fact is often not important to the competition's host.

Investment algorithms, however, are very different. As long as the top ones differ from each other—in other words, they're not just essentially replications of the best performer—they can be productively combined to deliver higher overall returns to investors than could be achieved from using only one algorithm, no matter how good it was. This insight—about the importance of putting together an optimal portfolio of investments—was significant enough to merit a Nobel Prize in economics for Henry Markowitz, its originator. It was also ideally suited for a crowd-based environment that could generate lots of well-performing but dissimilar quantitative investment ideas. As Fawcett told us, "The way I frame the problem for

Quantopian is, 'How do we maximize the probability that we're going to discover lots of strategies that have low correlation and good structure?' "*

One way to do this is to have lots of people show up and suggest quantitative investment strategies. By the middle of 2016, Quantopian had attracted to its platform more than 100,000 prospective algo traders from 180 countries, and over 400,000 algorithms. Who are these traders? According to Fawcett, "The thing they often have in common is that they've got a degree or an advanced degree or years in a profession where they know how to build models. They're an astrophysicist, or a computational fluid dynamicist. By and large, they're new to finance; they might work in ad tech, or oil and gas. We have students and professionals. I think the age range is undergraduates to . . . a pair of brothers who are retirees that build stuff together that were very successful scientists in their first career."

This population is largely male, and one of Quantopian's priorities is to attract more female participants because, as Fawcett told us, "We're trying to get the community to produce diverse strategies, and there's loads of studies that men and women perceive risk differently. They think about investment very, very differently. So it would be amazing [to have more women in our community]. . . . You will outperform because the thing that the market will pay for is a return stream that looks different from all the other return streams."

How is Quantopian's crowd doing against the core of professional investors? By the end of 2016, it had hosted nineteen contests. Four of them were won by professional quants, and one by an investment professional who was not an algorithmic trader. The other fourteen

---

* For Quantopian, an investment algorithm has "good structure" if it does not rely too heavily on one type of asset, is not excessively leveraged (in other words, reliant on debt), and is able to generate good returns under a wide range of market conditions.

winners were complete outsiders. The real test of insiders versus outsiders, and of the concept of crowdsourced algorithmic investment, will come in 2017, when the company plans to offer to qualified investors its own quantitative investment fund. Its performance compared to that of other hedge funds, especially quant funds, will help us understand where the true experts are in this domain, and how powerful the crowd can be.

At least one stalwart of the investment community's core believes enough in Quantopian to trust it with his own money. In July of 2016, Steven Cohen, one of the best-known hedge fund managers of all time, announced that he was making a venture investment in Quantopian and also giving it $250 million from his family office to invest in its crowdsourced portfolio of quant algorithms. Matthew Granade, Cohen's head of research and venture investment, said that "the scarce resource in quantitative investing is talent, [and] Quantopian has demonstrated an innovative approach to finding that talent."

We find Quantopian fascinating because it illustrates all three of the technology trends that are reshaping the business world. It's bringing together minds and machines in fresh ways to rethink how investment decisions are made, and substituting data and code for human experience, judgment, and intuition. It's also building a platform for quantitative investment rather than introducing a specific product (such as a backtester). This platform is open and noncredentialist, aims to take advantage of network effects (the more good investment algorithms it holds, the more capital it will attract; the more capital it holds, the more algo traders it will attract), and to provide a smooth interface and experience to its traders. And it's bringing together an online crowd to challenge the core and its experts in a large and critically important industry.

How will this all work out? We can't wait to see.

Voice of the World

The examples we've presented in this chapter might give the impression that the crowd today exists largely to serve the needs of the core, or to do battle with it. But this is not the case; very often, the crowd's work simply helps the crowd's members. The peer-to-peer, distributed, often not-for-profit communities that Robert Wright observed and celebrated in his 1993 "Voice of America" essay are alive and well.

The newsgroups of the pre-web Usenet system have evolved into thousands upon thousands of online user groups, community forums, message boards, and other spaces where people can find information supplied by their peers and can ask and answer questions. These cover every conceivable topic, from makeup to car repair to analyzing what happened on the last episode of a hit TV show.

As fans of innovation, we're particularly excited about the "maker movement," a broad term for the tinkerers, do-it-yourselfers, spare-time fabricators, engineers, and scientists who help each other out online. They share step-by-step instructions, recipes, blueprints, schematics for electronic circuits, files for generating 3D-printed parts, and troubleshooting tips for an astonishing range of products—everything from autonomous go-carts to homemade Geiger counters.

The maker movement keeps expanding. It's now possible to buy inexpensive kits and materials for synthetic biology, or "the design and construction of novel artificial biological pathways, organisms, or devices, or the redesign of existing ones," as the synthetic biology project defines it. Around the world, members of the "DIY bio" movement create their own useful strings of the amino acids denoted G, C, T, and A that carry the code of life, then share their recipes over the net. The biohacking movement got a huge boost with the 2012 discovery of the CRISPR-Cas9 gene-editing tool, which gave researchers unprecedented precision in modifying the DNA molecule.

Former NASA scientist Josiah Zayner wanted this technology to be as broadly available as possible. In 2015 he launched an Indiegogo campaign to develop a "DIY Bacterial Gene Engineering CRISPR Kit." The campaign attracted over $70,000 in support (which was 333% of its goal) and led to a $140 kit available for purchase from the biohacking collective The ODIN. Does it work? In June 2016 the consumer electronics and gear blog *Engadget* reported, "I played God with The Odin's DIY CRISPR Kit. And lo, it was glorious."

Even the ancient human activity of farming is being remade by makers. Caleb Harper of the MIT Media Lab has developed "food computers," or enclosed environments of various sizes for growing crops. The energy, water, and mineral use of each computer can be precisely monitored and controlled, as can parameters including humidity, temperature, and levels of carbon dioxide and dissolved oxygen. Growers can experiment with different "climate recipes" to produce characteristics they want in their crops, share the recipes they come up with, and work to improve others' recipes. The goal of Harper's Open Agriculture Initiative is to allow climate recipe experimentation and innovation at scales ranging from the desktop-sized personal food computer to warehouse-sized spaces.

Hand, Made

Medical devices sound like one product category that we might *not* want to entrust to the crowd. Don't these need to come from the core of the health care system, or at least be tested and approved by it, in order to ensure safety and quality?

Not always, it turns out, and artificial hands provide a great illustration of how a crowd of makers can assemble. Their work illustrates the potential benefits when such a self-organizing crowd dives in on a problem and engages in what the technology scholar Adam Thierer calls "permissionless innovation."

In April of 2011, South African carpenter Richard Van As lost control of a table saw and cut off two fingers of his right hand. The prostheses available at the time cost thousands of dollars, so Van As started looking around for cheaper alternatives. He came across a video uploaded to YouTube earlier that year by Ivan Owen, a "mechanical special effects artist" who had built a giant metal extension of his own hand as part of a costume for a "steampunk" convention.*

Although separated by more than 10,000 miles, Van As and Owen collaborated via e-mail and Skype to build a functional prosthetic finger. Their work was greatly accelerated when the 3D printer company MakerBot donated two of its desktop Replicator 2 machines to the effort. These enabled the makers to iterate and generate prototypes much more quickly, and eventually to come up with working mechanical digits for Van As.

They uploaded a video of their creation to YouTube, where it was seen by Yolandi Dippenaar, a South African woman whose son Liam, then five, had been born without fingers on his right hand. The Dippenaars asked for help, which Owen and Van As were happy to provide. While doing online research on possible solutions, they came across the "Corporal Coles hand," an amazing device built in the middle of the nineteenth century in Adelaide, Australia, by the dental surgeon Robert Norman.

Corporal John Coles had lost all four fingers on his right hand in a parade-ground accident involving a cannon. Norman made a prosthetic for him out of whalebone and catgut that not only looked much like a hand, but also operated like one in some ways. The fingers could flex, and "Corporal Coles could pick up a button or a sixpence with pleasing facility," as a contemporary description of the hand put it. Norman accomplished this impressive feat by precisely carving finger segments out of whalebone, snapping them together,

---

* Steampunk is a genre of science fiction that imagines, among other things, Victorian-era mechanical computers powered by steam. Many of its fans enjoy dressing up.

and connecting them with an inner system of pulleys and catgut string controlled by a ring worn on Coles's thumb.

Norman's work was available to inspire later innovators because a precise description of it existed in the collection of the National Library of Australia, and because the library had digitized the description and made it available via the web. When Owen and Van As came across the Corporal Coles hand during their online searches, they realized its brilliance. They soon built their own version of it, called "Robohand," for Liam. The two makers also realized that, thanks to 3D printers and powerful design software, endless variants of the hand could be designed and built both quickly and cheaply. Instead of filing for patents, they uploaded the plans for Robohand's parts to Thingiverse, a site where the crowd shares 3D printing files.

Since then, more than 1,800 plastic, 3D-printed hands have been created, assembled, and delivered to people in over forty-five countries.[*] This work is highly decentralized; its main points of coordination are a website and Google document that any interested person can join and edit. As economist Robert Graboyes points out, this crowd's creations are both cheap and innovative:

> The cost of a workable prosthetic plunged overnight by more than 99 percent. 3D-printed models weren't the same as $5,000 models, but they were functional and so inexpensive to build that makers could give them to users free-of-charge.
>
> Working together, users and makers modified designs. The original boxy-looking hand became sleeker. Time-consuming nuts and bolts gave way to snap-on joints, and the total cost dropped

---

[*] This is a conservative estimate, including only the prostheses built and delivered through the e-NABLE online community. According to e-NABLE's Jennifer Owen, "Anecdotal reports indicate that an equivalent number have been produced outside of our community's documented process." Enabling the Future, "Media FAQ," accessed February 8, 2017, http://enablingthefuture.org/faqs/media-faq.

to as little as $35 in materials for some designs. . . . Users and makers realized that prosthetics need not replicate the human hand. One father, wanting his son to have better grip, built a hand with two thumbs—one on each end. His son, fortuitously named Luke, became "Cool Hand Luke." Others built hands custom-designed for specific purposes—bike-riding, rock-climbing, trumpet-playing.

As all these examples show, the online crowd is growing and thriving. It interacts in many ways with the core and is facilitated by it. We think this trend is both healthy and productive, and not at all a betrayal of the original spirit of the Internet. As better devices and networks continue to bring the net to more and more people around the world, the crowd will only become bigger, smarter, and more multivoiced.

We're excited about future developments in artificial intelligence, as they change the boundaries between mind and machine, but we're probably even more excited at the prospect of bringing billions more human intelligences into the globally connected community. They can give each other a hand.

Chapter Summary

▶ Over and over again, the recognized experts of the core see their performance beaten by uncredentialed and conventionally inexperienced members of the crowd.

▶ One reason for the success of the crowd is that the core is often mismatched for the problems it's most interested in.

▶ The mismatch of the core happens because the knowledge necessary to most effectively address a problem often comes from a domain that's "far away" from that of the problem itself. It's very hard to predict where the relevant knowledge for solving a problem actually resides.

▶ There are many ways for the core to tap into the crowd's accumulated knowledge and expertise; the core and the crowd do not have to remain separate.

▶ The crowd can now accomplish a lot without ever needing much of a core. Technology helps people find knowledge, interact productively, and build things together with only minimal centralization.

▶ Established companies are finding novel ways to work with the crowd. At the same time, crowd-based startups are now challenging many successful incumbent companies at their core activities.

Questions

1. How and how often do you look outside your group of identified internal and external experts for help with your challenges and opportunities?

2. What experiments could you run to see whether you can put the crowd to work for your organization? How would you judge the results of such experiments?

3. In the past five to ten years, how much have you changed your methods for acquiring new customers and assessing demand and willingness to pay for new products you're considering?

4. In the past five to ten years, have you expanded the number of people that you or your organization regularly interacts with?

5. If the crowd comes up with a better idea, how will you bring it into your core?

CHAPTER 12

THE DREAM OF DECENTRALIZING ALL THE THINGS

The freedom of all is essential to my freedom.

— *Mikhail Bakunin, 1871*

WE'VE KNOWN FOR A WHILE THAT DECEASED ECONOMISTS can greatly influence the world. We recently learned that anonymous hackers can too.

John Maynard Keynes, himself an economist of immense influence, observed in his 1936 masterpiece *The General Theory of Employment, Interest, and Money* that "practical men, who believe themselves to be quite exempt from any intellectual influence, are usually the slaves of some defunct economist. Madmen in authority, who hear voices in the air, are distilling their frenzy from some academic scribbler of a few years back. I am sure that the power of vested interests is vastly exaggerated compared with the gradual encroachment of ideas."

"Indeed," Keynes wrote, "the world is ruled by little else."

Keynes saw that the ideas of prominent "worldly philosophers"*

---

* Robert Heilbroner coined this label for economists in his 1953 book *The Worldly Philosophers: The Lives, Times and Ideas of the Great Economic Thinkers.*

like Adam Smith, Karl Marx, David Ricardo, Friedrich Hayek, and Joseph Schumpeter reach far outside the discipline of economics. They change how people think about fairness and justice, how companies organize themselves and innovate, how governments approach taxation and trade, and so on. Economists think about exchange, a fundamental and universal human activity, so their biggest ideas on the subject have had a huge impact.

Bitcoin: The Pseudonymous Revolution

Satoshi Nakamoto's ideas have also had a huge impact, even though nobody knows who he or she is.* On October 31, 2008, a person or group going by that name posted online a short paper titled "Bitcoin: A Peer-to-Peer Electronic Cash System." It addressed a straightforward question: Why do online payments have to involve banks, credit card companies, and other financial intermediaries? Why can't they be like cash payments in the physical world? Cash transactions have two attractive properties: there are no fees associated with them, and they preserve anonymity; you are usually not asked for your ID when you pay cash. Physical cash is also durable and reusable; it keeps circulating throughout our economy, being used to pay for things over and over.

Governments have not yet shown much willingness to create digi-

---

* Beginning in 2008, Nakamoto shared a vision with the world via pseudonymous e-mails, blog posts, and elements of the source code needed to build the Bitcoin system. Nakamoto's final public communications were in late 2010. Since then there have been a number of unsuccessful attempts to identify Nakamoto. One thing that is known about the Bitcoin creator is that she or he holds almost a million BTCs (the Bitcoin trading acronym) worth over $600 million by September 2016 and equivalent to almost 7% of all the Bitcoins in circulation.

tal dollars, euros, yen, renminbi, and so on.* So Nakamoto proposed, with considerable ambition, to create an entirely new and completely independent digital currency, called Bitcoin. Because it relied heavily on many of the same algorithms and mathematics as cryptography (the art and science of making and breaking codes), Bitcoin came to be known as a "cryptocurrency." American dollars, Japanese yen, Turkish lira, Nigerian naira, and all the other money issued by nations around the world, meanwhile, are called "fiat currencies" because they exist by government fiat, or order; governments simply declare them to be legal tender.†

Existing combinations of "crypto" code and math helped Nakamoto solve the tough problem of identifying who owned Bitcoins as they got used over time and all over the web to pay for things. Participants would use their digital signatures during transactions to sign over the right quantity of Bitcoins from the buyer to the seller. Digital signatures have been around for a while and are known to work well. They are easy for anyone to generate and verify, very hard to forge, and "pseudonymous": a person could generate digital signatures without revealing their true identity. As Bitcoin transactions happened, Nakamoto proposed, they would all be recorded in a ledger that logged exactly which Bitcoins were spent and the pseudonymous identity of both the buyer and the seller, as verified by their signatures.

---

* Some national governments have begun looking into digital cash. The Bank of England, for example, has announced that it is undertaking "a multi-year research programme looking to assess the main economic, technology and regulatory impacts of introducing central bank-issued digital currency." Bank of England, "Digital Currencies," accessed February 8, 2017, http://www.bankofengland.co.uk/banknotes/Pages/digitalcurrencies/default.aspx.

† From 1873 to 1971, US dollars were convertible to a fixed quantity of gold. The US "gold standard" ended with a series of economic measures, introduced by President Richard Nixon, that converted dollars to a fiat currency.

How Do We Get This Information to Stop . . . Behaving like Information?

A universal, easily consultable ledger was essential for the Bitcoin system in order to deal with the "double spend problem." This problem arises because Bitcoins are purely and only pieces of information, yet it's essential that they not all follow the free, perfect, and instant economics of information goods that we discussed in Chapter 6. If Bitcoins could be freely, perfectly, and instantly copied, forgery would be rampant. Bad actors, protected by their pseudonyms, would spend the same coins over and over until they were caught, merchants would get cheated, trust would evaporate, and the system would very quickly collapse.

A trusted, universally accessible online ledger would solve the double spend problem by enabling merchants (or anyone else) to verify that a prospective buyer actually has the Bitcoins they say they do, and that they haven't been already spent anywhere else.

But who should be responsible for creating, maintaining, and ensuring the integrity of this ledger? It can't be a bank or credit card company, or combination of them, because the whole point of the system proposed by Nakamoto is that it wouldn't rely at all on existing financial institutions. Or on governments: the Bitcoin system needed to operate entirely independent of them. In fact, it had to operate in a completely decentralized way—unreliant on any core set of organizations or institutions and able to survive and thrive no matter how its participants change over time. But how on Earth could this philosophy of radical and permanent decentralization ever be reconciled with the absolute need for a single, permanent, universally trusted ledger?

By another ingenious combination of math and programming, combined with a healthy dose of self-interest. Nakamoto proposed an online system that would work as follows:

1. As each transaction between buyers and sellers happens, it is broadcast throughout the system.

2. Specialized computers called "nodes" periodically collect all the transactions and verify that they're legitimate by checking that the Bitcoins involved weren't previously spent elsewhere. The set of good transactions over a period of time is called a "block."

3. At the same time that they're doing this work on transactions, the nodes are also involved in a competition with each other, consisting of trying to find a short numeric summary, called a "hash," of the current block. The first node to find a hash of the right form wins the competition. Finding the right hash is a trial-and-error process; it takes a lot of computational work and so is called "proof of work." The more computing power a node has, the more likely it is to be the first to complete this task. The proof of work is included in the block in such a way that in order to change the block's contents, another node would have to redo all of the work.

4. The winning node—the first one to successfully complete the proof of work—broadcasts its just-finished block throughout the system. As its reward, it is allowed to create and keep for itself a predetermined number of Bitcoins.[*] The creation of these Bitcoins is itself recorded in the block.

---

* The original reward was set at 50 Bitcoins. It fell to 25 in November 2012 and to 12.5 in June 2016. This process, known as "halving," happens every 210,000 blocks and is built into the Bitcoin software. There will be a maximum of sixty-four halvings, yielding a total 21 million Bitcoins, after which no more will be created (Jacob Donnelly, "What Is the 'Halving'? A Primer to Bitcoin's Big Mining Change," Coin-Desk, June 12, 2016, http://www.coindesk.com/making-sense-bitcoins-halving). All

5. The other nodes double-check this block, verifying that all the transactions it contains are legitimate, as is the proof of work. They have ample incentive to do this because if they find illegitimate transactions or an incorrectly done proof of work, the entire block is invalid, which means that its associated Bitcoins are still up for grabs.

6. Once nodes convince themselves that a block is correct and complete, they start putting together the next one and carrying out its proof of work, and the entire block creation process starts over again. Nakamoto designed the system so that a new block would be created and Bitcoins awarded about every ten minutes. Nakamoto noted that "the steady addition of a constant amount of new coins is analogous to gold miners expending resources to add gold to circulation." The analogy stuck, and the people and organizations that managed nodes around the world came to be known as Bitcoin "miners."

This Thing Might Actually Work

Many readers of Nakamoto's paper came to believe that the system he described could actually be built and would be valuable. The math and the programming seemed to work. More impressively, so did the incentives.

The miners could conduct their activities without coordination and entirely selfishly, motivated only by their desire for Bitcoins and

---

participants in Bitcoin therefore know both how and how much of the currency will be issued over time. The same is not true of dollars, euros, yen, or other currency issued by the world's governments, which reserve the right to simply print more money as they see fit. When they make the unwise decision to print too much of it, too quickly, the result is hyperinflation.

not at all by altruism or community spirit, and the system would still accomplish its goals and grow over time. Bitcoin participants would not need to coordinate with each other; they'd only need to broadcast their transactions and completed blocks. In fact, it would be better if the miners *didn't* coordinate with each other, because coordination could pretty easily and quickly turn into collusion: a group of miners getting together and, for example, altering the historical record to make all the Bitcoins belong to them.

Nakamoto's brilliant design offered two main defenses against such attacks. The first is the proof of work: the computationally intensive task of coming up with the right hash for each block. It gets exponentially harder with each new block, and the blocks are mathematically chained together so that attackers wouldn't just need to redo the proof of work for the block they were interested in; they would instead need to do it for every block in the chain—in other words, for every block ever created. Because the blocks are inextricably linked, the complete historical record of all transactions is called the "blockchain."

The fact that the proof of work keeps getting harder has another important effect. The amount of computing power needed to "take over" the entire Bitcoin system* keeps growing exponentially over time, and quickly becomes uneconomical. Many miners found it worthwhile to keep investing over time in specialized mining hardware in hopes of winning the block-by-block competition for Bitcoins. To take over the whole system, an attacker would have to outspend all the rest of them put together.

The second main defense against attacks on the system is that they'd be inherently self-defeating. If the people and organizations

---

* An entity could take over the Bitcoin system by having more than 50% of the system's total processing power, thus virtually always being able to complete the proof of work first and thereby to decide which transactions are valid.

interested in Bitcoin came to believe that the system had been taken over by bad actors, they would quickly lose interest in it and move on to other projects or payment methods. Bitcoins would then quickly lose value. So why would attackers spend all the money required to take over the entire blockchain, only to see the asset they had thereby acquired—a huge trove of Bitcoins—rendered worthless? It would make no economic sense, so the only attackers to worry about, it appeared, would be extremely well financed nihilists, or at least those with some more subtle, complex incentive for controlling the blockchain.* Nakamoto reasoned that there are not very many of these, or at least that they would be substantially outnumbered by Bitcoin participants who want to see their assets appreciate.

In short, the blueprint that Nakamoto's brief paper laid out looked workable; it was both technically feasible and economically sound. It also appeared in late 2008, a time when many people around the world were losing faith in the existing financial system, from mortgage companies to central banks themselves. The bankruptcies, bailouts, and other dislocations of the Great Recession convinced many that the global status quo was unfair, unsustainable, or both. The idea of a new currency independent of any and all governments appealed to many. So did the possibility of making money, of both the old and new varieties. Conditions were ripe for interesting things to happen. Many did.

▶ In May 2010 Laszlo Hanyecz, a programmer living in Jacksonville, Florida, posted a request on a Bitcoin forum to trade 10,000 Bitcoins in exchange for "a couple of pizzas." Four days later,

---

* The value of the Bitcoin might not collapse after a takeover. After all, fiat currency typically has value as long as the issuer, who can create more at will, is somewhat trusted.

eighteen-year-old Jeremy Sturdivant accepted the offer and purchased the food via the Papa John's website. This was the first known trade of Bitcoin for a physical product and gave the fledgling currency a value of about $0.003 per Bitcoin, since Sturdivant paid $30 for the pizza. If he had kept the Bitcoins that he received in exchange for his food delivery, they would have been worth over $8.3 million by mid-January of 2017.

▶ As Bitcoins gained in popularity, numerous marketplaces appeared to facilitate trading them. These exchanges enabled people to create orders to buy or sell Bitcoins for a certain price, usually denominated in fiat currencies like the US dollar or British pound. When the conditions of both the buyer and seller were met, the trade was executed. The largest and most infamous of these exchanges was Mt. Gox, a Tokyo-based firm that accounted for 80% of all Bitcoin trading at its peak. Mt. Gox was plagued with difficulties from the time it was founded, including at least one major hack that resulted in a loss of $8.75 million in 2011. Despite this cybertheft, Mt. Gox continued to gain momentum until February of 2014, when management uncovered a security flaw that had left it exposed for several years. Mt. Gox suspended trading, closed the website, and filed for bankruptcy after confirming that the exchange "had weaknesses" in its system and that "bitcoins vanished." At the time of the collapse, total losses were approximately $470 million in Bitcoins and $27 million in cash.

▶ When Bitcoin first emerged, the work of mining, although computationally intensive, could be done using open-source software and personal computers. But the proof of work required for successful mining becomes exponentially difficult with each successive block. The result has been a sharp rise in the scale of resources being deployed. By January 2015 the processing capability of the Bitcoin network was 13,000 times greater than the world's 500 most powerful supercomputers combined. In their search for cheap electricity, successful miners set up operations in, among many other places, Iceland, Washington State, and Inner Mongolia. Soon a market developed for specialized computer chips, ASICs (application-specific integrated circuits), optimized for Bitcoin mining.

▶ The saddest story of the Bitcoin era so far might be that of James Howells, a Welsh technology professional who began mining Bitcoins in 2009, when they were almost free to create but also had little or no value. He dismantled the computer he had used for mining after spilling a drink on it. The good news was that he kept its hard drive, which contained the only record of all his Bitcoins, in a drawer. The bad news is that he threw the drive away during a housecleaning in 2013. When he heard news stories about the price of Bitcoins later that year, he remembered his previous mining, realized what he had done, and went to the dump that received his trash. The manager told him that the hard drive would most likely be buried under several feet of refuse somewhere in an area the size of a football field. Even though the 7,500 Bitcoins on the hard drive were at that time worth about $7.5 million, Howells did not mount a search for it.

The miners and others who built the Bitcoin network were behaving just as Keynes had predicted, but with some fascinating twists. They weren't madmen, and most of them weren't in authority, but they were still "distilling their frenzy" not from some academic scribbler, but instead from a pseudonymous one: Satoshi Nakamoto.

The Ledger, Not the Currency:
Waking Up to the Blockchain's Potential

Throughout this time, most mainstream economists were skeptical, even dismissive, of Bitcoin's potential as a rival to the world's established currencies. Two of the main functions of any money, they pointed out, were a means of exchange (I give you these dollars or euros or yen and you give me that house or car or chicken dinner) and a store of value (my total net worth is X dollars, euros, or yen; with this amount of wealth I can buy so many houses, cars, or chicken dinners). For both of these functions, stability of the currency is critical. In order to guide their activities and plan their futures, people need to know that the purchasing power of their money will remain relatively constant, or at least that it will change at a predictable rate.

But the value of the Bitcoin, as expressed by its exchange rate against currencies like the dollar, fluctuated wildly, rising to a high of over $1,100 in November 2013 before plummeting 77% to less than $250 in January 2015 and then recovering to more than $830 two years later. This volatility made the digital currency interesting for risk-tolerant investors[*] but unsuitable as a mainstream means of exchange or store of value.

While the debate about Bitcoin's ability to ever be a true currency was unfolding, a small group of people began to make a different point: that the truly valuable innovation was not the new digital money, but instead the distributed ledger that it rested on. It was the blockchain that really mattered, not Bitcoins.

Bitcoin's tumultuous history was evidence that the blockchain could actually work. For years, it functioned as designed: as a completely decentralized, undirected, apparently immutable record of

---

[*] In practice, this usually meant wealthy speculators.

transactions.* The transactions it was originally intended to record were limited to the mining and exchange of Bitcoins, but why stop there? The blockchain could conceivably be used to record all kinds of things: transfer of ownership, or "title," of a piece of land; the issuance of a company's stock to a group of people; the fact that both the buyer and the seller of an office building agreed that all the conditions of the sale had been met; the name, birthplace, and parents of a baby born in Hawaii; and so on. All of these events would be universally visible—they would be real public records—and they would also be undeniable and unalterable, no matter who wanted to rewrite history.

This would truly be something new under the sun, and it would truly be valuable. The blockchain operated for years, under intense scrutiny and stress testing, as a global, transparent, immutable ledger, accessible to all on the web with zero entrance, participation, or transaction fees.† Its existence opened up many possibilities, and innovators and entrepreneurs soon begin exploring them.

▶ The University of Nicosia in Cyprus and the Holberton School of Software Engineering in San Francisco were early examples of academic institutions using the blockchain to share certified student transcripts.

▶ The Kimberley Process is the UN-supported organization that manages a certification intended to reduce the number of con-

---

* The hackers who successfully attacked the Mt. Gox exchange and other Bitcoin exchanges didn't compromise the blockchain itself. Instead, it appears that the Bitcoins were stolen from the exchange's "hot wallet," an Internet-connected bank account for Bitcoins that is not part of the blockchain.

† The parties involved in a blockchain transaction can decide to include a transaction fee, which will be awarded to the miner that creates the block. These voluntary fees are intended as an additional incentive to miners.

flict diamonds entering the market. It has traditionally relied on paper-based certificates of provenance, but in 2016 the body's chairman reported that they were working on a blockchain pilot to understand how the immutable ledger can improve their existing system. A London-based startup, Everledger, is using similar technology to certify precious stones for consumer insurance purposes.

▶ Customs officials seized $50 million of counterfeit shoes entering the United States in 2014, a small fraction of the $461 billion of fake goods that are traded internationally every year. To prevent against this type of fraud, shoe designer Greats released its Beastmode 2.0 Royale Chukkah collection in 2016 with a blockchain-enabled smart tag that enables enthusiasts to confirm the authenticity of their sneakers with their smartphone.

▶ Patrick Byrne, CEO of online retailer Overstock.com, has been a blockchain advocate since the early days of Bitcoin. Overstock became the first major e-commerce store to accept the digital currency, in September 2014. Byrne went on to create a subsidiary, TØ.com, that uses blockchain to track the exchange of financial assets. The name comes from the fact that trades on the platform settle in zero days as opposed to three days later (T+3), which is the norm on Wall Street. Overstock used TØ.com to offer $25 million in corporate bonds in June of 2015. In March of 2016 it announced it was making a public offering of preferred stock, utilizing blockchain. Both of these were world firsts.

▶ In October of 2015, Nasdaq launched Linq, a solution enabling private companies to digitally record share ownership using blockchain technology. Although Linq initially focused on private companies, Nasdaq believes a similar system could be used in public markets, reducing settlement risk exposure[*] by over 90% as well as "dramatically lowering capital costs."

▶ When Ornua, an Irish agricultural food company, shipped $100,000 worth of cheese to the Seychelles Trading Company in September 2016, it was the first international trade transaction that used the blockchain to record all details of its trade financing. Trade across borders typically doesn't happen until two conditions are met. First, the parties involved have ironed out all details about the trade financing: insuring the goods while they're in transit, identifying exactly when ownership is transferred, and so on. Second, all involved parties have satisfied themselves that they have received identical sets of properly signed legal documents related to this financing. Posting all documentation for the Ornua–Seychelles Trading transaction on the blockchain reduced a seven-day process to four hours.

▶ In June of 2016 the Republic of Georgia announced a project in conjunction with economist Hernando de Soto to design and pilot a blockchain-based system for land title registry in the country. It is expected that moving elements of the process onto the blockchain can reduce costs for homeowners and other users, while also reducing possibilities for corruption (since the land records, like everything else on the blockchain, will be unalterable).

Why Not Get Smart about Contracts?

As it became apparent that the blockchain could be used to record all kinds of transactions, not just those related to Bitcoins, it also

---

* Settlement risk is the possibility that one side of the transaction might not deliver the shares as promised once the other party has paid for them, or vice versa.

became clear to some that a distributed ledger was the ideal home for digital "smart contracts." This was a phrase coined in the mid-1990s by Nick Szabo, a computer scientist and legal scholar.* Szabo observed that business contracts, one of the foundations of modern capitalist economies, are similar to computer programs in many ways. Both involve clear definitions (in programs, of variables; in contracts, of the parties involved and their roles), and both specify what will happen under different conditions. A contract between book authors and a publisher, for example, might specify that the authors will receive a specified payment when they deliver the manuscript to the publisher, and that the royalties paid to the authors will increase if total hardcover sales pass a certain level. Any decent programmer could write the equivalent of these conditions in a few lines of computer code.

But so what? Even if the two of us wrote our contract with Norton (the publisher of this book) in the form of a program, it's not clear how this would be better than the standard paper-only, word-based contract. Wouldn't we still need our editor to tell his company's accounts payable department that he'd received the manuscript, and that we were therefore due a payment? And wouldn't we still need accountants at Norton to monitor sales and send us royalty checks? And courts to settle any disputes we couldn't resolve ourselves, or to determine which version of the contract was the "right" one if (either through honest mistakes or tampering) we held a contract that said one thing, and Norton held one that said another? Most fundamentally, don't we and the publisher really need to have a pretty high level of trust—trust that the other party will be honest, respect the terms of the contract, and not engage in bad behavior?

---

* Many believe that Szabo is, in fact, Satoshi Nakamoto. He has repeatedly denied this claim.

We do trust Norton a lot, but that's largely because we've already published one book with them and had a great experience with it. And we decided to do the first book with them in large part because they've been around a long time, have an excellent reputation, publish authors whom we respect greatly, and came highly recommended by our literary agent.[*] There were a lot of signals, in short, that Norton would be a trustworthy partner for us.[†]

Advocates of smart contracts would look at this situation very differently. They would note that, instead of trusting Norton to accurately report book sales to us, we could instead rely on third parties like Nielsen BookScan. We could then write a program that would access the web, BookScan, and Norton's bank account and our bank accounts, and would have the following logic:

▶ Present a web page to the authors and the editor, asking each to click on a button to certify that the manuscript has been submitted. Once all parties have clicked this button, transfer funds from Norton's bank account to the authors.

▶ Begin monitoring hardcover book sales using BookScan. If hardcover sales pass a certain number, increase the royalty rate in all future payments to authors.

Any actual smart contract between us would obviously be more formal and complicated than this, but it wouldn't need any esoteric data or code. It would be easy to write.

But what about the potential problems of having multiple versions of the contract, or of tampering with it? This is where the blockchain

---

[*] Our literary agent is the eminently trustworthy Raphael Sagalyn.

[†] There were fewer signals to Norton that the two of us would be good authors for them to work with. We're grateful that they took a chance on us.

comes in and offers an apparently ideal solution: after we and Norton agree on the contract, we simply sign it with our digital signatures and add it to the blockchain. The contract then has all the same properties as all the transactions recorded in that ledger. It's permanently there, visible and verifiable. Most important, it's immutable: neither we nor Norton nor anyone else can tamper with it after the fact. We'd probably want to include the ability to renegotiate this smart contract by using our digital signatures to open it back up or delete it, but outside of this possibility, the proven integrity of the blockchain would ensure the integrity of our contract.

A major advantage of this kind of contract is that it removes the need for many kinds of trust. We don't need to trust that Norton will count our sales accurately, since the contract relies on BookScan data for that. Or that the publisher will actually raise our royalty rate if we meet the hardcover sales target, since that increase is part of the immutable code.* We don't even need to trust that the courts in our area will be competent, impartial, and expedient, since the smart contract doesn't rely on them to enforce its terms or verify its legitimacy. This contract just exists and runs on the blockchain, taking advantage of its openness, verifiability, and immutability.

In 1996, smart-contract pioneer Nick Szabo wrote,

A broad statement of the key idea of smart contracts, then, is to say that contracts should be *embedded in the world*. The mechanisms of the world should be structured in such a way as to make the contracts

   (a) robust against naive vandalism, and
   (b) robust against sophisticated, incentive compatible (rational) breach.

---

* If we were worried that Norton might not have enough money to pay us, we could include an escrow account or other contingency within the smart contract.

Almost twenty years later, the world of the blockchain appeared and seemed to provide exactly the structure and world that Szabo was describing. Entrepreneurs, programmers, and visionaries took notice, and efforts to combine distributed ledgers and smart contracts blossomed.

By the end of 2016, the best known of these was probably Ethereum, which described itself as "a decentralized platform that runs smart contracts: applications that run exactly as programmed without any possibility of downtime, censorship, fraud or third party interference." A number of ambitious efforts were launched on the Ethereum platform, one of which we'll encounter in the next chapter.

Toppling the Stacks: The Crypto Assault on the Core

At least some efforts involving cryptocurrencies, distributed ledgers, and smart contracts seemed to be motivated by a desire to decentralize activities and information that had previously been concentrated, and to explicitly favor the crowd over the core. There were many reasons for this, not least of which was the feeling that the core had become too powerful and could not be trusted.

In a 2012 onstage conversation at a WELL conference, the science fiction author Bruce Sterling introduced the idea of a small group of "stacks" within the high-tech industry. He said that it "made less and less sense to talk about 'the Internet,' 'the PC business,' 'telephones,' 'Silicon Valley,' or 'the media,' and much more sense to just study Google, Apple, Facebook, Amazon and Microsoft." Sterling opined that "these big five American vertically organized silos are re-making the world in their image."

Writing in the *Atlantic* shortly after the conference, Alexis Madrigal pondered the effects of the stacks:

What will the world that they create look like? Here's what I think: Your technology will work perfectly within the silo and with an individual stacks's [*sic*] (temporary) allies. But it will be perfectly broken at the interfaces between itself and its competitors.

That moment where you are trying to do something that has no reason not to work, but it just doesn't and there is no way around it without changing some piece of your software to fit more neatly within the silo?

That's gonna happen a lot.

The argument was that the companies forming the innermost core of the tech industry could not be trusted to look after consumers' interests as they looked after their own. And the power of the stacks seemed only to grow, and to make Sterling look prescient. In late July of 2016, for example, the five companies he had named more than three years earlier became the five publicly traded companies with the highest stock market valuations in the world.

Distrust was not limited to high tech. In the years following the recession, surveys conducted by the public relations firm Edelman found that financial services was the world's least-trusted industry. But how could the large, powerful companies in this industry be disrupted, especially in a way that didn't automatically create other large, powerful companies with the same weaknesses and faults?

Restructuring the Entire Economy?
There's an App for That

A beguilingly simple way forward was suggested by the title of a January 2015 article on the website TechCrunch by Jon Evans: "Decentralize All the Things." Why not take the philosophies, processes, and technologies underlying Bitcoin, blockchain, and smart contracts, he argued, and apply them more broadly? The cryptocurrency experiment sparked by Nakamoto had shown something remarkable: that a crowd of independent and self-interested actors could, when held together with nothing more than a little communication and a lot of math and code, create something of great value to the group as a whole and beat the core at its own game of, in this case, maintaining an accurate ledger of important transactions. How broadly applicable was this lesson? Where were its boundaries?

Evans's article both acknowledged that there were obstacles to this vision and expressed confidence that they could be overcome. It was an excellent example of "solutionism": the belief that tough problems could be solved with the right combination of entrepreneurial energy and technological innovation. The term "solutionism" was originally intended as an insult; the writer Evgeny Morozov coined the phrase to refer to "an intellectual pathology." Instead of taking offense at being called solutionists, however, many technologists embraced the term; in 2014, Marc Andreessen described himself in his Twitter profile as a "proud solutionist since 1994."

Bitcoins and the blockchain lend themselves wonderfully to solutionism. Smart contracts and related innovations hold out the promise of making the blockchain something much broader than just a ledger, while maintaining its most desirable properties. The solutionist vision is for the blockchain to become an open, transparent, global, free-to-use (or at least very cheap), universally available, immutable repository not just of Bitcoin transactions, but for all kinds of information goods.

Who Needs Companies Anymore Anyway?

Information goods could include contracts and software. Imagine, the crowd cryptocurrency solutionists said, if people and organizations allowed programs to access information assets such as bank accounts, insurance policies, escrow funds, investment portfolios, and so on. Imagine also that these programs could access the blockchain, enter transactions into it, and also themselves be recorded within it. Such a system would provide assurance, thanks to the chain's immutability, that the programs' code had not been altered or hacked, and that the programs were therefore operating as originally intended. Then, strange new things would become possible: contracts and complicated transactions with real-world impact that execute automatically, costlessly, and without the oversight or blessing of any central authority.

Some felt that the blockchain was powerful enough to directly challenge the stacks—the large tech companies that, according to Bruce Sterling and others, controlled much of the web. In their 2016 book *Blockchain Revolution*, father and son authors Don and Alex Tapscott wrote,

> Corporate forces have captured many . . . wonderful peer-to-peer, democratic, and open technologies and are using them to extract an inordinate share of value . . . powerful "digital conglomerates" such as Amazon, Google, Apple, and Facebook . . . are capturing the treasure troves of data that citizens and institutions generate. . . . Now, with blockchain technology, a world of new possibilities has opened up to reverse all these trends. We now have a true peer-to-peer platform that . . . can start to change the way wealth is distributed—how it is created in the first place, as people everywhere from farmers to musicians can share more fully, a priori, in the wealth they create. The sky does seem to be the limit.

In the developed world, many felt that large companies, especially those in finance and high tech, were becoming too powerful. In much of the developing world, meanwhile, courts are relatively weak, trust between strangers is low, and governments pursue policies that damage their currencies. In both situations, cryptocurrency advocates argued, the results are the same: exchange is throttled, opportunities are wasted, and people are worse off than they otherwise would be.

Many people worked on Bitcoin, the blockchain, and smart contracts because they wanted to improve this situation by, in essence, moving important aspects of market-based economies from the core to the crowd—from central banks, companies, and the legal system to a huge number of computers humming away around the world, running code that attempted to decentralize all the things.

How well would this work?

Chapter Summary

▶ Bitcoin shows the potential of completely decentralized communities. By combining math (cryptography), economics, code, and networks, they can create something as fundamental and critical as money.

▶ The blockchain might well be more important than Bitcoin. It's open, transparent, global, flexible, and immutable ledger is clearly valuable, especially if it's combined with smart contracts and other digital innovations.

▶ The most remarkable thing about Bitcoin and the blockchain might be how they enable a global crowd of people and organizations, all acting in their own interest, to create something of immense shared value.

▶ Bitcoin and the blockchain have sparked a wave of innovation and entrepreneurship, and it's not at all clear now what roles they'll eventually play in economies and societies.

▶ Some people believe that large organizations, from banks to technology companies, have become too powerful, and that a viable alternative to them now exists because of the new technologies of extreme decentralization.

▶ Early initiatives indicate that there's a lot of demand for new ledger technologies. That may make many existing business processes cheaper and faster and, perhaps more important, enable new ones.

Questions

1. How might an open, transparent, global, flexible, immutable ledger be valuable to you? What kinds of documents, records, or transactions would you put in it? What partners—customers, suppliers, third parties, government entities, and so on—would you have join you? How much time and money do you think such a ledger could save you?

2. In order for it to be valuable to you, would this ledger also need to be radically decentralized, or could it be owned and controlled by one or more organizations?

3. How important might Bitcoin and other cryptocurrencies be to you? Are you planning to accept them as payment?

4. What would be the first "smart contracts" (contracts that execute 100% automatically) you would attempt to write?

5. Where, if anywhere, do you think massive decentralization will upset the core and replace it (entirely or largely) with a crowd in the next five to ten years?

CHAPTER 13

ARE COMPANIES PASSÉ? (HINT: NO)

> Some people regard private enterprise as a pred-
> atory tiger to be shot. Others look on it as a cow
> they can milk. Not enough people see it as a
> healthy horse, pulling a sturdy wagon.
>
> — *attributed to Winston Churchill (1874–1965)*

IN THIS ERA OF POWERFUL NEW TECHNOLOGIES, DO WE STILL need companies? Many observers assert that real alternatives to companies are now available. These alternatives make use of many of the digital innovations described in this book, especially the radically decentralized, crowd-based technologies of cryptocurrencies, distributed ledgers, and smart contracts that we described in the previous chapter. Companies are squarely at the core of modern capitalism, but as we've shown repeatedly throughout this section of the book, the core can often be beaten by a technology-enabled crowd. So, what will happen to companies?

To start addressing this important question, let's look at what has transpired with two recent efforts to substitute a crowd for a company: The DAO (a "decentralized autonomous organization") and the Bitcoin/blockchain effort. The recent histories of these two specific efforts, when understood in light of relevant economic theory, tell us a great deal about the future of companies in general.

The Way of The DAO

At 9:00 a.m. GMT on May 28, 2016, the purest expression of the crowd that the capitalist business world had ever seen closed the largest round of crowdfunding ever. The entity involved was the first truly decentralized autonomous organization ever created, "The DAO"—an entity that, as its manifesto explained, existed "simultaneously nowhere and everywhere and operat[ed] solely with the steadfast iron will of immutable code"* It was something like a venture capital fund, but one that followed the principle of decentralizing all the things.

The DAO existed only as open-source, distributed software for executing smart contracts. It was built within the Ethereum project (which we described in the previous chapter) and made use of its ether cryptocurrency. Like a venture capital fund, it existed to approve and invest in projects. But The DAO differed from a standard venture capital fund in two ways. First, not all projects had to promise a financial return; the organization could support not-for-profit efforts as well. Second, the projects to be supported would be picked not by a core group of partners or evaluators, but instead by the entire crowd that funded The DAO's creation; members of this crowd would get voting power in proportion to their initial investment.

There was no human or institutional layer outside of The DAO's software—no CEO, board of directors, or employees, and not even a steering committee like the one Linus Torvalds ran for Linux. The

---

* "The Dao" (sometimes spelled "Tao") is also a set of teachings that, according to tradition, originated in China in the sixth century BCE with the publication of the *Tao Te Ching* text. The Dao, most often translated as "the way," holds that the essence of existence and nature is both dynamic and diffuse. It is often cited as the inspiration for "The Force" in the *Star Wars* movies. The technologists who created the distributed autonomous organization were almost certainly aware of the associations its acronym would evoke.

DAO was software and software alone, the functionality of which would be changed only if a majority of its participants decided to install on their computers a new version of it. Unless and until that happened, The DAO would continue to operate as originally programmed, with no interruptions or human interventions possible. There was no one with the formal authority to change The DAO, no one to negotiate with or appeal to in order to alter it, and no one to sue or pursue in court if a perceived injustice was perpetrated through it.

Many felt that this kind of software was exactly what was needed to overcome the biases and deficiencies of the core. Commentators called it a "paradigm shift" that could "offer new opportunities to democratize business." *Forbes* reported that it would enable "entrepreneurs of the future . . . to 'design' their own organizations customized to the optimal needs of their mission, vision, and strategy to change the world." Real money poured in to support this entirely virtual organization: $162 million within a twenty-eight-day period in May of 2016.

That Didn't Take Long

Shortly before The DAO's funding window closed, however, a group of computer scientists who had analyzed its code released a paper pointing out what they said were serious flaws with the community voting process embedded in the software.[*] The authors wrote that they were publicly discussing these issues not to destroy The DAO just as it was coming into existence, but instead to strengthen it: "We discuss these attacks, and provide concrete and simple suggestions

---

[*] The paper was written by Dino Mark, Vlad Zamfir, and Emin Gün Sirer. Many of the weaknesses were not just software holes, but economic flaws that gave investors incentives to behave in ways that were at odds with the group's best interest. Cade Metz, "The Biggest Crowdfunding Project Ever—The DAO—Is Kind of a Mess," *Wired*, June 6, 2016, https://www.wired.com/2016/06/biggest-crowdfunding-project-ever-dao-mess.

that will mitigate the attacks, or in some cases make them completely impossible."

The anonymous hacker who stole approximately one-third of The DAO's money shortly after it went live, however, was probably not as community minded. After examining its code, this person or persons realized that it would be straightforward to essentially make The DAO operate like an ATM full of cash that kept dispensing money even though the requesting account had a zero balance.

This was done publicly—after all, The DAO was radically transparent—and it was completely legal; the software's licensing terms were clear that users must stoically accept everything that happened within the decentralized autonomous organization.

Questions were raised about why the hacker would attempt this exploit, since the ethers siphoned off couldn't immediately be converted into dollars or any other fiat currency. One explanation, advanced by Daniel Krawisz of the Satoshi Nakamoto Institute, was that the hacker could have made approximately $3 million by shorting ethers in one of the cryptocurrency exchanges operating online, correctly betting that once the hack became public, the ether's value would plummet.

But the important questions were not about the hacker's motivations. They were instead about the vulnerabilities of cryptocurrencies and smart contracts revealed by the exploit. The Nakamoto Institute's withering assessment was that Ethereum was "doomed." Its combination of poor programming and terms of use that essentially made this lousy programming legally binding spelled disaster.

Believers in the dream of decentralizing all the things, however, weren't yet ready to give up. In July of 2016, Vitalik Buterin, one of Ethereum's cofounders and the author (at nineteen years old) of the influential 2013 "Ethereum White Paper," announced a "hard fork" in the cryptocurrency and its blockchain. If a majority of participants in The DAO accepted this fork (which was embodied in a new version of the Ethereum software), all previous transactions that occurred within the decentralized autonomous organization would be essentially forgotten, and all involved ethers would be returned to their original owners.

The hard fork was, in fact, adopted by a majority of The DAO's members, but a substantial minority was left howling mad. The (possibly pseudonymous) writer E. J. Spode explained why in the online magazine *Aeon*: "In [minority members'] view, the hard fork undermined the core principle of Ethereum, which was, after all, to bypass all the meddling humans—the corrupt bureaucrats and politicians and board directors and CEOs and lawyers. The code was supposed to be the law. If you didn't see the weakness in the software, that was your problem, since the software was publicly available."

Spode's list of meddling humans should probably have included central bankers, who were often accused of manipulating the value of fiat currencies. The hard fork, many felt, did something much worse. It didn't arbitrarily change the value of ethers; it actually changed who owned them. Some participants in the original DAO refused to go along with the hard fork, continued to use the original version of the distributed software, and named their system "Ethereum Classic." As we write this in early 2017, Ethereum and Ethereum Classic continue to exist in parallel.

Bitcoin's Bitter End?

Despite ample worldwide enthusiasm for them, Bitcoin and the blockchain have also experienced trouble. In January of 2016 Mike Hearn, who had been a prolific and respected contributor to programming for the blockchain, and who had believed in its promise so deeply that he had quit his job at Google to devote himself full-time to it, sold all his Bitcoins and walked away from the project. The blog post he wrote explaining his decision was titled "The Resolution of the Bitcoin Experiment." In Hearn's view this resolution was failure. And the failure occurred not because of intractable problems with mining or newly discovered vulnerabilities of the cryptocurrency itself, but instead for organizational reasons. As Hearn wrote,

> It has failed because the community has failed. What was meant to be a new, decentralized form of money that lacked "systemically important institutions" and "too big to fail" has become something even worse: a system completely controlled by just a handful of people. Worse still, the network is on the brink of technical collapse. The mechanisms that should have prevented this outcome have broken down, and as a result there's no longer much reason to think Bitcoin can actually be better than the existing financial system.

Problems arose because of a difference in opinion about how to handle the system's continued growth. Two camps emerged, each led by senior programmers. Instead of resolving their differences, they hardened their positions over time. Each side felt it was remaining true to the founding principles of Bitcoin and the blockchain (and some members of each side were associated with venture capital–backed cryptocurrency startups or other commercial interests). Satoshi Nakamoto remained silent on the matter, having left all discussions years earlier. While this impasse continued, the performance of the Bitcoin system suffered, increasing the risk that some blockchain transactions would be delayed or ignored altogether.

The dispute over the architecture and future of the Bitcoin system coincided with another worrying trend: the concentration of a great deal of the world's total Bitcoin-mining power in China. By the middle of 2016, Chinese exchanges accounted for 42% of all Bitcoin transactions and an estimated 70% of all Bitcoin-mining gear in the world. For many within the community, any large concentration was undesirable, since it could lead to disproportionate influence over the system's evolution, and the whole point was to avoid such influence by maintaining decentralization. In particular, any entity or coordinated group that controlled more than 50% of total mining could unilaterally decide which transactions were valid, disenfranchising everyone else.

The fact that the concentration was occurring within China was particularly troubling. The government there had a long tradition of overseeing its financial institutions closely and sometimes intervening in them directly, and this kind of activity seems fundamentally at odds with the cryptocurrency dream of complete freedom from government meddling. Having control over Bitcoin and the blockchain behind the great firewall of China, many felt, would turn the dream into a nightmare.

The Technologies of Disruption . . .

The troubles experienced by The DAO and the Bitcoin-mining network highlight a fundamental question about the rise of cryptocurrencies, smart contracts, powerful platforms, and other recent digital developments. The question, which we posed at the start of this chapter, is a simple one: Are companies becoming passé? As we get better at writing smart contracts, building networks that brilliantly combine self-interest and collective benefit, and increasingly democratizing powerful tools for production and innovation, will we still rely so much on industrial-era companies to get work done?

We've made the case throughout this book that minds and machines and products and platforms are being combined and recombined in powerful ways thanks to a surge in digital progress. As this happens, will the crowd come to dominate or even overwhelm the core?

Many people believe and hope that this will be the case. Antiestablishment philosophies have been around as long as establishments have, of course, but the dislocations and perceived unfairness of the Great Recession and the slow, uneven recovery that followed provided new nourishment for them. Many people saw ample evidence that companies, especially large ones, could never be trusted, and considered them engines of deprivation and exploitation instead of prosperity.*

If big companies are the problem, then the solution is clear: decentralize all the things. Technological progress certainly seems to be enabling this vision. 3D printers (which we discussed in Chapter 4) could let individuals make anything, removing the need for large-scale facilities full of specialized equipment. This is the new vision of production espoused by our MIT colleague Neil Gershenfeld and others.† For many crops, large farms could be replaced by precisely monitored and controlled microcontainers (Chapter 11). Cryptocurrencies and smart contracts could take care of financial services and other information goods (Chapter 12). The web has already greatly democratized access to information and educational resources (Chapter 10). Futurist Ray Kurzweil said in 2012 that "a kid in Africa with a smartphone has access to more information than the president of the United States did 15 years ago," and this diffusion of knowledge will certainly continue. And Moore's law will continue to operate, driving prices down and performance up for all manner of digital goods, at rates unheard of in history prior to the computer era.

So the technology seems to support decentralizing all the things.

---

* We do not share this view. Capitalism can be an enormous force for good, but "crony capitalism"—the act of distorting markets so that friends of the powerful can enrich themselves—should always be rooted out.

† See, for example, Neil A. Gershenfeld, *Fab: The Coming Revolution on Your Desktop—From Personal Computers to Personal Fabrication* (New York: Basic Books, 2005).

What about the economics? What does economic theory and evidence have to say about how tech progress changes companies and other ways we organize to get work done? Quite a lot, actually.

. . . Meet the Economics of the Firm

In November 1937, when he was just twenty-six, the economist Ronald Coase published his landmark paper "The Nature of the Firm." In it, he posed a very basic question: If markets are so great, why does so much happen inside companies? Why, in other words, do we choose to conduct so much economic activity within these stable, hierarchical, often large and bureaucratic structures called companies, rather than just all working as independent freelancers, coming together as needed and for only as long as necessary to complete a particular project, then going our own way afterward? In practice, the "visible hand" of managers is very much at work in day-to-day business; after all, companies are all over the place.* If market share is the ultimate test of the success of an idea, then one could argue that markets themselves have failed the market test.

It's easy to see why a pure, atomistic market wouldn't work in an environment where business law was underdeveloped, courts were weak, and contracts therefore could not be trusted. But this was not the case in the United States and the other advanced economies of the 1930s. So, why so many companies? Coase's analysis of this question proves again how right Keynes was about the enduring influence of dead economists: "The Nature of the Firm" is frequently cited by

---

* In his classic book *The Visible Hand*, Alfred Chandler argued that management, especially middle management, had become the most powerful institution in the US economy by the middle of the twentieth century. Alfred Chandler, *The Visible Hand* (Cambridge, MA: Belknap Press, 1977).

geeks and technologists. In fact, it's almost the only economics paper we've heard them mention.

We're amazed at how often we've heard Coase's name invoked by digital entrepreneurs, innovators, and futurists. But we probably shouldn't be, because he indicated to them how important their work could be, and how it could reshape entire economies.*

Coase's Choice: Organization or Market?

Coase proposed that the choice between firms and markets was essentially a cost minimization exercise. It almost had to be, in fact, because competition tends to drive out high-cost players. The boundary of the firm was incredibly flexible; it could be set either to encompass thousands of people and billions of dollars of assets or much more narrowly, with most people working as independent contractors, owning or renting the necessary equipment, and buying and selling goods and services from others. Companies must be so large and powerful, then, because they are often able to produce goods and services at a lower total cost than pure markets can.

But why is this? Aren't markets supposed to be super efficient? They are in some ways, Coase argued, but they also tend to have higher costs in several areas. These include

▶ The costs of searching and discovering the relevant prices

▶ The costs of negotiating and making decisions

---

* With over 35,000 citations on Google Scholar, Coase's paper on the nature of the firm has long been one of the most cited papers in economics. In 1972 he noted that it was "much cited and little used," but the subsequent generation of economists and business executives has made it a workhorse for understanding business organization. R. H. Coase, "Industrial Organization: A Proposal for Research," in *Economic Research: Retrospect and Prospect*, vol. 3, *Policy Issues and Research Opportunities in Industrial Organization*, ed. Victor R. Fuchs (New York: National Bureau of Economic Research, 1972), 62, http://www.nber.org/chapters/c7618.pdf.

▶ The costs of concluding a separate contract

▶ The costs of monitoring and enforcing the contract

Can you see now why Coase is so influential and beloved among the geeks? Digital technologies clearly lower many of the costs that cause firms to dominate markets; they might reverse this domination and cause markets to flourish. This argument was made most clearly by Tom Malone, Joanne Yates, and Robert Benjamin in their 1987 article "Electronic Markets and Electronic Hierarchies."[*]

So what happened? We're about thirty-five years into the PC era, twenty into the age of the web, and ten into the time of the smartphone. These are novel and powerful tools, especially when combined, for lowering the costs that Coase identified. And they are, in many ways, ushering in a great shift toward markets and away from large companies. Indeed, Malone, Yates, and Benjamin predicted the rise of electronic commerce and even some of the market-based organizations like Upwork and O2O platforms.

Companies Must Be Doing Something Right

Despite the apparent trend away from big companies, their demise is simply not evident. Instead, we're seeing the opposite: the increasing dominance of big companies. The US economy both generates the most digital technologies and uses them most heavily, so it's where we would most expect big companies to be withering if the geek interpretation of Coase is correct. What's been happening, though, is actually increasing concentration: in most industries, more and more of the total sales and profits have been going to a smaller number

---

[*] The title of their article intentionally echoed Oliver Williamson's widely cited book *Markets and Hierarchies*, which built heavily on Coase's insights. Oliver E. Williamson, *Markets and Hierarchies, Analysis and Antitrust Implications: A Study in the Economics of Internal Organization* (New York: Free Press, 1975).

of large firms. For example, the *Economist* researched 893 different US industries and found that the weighted-average market share of the top four firms' revenues had risen from 26% to 32% of the total between 1997 and 2012. As we wrote in 2008, IT is making competition more "Schumpeterian," enabling companies to scale up rapidly and gain dominant market share, but also making it easier for new entrants to supplant them and increase turbulence.

Why is this? Why are big companies growing instead of shrinking as the economy becomes more digitized? It could be that the digital tools that favor markets are not yet diffused widely enough, or that they remain immature. If this is the case, then cryptocurrencies, blockchains, smart contracts, and other innovative new technologies might be just what's needed to realize the geek vision of Coase's arguments. The problems that we've described with The DAO and the Bitcoin/blockchain infrastructure could be simply the growing pains of a young colossus. As has often been said, we tend to overestimate the potential of new technologies in the short term, but underestimate it in the long term. And we think it's very easy to underestimate the new distributed ledgers and their kin. Satoshi Nakamoto, whoever that is, really did bring something new and powerful into the world.

But not powerful enough to make companies go away, or even to significantly reduce their importance in the world's economies. To see why, we need to go back to Coase's work, but not stop there. Instead, we need to understand subsequent insights from transaction cost economics (TCE), the discipline he was instrumental in founding.

The Latest Thinking on Why Companies Are So Common

TCE deals with the very basic question of why economic activity is organized the way it is—why, for example, we see markets and companies in the mix that we do. Often called the theory of the firm, TCE is a branch of economics important enough to have merited three Nobel prizes: the first in 1991 to Coase; the second in 2009 to his student Oliver Williamson, who was recognized along with Elinor Ostrom;[*] and most recently a third, to Oliver Hart and Bengt Holm-ström, who were recognized in 2016. As you've no doubt inferred from the name, transaction costs turn out to be deeply important: when markets have lower total transaction costs, they win out over hierarchies, and vice versa.

We can't possibly do a fair job of conveying here all the insights of transaction cost economics; there's too much rich and excellent work. Instead, we want to concentrate on one aspect of TCE that's especially helpful for understanding the impact of the powerful new digital technologies of the crowd. It starts with the basic rule of thumb that markets often have lower production costs (all the costs that come with making goods and services), while hierarchies typically have lower coordination costs (all the costs associated with setting up the production and keeping it running smoothly). The technologies discussed in this book are great cost reducers, and especially good at reducing coordination costs. It's easy to see how search engines, cheap global communication networks, and the free, perfect, and instant economies of information goods in general would drive down coordination costs.

Logic dictates that as coordination costs go down, markets become more and more attractive, because their comparative disadvantage shrinks. This implies that we should see markets being used more and hierarchies being used less, as Tom Malone and his coauthors predicted. And in some important ways this is exactly what we do see. Outsourcing, offshoring, freelancing, and other aspects of "unbun-

---

* Like Daniel Kahneman, Ostrom was awarded the prize despite not being an economist.

dling the firm" have increased substantially in recent years as digital technologies have improved and diffused. It's pretty clear that a large movement is under way to take much of the work that used to be done within the single hierarchy of the firm and move it to the market.

It's also clear, however, that firms are still going strong, and that in many ways their economic influence is growing, not shrinking. So, is TCE's basic rule of thumb wrong? No, it's not, but it needs to be modernized. Eighty years of research has built on and enhanced Coase's findings since "The Nature of the Firm" appeared. Continuing to rely on it alone is a bit like treating Gregor Mendel's mid-nineteenth-century work as the last word on genetics and ignoring Watson and Crick, the discovery of DNA, and everything that came after.

No Matter How Smart They Get, Contracts Will Still Be Incomplete

Of the many elaborations of TCE, those that are most relevant here are the concepts of incomplete contracts and residual rights of control. In pathbreaking work, Sandy Grossman and Oliver Hart asked, "What rights does the owner of a firm have that a non-owner doesn't?" They reasoned that ownership has value only to the extent that contracts are incomplete; if every possible contingency for use of a building, machine, or patent were spelled out in contracts, then labeling one party the "owner" of the asset would confer no additional rights.

However, when contracts are incomplete, owners have the residual rights of control, meaning they can do whatever they want with the asset except for what's in the contract.* If there's nothing in any contract about what colors you can paint your car, or when to change the

---

* Within certain limits of law and morality.

oil, or whether to replace the music system, or even whether to sell it to a little old lady down the street for $1, then you, as the owner, pretty much have the right to make those decisions. Hart dove deeper into these questions, including through a particularly influential set of papers with John Moore* and with Bengt Holmström.†

But why assume, a fan of decentralizing all the things might ask, that contracts must always be incomplete? Maybe we can succeed at writing complete contracts if we try harder. Perhaps two or more parties can, in fact, write down a complete set of roles, rights, responsibilities, and rewards with respect to that car (or other asset), no matter what happens to it over time, or to them. If such a complete contract really were possible, then there would be no residual rights of control, and no need to worry about who actually owned the car. In essence, this is what The DAO assumed could be done—that every future decision could be adjudicated by a comprehensive contract.

Virtually every economist who has studied the issue, however, argues that, in practice, complete contracts are not possible. The world is a complicated place, the future is largely unknowable, and we humans have limited intelligence. These and other factors combine to make it prohibitively difficult, and most likely actually impossible, to

---

* Oliver Hart and John Moore, "Property Rights and the Nature of the Firm," *Journal of Political Economy* 98, no. 6 (1990): 1119–58.

† For example, Oliver Hart and Bengt Holmstrom, *The Theory of Contracts*, MIT Department of Economics Working Paper 418 (March 1986), https://dspace.mit.edu/bitstream/handle/1721.1/64265/theoryofcontract00hart.pdf%3Bjsessionid%3DD2F89D14123801EBB5A616B328AB8CFC?sequence%3D1. Holmström's earlier, pathbreaking work on the "principal-agent problem" (Bengt Holmström, "Moral Hazard and Observability," *Bell Journal of Economics* 10, no. 1 [1979]: 74–91, http://www.jstor.org/stable/3003320), provided a foundation for a large subsequent economic literature on the economics of incentive contracts, including incomplete contracts theory. As Holmström and Paul Milgrom noted, the firm itself, including all its rules and norms, can be usefully thought of as an incentive system. Bengt Holmström and Paul Milgrom, "The Firm as an Incentive System," *American Economic Review* 84, no. 4 (1994): 972–91, http://www.jstor.org/stable/2118041.

write a complete contract—one that truly does away with the need for ownership—for any realistic business situation.

In practice, this means that when two people work together on a project and one of them owns an essential asset, like a machine or factory necessary to produce the output, then that owner has the residual rights of control. If either of them comes up with some great new idea to increase the output of the machine, the owner can implement it without further consultation. The nonowner, in contrast, needs the owner's permission. That requirement gives the owner bargaining power to, for example, insist on a cut of the additional output. TCE calls this the "hold-up problem." As a result, ownership affects the incentives for innovation, whether large (like a new product idea) or small (like a better way to sort inventory).

The bottom line is that changing ownership changes incentives, and therefore results. Employees working with someone else's assets have different incentives from those of independent contractors who own their own assets. That's an important reason why firm boundaries matter. A crucial question in the efficient design of a company, a supply chain, or a whole economy is how the assets, and thus incentives, are arranged.

One of the fundamental reasons that firms exist, then, is that it's just not possible for market participants to get together and write complete contracts—ones that specify who does what, and who gets what, in all possible contingencies: all the ways the real world could unfold in the future. The company is, in effect, a solution to this problem. It's a predefined way to determine who gets to exercise residual rights of control (that's management's job, on behalf of the owners of the company) and who reaps rewards (the company's stakeholders, which include the owners, but possibly others[*] who have bargaining

---

[*] These might include labor unions, local communities, central governments, powerful customers, or key suppliers.

power as well, get to divide up the value generated after all contractual requirements have been satisfied).

There's no guarantee, of course, that this arrangement will work out well. Management can be indecisive, incompetent, corrupt, or simply wrong, and shareholders can lose their money. But firms exist and endure because they work, and they work, in part, because they address the problem of incomplete contracts and residual rights of control that plague markets.

The Failure Modes of Decentralized Things

These insights help us understand the recent problems of Bitcoin, the blockchain, Ethereum, and The DAO discussed earlier in this chapter. The blockchain was designed from the start to be as decentralized and uncontrollable as possible; it was meant to be the ultimate antihierarchy. But then, what recourse is available to its enthusiasts if it evolves in a direction they don't like—if, for example, it begins to operate more and more behind the great firewall of China? This is in many ways the opposite of the original vision for the cryptocurrency and its distributed ledger. But it's also virtually impossible for the original Bitcoin enthusiasts to change or undo—about as hard as it would be for a small group of traders to change the trend of an entire stock market.

It's bad enough that Bitcoin and blockchain programmers have split into two adversarial camps without any single authority (either a formal or an informal one) to make final decisions. It's still worse when their creation increasingly falls under the control of an authoritarian government with a track record of heavy interventions in both technologies and markets. The contracts that hold the blockchain together, embedded entirely in code and supported by math, didn't specify what would or should be done if the mining network became too geographically concentrated. And there was no owner to fall back on once this contractual incompleteness became an obvious issue.

The DAO's problem was even more severe, since it was explicitly intended to be simultaneously 100% hierarchy-free and a 100% complete contract. Its members signed up to participate and commit their capital within an online environment where all decisions would be made by the crowd without oversight, review, or recourse—in other words, without hierarchy, management, or centralized ownership of any kind. There was only a distributed blockchain and body of code that took in money, accepted proposals, counted votes for them, and distributed money according to the results. The DAO made clear that there would be no second-guessing the decisions and outcomes it generated. So when it sent a third of its ethers to an anonymous hacker, that was a legitimate outcome under its complete contract. The hard fork in the Ethereum software announced in July of 2016 undid the hacker's work. However, the fork also infuriated many members of that cryptocurrency's community, who saw it as exactly the kind of thing that an owner would do, and the whole point of Ethereum was not only that it had no owners, but more fundamentally that it was not ownable. As a result, the Ethereum community split in two. Someone well versed in transaction cost economics and the realities of incomplete contracting might have predicted an outcome like this.

The two of us are pessimistic that totally decentralized, purely crowd-based entities like The DAO will ever be economically dominant, no matter how technologically solid they become. They simply can't solve the problems of incomplete contracting and residual rights of control that a company solves by letting management make all the decisions not explicitly assigned to other parties. Smart contracts are interesting and powerful new tools and there will be a place for them, but they don't address the fundamental problem that keeps companies, as it were, in business. Companies exist in large part because well-functioning complete contracts are impossible to write, not because they're too difficult or costly to enforce.

But will future technologies eventually make it possible to write complete contracts? Some technologies could help. For instance, increasingly ubiquitous sensors, as we are seeing with the Internet of things, could make possible the monitoring of far more of our actions and outcomes. Increased computer power could make it possible to simulate, choose, and store decisions for many future possible outcomes, and networks could make it possible to bring all this data and information to central clearinghouses for adjudication and resolution. But as fast as computers enable one party to anticipate outcomes, they enable other parties to consider more complex possibilities. Like the Red Queen in *Alice in Wonderland*, machines would have to run ever faster just to keep track of all the contingencies being generated. In the end, contracts would still be incomplete.

The Company of the Future Will Actually Be Pretty Boring

Companies also exist because they serve several other economic and legal functions that would be difficult to replicate in a world made up only of freelancers who constantly wrote contracts to work together. Companies are assumed to endure indefinitely, for example, which makes them suitable for long-term projects and investments. They are also governed by a large and well-developed set of laws (different from those that apply to individuals) that provide predictability and confidence. As a result, companies remain the preferred vehicle for conducting many kinds of business.

In fact, even in the parts of the economy where digital technologies are having their greatest impact—where the machines, platforms, and crowds are farthest along—we still see good old-fashioned companies everywhere. It's true that many of them are doing some things differently from the norm of fifty or a hundred years ago. Platform companies like Airbnb, Uber, and ClassPass are working with large and fluid networks of people and organizations, instead of a small and stable group of them. These companies are trying to make it as easy as possible for some types of partners to enter and leave a business relationship with them, giving rise to the notion of an "on-demand economy." Other companies are exploring how to deliver value with blockchains, smart contracts, and other technologies of extreme decentralization. But they're almost all pursuing these radical goals within the highly traditional structure of a joint-stock company, an organizational form that has existed for well over four centuries.*

When we visit these companies, we're struck by how normal they look. They all have employees, job titles, managers, and executives. They all have a CEO and a board of directors. Very few of them are purely virtual; instead, they have physical office space, desks, and meeting rooms. They might have bigger computer screens, more foos-ball and Ping-Pong tables, and better perks like free snacks and meals than a lot of the other companies we've seen in our careers, but are these major differences?

Why Management Matters

Corporate managers have been one of the most maligned groups within the standard arrangement. Their portrayals in popular culture, from the movie *Office Space* to the British and American TV shows *The Office*, are almost always negative. They are seen as bumblers who have no value while sapping employees' enthusiasm, wasting their time, and thwarting their ambitions. Once enough computers and networks came along, many hoped, middle managers' paper-

---

* Joint-stock companies issue shares that can be bought and sold by people without affecting the operation of the company. They date back at least as far as 1602, when the Dutch East India Company issued shares on the Amsterdam Stock Exchange. Andrew Beattie, "What Was the First Company to Issue Stock?" Investopedia, accessed March 13, 2017, http://www.investopedia.com/ask/answers/08/first-company-issue-stock -dutch-east-india.asp.

pushing and reporting functions would be automated, and fewer of them would be needed.

But things have not worked out that way. According to the Bureau of Labor Statistics, managers represented approximately 12.3% of the US workforce in 1998, but by 2015 this figure had increased to 15.4%. And there's strong evidence that a lot of other jobs have become substantially more management-like over time. In 2015, economist David Deming published an intriguing study that looked at the demand for different skills throughout the US economy between 1980 and 2012. As expected, demand for routine skills, both cognitive and physical, declined sharply over this period as the standard partnership between minds and machines, which we described in Chapter 2, spread throughout the economy.

Deming was also able to assess demand shifts for what he calls the "social skills" of coordination, negotiation, persuasion, and social perceptiveness. He found that "social skill task inputs"—in other words, the overall use of these tasks—increased 24% between 1980 and 2012, while the use of "non routine and analytical skills" grew only 11%. What's more, jobs that required high social skills increased as a share of total employment during this period, whether or not those jobs also required high math skills. Not all of these jobs are managerial, but it's clear that the economy as a whole has, over the years, been demanding more of the things that good managers excel at: sensing people's emotions and priorities, and getting them to work well together.

What's going on? Why is the business world coming to need proportionately more managers, and more workers skilled at social tasks, even as the powerful digital technologies spread? We think there are three main reasons, all highly interdependent, for the continued centrality of management and social skills.

The first and most obvious is simply that the world is a very complex and fast-changing place. Thriving within it requires a great deal of constant coordination, not all of which can be accomplished via automatic updates and conversations among peers on social media. Such activities are highly valuable, but they don't remove the need for the "transmission belts" of the organization, which is our MIT colleague Paul Osterman's excellent image of middle managers. These people solve small problems, escalate large ones, interpret and clarify communications both upward and downward, negotiate and discuss with their peers, and exercise their social skills in many other ways. The old definition of a great lawyer is one who makes problems go away before they show up in court. Really good managers are much the same; they make the transmission of an organization work smoothly, and prevent it from seizing up.

The second reason human social skills remain so valuable is that most of us don't find numbers and algorithms alone very persuasive. We're much more swayed by a good story or compelling anecdote then we are by a table full of statistically significant results. This is another of our cognitive biases, obviously, but one that none of us can afford to ignore. So, smart companies invest heavily in the gentle art of persuasion, not only of their customers but also of their own people. This is why, as Deming found, analytical ability is even more valuable when it's paired with high social skills; this combination is what helps good ideas spread and be accepted.

The third reason is the most nebulous, but also probably the most important. It's that we humans want to work together and help each other out, and we can and should be encouraged to do so. There are many social animals in the world, but as the primatologist Michael Tomasello beautifully summarized, "It is inconceivable that you would ever see two chimpanzees carrying a log together." And in virtually every large human group that's ever existed, some subset of people has taken on the role of defining and shaping the work to be done. When this goes poorly, we get tyrants, demagogues, manipulators, and oligarchies—every flavor of bad boss or clique. When it goes well, we get phenomena that have been trivialized by the overuse of words like "leadership" and "empowerment" and organizations that can build amazingly complex things like a double-decker jetliner, a 2,700-foot-tall skyscraper, a pocket-sized computer, and a global, digital encyclopedia.

Leading Past the Standard Partnership

This is not the place for a deep exploration of how to lead an organization—again, there are countless books on the topic—but we do want to point out two consistent features of the management styles we've observed at the successful and technologically sophisticated companies we've worked with. The first is egalitarianism, especially of ideas. While these companies have a clear organizational structure and management hierarchy, they also have a practice of listening to ideas even if they come from junior or low-level people, and even if they originate far from the R&D department or other parts of the core. Sometimes the upward percolation of these ideas is facilitated by technology, and sometimes it happens via the old routes: meetings and conversations.

In either case, the key practice for managers within these companies is that they try not to let their own biases and judgments play too large a role in determining which of the ideas they hear are the good ones, and thus worthy of implementation. Instead, they fall back whenever possible on the processes of iteration and experimentation to find unbiased evidence on the quality of a new idea. Managers, in other words, step away from their traditional roles as evaluators and gatekeepers of ideas. This shift is uncomfortable for some, who fear (with justification) that some bad ideas will see the light of day, but many of the most impressive companies and managers we've encountered believe the benefits are far greater than the risks. At the online education company Udacity, for example, egalitarianism about ideas led to a major positive change to the company's business model and cost structure.

Udacity offers many computer programming courses, all of which are project based; instead of taking exams, students write and submit code. This code was originally evaluated by Udacity employees, who took, on average, two weeks to send their feedback to students. Developer Oliver Cameron wanted to see whether outsiders could do the student evaluations as well as Udacity's employees could, and perhaps also faster. As then-COO Vish Makhijani (who was later promoted to CEO) told us,

> Oliver did the experiment where he essentially got project submissions and recruited people to look at them: project comes in, internal person does it, we go find somebody else external [and compare the two].
>
> "Oh, wow, they look pretty similar." Do that a few times.
>
> "Oh my gosh, you know what? There's talented people all over the place. We don't have to hire them here in Mountain View. They can actually provide just as meaningful feedback, if not better."
>
> Then we started thinking, "What do we have to pay for this stuff?"
>
> We started experimenting with different amounts of pay. "Wow, we could do it for 30%." He manually tested his way to build the product that he launched in six weeks.

When we asked Makhijani if he had formally approved opening up Udacity's grading to outsiders, he said he had not.

> I just said, "That sounds pretty cool. Keep going." And he did. It's funny, [Udacity founder] Sebastian [Thrun] says it the best:

"When we make a change to the mobile app, I find out because it's in the app store." There's no product reviews here, there's no sense that you must clear your idea with Vish or anything like that. I don't have this absolute perfect filter of what should be in the market and what shouldn't, let alone the creativity to do it all. So why not tap the collective brains of everybody here?

In addition to egalitarianism, and often in support of it, second-machine-age companies have high levels of transparency: they share more information more widely than has been typical. *Wall Street Journal* technology columnist Christopher Mims points out that information transparency and a flat, fast, evidence-based management style are highly complementary. As he puts it, "What makes this relatively flat hierarchy possible is that front-line workers have essentially unlimited access to data that used to be difficult to obtain, or required more senior managers to interpret." Mims summarizes that the combination of egalitarianism and transparency "isn't the end of middle management, but it is an evolution. Every company I talked to had middle and even senior managers who operated as player-coaches, tasked with both doing things and directing others."

We see the same phenomenon. We also see that after at least two decades, the standard division between mind and machine is giving way to something quite different. Second-machine-age companies are combining modern technologies with a better understanding of Daniel Kahneman's System 1 and System 2 (discussed in Chapter 2), and of human abilities and biases, to change how they make and evaluate decisions, how they generate and refine new ideas, and how they move forward in a highly uncertain world.

While new marketplaces are emerging and thriving, we see no evidence in the economic data to indicate that companies are becoming passé, or are going to be wholly replaced by any variety of technology-enabled distributed autonomous organizations. TCE, incomplete contracts theory, and insights from other disciplines reveal several reasons why this won't be the case. But this scholarship, as valuable as it is, provides far too narrow an aperture for viewing the issue.

Incomplete contracting and residual rights of control will probably always necessitate the existence of companies. But companies will also exist for a much more important reason: they are one of the best ways we've ever come up with to get big things done in the world. To feed people and improve their health; to provide entertainment and access to knowledge; to improve material conditions of life and to do so for more and more people over time, all around the planet. The new technologies of the crowd will help greatly with all this, but they will not displace companies, which are one of the cornerstone technologies of the core.

Chapter Summary

▶ The failure of The DAO and challenges within the Bitcoin-mining network show that there are problems with the idea of completely decentralized organizations.

▶ Transaction cost economics and the theory of the firm are excellent bases for understanding these problems.

▶ It is true that technological progress has lowered transaction and coordination costs, which has helped new market and market-oriented business models to emerge.

▶ It is also true, though, that in most industries and geographies, economic activity is concentrating instead of dispersing: a smaller number of companies are capturing more of the value.

▶ Companies and other nonmarket organizations are needed to deal with the problem of incomplete contracting—the fact that contracts cannot realistically specify all possible contingencies in the messy real world. Within companies, managers—on behalf of owners and other stakeholders—have the residual rights of control: the right to make decisions not specified in contracts.

▶ Corporate leaders and managers do much more than simply make decisions that are not contractually delegated elsewhere. They get people to work together; articulate goals, visions, and strategies; shape culture and values; and do many other essential things.

▶ Technology is progressing, but because companies deal effectively with the shortcomings of contracts and also provide many other benefits, they will be part of the economic landscape for a long time to come.

▶ The leading companies of the second machine age may look very different from those of the industrial era, but they will almost all be easily recognizable as companies.

Questions

1. In the face of the technology surge now under way, how do you want your organization to be different in three to five years? How do you want to change the balance between minds and machines, products and platforms, and the core and the crowd?

2. What decisions do you most want to keep for yourself? What assets do you need to own in order to keep them?

3. What are the most important steps you'll take in the next quarter to move past the standard partnership?

4. Would your goals be better served by orchestrating a platform, participating in another platform, focusing on your own products, or some combination of strategies?

5. How far are you willing to push being less centralized and more distributed? Less hands-on and more autonomous?

6. How frequently do managers act as gatekeepers for ideas in your organization? Why is this? Are you exploring alternatives?

ECONOMIES AND SOCIETIES BEYOND COMPUTATION

> It is not enough that you should understand about applied science in order that your work may increase man's blessings. Concern for the man himself and his fate must always form the chief interest of all technical endeavors; concern for the great unsolved problems of the organization of labor and the distribution of goods in order that the creations of our mind shall be a blessing and not a curse to mankind. Never forget this in the midst of your diagrams and equations.
>
> — *Albert Einstein, 1931*

OVER THE NEXT TEN YEARS, YOU WILL HAVE AT YOUR DIS- posal 100 times more computer power than you do today. Billions of brains and trillions of devices will be connected to the Internet, not only gaining access to the collective knowledge of our humanity, but also contributing to it. And by the end of the decade, more and more of that knowledge will be accessed by software agents, and created by them.

The people alive today have the unique experience of witnessing the emergence of effective artificial intelligence in domains as diverse as health care, transportation, and retailing. We are working alongside machines that understand what we say and respond appropriately, robots that can manipulate objects and move through the environment, and vehicles that can pilot themselves.

Understanding the implications of these developments for business can make the difference between thriving and merely surviving. Or between surviving and perishing.

Technological progress tests firms. Indeed, the average life span of the most valuable US companies, those listed in the S&P 500, has fallen from about sixty years in 1960 to less than twenty years today. A lot of Joseph Schumpeter's "creative destruction" has taken place in this digital era, and most of this book has focused on how executives can navigate that destruction successfully.

But although we field many requests for advice on how a company can thrive in the digital era, some of the most common questions we get take a broader view: What does the machine-platform-crowd transformation mean for society? Will machines leave people unemployed? Will powerful platforms control all our economic decisions? Will individuals have less freedom to decide how and when they work, where they live, and who their friends are?

These are profoundly important issues. But too often, they are variants of a single question: What will technology do to us?

And that's not the right question. Technology is a tool. That is true whether it's a hammer or a deep neural network. Tools don't decide what happens to people. We decide. The lesson we've learned from studying thousands of companies over our careers is that while technology creates options, success depends on how people take advantage of these options. The success of a venture almost never turns on how much technology it can access, but on how its people use that technology, and on what values they imbue in the organization.

We have more powerful technology at our disposal than ever before, both as individuals and as a society. This means we have more power to change the world than ever before. Fundamentally, we have more freedom to do things that simply could not have been done by earlier generations. Rather than being locked into any one future, we have a greater ability to shape the future.

So we should ask not "What will technology do to us?" but rather "What do we want to do with technology?" More than ever before, what matters is thinking deeply about what we want. Having more power and more choices means that our values are more important than ever.

In this book, we've described the three great rebalancings of this digital era: minds and machines, products and platforms, and the core and the crowd. Although important patterns and principles are at work, our research finds no single formula for success. Machines can make better decisions in an increasing variety of fields, but there's still a huge role for humans. Likewise, turning the dial all the way to "platform" or all the way to "crowd" does not guarantee success.

What's more, there's not just one single optimal balance point for a company along each of the three dimensions. Instead, there is always a range of potentially successful strategies. Few companies are more successful than Apple and Google, but while both leverage platforms, they've done it in different ways, with different degrees of openness and varying dependence on the crowd. And in addition to the principles we describe, many other factors, of course, are involved, from the creativity of a good designer, to the support of a key business partner, to the luck of a technical breakthrough. Just as the race doesn't always go to the swiftest, or to those with the best running form, business success does not always accrue to those with the best products or the best understanding of strategy.

It's not just chance or randomness in outcomes. It's that there are multiple equilibria, each of which might be fairly stable and lasting. Two seemingly similar gaming apps might be launched at the same time, but if, through a series of small decisions and events, one of them gets a bigger share of consumers' attention, that advantage can feed on itself until the game vastly dominates its competitor. Network effects, economies of scale, complementarities, two-sided networks, learning curves, and a variety of other factors can create very strong path dependencies, amplifying the impact of small initial decisions. Noneconomic forces are also important. A successful organization creates a sense of purpose, a mission, and a community.

Just as there is no single equilibrium for a company or market, there is no inevitable future path determined by the technological forces unfolding today. What's more, each of our individual decisions shapes, and can change, the path of history. As Friedrich Hayek stressed, no single mind has access to all the knowledge needed to make decisions in the economy. Each of us has some piece of essential knowledge, whether it's resources that we are uniquely informed about, or our own capabilities, or even our own wants and desires. The genius of the free market system has been its ability to channel much of this knowledge toward productive use, coordinating, through the price system and well-defined property rights, the decisions of people who may not ever have met or spoken to each other.

But now digitization is creating a new wave of challenges. Millions of people have legitimate worries that their jobs will disappear as technology improves, and they are uncertain they will find equally rewarding work afterward. Wages have shrunk as a share of GDP in most advanced countries, and real wages for people in the bottom half of the distribution are lower now than they were twenty years ago. In addition, the workforce disruptions of technology are not nearly finished. A study published in January 2017 by James Manyika and his colleagues at the McKinsey Global Institute estimated that "about half of all the activities people are paid to do in the world's workforce could potentially be automated by adapting currently demonstrated technologies."

At the same time, there's never been a better time to be a person with the skill, talent, or luck to produce a good that can be delivered via the global digital infrastructure. Being able to reach millions or even billions of customers makes it possible to create and capture value on an unprecedented scale. This value creation is an engine of growth far beyond what is reflected in the official GDP or productivity statistics. Now there are huge opportunities to have more people contribute and to use technology to create more widely shared prosperity.

Shaping how society will use technology is not just, or even mainly, a job for government or government leaders. It's something that arises from all parts of society. It emerges from the decisions of entrepreneurs and managers who think about how technologies are implemented and how they are used. And it springs from the decisions of millions of individuals in their daily lives and the ways they manage their affairs.

Today, millions of people work in jobs that create goods and services our grandparents couldn't even imagine. One of the things our economy needs most are people who specialize in inventing these new jobs. This task requires designing and implementing new combinations of technologies, human skills, and other resources and assets to solve problems and meet the needs of potential customers. Machines are not very good at this sort of large-scale creativity and planning, but humans are. That is why being an entrepreneur is one of the most rewarding jobs both for individuals and for society. Matching new technologies with the right people can lead to more sustainable, inclusive, productive, and higher-paying jobs, benefiting employers, employees, and customers alike.

Consider 99Degrees Custom, a Lawrence, Massachusetts, apparel maker. You seemingly couldn't get any more antiquated than making clothes, especially in an old mill in a New England textile manufacturing city that's seen better days. But unlike the Luddites who smashed machines in 1815, the team at 99Degrees Custom embraces a highly engineered, partially automated production line to make highly customized textile products. They've created a lot of new jobs that are better than the old factory jobs. The work is more varied, more highly skilled, and better paid. The net effect has been to create more value for more people.

Another example of an organization using technology to complement human labor is Iora Health, which (as we discussed in Chapter 5) employs health coaches. Coaches work with patients to help them stick to a diet or exercise regimen, or to remember to take their pills. These coaches don't have medical degrees, but they add value through their compassion, motivational skills, and emotional intelligence. Studies show that this approach can make the difference between a patient's recovering or incurring the expense of another stay in the hospital. The cost savings can be as much as 15%–20% while leaving patients and workers better off.

Depending on how they are used, machines, platforms, and the crowd can have very different effects. They can concentrate power and wealth or distribute decision making and prosperity. They can increase privacy, enhance openness, or even do both at the same time. They can create a workplace imbued with inspiration and purpose, or one that is driven by greed and fear. As the power of our technologies grows, so do our future possibilities. This potential increases the importance of having clarity in our goals and thinking more deeply about our values.

Ultimately, we have an optimistic vision for the future. The next few decades could and should be better than any other that humans have witnessed so far. This is not a prediction; it's a possibility and a goal. No single future is predetermined. Just as individuals can chart their own courses, so can companies, and so can a society.

We hope this book has helped you chart your course.

NOTES

Chapter 1
THE TRIPLE REVOLUTION

1 **at least 2,500 years ago:** Alan Levinovitz, "The Mystery of Go, the Ancient Game That Computers Still Can't Win," *Wired*, May 12, 2014, https://www.wired.com/2014/05/the-world-of-computer-go.

1 **"gentlemen should not waste their time":** American Go Association, "Notable Quotes about Go," accessed January 11, 2017, http://www.usgo.org/notable-quotes-about-go.

2 **"While the Baroque rules of chess":** Ibid.

2 **about 2×10^{170}:** Mike James, "Number of Legal Go Positions Finally Worked Out," *I Programmer*, February 3, 2016, http://www.i-programmer.info/news/112-theory/9384-number-of-legal-go-positions-finally-worked-out.html.

2 **about 10^{82} atoms:** John Carl Villanueva, "How Many Atoms Are There in the Universe?" *Universe Today*, December 24, 2015, http://www.universetoday.com/36302/atoms-in-the-universe.

2 **"I'll see a move":** Levinovitz, "Mystery of Go."

3 **"another ten years":** Ibid.

4 **"Mastering the Game of Go":** David Silver et al., "Mastering the Game of Go with Deep Neural Networks and Search Trees," *Nature* 529 (2016): 484–89, http://www.nature.com/nature/journal/v529/n7587/full/nature16961.html.

4 **Work on AlphaGo began in 2014:** John Ribeiro, "AlphaGo's Unusual Moves Prove Its AI Prowess, Experts Say," *PC World*, March 14, 2016, http://www.pcworld.com/article/3043668/analytics/alphagos-unusual-moves-prove-its-ai-prowess-experts-say.html.

5 **"Go is scarcely a sport in Europe":** Silver et al., "Mastering the Game of Go."

5 **"intuitive, unpredictable, creative":** Sam Byford, "Google vs. Go: Can AI Beat the Ultimate Board Game?" *Verge*, March 8, 2016, http://www.theverge.com/2016/3/8/11178462/google-deepmind-go-challenge-ai-vs-lee-sedol.

5 **"There is a beauty to the game of Go":** Ibid.

5 **"Looking at the match in October":** "S. Korean Go Player Confident of Beating

Google's AI," *Yonhap News Agency*, February 23, 2016, http://english.yonhapnews
.co.kr/search1/2603000000.html?cid=AEN20160223003651315.

6 **"I kind of felt powerless":** Jordan Novet, "Go Board Game Champion Lee Sedol
Apologizes for Losing to Google's AI," *VentureBeat*, March 12, 2016, http://
venturebeat.com/2016/03/12/go-board-game-champion-lee-sedol-apologizes
-for-losing-to-googles-ai.

6 **"Uber, the world's largest taxi company":** Tom Goodwin, "The Battle Is for the Customer Interface," TechCrunch, March 3, 2015, https://
techcrunch.com/2015/03/03/in-the-age-of-disintermediation-the-battle-is-all-for
-the-customer-interface.

7 **over a million people:** Ellen Huet, "Uber Says It's Doing 1 Million Rides
per Day, 140 Million in the Last Year," *Forbes*, December 17, 2014, http://
www.forbes.com/sites/ellenhuet/2014/12/17/uber-says-its-doing-1-million-rides
-per-day-140-million-in-last-year.

7 **one of 300 cities in 60 countries:** Anne Freier, "Uber Usage Statistics and Revenue," *Business of Apps*, September 14, 2015, http://www.businessofapps.com/
uber-usage-statistics-and-revenue.

7 **640,000 different lodging options:** Chip Conley, "Airbnb Open: What I
Learned from You," *Airbnb* (blog), November 25, 2014, http://blog.airbnb.com/
airbnb-open-chips-takeaways.

7 **191 countries:** Airbnb, "Airbnb Summer Travel Report: 2015," accessed January 11, 2017, http://blog.airbnb.com/wp-content/uploads/2015/09/Airbnb
-Summer-Travel-Report-1.pdf.

7 **a yurt in Mongolia:** Airbnb, "Nomadic Life in the Countryside," accessed January 11, 2017, https://www.airbnb.com/rooms/13512229?s=zcoAwTWQ.

7 **James Joyce's childhood home:** Airbnb, "James Joyce's Childhood Home Dub-
lin," accessed January 11, 2017, https://www.airbnb.ie/rooms/4480268.

7 **4,500 shops across the United States:** Wal-Mart, "Our Locations," accessed
January 13, 2017, http://corporate.walmart.com/our-story/our-locations.

7 **$180 billion of property and equipment assets:** US Securities and Exchange
Commission, "Form 10-Q: Wal-Mart Stores, Inc.," December 1, 2016, http://
d18rn0p25nwr6d.cloudfront.net/CIK-0000104169/2b25dfe5-6d4a-4d2d-857f
-08dda979d6b9.pdf.

7 **number of Chinese people using Alibaba's apps:** Alibaba Group, "Consumer
Engagement Driving Growth for Mobile Taobao (Alizila News)," June 28, 2016,
http://www.alibabagroup.com/en/ir/article?news=p160628.

8 **sales of $17.8 billion:** Cheang Ming, "Singles' Day: Alibaba Smashes Records
at World's Largest Online Shopping Event," *CNBC*, November 11, 2016, http://
www.cnbc.com/2016/11/11/singles-day-news-alibaba-poised-to-smash-records
-at-worlds-largest-online-shopping-event.html.

8 **visited daily by 936 million people:** US Securities and Exchange Commission,
"Form 10-Q: Facebook, Inc.," April 23, 2015, http://d1lge852tjjqow.cloudfront.net/
CIK-0001326801/a1186095-bc85-4bf7-849f-baa62dfa13ef.pdf.

8   **an average of fifty minutes per day:** James B. Stewart, "Facebook Has 50 Minutes of Your Time Each Day. It Wants More," *New York Times*, May 5, 2016, http://www.nytimes.com/2016/05/06/business/facebook-bends-the-rules-of-audience-engagement-to-its-advantage.html.

8   **$6.4 billion. Profits were $2 billion:** Facebook, "Facebook Q2 2016 Results," accessed January 13, 2017, https://s21.q4cdn.com/399680738/files/doc_presentations/FB-Q216-Earnings-Slides.pdf.

9   **"Half the money I spend":** John Wanamaker, "Quotation Details: Quotation #1992," *Quotations Page*, accessed January 13, 2017, http://www.quotationspage.com/quote/1992.html.

9   **"indescribably thin layer":** Goodwin, "Battle Is for the Customer Interface."

9   **"Airbnb is facing an existential expansion problem":** Tom Slee, "Airbnb Is Facing an Existential Expansion Problem," *Harvard Business Review*, July 11, 2016, https://hbr.org/2016/07/airbnb-is-facing-an-existential-expansion-problem.

9   **introduced in 2014:** Alex, "Announcing UberPool," *Uber Newsroom* (blog), August 5, 2014, https://newsroom.uber.com/announcing-uberpool.

9   **all weekly rush-hour UberPool rides:** Mikaela, "New $5 Commuter Flat Rates with uberPOOL," *Uber Newsroom* (blog), May 8, 2016, https://newsroom.uber.com/us-new-york/new-5-commuter-flat-rates-with-uberpool.

9   **a special offer allowed New Yorkers:** Alison Griswold, "Commuting with Uber in New York Is Cheaper than Taking the Subway This Summer," *Quartz*, last modified July 11, 2016, http://qz.com/728871/commuting-with-uber-in-new-york-is-cheaper-than-taking-the-subway-this-summer.

10   **via Facebook than from Google:** Matthew Ingram, "Facebook Has Taken Over from Google as a Traffic Source for News," *Fortune*, August 18, 2015, http://fortune.com/2015/08/18/facebook-google.

10   **the company's ten-year road map:** Adario Strange, "Everything You Need to Know about Facebook's 10-Year Plan," *Mashable*, April 12, 2016, http://mashable.com/2016/04/12/facebook-10-year-plan/#pcbrzJRndSqS.

10   **"Something interesting is happening":** Goodwin, "Battle Is for the Customer Interface."

10   **GE was selected in 1896:** Quasimodos.com, "The First 120 Years of the Dow Jones: An Historical Timeline of the DJIA Components. 1884–2003," accessed January 19, 2017. http://www.quasimodos.com/info/dowhistory.html.

11   **"create marketing innovation internally":** Christine Moorman, "Marketing in a Technology Company: GE's Organizational Platform for Innovation," *Forbes*, January 29, 2013, http://www.forbes.com/sites/christinemoorman/2013/01/29/marketing-in-a-technology-company-ges-organizational-platform-for-innovation/#57f9333762c9.

11   **annual budget of $5.2 billion for R&D:** US Securities and Exchange Commission, "Form 10-K: General Electric Company," February 26, 2016, http://api40.10kwizard.com/cgi/convert/pdf/GE-20160226-10K-20151231.pdf?ipage=10776107&xml=1&quest=1&rid=23&section=1&sequence=-1&pdf=1&dn=1.

11 **$393 million on marketing:** Bradley Johnson, "Big Spender on a Budget: What Top 200 U.S. Advertisers Are Doing to Spend Smarter," *Advertising Age*, July 5, 2015, http://adage.com/article/advertising/big-spenders-facts-stats-top -200-u-s-advertisers/299270.

11 **"co-creation community that is changing":** FirstBuild, "[About]," accessed August 1, 2016, https://firstbuild.com/about.

12 **"munchable ice sells like hotcakes":** Ilan Brat, "Chew This Over: Munchable Ice Sells like Hot Cakes," *Wall Street Journal*, January 30, 2008, http:// www.wsj.com/articles/SB120165510390727145.

13 **"launchpad for creative and entrepreneurial ideas":** Google Play, "Indiegogo," accessed February 10, 2017, https://play.google.com/store/apps/dev?id=8186897 092162507742&hl=en.

13 **Within a few hours the campaign raised:** Jonathan Shieber, "GE FirstBuild Launches Indiegogo Campaign for Next Generation Icemaker," *TechCrunch*, July 28, 2015, https://techcrunch.com/2015/07/28/ge-firstbuild-launches-indie gogo-campaign-for-next-generation-icemaker.

13 **in excess of $1.3 million:** Samantha Hurst, "FirstBuild's Opal Nugget Ice Maker Captures $1.3M during First Week on Indiegogo," *Crowdfund Insider*, August 3, 2015, http://www.crowdfundinsider.com/2015/08/72196-firstbuilds -opal-nugget-ice-maker-captures-1-3m-during-first-week-on-indiegogo.

13 **the Opal campaign had attracted more than $2.7 million:** "FirstBuild Launches Affordable Nugget Ice Machine," *Louisville Business First*, July 22, 2015, http://www.bizjournals.com/louisville/news/2015/07/22/firstbuild-launches -affordable-nugget-ice-machine.html.

13 **more than 5,000 preorder customers:** Indiegogo, "Opal Nugget Ice Maker."

16 **"You can see the computer age":** Robert M. Solow, "We'd Better Watch Out," *New York Times*, July 21, 1987, http://www.standupeconomist.com/pdf/misc/ solow-computer-productivity.pdf.

17 **more than a billion users of smartphones:** Don Reisinger, "Worldwide Smartphone User Base Hits 1 Billion," *CNET*, October 17, 2012, https://www .cnet.com/news/worldwide-smartphone-user-base-hits-1-billion.

18 **more than 40% of the adults:** Jacob Poushter, "Smartphone Ownership and Internet Usage Continues to Climb in Emerging Economies," Pew Research Center, February 22, 2016, http://www.pewglobal.org/2016/02/22/smartphone -ownership-and-internet-usage-continues-to-climb-in-emerging-economies.

18 **approximately 1.5 billion more were sold:** Tess Stynes, "IDC Cuts Outlook for 2016 Global Smartphone Shipments," *Wall Street Journal*, September 1, 2016, http://www.wsj.com/articles/idc-cuts-outlook-for-2016-global-smartphone -shipments-1472740414.

19 **"There were many factories":** Warren D. Devine Jr., "From Shafts to Wires: Historical Perspective on Electrification," *Journal of Economic History* 43, no. 2 (1983): 347–72, http://www.j-bradford-delong.net/teaching_Folder/Econ_210c_ spring_2002/Readings/Devine.pdf.

20 **"the merits of driving machines in groups":** Ibid.

21 **"curse of knowledge":** Scott Sleek, "The Curse of Knowledge: Pinker Describes a Key Cause of Bad Writing," *Observer* 28, no. 6 (July/August 2015), http://www.psychologicalscience.org/observer/the-curse-of-knowledge-pinker-describes-a-key-cause-of-bad-writing#.WJodJhiZOi5.

21 **"At the beginning of the transition":** Andrew Atkeson and Patrick J. Kehoe, *The Transition to a New Economy after the Second Industrial Revolution*, Federal Reserve Bank of Minneapolis Research Department Working Paper 606 (July 2001), http://citeseerx.ist.psu.edu/viewdoc/download?doi=10.1.1.147.7979&rep=rep1&type=pdf.

21 **"the need for organizational":** Paul A. David and Gavin Wright, *General Purpose Technologies and Surges in Productivity: Historical Reflections on the Future of the ICT Revolution*, University of Oxford Discussion Papers in Economic and Social History 31 (September 1999), 12, http://sites-final.uclouvain.be/econ/DW/DOCTORALWS2004/bruno/adoption/david%20wright.pdf.

22 **more than 300 such trusts:** John Moody, *The Truth about Trusts: A Description and Analysis of the American Trust Movement* (New York: Moody, 1904), 467, https://archive.org/details/truthabouttrust01moodgoog.

22 **"'limping' units":** Shaw Livermore, "The Success of Industrial Mergers," *Quarterly Journal of Economics* 50, no. 1 (1935): 68–96.

23 **A study by economist Richard Caves:** Richard E. Caves, Michael Fortunato, and Pankaj Ghemawat, "The Decline of Dominant Firms, 1905–1929," *Quarterly Journal of Economics* 99, no. 3 (1984): 523–46.

25 **"Economic theory is concerned":** Carl Menger, *Principles of Economics* (Vienna: Braumüller, 1871), 48.

Chapter 2
THE HARDEST THING TO ACCEPT ABOUT OURSELVES

32 **"Paperwork Mine":** David Fahrenthold, "Sinkhole of Bureaucracy," *Washington Post*, March 22, 2014, http://www.washingtonpost.com/sf/national/2014/03/22/sinkhole-of-bureaucracy.

32 **twenty-five most influential business books of all time:** Roya Wolverson, "The 25 Most Influential Business Management Books," *Time*, August 9, 2011, http://content.time.com/time/specials/packages/article/0,28804,2086680_2086683_2087684,00.html.

32 **"Reengineering is new":** Thomas A. Stewart and Joyce E. Davis, "Reengineering the Hot New Managing Tool," *Fortune*, August 23, 1993, http://archive.fortune.com/magazines/fortune/fortune_archive/1993/08/23/78237/index.htm.

33 **over 60% of the Fortune 1000:** Flylib.com, "ERP Market Penetration," accessed January 22, 2017, http://flylib.com/books/en/1.20.1.44/1/.

33 **A study by Erik and his colleagues:** Sinan Aral, D. J. Wu, and Erik Brynjolfsson, "Which Came First, IT or Productivity? The Virtuous Cycle of Investment and Use in Enterprise Systems," paper presented at the Twenty Seventh International Conference on Information Systems, Milwaukee, 2006, http://ebusiness.mit.edu/research/papers/2006.11_Aral_Brynjolfsson_Wu_Which%20Came%20First_279.pdf.

33 **The web was born in 1989:** Tim Berners-Lee, "Information Management: A Proposal," last modified May 1990, https://www.w3.org/History/1989/proposal.html.

34 **This multimedia wonder:** Chris Anderson, "The Man Who Makes the Future: *Wired* Icon Marc Andreessen," April 24, 2012, https://www.wired.com/2012/04/ff_andreessen.

34 **10% of nonfood, nonautomotive retail sales:** Matthew Yglesias, "Online Shopping Really Is Killing Shopping Malls," *Vox*, January 4, 2015, http://www.vox.com/2015/1/4/7490013/ecommerce-shopping-mall.

35 **"Most of the checking":** Michael Hammer and James Champy, *Reengineering the Corporation: A Manifesto for Business Revolution* (New York: Harper Collins, 2013), Kindle ed., p. 73.

36 **"System 1 operates automatically":** Daniel Kahneman, *Thinking, Fast and Slow* (New York: Macmillan, 2011), Kindle ed., pp. 20–21.

37 ***Straight from the Gut* and *Tough Choices*:** Jack Welch, *Jack: Straight from the Gut* (London: Warner, 2001); Carly Fiorina, *Tough Choices: A Memoir* (New York: Portfolio, 2006).

37 **"building judgment and intuition":** Srikant M. Datar, David A. Garvin, and Patrick G. Cullen, *Rethinking the MBA: Business Education at a Crossroads* (Boston: Harvard Business Press, 2010), Kindle ed., p. 9.

38 **Sociology professor Chris Snijders used 5,200:** Chris Snijders, Frits Tazelaar, and Ronald Batenburg, "Electronic Decision Support for Procurement Management: Evidence on Whether Computers Can Make Better Procurement Decisions," *Journal of Purchasing and Supply Management* 9, no. 5–6 (September–November 2003): 191–98, http://www.sciencedirect.com/science/article/pii/S1478409203000463.

38 **"one of the most interesting issues":** Orley Ashenfelter, "Predicting the Quality and Prices of Bordeaux Wine," *Economic Journal* 118, no. 529 (June 2008): F174–84, http://onlinelibrary.wiley.com/doi/10.1111/j.1468-0297.2008.02148.x/abstract.

39 **Erik worked with Lynn Wu:** Lynn Wu and Erik Brynjolfsson, "The Future of Prediction: How Google Searches Foreshadow Housing Prices and Sales," in *Economic Analysis of the Digital Economy*, ed. Avi Goldfarb, Shane M. Greenstein, and Catherine E. Tucker (Chicago: University of Chicago Press, 2015), 89–118.

39 **A separate project by Erik:** D. Bertsimas et al., "Tenure Analytics: Models for Predicting Research Impact," *Operations Research* 63, no. 6 (2015): 1246–61; and Brynjolfsson and Silberholz, "'Moneyball' for Professors?" *Sloan*

Management Review, December 14, 2016. http://sloanreview.mit.edu/article/moneyball-for-professors.

39 **Israeli judges were more likely:** Shai Danzinger, Jonathan Levav, and Liora Avnaim-Pesso, "Extraneous Factors in Judicial Decisions," *PNAS* 108, no. 17 (2010): 6889–92, http://www.pnas.org/content/108/17/6889.full.pdf.

40 **Economists Ozkan Eren and Naci Mocan found:** Ozkan Eren and Naci Mocan, *Emotional Judges and Unlucky Juveniles*, NBER Working Paper 22611 (September 2016), http://www.nber.org/papers/w22611.

40 **In the Broward County, Florida, school district:** David Card and Laura Giuliano, *Can Universal Screening Increase the Representation of Low Income and Minority Students in Gifted Education?* NBER Working Paper 21519 (September 2015), http://www.nber.org/papers/w21519.pdf.

40 **Law professors Ted Ruger and Pauline Kim:** Theodore W. Ruger et al., "The Supreme Court Forecasting Project: Legal and Political Science Approaches to Predicting Supreme Court Decisionmaking," *Columbia Law Review* 104 (2004): 1150–1210, http://sites.lsa.umich.edu/admart/wp-content/uploads/sites/127/2014/08/columbia04.pdf.

41 **A team led by psychologist William Grove:** William M. Grove et al., "Clinical versus Mechanical Prediction: A Meta-analysis," *Psychological Assessment* 12, no. 1 (2000): 19–30, http://zaldlab.psy.vanderbilt.edu/resources/wmg00pa.pdf.

41 **"the clinicians received more data":** Ibid.

41 **"There is no controversy":** Paul E. Meehl, "Causes and Effects of My Disturbing Little Book," *Journal of Personality Assessment* 50, no. 3 (1986): 370–75, http://www.tandfonline.com/doi/abs/10.1207/s15327752jpa5003_6.

42 **Working with the US Census Bureau:** Erik Brynjolfsson and Kristina McElheran, "Data in Action: Data-Driven Decision Making in US Manufacturing," 2016, https://papers.ssrn.com/sol3/papers2.cfm?abstract_id=2722502. Early work using a smaller sample found similar results: Erik Brynjolfsson, Lorin M. Hitt, and Heekyung Hellen Kim, "Strength in Numbers: How Does Data-Driven Decisionmaking Affect Firm Performance?" 2011, https://papers.ssrn.com/sol3/papers2.cfm?abstract_id=1819486.

43 **7.5 billion:** Worldometers, "Current World Population," accessed February 26, 2017, http://www.worldometers.info/world-population.

43 **"Because System 1 operates automatically":** Kahneman, *Thinking, Fast and Slow*, p. 28.

44 **"1. Information overload sucks":** Buster Benson, "Cognitive Bias Cheat Sheet," *Better Humans*, September 1, 2016, https://betterhumans.coach.me/cognitive-bias-cheat-sheet-55a472476b18#.qtwg334q8.

45 **"Judgment and justification are two separate processes":** Jonathan Haidt, "Moral Psychology and the Law: How Intuitions Drive Reasoning, Judgment, and the Search for Evidence," *Alabama Law Review* 64, no. 4 (2013): 867–80, https://www.law.ua.edu/pubs/lrarticles/Volume%2064/Issue%204/4%20Haidt%20867-880.pdf.

45 **"telling more than we can know"**: Richard E. Nisbett and Timothy DeCamp Wilson, "Telling More Than We Can Know: Verbal Reports on Mental Processes," *Psychological Review* 84, no. 3 (1977): 231–60, http://www.people.virginia.edu/~tdw/nisbett&wilson.pdf.

45 **the acronym HiPPO:** Experimentation Platform, "HiPPO FAQ," accessed February 26, 2017, http://www.exp-platform.com/Pages/HiPPO_explained.aspx.

46 **"no [human being] even looks":** P. Nadler, "Weekly Adviser: Horror at Credit Scoring Is Not Just Foot-Dragging," *American Banker*, no. 211 (November 2, 1999), https://www.americanbanker.com/news/weekly-adviser-horror-at-credit-scoring-is-not-just-foot-dragging.

47 **"reduces the opportunities for engaging in":** Board of Governors of the Federal Reserve System, *Report to the Congress on Credit Scoring and Its Effects on the Availability and Affordability of Credit*, August 2007, pp. 36 and S-4, https://www.federalreserve.gov/boarddocs/rptcongress/creditscore/creditscore.pdf.

47 **35% of its sales are from cross-selling activities:** Chuck Cohn, "Beginner's Guide to Upselling and Cross-Selling," *Entrepreneurs* (blog), *Forbes*, May 15, 2015, http://www.forbes.com/sites/chuckcohn/2015/05/15/a-beginners-guide-to-upselling-and-cross-selling/#4c310dec572e (the article cites this article: http://www.the-future-of-commerce.com/2013/10/14/ecommerce-cross-sell-up-sell).

47 **Amazon and Walmart altered the prices:** 360pi, "360pi Cyber Monday Recap: Amazon Maintains Overall Price Leadership on Record-Setting Online Shopping Day, but Best Sellers Take Priority," December 9, 2015, http://360pi.com/press_release/360pi-cyber-monday-recap-amazon-maintains-overall-price-leadership-record-setting-online-shopping-day-best-sellers-take-priority.

47 **"second economy":** W. Brian Arthur, "The Second Economy," *McKinsey Quarterly*, October 2011, http://www.mckinsey.com/business-functions/strategy-and-corporate-finance/our-insights/the-second-economy.

48 **the agency at the center of the hit TV drama *Mad Men*:** Andrea Ovans, "That Mad Men Computer, Explained by HBR in 1969," *Harvard Business Review*, May 15, 2014, https://hbr.org/2014/05/that-mad-men-computer-explained-by-hbr-in-1969.

48 **Using machine learning:** Dan Wagner, interview by the authors, July 2015.

50 **"We ended up buying":** Ibid.

50 **"If you're selling expensive tires":** Ibid.

51 **"overall evaluation criterion":** Ron Kohavi, Randal M. Henne, and Dan Sommerfield, "Practical Guide to Controlled Experiments on the Web: Listen to Your Customers Not to the HiPPO," 2007, https://ai.stanford.edu/~ronnyk/2007GuideControlledExperiments.pdf.

52 **"Latanya Sweeney, Arrested?":** "Racism Is Poisoning Online Ad Delivery, Says Harvard Professor," *MIT Technology Review*, February 4, 2013, https://www.technologyreview.com/s/510646/racism-is-poisoning-online-ad-delivery-says-harvard-professor.

52 **With further research, Sweeney found:** Latanya Sweeney. "Discrimination in Online Ad Delivery," *Queue* 11, no. 3 (2013): 10.

52 **In an article in *Nature*:** Kate Crawford and Ryan Calo, "There Is a Blind Spot in AI Research," *Nature* 538, no. 7625 (2016): 311. Also relevant is Danah Boyd's dissertation: "The Networked Nature of Algorithmic Discrimination" (PhD diss., Fordham University, 2014).

53 **There's an old joke:** Mark Fisher, *The Millionaire's Book of Quotations* (New York: Thorsons, 1991), quoted in Barry Popik, "The Factory of the Future Will Have Only Two Employees, a Man and a Dog," *Barrypopik.com* (blog), December 2, 2015, http://www.barrypopik.com/index.php/new_york_city/entry/the_factory_of_the_future.

54 **"broken leg role":** Paul E. Meehl, *Clinical versus Statistical Prediction* (Minneapolis: University of Minnesota Press, 1954).

54 **"distinct, unanticipated factors":** Ibid.

54 **"look out of the window":** Stuart Lauchlan, "SPSS Directions: Thomas Davenport on Competing through Analytics," MyCustomer, May 14, 2007, http://www.mycustomer.com/marketing/strategy/spss-directions-thomas-davenport-on-competing-through-analytics.

55 **This practice earned the company:** "Uber 'Truly Sorry' for Price Surge during Sydney Siege," *BBC News*, December 24, 2014, http://www.bbc.com/news/technology-30595406.

55 **"We didn't stop surge pricing immediately":** "Uber 'Truly Sorry' for Hiking Prices during Sydney Siege," *Telegraph*, December 24, 2014, http://www.telegraph.co.uk/news/worldnews/australiaandthepacific/australia/11312238/Uber-truly-sorry-for-hiking-prices-during-Sydney-siege.html.

55 **Within thirty minutes of the first one:** Andrew J. Hawkings, "Tracing the Spread of Uber Rumors during Paris Terrorist Attacks," *Verge*, November 16, 2015, http://www.theverge.com/2015/11/16/9745782/uber-paris-terrorism-rumors-twitter-facebook.

55 **"what you usually see":** Ian Ayres, *Super Crunchers: Why Thinking-by-Numbers Is the New Way to Be Smart* (New York: Random House, 2007), Kindle ed., loc. 1801.

56 **"You should never trust your gut":** Daniel Kahneman and Gary Klein, "Strategic Decisions: When Can You Trust Your Gut?" *McKinsey Quarterly*, March 2010, http://www.mckinsey.com/business-functions/strategy-and-corporate-finance/our-insights/strategic-decisions-when-can-you-trust-your-gut.

57 **"they create a situation where":** Laszlo Bock, "Here's Google's Secret to Hiring the Best People," *Wired*, April 7, 2015, https://www.wired.com/2015/04/hire-like-google.

57 **"We then score the interview":** Ibid.

58 **"You'll see a clear line":** Ibid.

59 **"humanity barely bests [a] chimp":** P. Tetlock, *Expert Political Judgment: How Good Is It? How Can We Know?* (Princeton, NJ: Princeton University Press, 2005), P52.

62 **"It's often small ideas":** Matt Marshall, "How Travel Giant Priceline Drives Growth through a Series of A/B Tweaks—like Using a 'Free Parking' Button,"

VentureBeat, August 13, 2015, http://venturebeat.com/2015/08/13/how-travel
-giant-priceline-drives-growth-through-a-series-of-ab-tweaks-like-using-a-free
-parking-button.

62 **lingerie company Adore Me found:** Rebecca Greenfield, "This Lingerie Company A/B Tests the World's Hottest Women to See Who Makes You Click 'Buy,'" *Fast Company*, November 21, 2014, https://www.fastcompany.com/3038740/most-creative-people/this-lingerie-company-a-b-tests-the-worlds-hottest-women-to-see-who-mak.

62 **"multiunit enterprises" (MUEs):** David A. Garvin and Lynne C. Levesque, "The Multiunit Enterprise," *Harvard Business Review*, June 2008, https://hbr.org/2008/06/the-multiunit-enterprise.

62 **According to innovation scholar Stefan Thomke:** Stefan Thomke and Jim Manzi, "The Discipline of Business Experimentation," *Harvard Business Review*, December 2014, https://hbr.org/2014/12/the-discipline-of-business-experimentation.

Chapter 3
OUR MOST MIND-LIKE MACHINES

67 **"science and engineering of making intelligent machines":** AISB (Society for the Study of Artificial Intelligence and Simulation of Behaviour), "What Is Artificial Intelligence?" accessed March 1, 2017, http://www.aisb.org.uk/public-engagement/what-is-ai.

69 **"responded with delight":** Pamela McCorduck, *Machines Who Think*, 2nd ed. (Natick, MA: A. K. Peters, 2004), 167.

69 **"invented a thinking machine":** Ibid., 138.

69 **According to a 1979 collection of anecdotes:** Paul Lee Tan, *Encyclopedia of 7700 Illustrations* (Rockville, MD: Assurance, 1979), 717.

70 **"adjectives in English absolutely have to be in this order":** Mark Forsyth, *The Elements of Eloquence: How to Turn the Perfect English Phrase* (London: Icon, 2013), 46.

71 **"As of 2014, few commercial systems":** Ernest Davis and Gary Marcus, "Commonsense Reasoning and Commonsense Knowledge in Artificial Intelligence," *Communications of the ACM* 58, no. 9 (2015): 92–103, http://cacm.acm.org/magazines/2015/9/191169-commonsense-reasoning-and-commonsense-knowledge-in-artificial-intelligence/abstract.

71 **"In doing commonsense reasoning":** Ibid.

72 **"The scope for this kind of substitution":** David H. Autor, "Why Are There Still So Many Jobs? The History and Future of Workplace Automation," *Journal of Economic Perspectives* 29, no. 3 (2015): 3–30, http://pubs.aeaweb.org/doi/pdfplus/10.1257/jep.29.3.3.

72 **The goal with the Perceptron:** Daniela Hernandez, "How Computers Will Think," *Fusion*, February 3, 2015, http://fusion.net/story/35648/how-computers-will-think.

72 **as many as 10,000 of its neighbors:** John H. Byrne, "Introduction to Neurons and Neuronal Networks," *Neuroscience Online*, accessed January 26, 2017, http://neuroscience.uth.tmc.edu/s1/introduction.html.

73 **"the embryo of an electronic computer":** Mikel Olazaran, "A Sociological Study of the Official History of the Perceptrons Controversy," *Social Studies of Science* 26 (1996): 611–59, http://journals.sagepub.com/doi/pdf/10.1177/030631296026003005.

74 **Paul Werbos:** Jürgen Schmidhuber, "Who Invented Backpropagation?" last modified 2015, http://people.idsia.ch/~juergen/who-invented-backpropagation.html.

74 **Geoff Hinton:** David E. Rumelhart, Geoffrey E. Hinton, and Ronald J. Williams, "Learning Representations by Back-propagating Errors," *Nature* 323 (1986): 533–36, http://www.nature.com/nature/journal/v323/n6088/abs/323533a0.html.

74 **Yann LeCun:** Jürgen Schmidhuber, *Deep Learning in Neural Networks: An Overview*, Technical Report IDSIA-03-14, October 8, 2014, https://arxiv.org/pdf/1404.7828v4.pdf.

74 **as many as 20% of all handwritten checks:** Yann LeCun, "Biographical Sketch," accessed January 26, 2017, http://yann.lecun.com/ex/bio.html.

74 **"a new approach to computer Go":** David Silver et al., "Mastering the Game of Go with Deep Neural Networks and Search Trees," *Nature* 529 (2016): 484–89, http://www.nature.com/nature/journal/v529/n7587/full/nature16961.html.

75 **approximately $13,000 by the fall of 2016:** Elliott Turner, *Twitter* post, September 30, 2016 (9:18 a.m.), https://twitter.com/eturner303/status/781900528733261824.

75 **"the teams at the leading edge":** Andrew Ng, interview by the authors, August 2015.

76 **"Retrospectively, [success with machine learning]":** Paul Voosen, "The Believers," *Chronicle of Higher Education*, February 23, 2015, http://www.chronicle.com/article/The-Believers/190147.

76 **His 2006 paper:** G. Hinton, S. Osindero, and Y. Teh, "A Fast Learning Algorithm for Deep Belief Nets," *Neural Computation* 18, no. 7 (2006): 1527–54.

77 **The software engineer Jeff Dean:** Jeff Dean, "Large-Scale Deep Learning for Intelligent Computer Systems," accessed January 26, 2017, http://www.wsdm-conference.org/2016/slides/WSDM2016-Jeff-Dean.pdf.

78 **When control of an actual data center:** Richard Evans and Jim Gao, "DeepMind AI Reduces Google Data Centre Cooling Bill by 40%," *DeepMind*, July 20, 2016, https://deepmind.com/blog/deepmind-ai-reduces-google-data-centre-cooling-bill-40.

79 **Tech giants including Microsoft:** Tom Simonite, "Google and Microsoft Want Every Company to Scrutinize You with AI," *MIT Technology Review*, August 1, 2016, https://www.technologyreview.com/s/602037/google-and-microsoft-want-every-company-to-scrutinize-you-with-ai.

79 **nonrice farms in Japan average only 1.5 hectares:** "Field Work: Farming in Japan," *Economist*, April 13, 2013, http://www.economist.com/news/

asia/21576154-fewer-bigger-plots-and-fewer-part-time-farmers-agriculture-could
-compete-field-work.

80 **about one and a half baseball fields:** Metric Views, "How Big Is a Hectare?"
November 11, 2016, http://metricviews.org.uk/2007/11/how-big-hectare.

80 **Makoto was impressed:** Kaz Sato, "How a Japanese Cucumber Farmer Is
Using Deep Learning and TensorFlow," *Google*, August 31, 2016, https://
cloud.google.com/blog/big-data/2016/08/how-a-japanese-cucumber-farmer-is-using
-deep-learning-and-tensorflow.

80 **"I can't wait to try it":** Ibid.

80 **"It's not hyperbole":** Ibid.

80 **"If intelligence was a cake":** Carlos E. Perez, " 'Predictive Learning' Is the New
Buzzword in Deep Learning," Intuition Machine, December 6, 2016, https://
medium.com/intuitionmachine/predictive-learning-is-the-key-to-deep-learning
-acceleration-93e063195fd0#.13qh1nti1.

81 **Joshua Brown's Tesla crashed:** Anjali Singhvi and Karl Russell, "Inside the
Self-Driving Tesla Fatal Accident," *New York Times*, July 12, 2016, https://
www.nytimes.com/interactive/2016/07/01/business/inside-tesla-accident.html.

82 **it appears that neither Brown:** Tesla, "A Tragic Loss," June 30, 2016, https://
www.tesla.com/blog/tragic-loss.

82 **"Conventional wisdom would say":** Chris Urmson, "How a Driverless Car
Sees the Road," TED Talk, June 2015, 15:29, https://www.ted.com/talks/
chris_urmson_how_a_driverless_car_sees_the_road/transcript?language=en.

82 **"Our vehicles were driving through Mountain View":** Ibid.

83 **The Japanese insurer Fukoku Mutual Life:** Dave Gershgorn, "Japanese White-
Collar Workers Are Already Being Replaced by Artificial Intelligence," *Quartz*,
January 2, 2017, https://qz.com/875491/japanese-white-collar-workers-are
-already-being-replaced-by-artificial-intelligence.

83 **"learn the history of past payment assessment":** Google Translate, "December
26, Heisei 28, Fukoku Life Insurance Company," accessed January 30, 2017,
https://translate.google.com/translate?depth=1&hl=en&prev=search&rurl=trans
late.google.com&sl=ja&sp=nmt4&u=http://www.fukoku-life.co.jp/about/news/
download/20161226.pdf.

84 **In October of 2016:** Allison Linn, "Historic Achievement: Microsoft Researchers Reach Human Parity in Conversational Speech Recognition," *Microsoft*
(blog), October 18, 2016, http://blogs.microsoft.com/next/2016/10/18/historic
-achievement-microsoft-researchers-reach-human-parity-conversational-speech
-recognition/#sm.0001d0t49dx0veqdsh21cccecz0e3.

84 **"I must confess that I never thought":** Mark Liberman, "Human Parity in
Conversational Speech Recognition," *Language Log* (blog), October 18, 2016,
http://languagelog.ldc.upenn.edu/nll/?p=28894.

84 **"Every time I fire a linguist":** Julia Hirschberg, " 'Every Time I Fire a Linguist,
My Performance Goes Up,' and Other Myths of the Statistical Natural Language
Processing Revolution" (speech, 15th National Conference on Artificial Intelli-
gence, Madison, WI, July 29, 1998).

84 **"AI-first world":** Julie Bort, "Salesforce CEO Marc Benioff Just Made a Bold Prediction about the Future of Tech," *Business Insider*, May 18, 2016, http://www.businessinsider.com/salesforce-ceo-i-see-an-ai-first-world-2016-5.

85 **"Many businesses still make important decisions":** Marc Benioff, "On the Cusp of an AI Revolution," Project Syndicate, September 13, 2016, https://www.project-syndicate.org/commentary/artificial-intelligence-revolution-by-marc-benioff-2016-09.

Chapter 4
HI, ROBOT

88 **"It's a restaurant":** Candice G., Eatsa review, *Yelp*, July 5, 2016, https://www.yelp.com/biz/eatsa-san-francisco-2?hrid=WODfZ9W7ZQ0ChbW1lQnpag.

90 **total number of bank tellers in the United States:** Number of bank tellers in 2007: Political Calculations, "Trends in the Number of Bank Tellers and ATMs in the U.S.," June 28, 2011, http://politicalcalculations.blogspot.com/2011/06/trends-in-number-of-bank-tellers-and.html#.WLMqPxIrJBw. Number of bank tellers in 2015: US Bureau of Labor Statistics, "Occupational Employment and Wages, May 2015," accessed March 1, 2017, https://www.bls.gov/oes/current/oes433071.htm.

90 **"because of technical problems":** Virginia Postrel, "Robots Won't Rule the Checkout Lane," Bloomberg, August 10, 2015, https://www.bloomberg.com/view/articles/2015-08-10/robots-won-t-rule-the-checkout-lane.

90 **Amazon Go, an 1,800-square-foot convenience store:** Laura Stevens and Khadeeja Safdar, "Amazon Working on Several Grocery-Store Formats, Could Open More than 2,000 Locations," *Wall Street Journal*, December 5, 2016, http://www.wsj.com/articles/amazon-grocery-store-concept-to-open-in-seattle-in-early-2017-1480959119.

90 **"Amazon Go is not a grocery store":** Lloyd Alter, "Amazon Go Is More than Just a Grocery Store with No Checkout," Mother Nature Network, December 19, 2016, http://www.mnn.com/green-tech/research-innovations/blogs/amazon-go-lot-more-just-checkout-free-grocery-store.

91 **Wealthfront's clients tend to be younger:** Gabrielle Karol, "High-Tech Investing Startup for Millennials Hits $1 Billion in Assets," *Fox Business*, June 5, 2014, http://www.foxbusiness.com/markets/2014/06/05/high-tech-investing-startup-for-millennials-hits-1-billion-mark.html.

92 **By November 2016 it had installed:** Stephanie Strom, "McDonald's Introduces Screen Ordering and Table Service," *New York Times*, November 17, 2016, https://www.nytimes.com/2016/11/18/business/mcdonalds-introduces-screen-ordering-and-table-service.html.

92 **The Discover credit card:** Maryann Fudacz, Facebook post on Discover's timeline, June 6, 2013, https://www.facebook.com/discover/posts/10151622117196380.

92 **One of the ads even suggested:** " 'Live Customer Service' Discover It Card Commercial," YouTube, April 27, 2016, 0:30, https://youtu.be/xK-je8YKkNw.

93 **At one restaurant in China's Heilongjiang Province:** "Robot Chefs Take Over Chinese Restaurant," *BBC News*, April 22, 2014, 1:22, http://www.bbc.com/news/world-asia-china-27107248.

94 **"It's good":** James Vincent, "I Ate Crab Bisque Cooked by a Robot Chef," *Verge*, July 31, 2015, http://www.theverge.com/2015/7/31/9076221/robot-chef-moley-robotics-crab-bisque.

95 **"Today, technological developments":** Gill A. Pratt, "Is a Cambrian Explosion Coming for Robotics?" *Journal of Economic Perspectives* 29, no. 3 (2015): 51–60, http://pubs.aeaweb.org/doi/pdfplus/10.1257/jep.29.3.51.

95 **90% of all the digital data:** IBM, "What Is Big Data?" accessed January 30, 2017, https://www-01.ibm.com/software/data/bigdata/what-is-big-data.html.

96 **"Moore's law and some very clever technical work":** Andrew Ng, interview by the authors, August 2015.

96 **Both AT&T and Verizon:** David Samberg, "Verizon Sets Roadmap to 5G Technology in U.S.; Field Trials to Start in 2016," *Verizon*, September 8, 2015, http://www.verizon.com/about/news/verizon-sets-roadmap-5g-technology-us-field-trials-start-2016.

97 **"Human beings take decades":** Pratt, "Is a Cambrian Explosion Coming for Robotics?"

98 **"This is a gyro sensor":** Chris Anderson, interview by the authors, October 2015.

98 **"peace dividend of the smartphone wars":** Benjamin Pauker, "Epiphanies from Chris Anderson," *Foreign Policy*, April 29, 2013, http://foreignpolicy.com/2013/04/29/epiphanies-from-chris-anderson.

100 **Sky Futures, a UK company:** Olivia Solon, "Robots Replace Oil Roughnecks," Bloomberg, August 21, 2015, https://www.bloomberg.com/news/articles/2015-08-21/flying-robots-replace-oil-roughnecks.

100 **In 2015, Rio Tinto became the first company:** Jamie Smyth, "Rio Tinto Shifts to Driverless Trucks in Australia." *Financial Times*, October 19, 2015, https://www.ft.com/content/43f7436a-7632-11e5-a95a-27d368e1ddf7.

100 **The driverless vehicles run twenty-four hours a day:** Rio Tinto, "Driving Productivity in the Pilbara," June 1, 2016, http://www.riotinto.com/ourcommitment/spotlight-18130_18328.aspx.

101 **Automated milking systems:** Janet Beekman and Robert Bodde, "Milking Automation Is Gaining Popularity," *Dairy Global*, January 15, 2015, http://www.dairyglobal.net/Articles/General/2015/1/Milking-automation-is-gaining-popularity-1568767W.

101 **Ninety percent of all crop spraying:** Alltech, "Drones and the Potential for Precision Agriculture," accessed January 30, 2017, http://ag.alltech.com/en/blog/drones-and-potential-precision-agriculture.

101 **"radically simplify[ing] the environment":** David H. Autor, "Why Are There Still So Many Jobs? The History and Future of Workplace Automation," *Journal of Economic Perspectives* 29, no. 3 (2015): 3–30, http://pubs.aeaweb.org/doi/pdfplus/10.1257/jep.29.3.3.

101 **"Do you think when my grandfather":** Brian Scott, "55 Years of Agricultural Evolution," *Farmer's Life* (blog), November 9, 2015, http://thefarmerslife .com/55-years-of-agricultural-evolution-in-john-deere-combines.

102 **Kiva was bought by Amazon in 2012:** John Letzing, "Amazon Adds That Robotic Touch," *Wall Street Journal*, March 20, 2012, http://www.wsj.com/ articles/SB10001424052702304724404577291903244796214.

103 **When Gill Pratt was a program manager at DARPA:** John Dzieza, "Behind the Scenes at the Final DARPA Robotics Challenge," *Verge*, June 12, 2015, http:// www.theverge.com/2015/6/12/8768871/darpa-robotics-challenge-2015-winners.

104 **250 million tons:** PlasticsEurope, "Plastics—the Facts 2014/2015: An Analysis of European Plastics Production, Demand and Waste Data," 2015, http:// www.plasticseurope.org/documents/document/20150227150049-final_plastics_ the_facts_2014_2015_260215.pdf.

105 **About thirty years ago:** PlasticsEurope, "Automotive: The World Moves with Plastics," 2013, http://www.plasticseurope.org/cust/documentrequest.aspx?DocID= 58353.

105 **For one thing, complexity would be free:** Thomas L. Friedman, "When Complexity Is Free," *New York Times*, September 14, 2013, http://www .nytimes.com/2013/09/15/opinion/sunday/friedman-when-complexity-is-free .html.

106 **20%–35% faster:** Guillaume Vansteenkiste, "Training: Laser Melting and Conformal Cooling," PEP Centre Technique de la Plasturgie, accessed January 30, 2017, http://www.alplastics.net/Portals/0/Files/Summer%20school%20 presentations/ALPlastics_Conformal_Cooling.pdf.

106 **with greater quality:** Eos, "[Tooling]," accessed January 30, 2017, https:// www.eos.info/tooling.

106 **3D-printed tumor model:** Yu Zhao et al., "Three-Dimensional Printing of Hela Cells for Cervical Tumor Model *in vitro*," *Biofabrication* 6, no. 3 (April 11, 2014), http://iopscience.iop.org/article/10.1088/1758-5082/6/3/035001.

107 **"I think additive manufacturing":** Carl Bass, interview by the authors, summer 2015.

Chapter 5
WHERE TECHNOLOGY AND INDUSTRY STILL NEED HUMANITY

113 **"Most words we use":** John Brockman, "Consciousness Is a Big Suitcase: A Talk with Marvin Minsky," *Edge*, February 26, 1998, https://www.edge.org/ conversation/marvin_minsky-consciousness-is-a-big-suitcase.

113 **Starting in 2013, Autodesk teamed up:** Daniel Terdiman, "Inside the Hack Rod, the World's First AI-Designed Car," *Fast Company*, December 1, 2015, accessed 30 Jan 2017, https://www.fastcompany.com/3054028/inside-the-hack-rod-the -worlds-first-ai-designed-car.

116 **A clever study by computational biologists:** Scott Spangler et al., "Automated

Hypothesis Generation Based on Mining Scientific Literature," in *Proceedings of the 20th ACM SIGKDD International Conference on Knowledge Discovery and Data Mining* (New York: ACM, 2014), 1877–86, http://scholar.harvard.edu/files/alacoste/files/p1877-spangler.pdf.

116 **70,000 scientific papers:** IBM, "IBM Watson Ushers In a New Era of Data-Driven Discoveries," August 28, 2014, https://www-03.ibm.com/press/us/en/pressrelease/44697.wss.

117 **Simon Colton's program The Painting Fool:** The Painting Fool, "About Me . . . ," accessed January 30, 2017, http://www.thepaintingfool.com/about/index.html.

117 **Patrick Tresset has built:** PatrickTresset.com, accessed January 30, 2017, http://patricktresset.com/new.

117 **Emily Howell, a program developed:** "Emily Howell," accessed January 30, 2017, http://artsites.ucsc.edu/faculty/cope/Emily-howell.htm.

117 **"At one Santa Cruz concert":** Ryan Blitstein, "Triumph of the Cyborg Composer," *Pacific Standard*, February 22, 2010, https://psmag.com/triumph-of-the-cyborg-composer-620e5aead47e#.tkinbzy0l.

118 **a 128-story modern skyscraper:** Skyscraper Center, "Shanghai Tower," accessed January 30, 2017, http://skyscrapercenter.com/building/shanghai-tower/56.

118 **34,000 metric tons per year:** Gensler Design Update, "Sustainability Matters," accessed January 30, 2017, http://du.gensler.com/vol6/shanghai-tower/#/sustainability-matters.

118 **$58 million in construction costs:** Gensler Design Update, "Why This Shape?" accessed January 30, 2017, http://du.gensler.com/vol6/shanghai-tower/#/why-this-shape.

119 **"Most of what I've heard":** Blitstein, "Triumph of the Cyborg Composer."

119 **"Using [computer-aided design] tools":** Carl Bass, interview by the authors, summer 2015.

121 **"the only thing that separates":** Andrew Bird, "Natural History," *New York Times*, April 8, 2008, https://opinionator.blogs.nytimes.com/2008/04/08/natural-history.

121 **"there are major conceptual advances":** Quentin Hardy, "Facebook's Yann LeCun Discusses Digital Companions and Artificial Intelligence (and Emotions)," *New York Times*, March 26, 2015, https://bits.blogs.nytimes.com/2015/03/26/facebooks-yann-lecun-discusses-digital-companions-and-artificial-intelligence.

121 **"We have no idea how the brain works":** Andrew Ng, interview by the authors, August 2015.

121 **"a literary magazine written by machines, for people":** *CuratedAI*, accessed March 1, 2017, http://curatedai.com.

121 **"Chilly, and no recollection":** Deep Thunder, "The Music Is Satisfied with Mr. Bertram's Mind," *CuratedAI*, August 31, 2016, http://curatedai.com/prose/the-music-is-satisfied-with-mr-bertrams-mind.

124 **as much as $289 billion a year:** Meera Viswanathan et al., "Interventions to Improve Adherence to Self-Administered Medications for Chronic Diseases in

the United States: A Systematic Review," *Annals of Internal Medicine*, December 4, 2012, http://annals.org/article.aspx?articleid=1357338.

124 **"At one Iora site":** Sarah Shemkus, "Iora Health's Promise: Patients Come First," *Boston Globe*, May 4, 2015, https://www.bostonglobe.com/business/2015/05/03/iora-health-pioneers-new-primary-care-model/kc7V4W5V8OJ0gxFqY4zBrK/story.html.

Chapter 6
THE TOLL OF A NEW MACHINE

130 **13% of people:** The World Bank said 12.6% in 1995. World Bank, "Mobile Cellular Subscriptions (per 100 People): 1960–2015," accessed January 31, 2017, http://data.worldbank.org/indicator/IT.CEL.SETS.P2?locations=US&name_desc=true.

130 **In the mid-1990s, almost every American community:** Newspaper Association of America, "Annual Newspaper Ad Revenue," accessed May 2, 2016, http://www.naa.org/~/media/NAACorp/Public Files/TrendsAndNumbers/Newspaper-Revenue/Annual-Newspaper-Ad-Revenue.xls.

130 **well over 10,000 AM and FM stations:** Steven Waldman, "The Information Needs of Communities: The Changing Media Landscape in a Broadband Age," *Federal Communications Commission*, July 2011, 63, https://transition.fcc.gov/osp/inc-report/The_Information_Needs_of_Communities.pdf.

130 **In 2000, recorded music was a $14.3 billion industry:** RIAA (Recording Industry Association of America), "RIAA's Yearend Statistics," accessed March 9, 2017, http://www.icce.rug.nl/~soundscapes/VOLUME02/Trends_and_shifts_Appendix.shtml.

131 **In 1997, David Bowie:** Ed Christman, "The Whole Story behind David Bowie's $55 Million Wall Street Trailblaze," *Billboard*, January 13, 2016, http://www.billboard.com/articles/business/6843009/david-bowies-bowie-bonds-55-million-wall-street-prudential.

131 **which spanned twenty-one years and twenty-five albums:** Tom Espiner, " 'Bowie Bonds'—the Singer's Financial Innovation," *BBC News*, January 11, 2016, http://www.bbc.com/news/business-35280945.

131 **raising $55 million:** Ibid.

131 **Iron Maiden:** "Iron Maiden Rocks the Bond Market," *BBC News*, February 9, 1999, http://news.bbc.co.uk/2/hi/business/275760.stm.

131 **Rod Stewart and James Brown:** Roy Davies, "Who's Who in Bowie Bonds: The History of a Music Business Revolution," last modified June 5, 2007, http://projects.exeter.ac.uk/RDavies/arian/bowiebonds.

131 **America's love affair with shopping malls:** Richard A. Feinberg and Jennifer Meoli, "A Brief History of the Mall," *Advances in Consumer Research* 18 (1991): 426–27, http://www.acrwebsite.org/volumes/7196/volumes/v18/NA-18.

131 **1,500 were built from 1956 to 2005:** "A Dying Breed: The American Shop-

ping Mall," *CBS News*, March 23, 2014, http://www.cbsnews.com/news/a
-dying-breed-the-american-shopping-mall.

131   **a $10 billion industry in 1997:** Thomas C. Finnerty, "Kodak vs. Fuji: The Battle
for Global Market Share," 2000, https://www.pace.edu/emplibrary/tfinnerty.pdf.

131   **the Casio QV-10:** Sam Byford, "Casio QV-10, the First Consumer LCD Digital
Camera, Lauded as 'Essential' to Tech History," *Verge*, September 14, 2012, http://
www.theverge.com/2012/9/14/3330924/first-lcd-digital-camera-casio-qv-10.

131   **Its $900 price tag:** Richard Baguley, "The Gadget We Miss: The Casio QV-10
Digital Camera," *Medium*, August 31, 2013, https://medium.com/people-gadgets/
the-gadget-we-miss-the-casio-qv-10-digital-camera-c25ab786ce49#.3cbg1m3wu.

132   **print ad revenue had declined by 70%:** Mark J. Perry, "Creative Destruction:
Newspaper Ad Revenue Continued Its Precipitous Free Fall in 2013, and It's Probably Not Over Yet," *AEIdeas*, April 25, 2014, https://www.aei.org/publication/
creative-destruction-newspaper-ad-revenue-continued-its-precipitous-free-fall-in
-2013-and-its-probably-not-over-yet.

132   **$3.4 billion:** Pew Research Center, "State of the News Media 2015," April 29, 2015,
http://www.journalism.org/files/2015/04/FINAL-STATE-OF-THE-NEWS
-MEDIA1.pdf.

132   **"print dollars were being replaced by digital dimes":** Waldman, "Information
Needs of Communities."

132   **13,400 newspaper newsroom jobs:** Ibid.

132   *Tucson Citizen:* *Tucson Citizen*, accessed January 31, 2017, http://tucsoncitizen
.com.

132   *Rocky Mountain News:* Lynn DeBruin, "Rocky Mountain News to Close, Publish Final Edition Friday," *Rocky Mountain News*, February 26, 2009, http://
web.archive.org/web/20090228023426/http://www.rockymountainnews.com/
news/2009/feb/26/rocky-mountain-news-closes-friday-final-edition.

132   **lost more than 90% of their value:** Yahoo! Finance, "The McClatchy Company
(MNI)," accessed January 31, 2017, http://finance.yahoo.com/quote/MNI.

132   **On August 5, 2013, the *Washington Post*:** Paul Farhi, "Washington Post to Be
Sold to Jeff Bezos, the Founder of Amazon," *Washington Post*, August 5, 2013,
https://www.washingtonpost.com/national/washington-post-to-be-sold-to-jeff
-bezos/2013/08/05/ca537c9e-fe0c-11e2-9711-3708310f6f4d_story.html.

132   *Penthouse* **(General Media):** Bloomberg News, "Company News; General
Media's Plan to Leave Bankruptcy Is Approved," *New York Times*, August 13,
2004, http://www.nytimes.com/2004/08/13/business/company-news-general
-media-s-plan-to-leave-bankruptcy-is-approved.html.

132   *National Enquirer* **and** *Men's Fitness* **(American Media):** Eric Morath, "American Media Files for Bankruptcy," *Wall Street Journal*, November 17, 2010,
https://www.wsj.com/articles/SB10001424052748704648604575621053554
011206.

133   *Newsweek:* Rob Verger, "Newsweek's First Issue Debuted Today in 1933,"
Newsweek, February 17, 2014, http://www.newsweek.com/newsweeks-first-issue
-debuted-today-1933-229355.

133   **a circulation of 3.3 million:** Ryan Nakashima, "Newsweek Had Unique Troubles as Industry Recovers," *U.S. News & World Report*, October 19, 2012, http://www.usnews.com/news/business/articles/2012/10/19/newsweek-had-unique-troubles-as-industry-recovers.

133   **ceased publishing a print edition altogether in 2012:** "Newsweek's Future: Goodbye Ink," *Economist*, October 18, 2012, http://www.economist.com/blogs/schumpeter/2012/10/newsweek%E2%80%99s-future.

133   **The *New Republic*:** Dylan Byers, "The New Republic Is Sold by Facebook Co-founder Chris Hughes," *CNNMoney*, February 26, 2016, http://money.cnn.com/2016/02/26/media/new-republic-chris-hughes-win-mccormack.

133   **"required reading on Air Force One":** Desson Howe, " 'Glass': An Eye for the Lie," *Washington Post*, November 7, 2003, https://www.washingtonpost.com/archive/lifestyle/2003/11/07/glass-an-eye-for-the-lie/8a3e6ff0-4935-4e99-a354-9ce4eac6c472/?utm_term=.75dccd7041cb.

133   ***Playboy*'s announcement:** Ravi Somaiya, "Nudes Are Old News at Playboy," *New York Times*, October 12, 2015, https://www.nytimes.com/2015/10/13/business/media/nudes-are-old-news-at-playboy.html.

133   **Founder Hugh Hefner:** "Top Living Influential Americans," *Atlantic*, December 2006, https://www.theatlantic.com/magazine/archive/2006/12/top-living-influential-americans/305386.

133   **In February of 2017, Cooper Hefner:** Cooper Hefner, Twitter post, February 13, 2017 (7:55 a.m.), https://twitter.com/cooperhefner/status/831169811723939842.

134   **Worldwide sales of recorded music declined by 45%:** Tim Ingham, "Global Record Industry Income Drops below $15bn for First Time in Decades," Music Business Worldwide, April 14, 2015, http://www.musicbusinessworldwide.com/global-record-industry-income-drops-below-15bn-for-first-time-in-history.

134   **$27 billion:** Robert Cookson and Andrew Edgecliffe-Johnson, "Music Sales Hit First Upbeat since 1999," *Financial Times*, February 26, 2013, https://www.ft.com/content/f7b0f2b0-8009-11e2-adbd-00144feabdc0.

134   **$15 billion:** IFPI (International Federation of the Phonographic Industry), "[Global Statistics]," accessed January 31, 2017, http://www.ifpi.org/global-statistics.php.

134   **the same proportion of revenue:** IFPI (International Federation of the Phonographic Industry), "IFPI Digital Music Report 2015," 2015, http://www.ifpi.org/downloads/Digital-Music-Report-2015.pdf.

134   **75% of the world market:** Mike Wiser, "*The Way the Music Died*: Frequently Asked Questions," *Frontline*, accessed January 31, 2017, http://www.pbs.org/wgbh/pages/frontline/shows/music/inside/faqs.html.

134   **85% of music distributed in the United States:** Tim Ingham, "Independent Labels Trounce UMG, Sony and Warner in US Market Shares," Music Business Worldwide, July 29, 2015, http://www.musicbusinessworldwide.com/independent-label-us-market-share-trounces-universal-sony-warner.

134   **Tower Records went bankrupt in 2006:** Dan Glaister, "Tower Crumbles in

the Download Era," *Guardian*, October 9, 2006, https://www.theguardian.com/business/2006/oct/09/retail.usnews.

134   **HMV "called in the administrators":** Simon Bowers and Josephine Moulds, "HMV Calls in Administrators—Putting 4,500 Jobs at Risk," *Guardian*, January 15, 2013, https://www.theguardian.com/business/2013/jan/15/hmv-administrators-4500-jobs-at-risk.

134   **In 2004 the rating agency Moody's:** Jim Boulden, "David Bowie Made Financial History with Music Bond," *CNNMoney*, January 11, 2016, http://money.cnn.com/2016/01/11/media/bowie-bonds-royalties.

134   **In 2011, Goldman Sachs:** Josephine Moulds, "Bond Investors See Another Side of Bob Dylan—but Desire Isn't There," *Guardian*, August 31, 2012, https://www.theguardian.com/business/2012/aug/31/bob-dylan-bond-goldman-sachs.

134   **Between 2005 and 2015, 20%:** This report confirms 1,500 malls in 2005: "Dying Breed," *CBS News*. This report confirms 1,200 by 2015: Nelson D. Schwartz, "The Economics (and Nostalgia) of Dead Malls," *New York Times*, January 3, 2015, http://www.nytimes.com/2015/01/04/business/the-economics-and-nostalgia-of-dead-malls.html.

134   **When General Growth Properties:** Ilaina Jones and Emily Chasan, "General Growth Files Historic Real Estate Bankruptcy," *Reuters*, April 16, 2009, http://www.reuters.com/article/us-generalgrowth-bankruptcy-idUSLG52607220090416.

134   **$77 billion:** Federal Communications Commission, "FCC Releases Statistics of the Long Distance Telecommunications Industry Report," May 14, 2003, table 2, p. 9, year 2000 (interstate plus long distance combined), https://transition.fcc.gov/Bureaus/Common_Carrier/Reports/FCC-State_Link/IAD/ldrpt103.pdf.

134   **$16 billion:** Sarah Kahn, *Wired Telecommunications Carriers in the US*, IBISWorld Industry Report 51711c, December 2013, http://trace.lib.utk.edu/assets/Kuney/Fairpoint%20Communications/Research/Other/IBIS_51711C_Wired_Telecommunications_Carriers_in_the_US_industry_report.pdf.

135   **By 2015, 44% of American adults:** Business Wire, "GfK MRI: 44% of US Adults Live in Households with Cell Phones but No Landlines," April 02, 2015, http://www.businesswire.com/news/home/20150402005790/en#.VR2B1JOPoyS.

135   **$20 billion in 2000:** Greg Johnson, "Ad Revenue Slides for Radio, Magazines," *Los Angeles Times*, August 9, 2001, http://articles.latimes.com/2001/aug/09/business/fi-32280.

135   **$14 billion in 2010:** BIA/Kelsey, "BIA/Kelsey Reports Radio Industry Revenues Rose 5.4% to $14.1 Billion in 2010, Driven by Political Season and More Activity by National Advertisers," PR Newswire, April 4, 2011, http://www.prnewswire.com/news-releases/biakelsey-reports-radio-industry-revenues-rose-54-to-141-billion-in-2010-driven-by-political-season-and-more-activity-by-national-advertisers-119180284.html.

135   **Clear Channel:** Waldman, "Information Needs of Communities."

135 **"what happens when someone does something clever":** Thomas L. Friedman, *Thank You for Being Late: An Optimist's Guide to Thriving in the Age of Accelerations* (New York: Farrar, Straus, and Giroux, 2016), Kindle ed., loc. 414.

136 **cost $0.02:** Statistic Brain Research Institute, "Average Cost of Hard Drive Storage," accessed January 31, 2017, http://www.statisticbrain.com/average-cost-of-hard-drive-storage.

136 **$11 in 2000:** Matthew Komorowski, "A History of Storage Cost," last modified 2014, Mkomo.com. http://www.mkomo.com/cost-per-gigabyte.

137 **"the death of distance":** Francis Cairncross, *The Death of Distance: How the Communications Revolution Will Change Our Lives* (Boston: Harvard Business School Press, 1997).

138 **computer programmer Craig Newmark:** Craig Newmark, LinkedIn profile, accessed February 1, 2017, https://www.linkedin.com/in/craignewmark.

138 **to let people list local events in the San Francisco area:** Craigconnects, "Meet Craig," accessed February 1, 2017, http://craigconnects.org/about.

138 **700 local sites in seventy countries by 2014:** Craigslist, "[About > Factsheet]," accessed February 1, 2017, https://www.craigslist.org/about/factsheet.

138 **estimated profits of $25 million:** Henry Blodget, "Craigslist Valuation: $80 Million in 2008 Revenue, Worth $5 Billion," *Business Insider*, April 3, 2008, http://www.businessinsider.com/2008/4/craigslist-valuation-80-million-in-2008-revenue-worth-5-billion.

138 **charging fees for only a few categories of ads:** Craigslist, "[About > Help > Posting Fees]," accessed February 1, 2017, https://www.craigslist.org/about/help/posting_fees.

139 **over $5 billion between 2000 and 2007:** Robert Seamans and Feng Zhu, "Responses to Entry in Multi-sided Markets: The Impact of Craigslist on Local Newspapers," January 11, 2013, http://www.gc.cuny.edu/CUNY_GC/media/CUNY-Graduate-Center/PDF/Programs/Economics/Course%20Schedules/Seminar%20Sp.2013/seamans_zhu_craigslist%281%29.pdf.

139 **$22 billion of US marketers' budgets:** "More than Two-Thirds of US Digital Display Ad Spending Is Programmatic," *eMarketer*, April 5, 2016, https://www.emarketer.com/Article/More-Than-Two-Thirds-of-US-Digital-Display-Ad-Spending-Programmatic/1013789#sthash.OQclVXY5.dpuf.

139 **over 8,000 servers that, at peak times, can process 45 billion ad buys per day:** "Microsoft and AppNexus: Publishing at Its Best (Selling)," *AppNexus Impressionist* (blog), November 3, 2015, http://blog.appnexus.com/2015/microsoft-and-appnexus-publishing-at-its-best-selling.

139 **Belgian:** Matthew Lasar, "Google v. Belgium "Link War" Ends after Years of Conflict," *Ars Technica*, July 19, 2011, https://arstechnica.com/tech-policy/2011/07/google-versus-belgium-who-is-winning-nobody.

139 **German:** Harro Ten Wolde and Eric Auchard, "Germany's Top Publisher Bows to Google in News Licensing Row," *Reuters*, November 5, 2014, http://www.reuters.com/article/us-google-axel-sprngr-idUSKBN0IP1YT20141105.

139 **Spanish newspaper publishers:** Eric Auchard, "Google to Shut Down

News Site in Spain over Copyright Fees," *Reuters*, December 11, 2014, http://www.reuters.com/article/us-google-spain-news-idUSKBN0JP0QM20141211.

140 **by 2016 it had over a billion active users:** WhatsApp, "One Billion," *WhatsApp* (blog), February 1, 2016, https://blog.whatsapp.com/616/One-billion.

140 **more than 40 billion messages per day:** "WhatsApp Reaches a Billion Monthly Users," *BBC News*, February 1, 2016, http://www.bbc.com/news/technology-35459812.

141 **600 million monthly active users:** Alexei Oreskovic, "Facebook's WhatsApp Acquisition Now Has Price Tag of $22 Billion," *Reuters*, October 6, 2014, http://www.reuters.com/article/us-facebook-whatsapp-idUSKCN0HV1Q820141006.

141 **just 70 employees:** Ibid.

141 **50% more messages:** Benedict Evans, "WhatsApp Sails Past SMS, but Where Does Messaging Go Next?" *Benedict Evans* (blog), January 11, 2015, http://ben-evans.com/benedictevans/2015/1/11/whatsapp-sails-past-sms-but-where-does-messaging-go-next.

142 **CEO Jeff Bezos assigned Rick Dalzell the task:** Staci D. Kramer, "The Biggest Thing Amazon Got Right: The Platform," Gigaom, October 12, 2011, https://gigaom.com/2011/10/12/419-the-biggest-thing-amazon-got-right-the-platform.

142 **Dalzell was described as a bulldog:** Matt Rosoff, "Jeff Bezos 'Makes Ordinary Control Freaks Look like Stoned Hippies,' Says Former Engineer," *Business Insider*, October 12, 2011, http://www.businessinsider.com/jeff-bezos-makes-ordinary-control-freaks-look-like-stoned-hippies-says-former-engineer-2011-10.

143 **launched Amazon Web Services in 2006:** Amazon Web Services, "About AWS," accessed February 4, 2017, https://aws.amazon.com/about-aws.

143 **Amazon S3:** Amazon Web Services, "Amazon Simple Storage Service (Amazon S3)—Continuing Successes," July 11, 2006, https://aws.amazon.com/about-aws/whats-new/2006/07/11/amazon-simple-storage-service-amazon-s3---continuing-successes.

143 **Amazon EC2:** Amazon Web Services, "Announcing Amazon Elastic Compute Cloud (Amazon EC2)—Beta," August 24, 2006, https://aws.amazon.com/about-aws/whats-new/2006/08/24/announcing-amazon-elastic-compute-cloud-amazon-ec2---beta.

143 **more than 290,000 developers using the platform:** Amazon, "Ooyala Wins Amazon Web Services Start-up Challenge, Receives $100,000 in Cash and Services Credits Plus Investment Offer from Amazon.com," December 7, 2007, http://phx.corporate-ir.net/phoenix.zhtml?c=176060&p=irol-newsArticle&ID=1085141.

143 **9% of Amazon's total revenue:** Matthew Lynley, "Amazon's Web Services Are Shining in Its Latest Earnings Beat," TechCrunch, April 28, 2016, https://techcrunch.com/2016/04/28/amazon-is-spiking-after-posting-a-huge-earnings-beat.

143 **over half of the company's total operating income:** Nick Wingfield, "Amazon's

Cloud Business Lifts Its Profits to a Record," *New York Times*, April 28, 2016, https://www.nytimes.com/2016/04/29/technology/amazon-q1-earnings.html.

143 **In early 2016, AWS was called the fastest-growing:** Ben Sullivan, "AWS Heralded as 'Fastest-Growing Enterprise Technology Company in History,'" Silicon UK, November 4, 2015, http://www.silicon.co.uk/cloud/cloud-management/amazon-aws-cloud-160-valuation-179948.

143 **from $35.66 to $753.78:** Yahoo! Finance, "AMZN—Amazon.com, Inc.," accessed February 4, 2017, https://finance.yahoo.com/quote/AMZN/history.

143 **$37 billion:** IFPI (International Federation of the Phonographic Industry), "2000 Recording Industry World Sales," April 2001, http://www.ifpi.org/content/library/worldsales2000.pdf.

143 **$15 billion:** IFPI (International Federation of the Phonographic Industry), "IFPI Global Music Report 2016," April 12, 2016, http://www.ifpi.org/news/IFPI-GLOBAL-MUSIC-REPORT-2016.

144 **Napster, launched in 1999:** Tom Lamont, "Napster: The Day the Music Was Set Free," *Guardian*, February 23, 2013, https://www.theguardian.com/music/2013/feb/24/napster-music-free-file-sharing.

144 **LimeWire:** *Wikipedia*, s. v. "LimeWire," last modified January 16, 2017, https://en.wikipedia.org/wiki/LimeWire.

145 **CD albums outsold CD singles 179 to 1:** RIAA (Recording Industry Association of America), "U.S. Sales Database," accessed February 4, 2017, https://www.riaa.com/u-s-sales-database.

145 **"There's only two ways I know of":** Justin Fox, "How to Succeed in Business by Bundling—and Unbundling," *Harvard Business Review*, June 24, 2014, https://hbr.org/2014/06/how-to-succeed-in-business-by-bundling-and-unbundling.

147 **47% of total US music revenues:** Joshua Friedlander, "News and Notes on 2016 Mid-year RIAA Music Shipment and Revenue Statistics," RIAA (Recording Industry Association of America), accessed February 4, 2017, http://www.riaa.com/wp-content/uploads/2016/09/RIAA_Midyear_2016Final.pdf.

147 **approximately $0.007 per person:** Lizzie Plaugic, "Spotify's Year in Music Shows Just How Little We Pay Artists for Their Music," *Verge*, December 7, 2015, http://www.theverge.com/2015/12/7/9861372/spotify-year-in-review-artist-payment-royalties.

148 **"the absolute transformation of everything":** Jon Pareles, "David Bowie, 21st-Century Entrepreneur," *New York Times*, June 9, 2002, http://www.nytimes.com/2002/06/09/arts/david-bowie-21st-century-entrepreneur.html.

148 **"file sharing and streaming have shrunk":** Jack Linshi, "Here's Why Taylor Swift Pulled Her Music from Spotify," *Time*, November 3, 2014, http://time.com/3554468/why-taylor-swift-spotify.

148 **"as a result of the rise of the platform":** Geoffrey G. Parker, Marshall W. Van Alstyne, and Sangeet Paul Choudary, *Platform Revolution: How Networked Markets Are Transforming the Economy and How to Make Them Work for You* (New York: Norton, 2016).

Chapter 7
PAYING COMPLEMENTS, AND OTHER SMART STRATEGIES

151 **"$500? Fully subsidized? With a plan?":** "Ballmer Laughs at iPhone," YouTube, September 18, 2007, 2:22, https://www.youtube.com/watch?v=eywi0h_Y5_U.

152 **"When [the iPhone] first came out in early 2007":** Walter Isaacson, *Steve Jobs* (New York: Simon & Schuster, 2011), 501.

152 **"You don't want your phone to be like a PC":** John Markoff, "Phone Shows Apple's Impact on Consumer Products," *New York Times*, January 11, 2007, http://www.nytimes.com/2007/01/11/technology/11cnd-apple.html.

162 **Steve Jobs made a "nine-digit" acquisition offer:** Victoria Barret, "Dropbox: The Inside Story of Tech's Hottest Startup," *Forbes*, October 18, 2011, http://www.forbes.com/sites/victoriabarret/2011/10/18/dropbox-the-inside-story-of-techs-hottest-startup/#3b780ed92863.

162 **84% of total revenue for Facebook:** Facebook, "Facebook Reports Third Quarter 2016 Results," November 2, 2016, https://investor.fb.com/investor-news/press-release-details/2016/Facebook-Reports-Third-Quarter-2016-Results/default.aspx.

163 **"grand slam":** Apple, "iPhone App Store Downloads Top 10 Million in First Weekend," July 14, 2008, http://www.apple.com/pr/library/2008/07/14iPhone-App-Store-Downloads-Top-10-Million-in-First-Weekend.html.

164 **$6 billion:** Daisuke Wakabayashi, "Apple's App Store Sales Hit $20 Billion, Signs of Slower Growth Emerge," *Wall Street Journal*, January 6, 2016, https://www.wsj.com/articles/apples-app-store-sales-hit-20-billion-signs-of-slower-growth-emerge-1452087004.

165 **"Jobs soon figured out":** Isaacson, *Steve Jobs*, 501.

165 **Facebook's offer to publish:** Henry Mance, "UK Newspapers: Rewriting the Story," *Financial Times*, February 9, 2016, http://www.ft.com/intl/cms/s/0/0aa8beac-c44f-11e5-808f-8231cd71622e.html#axzz3znzgrkTq.

166 **"we only have the faintest idea":** Peter Rojas, "Google Buys Cellphone Software Company," *Engadget*, August 17, 2005, https://www.engadget.com/2005/08/17/google-buys-cellphone-software-company.

166 **"best deal ever":** Owen Thomas, "Google Exec: Android Was 'Best Deal Ever,'" *VentureBeat*, October 27, 2010, http://venturebeat.com/2010/10/27/google-exec-android-was-best-deal-ever.

166 **Android founder Andy Rubin:** Victor H., "Did You Know Samsung Could Buy Android First, but Laughed It Out of Court?" phoneArena.com, February 16, 2014, http://www.phonearena.com/news/Did-you-know-Samsung-could-buy-Android-first-but-laughed-it-out-of-court_id52685.

167 **Android had become the world's most popular:** Gartner, "Gartner Says Worldwide Smartphone Sales Soared in Fourth Quarter of 2011 with 47 Percent Growth," February 15, 2012, table 3, http://www.gartner.com/newsroom/id/1924314.

167 **88% of all smartphones:** Gartner, "Gartner Says Chinese Smartphone Vendors

Were Only Vendors in the Global Top Five to Increase Sales in the Third Quarter of 2016," November 17, 2016, table 2, http://www.gartner.com/newsroom/id/3516317.

167   **Microsoft, which had ambitions:** Brian X. Chen, "How Microsoft Hit CTRL+ALT+DEL on Windows Phone," *Wired*, November 8, 2010, https://www.wired.com/2010/11/making-windows-phone-7.

167   **Windows Phone:** Windows Central, "Windows Phone," last updated February 3, 2017, http://www.windowscentral.com/windows-phone.

167   **Microsoft bought the mobile phone business:** Microsoft, "Microsoft to Acquire Nokia's Devices & Services Business, License Nokia's Patents and Mapping Services," September 3, 2013, https://news.microsoft.com/2013/09/03/microsoft-to-acquire-nokias-devices-services-business-license-nokias-patents-and-mapping-services/#setSm8pEXtFGqGKU.99.

167   **including Snapchat:** Microsoft, "Top Free Apps," accessed February 5, 2017, https://www.microsoft.com/en-us/store/top-free/apps/mobile?target=apps..social.

167   **less than 1% of worldwide smartphone sales:** Gartner, "Gartner Says Worldwide Smartphone Sales Grew 3.9 Percent in First Quarter of 2016," May 19, 2016, table 2, https://www.gartner.com/newsroom/id/3323017.

167   **"Microsoft's Nokia experiment is over":** Tom Warren, "Microsoft Lays Off Hundreds as It Guts Its Phone Business," *Verge*, May 25, 2016, http://www.theverge.com/2016/5/25/11766344/microsoft-nokia-impairment-layoffs-may-2016.

168   **more than 20,000 layoffs:** ZDNet, "Worst Tech Mergers and Acquisitions: Nokia and Microsoft, AOL and Time Warner," *Between the Lines* (blog), February 13, 2016, http://www.zdnet.com/article/worst-tech-mergers-and-acquisitions-nokia-and-microsoft-aol-and-time-warner.

168   **almost $8 billion in write-downs:** Nick Wingfield, "Cutting Jobs, Microsoft Turns Page on Nokia Deal," *New York Times*, July 8, 2015, https://www.nytimes.com/2015/07/09/technology/microsoft-layoffs.html.

168   **the largest in Microsoft history:** Gregg Keizer, "Microsoft Writes Off $7.6B, Admits Failure of Nokia Acquisition," *Computerworld*, July 8, 2015, http://www.computerworld.com/article/2945371/smartphones/microsoft-writes-off-76b-admits-failure-of-nokia-acquisition.html.

168   **By 2009, the BlackBerry operating system powered 20%:** Statista, "Global Smartphone OS Market Share Held by RIM (BlackBerry) from 2007 to 2016, by Quarter," accessed February 5, 2017, https://www.statista.com/statistics/263439/global-market-share-held-by-rim-smartphones.

168   **By the end of 2016 the company had announced:** Andrew Griffin, "BlackBerry Announces It Will Make No More New Phones," *Independent*, September 28, 2016, http://www.independent.co.uk/life-style/gadgets-and-tech/news/blackberry-announces-it-will-make-no-more-new-phones-a7334911.html.

168   **saw its market value drop below $4 billion:** Google Finance, "BlackBerry Ltd (NASDAQ:BBRY)," accessed February 5, 2017, https://www.google.com/finance?cid=663276.

170 **"Make things as simple as possible, but not simpler":** *Wikiquote*, s. v. "Albert Einstein," last modified January 29, 2017, https://en.wikiquote.org/wiki/Albert_Einstein.

170 **The difference between the two:** Shane Rounce, "UX vs. UI," Dribbble, December 7, 2014, https://dribbble.com/shots/1837823-UX-vs-UI.

170 **Friendster:** Gary Rivlin, "Wallflower at the Web Party," *New York Times*, October 15, 2006, http://www.nytimes.com/2006/10/15/business/yourmoney/15friend.html.

170 **News Corp bought it for $580 million in 2005:** Vauhini Vara and Rebecca Buckman, "Friendster Gets $10 Million Infusion for Revival Bid," *Wall Street Journal*, August 21, 2006, https://www.wsj.com/articles/SB115612561104040731.

170 **"Of the people you know":** Fame Foundry, "DeadSpace: 7 Reasons Why MySpace Is as Good as Dead," August 1, 2009, http://www.famefoundry.com/382/deadspace-7-reasons-why-myspace-is-as-good-as-dead.

171 **MySpace was sold by News Corp:** Todd Spangler, "Time Inc. Buys Myspace Parent Company Viant," *Variety*, February 11, 2016, http://variety.com/2016/digital/news/time-inc-myspace-viant-1201703860.

171 **"Getting redirected [from within an app]":** Patrick Collison, interview by the authors, summer 2015.

172 **"It's hard to convey to outsiders":** Ibid.

173 **"We had the idea":** Ibid.

173 **Stripe had processed at least one payment:** Ingrid Lunden, "Payments Provider Stripe Has Raised Another $150M at a $9B Valuation," TechCrunch, November 25, 2016, https://techcrunch.com/2016/11/25/payments-provider-stripe-has-raised-another-150-at-a-9b-valuation.

173 **the company was valued at $9 billion:** Rolfe Winkler and Telis Demos, "Stripe's Valuation Nearly Doubles to $9.2 Billion," *Wall Street Journal*, November 25, 2016, https://www.wsj.com/articles/stripes-valuation-nearly-doubles-to-9-2-billion-1480075201.

173 **"Our customer Postmates is a logistics company":** Collison, interview, summer 2015.

174 **"We want to build the infrastructure":** Ibid.

Chapter 8
THE MATCH GAME: WHY PLATFORMS EXCEL

178 **"Be careful of what you wish for in youth":** James Joyce, *Ulysses* (Paris: Sylvia Beach, 1922), 180.

178 **"It worked.":** Payal Kadakia, "An Open Letter to Our Community from Our CEO," *Warm Up*, November 2, 2016, https://classpass.com/blog/2016/11/02/open-letter-to-community.

178 **"Many of you began to work out":** Ibid.

179 **"UGH. Hearing the news":** Nakesha Kouhestani, Twitter post, November 2, 2016 (8:49 a.m.), https://twitter.com/NakesaKou/status/7938424600236 23680.

179 **"People Are Freaking Out":** Avery Hartmans, "People Are Freaking Out about ClassPass Killing Its Unlimited Membership Plan," *Business Insider*, November 2, 2016, http://www.businessinsider.com/classpass-kills-unlimited-memberships -twitter-reacts-2016-11.

179 **"It can't be a long-term membership option":** Kadakia, "Open Letter to Our Community."

183 **As vice president of pricing and inventory Zach Apter told us:** Zachary Apter, LinkedIn profile, accessed February 5, 2017, https://www.linkedin.com/ in/zachary-apter-421a96.

183 **"We say, "Give us a couple weeks":** Zachary Apter, interview by the authors, February 2016.

186 **half of the items in the closet of an average American:** "Rent the Runway Annonces [*sic*] New Business | Fortune," YouTube, July 16, 2014, 24:59, https:// www.youtube.com/watch?v=hc0RdVK-qK0.

187 **$5 for costume jewelry earrings:** Rent the Runway, "Danielle Nicole: Grey Pearl Linear Cage Earrings," accessed February 5, 2017, https://www.renttherunway.com/ shop/designers/danielle_nicole/grey_pearl_linear_cage_earrings.

187 **largest dry-cleaning operation in America:** Rebecca Greenfield, "Inside Rent the Runway's Secret Dry-Cleaning Empire," *Fast Company*, October 28, 2014, https://www.fastcompany.com/3036876/most-creative-people/inside-rent-the -runways-secret-dry-cleaning-empire.

187 **a new handbag:** Erin Griffith, "Rent the Runway Unveils a Netflix Subscription for Your Closet," *Fortune*, July 16, 2014, http://fortune.com/2014/07/16/ rent-the-runway-unlimited-netflix-subscription-closet.

187 **By the spring of 2016:** Rent the Runway, "Want an Unlimited Winter Wardrobe?" accessed February 5, 2017, https://www.renttherunway.com/unlimited.

188 **revenues of $700 billion per year:** David Z. Morris, "Trucking? There's Finally an App for That," *Fortune*, July 9, 2015, http://fortune.com/2015/07/09/ trucker-path-app.

188 **15% of all miles driven:** DAT (Dial-A-Truck), "3rd DAT Carrier Benchmark Survey: Q1 2013," DAT Special Report, 2013, http://www.dat.com/Resources/~/ media/Files/DAT/Resources/Whitepapers/2013_Carrier_BenchMark_ Surveyfinal.ashx.

188 **estimated $80 billion in annual fees:** Connie Loizos, "Long-Haul Trucking Startup Transfix Lands $12 Million Series A," TechCrunch, November 10, 2015, https://techcrunch.com/2015/11/10/long-haul-trucking-startup-transfix -lands-12-million-series-a.

188 **Transfix:** Transfix, "[Ship with Us]," accessed February 5, 2017, https:// transfix.io/ship-with-us.

188 **Flexe:** Flexe, "About Flexe," accessed February 5, 2017, https://www.flexe.com/company.

189 **By 2016, Upwork was facilitating:** Upwork Global Inc., "About Us," accessed February 5, 2017, https://www.upwork.com/about.

189 **15,000 customers annually:** Cvent, "Cvent Announces Fourth Quarter and Full Year 2015 Financial Results," February 25, 2016, http://investors.cvent.com/press-releases/2016/02-25-2016-211735769.aspx.

189 **$9.2 billion:** Ibid.

190 **Frédéric Mazzella, Nicolas Brusson, and Francis Nappez:** BlaBlaCar, "Founders," accessed February 5, 2017, https://www.blablacar.com/about-us/founders.

190 **founded BlaBlaCar in 2006:** Murad Ahmed, "BlaBlaCar Sets Course to Hit All Points Other than the US," *Financial Times*, December 10, 2014, https://www.ft.com/content/4260cd4e-7c75-11e4-9a86-00144feabdc0?siteedition=uk#axzz3QsbvnchO.

190 **"BlaBlaCar drivers don't make a profit":** Laura Wagner, "What Does French Ride-Sharing Company BlaBlaCar Have That Uber Doesn't," *Two-Way*, September 16, 2015, http://www.npr.org/sections/thetwo-way/2015/09/16/440919462/what-has-french-ride-sharing-company-blablacar-got-that-uber-doesnt.

190 **the average BlaBlaCar trip is 200 miles:** "BlaBlaCar: Something to Chat About," *Economist*, October 22, 2015, http://www.economist.com/news/business/21676816-16-billion-french-startup-revs-up-something-chat-about.

190 **operating in twenty-one countries:** BlaBlaCar, accessed February 5, 2017, https://www.blablacar.com.

190 **facilitating over 10 million rides every quarter:** Rawn Shah, "Driving Ridesharing Success at BlaBlaCar with Online Community," *Forbes*, February 21, 2016, http://www.forbes.com/sites/rawnshah/2016/02/21/driving-ridesharing-success-at-blablacar-with-online-community/#5271e05b79a6.

191 **$550 million in investor funding:** Yoolim Lee, "Go-Jek Raises Over $550 Million in KKR, Warburg-Led Round," Bloomberg, last modified August 5, 2016, https://www.bloomberg.com/news/articles/2016-08-04/go-jek-said-to-raise-over-550-million-in-kkr-warburg-led-round.

191 **$15:** Steven Millward, "China's Top 'Uber for Laundry' Startup Cleans Up with $100M Series B Funding," Tech in Asia, August 7, 2015, https://www.techinasia.com/china-uber-for-laundry-edaixi-100-million-funding.

191 **100,000 orders per day:** Emma Lee, "Tencent-Backed Laundry App Edaixi Nabs $100M USD from Baidu," TechNode, August 6, 2015, http://technode.com/2015/08/06/edaixi-series-b.

191 **twenty-eight cities with a combined 110 million residents:** Edaixi, accessed February 5, 2017, http://www.edaixi.com/home/about. (English version: https://translate.google.com/translate?hl=en&sl=zh-CN&tl=en&u=http%3A%2F%2Fwww.edaixi.com%2Fhome%2Fabout.)

191 **Guagua Xiche:** Guagua Xiche, accessed February 5, 2017, http://www.guaguaxiche.com/web/about.html.

191 **$58 million in 2015:** C. Custer, "2015 Has Been Brutal to China's O2O Car Wash Services," Tech in Asia, November 2, 2015, https://www.techinasia.com/2015 -brutal-chinas-o2o-car-wash-services.

191 **Hao Chushi:** Hao Chushi, accessed February 5, 2017, http://www.chushi 007.com/index.html.

192 **approximately $15:** Jamie Fullerton, "China's New App Brings Chefs to Cook in Your Home," *Munchies*, April 8, 2015, https://munchies.vice.com/en/articles/ chinas-new-app-brings-world-class-chefs-to-cook-in-your-home.

192 **Ele.me, which raised over $1 billion:** C. Custer, "Confirmed: Alibaba Invested $1.25 Billion in China's Top Food Delivery Startup," Tech in Asia, April 13, 2016, https://www.techinasia.com/confirmed-alibaba-invested-125-billion-food -delivery-startup-eleme.

192 **58 Daojia:** 58.com, "58.com Subsidiary 58 Home Raises US$300 Million in Series A Funding," PR Newswire, October 12, 2015, http://www.prnewswire.com/ news-releases/58com-subsidiary-58-home-raises-us300-million-in-series-a-funding -300157755.html.

192 **Chinese search giant Baidu:** Paul Carsten, "Baidu to Invest $3.2 Billion in Online-to-Offline Services," *Reuters*, June 30, 2015, http://www.reuters.com/ article/us-baidu-investment-idUSKCN0PA0MH20150630.

195 **"they don't have to forecast their own success":** Charlie Songhurst, interview by the authors, October 2015.

196 **95% of the time:** Paul Barter, " 'Cars Are Parked 95% of the Time.' Let's Check!" Reinventing Parking, February 22, 2013, http://www.reinventingparking.org/ 2013/02/cars are-parked-95-of-time-lets-check.html.

197 **By 2013, people born in the 1980s:** Nicholas J. Klein and Michael J. Smart, "Millennials and Car Ownership: Less Money, Fewer Cars," *Transport Policy* 53 (January 2017): 20–29, http://www.sciencedirect.com/science/article/pii/ S0967070X16305571.

Chapter 9
DO PRODUCTS HAVE A PRAYER?

200 **"So," the company's website explains:** Uber, "[Our Story]," accessed February 5, 2017, https://www.uber.com/our-story.

200 **initially called UberCab:** Leena Rao, "UberCab Takes the Hassle Out of Booking a Car Service," TechCrunch, July 5, 2010, https://techcrunch.com/2010/07/05/ ubercab-takes-the-hassle-out-of-booking-a-car-service.

200 **"supercrazy freakin' small":** Fast Company, "Travis Kalanick, the Fall and Spectacular Rise of the Man behind Uber," *South China Morning Post*, September 25, 2015, http://www.scmp.com/magazines/post-magazine/article/1860723/ travis-kalanick-fall-and-spectacular-rise-man-behind-uber.

200 **By late 2010, Kalanick had begun:** Ibid.

200 **Eighteen months later they launched UberX:** Alexia Tsotsis, "Uber Opens Up

Platform to Non-limo Vehicles with 'Uber X,' Service Will Be 35% Less Expensive," *TechCrunch*, July 1, 2012, https://techcrunch.com/2012/07/01/uber-opens-up-platform-to-non-limo-vehicles-with-uber-x-service-will-be-35-less-expensive.

201 **UberPool, launched in August of 2014:** Alex, "Announcing UberPool," *Uber Newsroom* (blog), August 5, 2014, https://newsroom.uber.com/announcing-uberpool.

201 **$20 billion in annual gross bookings:** James Temperton, "Uber's 2016 Losses to Top $3bn According to Leaked Financials," *Wired*, December 20, 2016, http://www.wired.co.uk/article/uber-finances-losses-driverless-cars.

201 **Uber was valued at $68 billion:** Andrew Ross Sorkin, "Why Uber Keeps Raising Billions," *New York Times*, June 20, 2016, https://www.nytimes.com/2016/06/21/business/dealbook/why-uber-keeps-raising-billions.html.

201 **Traditional taxis provided 8.4 million trips:** UCLA Labor Center, "Ridesharing or Ridestealing? Changes in Taxi Ridership and Revenue in Los Angeles 2009–2014," Policy Brief, July 2015, table 1, p. 3, http://www.irle.ucla.edu/publications/documents/Taxi-Policy-Brief.pdf.

201 **Yellow Cab Cooperative, filed for bankruptcy:** Tom Corrigan, "San Francisco's Biggest Taxi Operator Seeks Bankruptcy Protection," *Wall Street Journal*, January 24, 2016, https://www.wsj.com/articles/san-franciscos-biggest-taxi-operator-seeks-bankruptcy-protection-1453677177.

201 **Less than three years later:** Simon Van Zuylen-Wood, "The Struggles of New York City's Taxi King," *Bloomberg BusinessWeek*, August 27, 2015, https://www.bloomberg.com/features/2015-taxi-medallion-king.

202 **Lawmakers in France:** "Uber Fined in France over UberPop," *BBC News*, June 9, 2016, http://www.bbc.com/news/business-36491926.

202 **In June 2015 the *Economist*:** "Why Fintech Won't Kill Banks," *Economist*, June 17, 2015, http://www.economist.com/blogs/economist-explains/2015/06/economist-explains-12.

202 **"a future as a sort of financial utility":** Ibid.

203 **$45 billion:** Juro Osawa, Gillian Wong, and Rick Carew, "Xiaomi Becomes World's Most Valuable Tech Startup," *Wall Street Journal*, last modified December 29, 2014, https://www.wsj.com/articles/xiaomi-becomes-worlds-most-valuable-tech-startup-1419843430.

203 **Xiaomi had sold 61 million smartphones:** Eva Dou, "China's Xiaomi under Pressure to Prove Value to Investors," *Wall Street Journal*, January 10, 2016, https://www.wsj.com/articles/chinas-xiaomi-under-pressure-to-prove-value-to-investors-1452454204.

203 **typically selling for $149 in 2015:** Eva Dou, "Xiaomi Ends 2015 as China's Smartphone King," *Wall Street Journal*, February 1, 2016, http://blogs.wsj.com/digits/2016/02/01/xiaomi-ends-2015-as-chinas-smartphone-king.

203 **less than 5% of revenue:** Kevin Kelleher, "Once a Darling, Xiaomi Is Facing Tough Questions about Its Future," *Time*, March 21, 2016, http://time.com/4265943/xiaomi-slowdown.

203 **Xiaomi's sales had dropped by almost 40%:** David Gilbert, "How Xiaomi

Lost $40bn: Where It All Went Wrong for the 'Apple of the East,'" *International Business Times*, August 18, 2016, http://www.ibtimes.co.uk/how-xiaomi-lost -40bn-where-it-all-went-wrong-apple-east-1576781.

203 **closer to $3.6 billion:** Ibid.

204 **Total unit sales in 2016:** James Titcomb, "Samsung Mobile Phone Sales Fall to Lowest Level in Five Years," *Telegraph*, January 24, 2017, http://www .telegraph.co.uk/technology/2017/01/24/samsung-mobile-phone-sales-fall -lowest-level-five-years.

204 **Apple captured 91% of global smartphone profits:** Philip Elmer-DeWitt, "How Apple Sucks the Profit Out of Mobile Phones," *Fortune*, February 14, 2016, http://fortune.com/2016/02/14/apple-mobile-profit-2015.

204 **analyst Tim Long of BMO Capital Markets estimated:** Mikey Campbell, "Apple Captures More than 103% of Smartphone Profits in Q3 despite Shrink- ing Shipments," November 3, 2016, http://appleinsider.com/articles/16/11/03/ apple-captures-more-than-103-of-smartphone-profits-in-q3-despite-shrinking -shipments.

204 **$22 billion in profits:** Joel Rosenblatt and Jack Clark, "Google's Android Gener- ates $31 Billion Revenue, Oracle Says," Bloomberg, January 21, 2016, https://www .bloomberg.com/news/articles/2016-01-21/google-s-android-generates-31-billion -revenue-oracle-says-ijor8hvt.

207 **"The Market for 'Lemons'":** George A. Akerlof, "The Market for 'Lemons': Quality Uncertainty and the Market Mechanism," *Quarterly Journal of Econom- ics* 84, no. 3 (1970): 488–500, https://doi.org/10.2307/1879431.

207 **"did not publish papers":** George A. Akerlof, "Writing the 'The Market for "Lem- ons"': A Personal and Interpretive Essay," Nobelprize.org, November 14, 2003, http://www.nobelprize.org/nobel_prizes/economic-sciences/laureates/2001/ akerlof-article.html.

207 **"if this paper were correct":** Ibid.

207 **50 million rides per month:** Eric Newcomer, "Lyft Is Gaining on Uber as It Spends Big for Growth," Bloomberg, last modified April 14, 2016, https:// www.bloomberg.com/news/articles/2016-04-14/lyft-is-gaining-on-uber-as-it -spends-big-for-growth.

208 **In 2013, California passed regulations:** Tomio Geron, "California Becomes First State to Regulate Ridesharing Services Lyft, Sidecar, UberX," *Forbes*, September 19, 2013, http://www.forbes.com/sites/tomiogeron/2013/09/19/california-becomes -first-state-to-regulate-ridesharing-services-lyft-sidecar-uberx/#6b22c10967fe.

208 **by August 2016, BlaBlaCar still did not require them:** BlaBlaCar, "Frequently Asked Questions: Is It Safe for Me to Enter My Govt. ID?" accessed February 6, 2017, https://www.blablacar.in/faq/question/is-it-safe-for-me-to-enter-my-id.

209 **"Many of the exchanges":** Alex Tabarrok and Tyler Cowen, "The End of Asymmetric Information," Cato Institute, April 6, 2015, https://www .cato-unbound.org/2015/04/06/alex-tabarrok-tyler-cowen/end-asymmetric -information.

209 **Airbnb CEO and cofounder Joe Gebbia:** Joe Gebbia, "How Airbnb Designs for Trust," TED Talk, February 2016, 15:51, https://www.ted.com/talks/ joe_gebbia_how_airbnb_designs_for_trust?language=en.

209 **"High reputation beats high similarity":** Ibid.

209 **"can actually help us overcome":** Ibid.

211 **SoulCycle:** SoulCycle, "All Studios," accessed February 6, 2017, https:// www.soul-cycle.com/studios/all.

217 **But if it's costly to switch:** See, for instance, Paul Klemperer, "Markets with Consumer Switching Costs," *Quarterly Journal of Economics* 102, no. 2 (1987): 375–94; and Joseph Farrell and Garth Saloner, "Installed Base and Compatibility: Innovation, Product Preannouncements, and Predation," *American Economic Review* (1986): 940–55.

219 **more than $15 billion in loans:** Douglas MacMillan, "Uber Raises $1.15 Billion from First Leveraged Loan," *Wall Street Journal*, July 7, 2016, https://www.wsj.com/ articles/uber-raises-1-15-billion-from-first-leveraged-loan-1467934151.

221 **The lodging-industry benchmarking company STR:** Bill McBride, "Hotels: Occupancy Rate on Track to Be 2nd Best Year," *Calculated Risk* (blog), October 17, 2016, http://www.calculatedriskblog.com/2016/10/hotels-occupancy-rate-on -track-to-be_17.html.

221 **In Los Angeles the daily hotel rate:** Hugo Martin, "Airbnb Takes a Toll on the U.S. Lodging Industry, but Los Angeles Hotels Continue to Thrive," *Los Angeles Times*, September 26, 2016, http://www.latimes.com/business/la-fi-airbnb -hotels-20160926-snap-story.html.

223 **Airbnb was responsible for a 10% decline:** Gregorios Zervas, Davide Proserpio, and John W. Byers, "The Rise of the Sharing Economy: Estimating the Impact of Airbnb on the Hotel Industry," last modified November 18, 2016, http://cs -people.bu.edu/dproserp/papers/airbnb.pdf.

Chapter 10
THAT ESCALATED QUICKLY: THE EMERGENCE OF THE CROWD

229 **the author Robert Wright:** Robert Wright, Twitter page, accessed February 6, 2017, https://twitter.com/robertwrighter.

229 **"Most newsgroup traffic":** Robert Wright, "Voice of America," *New Republic*, September 13, 1993, http://cyber.eserver.org/wright.txt.

230 **"The things [the Net] changes":** Ibid.

231 **An estimated 130 million books:** Leonid Taycher, "Books of the World, Stand Up and Be Counted! All 129,864,880 of You," *Google Books Search* (blog), August 5, 2010, http://booksearch.blogspot.com/2010/08/books-of-world-stand -up-and-be-counted.html.

231 **about 30 million are available:** Khazar University Library and Information Center, "10 Largest Libraries of the World," accessed February 6, 2017, http:// library.khazar.org/s101/10-largest--libraries-of-the-world/en.

231   **approximately 45 billion pages:** Antal van den Bosch, Toine Bogers, and Maurice de Kunder, "Estimating Search Engine Index Size Variability: A 9-Year Longitudinal Study," *Scientometrics*, July 27, 2015, http://www.dekunder.nl/Media/10.1007_s11192-016-1863-z.pdf; Maurice de Kunder, "The Size of the World Wide Web (the Internet)," WorldWideWebSize.com, accessed February 6, 2017, http://www.worldwidewebsize.com.

231   **at least 25 million of those books:** Stephen Heyman, "Google Books: A Complex and Controversial Experiment," *New York Times*, October 28, 2015, https://www.nytimes.com/2015/10/29/arts/international/google-books-a-complex-and-controversial-experiment.html.

231   **an estimated 80 million videos are on YouTube alone:** Chris Desadoy, "How Many Videos Have Been Uploaded to YouTube?" Quora, March 31, 2015, https://www.quora.com/How-many-videos-have-been-uploaded-to-YouTube.

233   **"The Internet is the world's largest library":** Quote verified via personal communication with Allen Paulos, March 2017.

233   **Their paper describing this approach:** Sergey Brin and Larry Page, "The Anatomy of a Large-Scale Hypertextual Web Search Engine," paper presented at the Seventh International World-Wide Web Conference, Brisbane, Australia, 1998, http://ilpubs.stanford.edu:8090/361.

234   **"Act in good faith":** Wikipedia, "Wikipedia:Five Pillars," last modified February 6, 2017, at 10:52, https://en.wikipedia.org/wiki/Wikipedia:Five_pillars.

236   **"the 'data' from which the economic calculus starts":** Friedrich A. Hayek, "The Use of Knowledge in Society," *American Economic Review* 35, no. 4 (1945): 519–30.

236   **"secure the best use of resources":** Ibid.

236   **Orwellian:** Geoffrey Nunberg, "Simpler Terms; If It's 'Orwellian,' It's Probably Not," *New York Times*, June 22, 2003, http://www.nytimes.com/2003/06/22/weekinreview/simpler-terms-if-it-s-orwellian-it-s-probably-not.html.

236   **Kafkaesque:** Joe Fassler, "What It Really Means to Be 'Kafkaesque,'" *Atlantic*, January 15, 2014, https://www.theatlantic.com/entertainment/archive/2014/01/what-it-really-means-to-be-kafkaesque/283096.

237   **"The marvel [of prices]":** Hayek, "Use of Knowledge in Society."

239   **"Prediction markets reflect a fundamental principle":** Kenneth J. Arrow et al., "The Promise of Prediction Markets," *Science* 320 (May 16, 2008): 877–78, http://mason.gmu.edu/~rhanson/PromisePredMkt.pdf.

240   **"Hello everybody out there using minix":** Derek Hildreth, "The First Linux Announcement from Linus Torvalds," Linux Daily, April 15, 2010, http://www.thelinuxdaily.com/2010/04/the-first-linux-announcement-from-linus-torvalds.

241   **over 1.5 billion Android phones and tablets:** Linus Torvalds, "The Mind behind Linux," TED Talk, February 2016, 21:30, https://www.ted.com/talks/linus_torvalds_the_mind_behind_linux?language=en.

241   **11,800 individual developers:** Linux Foundation, "Linux Kernel Development: How Fast It Is Going, Who Is Doing It, What They Are Doing, and Who

Is Sponsoring It [2015]," accessed February 7, 2017, https://www.linux.com/publications/linux-kernel-development-how-fast-it-going-who-doing-it-what-they-are-doing-and-who.

241 **including Samsung, IBM, Google, and Intel:** Linux Foundation, "The Linux Foundation Releases Linux Development Report," February 18, 2015, https://www.linuxfoundation.org/news-media/announcements/2015/02/linux-foundation-releases-linux-development-report.

242 **This was an early example:** Tim O'Reilly, "What Is Web 2.0," September 3, 2005, http://www.oreilly.com/pub/a/web2/archive/what-is-web-20.html.

242 **"There was no intention behind":** Torvalds, "Mind behind Linux," 21:30.

244 **Raspbian:** Raspbian.org, "Welcome to Raspbian," accessed February 7, 2017, https://www.raspbian.org.

244 **Raspberry Pi:** Gavin Thomas, "Raspbian Explained," *Gadget* [2015], accessed February 7, 2017, https://www.gadgetdaily.xyz/raspbian-explained.

244 **"I am not a visionary":** Torvalds, "Mind behind Linux," 17:00.

245 **"is about really seeing":** Ibid., 21:30.

246 **"sum of all human knowledge":** ARTFL Project, "Chambers' Cyclopaedia," accessed February 7, 2017, https://artfl-project.uchicago.edu/content/chambers-cyclopaedia.

246 **"We wish editors to be true experts":** Karim R. Lakhani and Andrew P. McAfee, "Wikipedia (A)," Harvard Business School Courseware, 2007, https://courseware.hbs.edu/public/cases/wikipedia.

247 **Nupedia had twelve completed articles:** Ibid.

247 **"Humor me":** Larry Sanger, "My Role in Wikipedia (Links)," LarrySanger.org, accessed February 8, 2017, http://larrysanger.org/roleinwp.html.

247 **By 2016 there were 36 million articles:** Wikipedia, s. v. "History of Wikipedia," accessed February 8, 2017, https://en.wikipedia.org/wiki/History_of_Wikipedia.

248 **Wikipedia was the sixth-most-popular website:** Alexa, "Wikipedia.org Traffic Statistics," last modified February 7, 2017, http://www.alexa.com/siteinfo/wikipedia.org.

248 **"other people using the encyclopedia can check":** Wikipedia, s. v. "Wikipedia:Verifiability," last modified February 27, 2017, https://en.wikipedia.org/wiki/Wikipedia:Verifiability.

249 **Slack, a group-level tool:** Josh Costine, "Slack's Rapid Growth Slows as It Hits 1.25M Paying Work Chatters," October 20, 2016, https://techcrunch.com/2016/10/20/slunk.

Chapter 11
WHY THE EXPERT YOU KNOW IS NOT THE EXPERT YOU NEED

252 **That's the conclusion:** Karim Lakhani et al., "Prize-Based Contests Can Provide Solutions to Computational Biology Problems," *Nature Biotechnology* 31, no. 2 (2013): 108–11, http://www.nature.com/nbt/journal/v31/n2/full/nbt.2495.html.

253 **The popular MegaBLAST algorithm:** Ibid.

253 **The idAb algorithm:** Ibid.

253 **Dr. Ramy Arnaout:** Dana-Farber/Harvard Cancer Center, "Ramy Arnaout, MD, PhD," accessed February 8, 2017, http://www.dfhcc.harvard.edu/insider/member-detail/member/ramy-arnaout-md-phd.

254 **"None were academic or industrial computational biologists":** Lakhani et al., "Prize-Based Contests."

255 **"In the more than 700 challenges":** Karim Lakhani, interview by the authors, October 2015.

258 **many problems, opportunities, and projects:** Anita Williams Woolley et al., "Evidence for a Collective Intelligence Factor in the Performance of Human Groups," *Science* 330, no. 6004 (2010): 686–88.

259 **"Given enough eyeballs, all bugs are shallow":** Eric Raymond, *The Cathedral and the Bazaar* (Sebastopol, CA: O'Reilly Media, 1999), 19.

259 **When Lakhani and Lars Bo Jeppesen studied:** Lars Bo Jeppesen and Karim R. Lakhani, "Marginality and Problem-Solving Effectiveness in Broadcast Search," *Organization Science*, February 22, 2010, http://pubsonline.informs.org/doi/abs/10.1287/orsc.1090.0491.

260 **Amazon's Mechanical Turk:** Jason Pontin, "Artificial Intelligence, with Help from the Humans," *New York Times*, March 25, 2007, http://www.nytimes.com/2007/03/25/business/yourmoney/25Stream.html.

260 **transcribing text from business cards into a spreadsheet:** Jeremy Wilson, "My Gruelling Day as an Amazon Mechanical Turk," *Kernel*, August 28, 2013, http://kernelmag.dailydot.com/features/report/4732/my-gruelling-day-as-an-amazon-mechanical-turk.

260 **"programming design pattern":** Michael Bernstein et al., "Soylent: A Word Processor with a Crowd Inside," 2010, http://courses.cse.tamu.edu/caverlee/csce438/readings/soylent.pdf.

260 **people who identify as designers:** Topcoder, "Topcoder Is Different," accessed February 8, 2017, https://www.topcoder.com/member-onboarding/topcoder-is-different.

261 **Kaggle:** Kaggle, accessed March 10, 2017, https://www.kaggle.com.

261 **officiating at a wedding:** JamieV2014, "Task of the Week: Perform My Marriage," *TaskRabbit* (blog), March 26, 2014, https://blog.taskrabbit.com/2014/03/26/task-of-the-week-perform-my-marriage.

261 **delivering ice cream cake:** LauraTaskRabbit, "Task of the Week: Deliver Ice Cream Cake to My Grandpa," *TaskRabbit* (blog), November 18, 2014, https://blog.taskrabbit.com/2014/11/18/task-of-the-week-deliver-ice-cream-cake-to-my-grandpa.

261 **waiting in line at the Apple Store:** JamieV2014, "We're First in Line at the Apple Store," *TaskRabbit* (blog), September 17, 2012, https://blog.taskrabbit.com/2012/09/17/were-first-in-line-at-the-apple-store.

261 **The TV show *Veronica Mars*:** IMDb, s. v. "Veronica Mars: TV Series (2004–2007)," accessed February 8, 2017, http://www.imdb.com/title/tt0412253.

262 **To find out, they launched a campaign:** Rob Thomas, "The Veronica Mars Movie Project," Kickstarter, accessed February 8, 2017, https://www.kickstarter .com/projects/559914737/the-veronica-mars-movie-project.

262 **offer of rewards for different levels of support:** Ibid.

262 **within the first twelve hours:** Sarah Rappaport, "Kickstarter Funding Brings 'Veronica Mars' Movie to Life," CNBC, March 12, 2014, http://www.cnbc.com/2014/03/12/kickstarter-funding-brings-veronica-mars-movie-to -life.html.

262 **The movie premiered on March 14, 2014:** Business Wire, "Warner Bros.' 'Veronica Mars' Movie Opens on March 14, 2014," December 6, 2013, http://www.businesswire.com/news/home/20131206005856/en/Warner-Bros.'-"Veronica -Mars"-Movie-Opens-March.

262 **"One could argue that":** Marc Andreessen, interview by the authors, August 2015.

263 **In early 2016, Indiegogo introduced:** Jacob Kastrenakes, "Indiegogo Wants Huge Companies to Crowdfund Their Next Big Products," *Verge*, January 6, 2016, http://www.theverge.com/2016/1/6/10691100/indiegogo -enterprise-crowdfunding-announced-ces-2016.

263 **"real-time customer feedback":** Indiegogo, "Indiegogo for Enterprise," accessed February 8, 2017, https://learn.indiegogo.com/enterprise.

263 **including some of the world's largest hedge funds:** Telis Demos and Peter Rude-geair, "LendingClub Held Talks on Funding Deals with Och-Ziff, Soros, Third Point," *Wall Street Journal*, last updated June 9, 2016, https://www.wsj.com/articles/ lendingclub-and-hedge-funds-have-discussed-major-funding-deals-1465476543.

263 **In 2014, well over half:** Shelly Banjo, "Wall Street Is Hogging the Peer-to-Peer Lending Market," *Quartz*, March 4, 2015, https://qz.com/355848/wall -street-is-hogging-the-peer-to-peer-lending-market.

264 **"Teespring is the modern method":** Andreessen, interview, August 2015.

264 **"In general it is not the owner":** Joseph Schumpeter, *The Theory of Economic Development: An Inquiry into Profits, Capital, Credit, Interest, and the Business Cycle* (Cambridge, MA: Harvard University Press, 1934), 66.

265 **Eric von Hippel:** Eric von Hippel, *Democratizing Innovation* (Cambridge, MA: MIT Press, 2006).

265 **"Wouldn't it be nice":** Alexia Tsotsis, "TaskRabbit Turns Grunt Work into a Game," *Wired*, July 15, 2011, https://www.wired.com/2011/07/mf_taskrabbit.

265 **Apple acquired 70 companies:** Wikipedia, s. v. "List of Mergers and Acquisitions by Apple," last modified January 21, 2017, https://en.wikipedia.org/wiki/ List_of_mergers_and_acquisitions_by_Apple.

265 **Facebook more than 50:** Wikipedia, s. v. "List of Mergers and Acquisitions by Facebook," last modified February 4, 2017, https://en.wikipedia.org/wiki/ List_of_mergers_and_acquisitions_by_Facebook.

265 **Google nearly 200:** Wikipedia, "List of Mergers and Acquisitions by Alphabet," last modified February 2, 2017, https://en.wikipedia.org/wiki/ List_of_mergers_and_acquisitions_by_Alphabet.

266 **Facebook paid $1 billion for Instagram:** Evelyn M. Rusli, "Facebook Buys Instagram for $1 Billion," *New York Times*, April 9, 2012, https:// dealbook.nytimes.com/2012/04/09/facebook-buys-instagram-for-1-billion.

266 **more than $20 billion for WhatsApp:** Facebook Newsroom, "Facebook to Acquire WhatsApp," February 19, 2014, http://newsroom.fb.com/news/2014/02/ facebook-to-acquire-whatsapp.

267 **D. E. Shaw had over $40 billion:** D. E. Shaw & Company, "[Who We Are]," accessed February 8, 2017, https://www.deshaw.com/WhoWeAre.shtml.

267 **12% annualized returns:** Cliffwater LLC, "Hedge Fund Investment Due Diligence Report: D. E. Shaw Composite Fund," June 2011, http://data.treasury .ri.gov/dataset/96dcb86f-e97e-4b05-8ce2-a40289e477a6/resource/ab68154d -9a7e-4a7d-82c9-d27998d1f2bc/download/DE-Shaw-Hedge-Fund-Investment -Due-Diligence-Report-0611Redacted.pdf.

267 **an annualized return of 15% over a decade:** Nathan Vardi, "Rich Formula: Math and Computer Wizards Now Billionaires Thanks to Quant Trading Secrets," *Forbes*, September 29, 2015, http://www.forbes.com/sites/nathanvardi/ 2015/09/29/rich-formula-math-and-computer-wizards-now-billionaires-thanks -to-quant-trading-secrets/4/#58ea036a3d61.

267 **It averaged a greater than 70% annual return:** Richard Rubin and Margaret Collins, "How an Exclusive Hedge Fund Turbocharged Its Retirement Plan," Bloomberg, June 16, 2015, https://www.bloomberg.com/news/articles/2015-06-16/ how-an-exclusive-hedge-fund-turbocharged-retirement-plan.

267 **"perhaps the world's greatest moneymaking machine":** Katherine Burton, "Inside a Moneymaking Machine like No Other," Bloomberg, November 21, 2016, https://www.bloomberg.com/news/articles/2016-11-21/how-renaissance -s-medallion-fund-became-finance-s-blackest-box.

267 **"That seemed way too low to me":** John Fawcett, interview by the authors, December 2016.

268 **"The way I frame the problem for Quantopian is":** Ibid.

269 **Quantopian had attracted to its platform:** Quantopian, accessed March 10, 2017, https://www.quantopian.com/100000.

269 **"The thing they often have in common":** Fawcett, interview, December 2016.

269 **"We're trying to get the community":** Ibid.

270 **"the scarce resource in quantitative investing is talent":** Taylor Hall, "Point72's Cohen Bets $250 Million on Crowd-Sourced Quantopian," Bloomberg, July 27, 2016, https://www.bloomberg.com/news/articles/2016-07-27/point72-s-cohen -bets-250-million-on-crowd-sourced-quantopian.

271 **"the design and construction":** Synthetic Biology Project, "What Is Synthetic Biology?" accessed February 8, 2017, http://www.synbioproject.org/topics/ synbio101/definition.

272 **The campaign attracted over $70,000:** Indiegogo, "DIY CRISPR Kits, Learn Modern Science by Doing," accessed February 8, 2017, https://www .indiegogo.com/projects/diy-crispr-kits-learn-modern-science-by-doing#.

272 **"I played God":** Andrew Tarantola, "I Played God with The Odin's DIY CRISPR

Kit," *Engadget*, June 30, 2016, https://www.engadget.com/2016/06/30/i-played-god-with-the-odins-diy-crispr-kit.

272 **Harper's Open Agriculture Initiative:** Open Agriculture Initiative, "Farming for the Future," accessed February 8, 2017, http://openag.media.mit.edu.

272 **"permissionless innovation":** Adam Thierer, *Permissionless Innovation: The Continuing Case for Comprehensive Technological Freedom* (Arlington, VA: Mercatus Center, 2014), section 1.02.

273 **He came across a video:** "Large Mechanical Hand," YouTube, April 2, 2011, 0:48, https://www.youtube.com/watch?v=dEHiAItVdiw.

273 **Van As and Owen collaborated via email and Skype:** Robert F. Graboyes, "A Hand for Innovation—Ivan Owen, Jon Schull and e-NABLE," InsideSources, October 19, 2016, http://www.insidesources.com/a-hand-for-innovation-ivan-owen-jon-schull-and-e-nable.

273 **"Corporal Coles could pick up a button":** eHive, "Corporal Coles Prosthetic Hand; Robert Norman; 1845; AR#1723," accessed February 8, 2017, https://ehive.com/collections/5254/objects/387275/corporal-coles-prosthetic-hand.

274 **"The cost of a workable prosthetic":** Graboyes, "Hand for Innovation."

Chapter 12
THE DREAM OF DECENTRALIZING ALL THE THINGS

278 **"practical men, who believe themselves":** John Maynard Keynes, *The General Theory of Employment, Interest, and Money* (London: Palgrave Macmillan, 1936), 383–84.

278 **"Indeed," Keynes wrote:** Ibid.

279 **On October 31, 2008:** Paul Vigna and Michael J. Casey, *The Age of Cryptocurrency: How Bitcoin and Digital Money Are Challenging the Global Economic Order* (New York: St. Martin's Press, 2015), 41.

279 **a short paper titled "Bitcoin":** Satoshi Nakamoto, "Bitcoin: A Peer-to-Peer Electronic Cash System," October 31, 2008, https://bitcoin.org/bitcoin.pdf.

283 **"the steady addition of a constant amount":** Ibid.

285 **Laszlo Hanyecz:** Bitcoinwhoswho, "A Living Currency: An Interview with 'Jercos,' Party to First Bitcoin Pizza Transaction," *Bitcoin Who's Who* (blog), January 30, 2016, http://bitcoinwhoswho.com/blog/2016/01/30/a-living-currency-an-interview-with-jercos-party-to-first-bitcoin-pizza-transaction.

286 **Mt. Gox, a Tokyo-based firm:** Yessi Bello Perez, "Mt Gox: The History of a Failed Bitcoin Exchange," CoinDesk, August 4, 2015, http://www.coindesk.com/mt-gox-the-history-of-a-failed-bitcoin-exchange.

286 **that the exchange "had weaknesses" in its system and that "bitcoins vanished":** Robert McMillan, "The Inside Story of Mt. Gox, Bitcoin's $460 Million Disaster," *Wired*, March 3, 2014, https://www.wired.com/2014/03/bitcoin-exchange.

286 **approximately $470 million in Bitcoins:** Robin Sidel, Eleanor Warnock, and

Takashi Mochizuki, "Almost Half a Billion Worth of Bitcoins Vanish," *Wall Street Journal*, February 28, 2014, https://www.wsj.com/news/article_email/SB10001424052702303801304579410010379087576.

286 **$27 million in cash:** Jake Adelstein and Nathalie-Kyoko Stucky, "Behind the Biggest Bitcoin Heist in History: Inside the Implosion of Mt. Gox," *Daily Beast*, May 19, 2016, http://www.thedailybeast.com/articles/2016/05/19/behind-the-biggest-bitcoin-heist-in-history-inside-the-implosion-of-mt-gox.html.

287 **By January 2015 the processing capability:** Michael J. Casey, "Bitcoin's Plunge Bites 'Miners,'" *Wall Street Journal*, January 14, 2015, https://www.wsj.com/articles/bitcoins-plunge-bites-miners-1421281616.

287 **Iceland, Washington State, and Inner Mongolia:** Simon Denyer, "The Bizarre World of Bitcoin 'Mining' Finds a New Home in Tibet," *Washington Post*, September 12, 2016, https://www.washingtonpost.com/world/asia_pacific/in-chinas-tibetan-highlands-the-bizarre-world-of-bitcoin-mining-finds-a-new-home/2016/09/12/7729cbea-657e-11e6-b4d8-33e931b5a26d_story.html?utm_term=.80e5d64087d2.

287 **James Howells:** "James Howells Searches for Hard Drive with £4m-Worth of Bitcoins Stored," *BBC News*, November 28, 2013, http://www.bbc.com/news/uk-wales-south-east-wales-25134289.

288 **rising to a high of over $1,100 in November 2013:** Blockchain, "BTC to USD: Bitcoin to US Dollar Market Price," accessed February 8, 2017, https://blockchain.info/charts/market-price.

289 **University of Nicosia:** University of Nicosia, "Academic Certificates on the Blockchain," accessed February 8, 2017, http://digitalcurrency.unic.ac.cy/free-introductory-mooc/academic-certificates-on-the-blockchain.

289 **Holberton School of Software Engineering:** Rebecca Campbell, "Holberton School Begins Tracking Student Academic Credentials on the Bitcoin Blockchain," Nasdaq, May 18, 2016, http://www.nasdaq.com/article/holberton-school-begins-tracking-student-academic-credentials-on-the-bitcoin-blockchain-cm623162#ixzz4Y8MUWUu2.

289 **Kimberley Process:** James Melik, "Diamonds: Does the Kimberley Process Work?" *BBC News*, June 28, 2010, http://www.bbc.com/news/10307046.

290 **in 2016 the body's chairman reported:** United Arab Emirates Ministry of Economy, "Kimberley Process: Mid-term Report," 2016, https://www.kimberleyprocess.com/en/system/files/documents/kimberley_process_mid-term_report.pdf.

290 **Everledger:** Everledger, accessed March 10, 2017, https://www.everledger.io.

290 **$50 million of counterfeit shoes:** US Department of Homeland Security, "Intellectual Property Rights Seizure Statistics: Fiscal Year 2014," accessed February 8, 2017, https://www.cbp.gov/sites/default/files/documents/2014%20IPR%20Stats.pdf.

290 **$461 billion of fake goods:** OECD (Organisation for Co-operation and Development), "Global Trade in Fake Goods Worth Nearly Half a Trillion Dollars a Year—OECD & EUIPO," April 18, 2016, https://www.oecd.org/industry/global-trade-in-fake-goods-worth-nearly-half-a-trillion-dollars-a-year.htm.

290 **Beastmode 2.0 Royale Chukkah:** John Brownlee, "How Sneaker Designers Are Busting Knock-Offs with Bitcoin Tech," *Fast Company*, June 3, 2016, https://www.fastcodesign.com/3060459/how-sneaker-designers-are-busting-knockoffs-with-bitcoin-tech.

290 **Overstock became the first:** Cade Metz, "The Grand Experiment Goes Live: Overstock.com Is Now Accepting Bitcoins," *Wired*, January 9, 2014, https://www.wired.com/2014/01/overstock-bitcoin-live.

290 **$25 million in corporate bonds:** Cade Metz, "Overstock Will Issue a Private Bond Powered by Bitcoin Tech," *Wired*, June 5, 2015, https://www.wired.com/2015/06/overstock-will-issue-private-bond-powered-bitcoin-tech.

290 **in June of 2015:** Overstock.com, "Overstock.com Launches Offering of World's First Cryptosecurity," June 5, 2015, http://investors.overstock.com/phoenix.zhtml?c=131091&p=irol-newsArticle&ID=2056957.

290 **In March of 2016:** Overstock.com, "Overstock.com Announces Historic Blockchain Public Offering," March 16, 2016, http://investors.overstock.com/mobile.view?c=131091&v=203&d=1&id=2148979.

291 **reducing settlement risk exposure by over 90%:** Nasdaq, "Nasdaq Linq Enables First-Ever Private Securities Issuance Documented with Blockchain Technology," December 30, 2015, http://ir.nasdaq.com/releasedetail.cfm?releaseid=948326.

291 **When Ornua, an Irish agricultural food company:** Jemima Kelly, "Barclays Says Conducts First Blockchain-Based Trade-Finance Deal," *Reuters*, September 7, 2016, http://www.reuters.com/article/us-banks-barclays-blockchain-idUSKCN11D23B.

294 **"A broad statement of the key idea":** Nick Szabo, "Smart Contracts: Building Blocks for Digital Markets," Alamut, 1996, http://www.alamut.com/subj/economics/nick_szabo/smartContracts.html.

295 **"a decentralized platform":** Ethereum, accessed February 8, 2017, https://www.ethereum.org.

295 **In a 2012 onstage conversation:** The Well, "Topic 459: State of the World 2013: Bruce Sterling and Jon Lebkowsky," accessed February 8, 2017, http://www.well.com/conf/inkwell.vue/topics/459/State-of-the-World-2013-Bruce-St-page01.html.

296 **"What will the world that they create look like?":** Alexis C. Madrigal, "Bruce Sterling on Why It Stopped Making Sense to Talk about 'The Internet' in 2012," *Atlantic*, December 27, 2012, https://www.theatlantic.com/technology/archive/2012/12/bruce-sterling-on-why-it-stopped-making-sense-to-talk-about-the-internet-in-2012/266674.

296 **the five companies he had named:** Will Oremus, "Tech Companies Are Dominating the Stock Market as Never Before," *Slate*, July 29, 2016, http://www.slate.com/blogs/moneybox/2016/07/29/the_world_s_5_most_valuable_companies_apple_google_microsoft_amazon_facebook.html.

296 **surveys conducted by the public relations firm Edelman:** Edelman, "2016 Edelman Trust Barometer," accessed February 9, 2017, http://www.edelman.com/

insights/intellectual-property/2016-edelman-trust-barometer/state-of-trust/trust-in-financial-services-trust-rebound.

296   **"Decentralize All the Things":** Jon Evans, "Decentralize All the Things!" Tech-Crunch, January 10, 2015, https://techcrunch.com/2015/01/10/decentralize-all-the-things.

297   **"an intellectual pathology":** Evgeny Morozov, "The Perils of Perfection," *New York Times*, March 2, 2013, http://www.nytimes.com/2013/03/03/opinion/sunday/the-perils-of-perfection.html.

297   **"proud solutionist since 1994":** Peter Sims, "How Andreessen Horo-witz Is Disrupting Silicon Valley," Silicon Guild, September 5, 2014, https://thoughts.siliconguild.com/how-andreessen-horowitz-is-disrupting-silicon-valley-208041d6375d#.jguk1gbxx.

298   **"Corporate forces have captured":** Don Tapscott and Alex Tapscott, *Blockchain Revolution: How the Technology behind Bitcoin Is Changing Money, Business, and the World* (New York: Portfolio, 2016).

Chapter 13
ARE COMPANIES PASSÉ? (HINT: NO)

302   **At 9:00 a.m. GMT:** The DAO, "Introduction to the DAO," last modified June 29, 2016, https://daowiki.atlassian.net/wiki/display/DAO/Introduction+to+the+DAO.

302   **"The DAO":** Will Dunn, "The Rise and Fall of The DAO, the First Code-Based Company," NS Tech, July 22, 2016, http://tech.newstatesman.com/feature/dao-code-based-company.

303   **"paradigm shift" that could "offer new opportunities":** Seth Bannon, "The Tao of 'The DAO' or: How the Autonomous Corporation Is Already Here," TechCrunch, May 16, 2016, https://techcrunch.com/2016/05/16/the-tao-of-the-dao-or-how-the-autonomous-corporation-is-already-here.

303   **"entrepreneurs of the future":** Joanna Belbey, "How to Invest in the Institutional Revolution of Blockchain," *Forbes*, January 18, 2017, http://www.forbes.com/sites/joannabelbey/2017/01/18/how-to-invest-in-the-institutional-revolution-of-blockchain/2/#5807c7603890.

303   **Real money:** Giulio Prisco, "The DAO Raises More than $117 Million in World's Largest Crowdfunding to Date," *Bitcoin Magazine*, May 16, 2016, https://bitcoinmagazine.com/articles/the-dao-raises-more-than-million-in-world-s-largest-crowdfunding-to-date-1463422191.

303   **$162 million:** The DAO, "Introduction."

303   **Shortly before The DAO's funding window closed:** Nathaniel Popper, "Paper Points Up Flaws in Venture Fund Based on Virtual Money," *New York Times*, May 27, 2016, https://www.nytimes.com/2016/05/28/business/dealbook/paper-points-up-flaws-in-venture-fund-based-on-virtual-money.html.

303 **"We discuss these attacks":** Dino Mark, Vlad Zamfir, and Emin Gün Sirer, "A Call for a Temporary Moratorium on 'The DAO,'" Draft (v0.3.2), last modified May 30, 2016, https://docs.google.com/document/d/10kTyCmGPhvZy 94F7VWyS-dQ4lsBacR2dUgGTtV98C40.

304 **The anonymous hacker:** Nathaniel Popper, "A Hacking of More than $50 Million Dashes Hopes in the World of Virtual Currency," *New York Times*, June 17, 2016, https://www.nytimes.com/2016/06/18/business/dealbook/hacker -may-have-removed-more-than-50-million-from-experimental-cybercurrency -project.html.

304 **Daniel Krawisz:** Daniel Krawisz, LinkedIn profile, accessed February 7, 2017, https://www.linkedin.com/in/daniel-krawisz-323bb121.

304 **The Nakamoto Institute's withering assessment:** Daniel Krawisz, "Ethereum Is Doomed," Satoshi Nakamoto Institute, June 20, 2016, http://nakamotoinstitute .org/mempool/ethereum-is-doomed.

304 **"hard fork":** E. J. Spode, "The Great Cryptocurrency Heist," *Aeon*, February 14, 2017, https://aeon.co/essays/trust-the-inside-story-of-the-rise-and-fall-of-ethereum.

305 **"In [minority members'] view":** Ibid.

305 **"Ethereum Classic":** Ibid.

306 **"The Resolution of the Bitcoin Experiment":** Mike Hearn, "The Resolution of the Bitcoin Experiment," *Mike's blog*, January 14, 2016, https://blog.plan99.net/ the-resolution-of-the-bitcoin-experiment-dabb30201f7#.rvh0ditgj.

306 **"It has failed because the community has failed":** Ibid.

306 **the performance of the Bitcoin system suffered:** Daniel Palmer, "Scalability Debate Continues as Bitcoin XT Proposal Stalls," CoinDesk, January 11, 2016, http://www.coindesk.com/scalability-debate-bitcoin-xt-proposal-stalls.

306 **Chinese exchanges accounted for 42%:** Nathaniel Popper, "How China Took Center Stage in Bitcoin's Civil War," *New York Times*, June 29, 2016, https:// www.nytimes.com/2016/07/03/business/dealbook/bitcoin-china.html.

306 **an estimated 70% of all Bitcoin-mining gear:** Danny Vincent, "We Looked inside a Secret Chinese Bitcoin Mine," *BBC News*, May 4, 2016, http://www.bbc.com/ future/story/20160504-we-looked-inside-a-secret-chinese-bitcoin-mine.

308 **"a kid in Africa with a smartphone":** Brandon Griggs, "Futurist: We'll Someday Accept Computers as Human," CNN, March 12, 2012, http://www .cnn.com/2012/03/12/tech/innovation/ray-kurzweil-sxsw.

309 **"The Nature of the Firm":** R. H. Coase, "The Nature of the Firm," *Economica* 4, no. 16 (1937): 386–405, http://www.richschwinn.com/richschwinn/ index/teaching/past%20courses/Econ%20340%20-%20Managerial%20 Economics/2013%20Fall%20340%20-%20The%20Nature%20of%20the%20 Firm.pdf.

311 **"Electronic Markets and Electronic Hierarchies":** Thomas W. Malone, Joanne Yates, and Robert I. Benjamin, "Electronic Markets and Electronic Hierarchies," *Communications of the ACM* 30, no. 6 (June 1987): 484–97.

312 **893 different US industries:** "Corporate Concentration," *Economist*, March 24, 2016, http://www.economist.com/blogs/graphicdetail/2016/03/daily-chart-13.

312 **As we wrote in 2008:** Andrew McAfee and Erik Brynjolfsson, "Investing in the IT That Makes a Competitive Difference," *Harvard Business Review* 86, no. 7/8 (2008): 98.

314 **Sandy Grossman and Oliver Hart asked:** Sanford J. Grossman and Oliver D. Hart, "The Costs and Benefits of Ownership: A Theory of Vertical and Lateral Integration," *Journal of Political Economy* 94, no. 4 (1986): 691–719.

321 **According to the Bureau of Labor Statistics:** US Bureau of Labor Statistics, "Occupational Employment Statistics," accessed March 11, 2017, https://www.bls.gov/oes/tables.htm.

321 **economist David Deming published an intriguing study:** David J. Deming, *The Growing Importance of Social Skills in the Labor Market*, NBER Working Paper 21473 (August 2015), http://www.nber.org/papers/w21473.

321 **He found that "social skill task inputs":** Ibid.

322 **"transmission belts":** Paul Osterman, *The Truth about Middle Managers: Who They Are, How They Work, Why They Matter* (Boston: Harvard Business School Press, 2009).

322 **"It is inconceivable":** Quoted in Jonathan Haidt, *The Righteous Mind: Why Good People Are Divided by Politics and Religion* (New York: Vintage Books, 2012), 237.

324 **"Oliver did the experiment":** Vishal Makhijani, interview by the authors, August 2015.

324 **"I just said, 'That sounds pretty cool'":** Ibid.

325 *Wall Street Journal* **technology columnist Christopher Mims points out:** Christopher Mims, "Data Is the New Middle Manager," *Wall Street Journal*, April 19, 2015, https://www.wsj.com/articles/data-is-the-new-middle-manager-1429478017.

Conclusion
ECONOMIES AND SOCIETIES BEYOND COMPUTATION

332 **Wages have shrunk as a share of GDP:** For median wages in the United States: Drew DeSilver, "For Most Workers, Real Wages Have Barely Budged for Decades," Pew Research Center, October 9, 2014, http://www.pewresearch.org/fact-tank/2014/10/09/for-most-workers-real-wages-have-barely-budged-for-decades. For share of labor in the OECD: "Workers' Share of National Income: Labour Pains," *Economist*, October 31, 2013, https://www.economist.com/news/finance-and-economics/21588900-all-around-world-labour-losing-out-capital-labour-pains.

332 **"about half of all the activities":** James Manyika et al., "Harnessing Automation for a Future That Works," McKinsey Global Institute, January 2017, http://www.mckinsey.com/global-themes/digital-disruption/harnessing-automation-for-a-future-that-works.

ACKNOWLEDGMENTS

Writing this book began as a highly social activity and ended as an intensely solitary one. Over the past three years we've spoken about the second machine age in front of well over 100,000 people, and we've had hundreds of conversations on the topic. We've given talks at academic, industry, government, and nonprofit conferences; met with elected officials, policy makers, management teams and boards of directors, educators, investors, and philanthropists; and participated in workshops with all types of wonks and geeks.

It's impossible for us to remember all of these events, let alone to thank all their organizers. But a couple stand out. Klaus Schwab and his colleagues have been including us in the World Economic Forum's annual meeting in Davos, Switzerland, for a few years now, which might be the event with the greatest hallway conversations ever. Its main rival in this regard is TED, where we both gave main-stage talks in 2013 and have been attending ever since. TED's curator, Chris Anderson (a different Chris Anderson from the 3D Robotics CEO we interviewed for this book), and his team bring together in Vancouver a group so rich in ideas that any of the audience members could easily be a speaker. We're fortunate to be part of that community.

At our professional home of MIT, Frank Levy organized for several years a superb academic seminar. It brought together many of the institute's top scientists, engineers, economists, and business scholars to learn from each other about the current state of technological progress and its economic and social implications. The label "cross-disciplinary" in academia is much like "world-class" in business: it signals aspiration much more often than reality. But Levy actually succeeded in convincing a group of busy people from throughout MIT to come together regularly. It's an impressive accomplishment, and one we've tried to carry on in the seminar series we organize at the MIT Sloan School of Management and a series of workshops we organized from 2014 to 2017. We're hugely grateful to all the people who have accepted our invitation to present there. Our book can't do justice to the insights we gleaned from the many stimulating conversations and presentations we had a chance to hear, but we're fortunate that MIT provides us an unparalleled hub for this invisible network of thinkers.

Conferences and seminars put a lot of ideas into our heads. To test, sharpen, and refine them, we needed to have more focused conversations with as many of our favorite alpha geeks as possible. So we made appointments in Cambridge, New York, London, San Francisco, Silicon Valley, Washington, DC, and other places, and set out. In addition to the interviewees who are quoted in this book, many others taught us a lot:

Daron Acemoglu
Susan Athey
David Autor
Jeff Bezos
Nick Bloom
Christian Catalini
Michael Chui
Paul Daugherty
Tom Davenport

Tom Friedman

Demis Hassabis

Reid Hoffman

Jeremy Howard

Dean Kamen

Andy Karsner

Christine Lagarde

Yann LeCun

Shane Legg

John Leonard

David Lipton

Tom Malone

James Manyika

Kristina McElheren

Tom Mitchell

Elon Musk

Ramez Naam

Tim O'Reilly

Gill Pratt

Francesa Rossi

Daniela Rus

Stuart Russell

Eric Schmidt

Mustafa Suleyman

Max Tegmark

Sebastian Thrun

But you can put off writing for only so long. After we had talked to a lot of people, and to each other a fair amount, it was time to put words on paper. This is an unavoidably solitary and strangely time-consuming activity. While it was going on, we needed our colleagues to carry on the work of the MIT Initiative on the Digital Economy. And they did, with more flair and tenacity than we had any right to expect. Joanne Batziotegos, Tammy Buzzell, Devin Wardell Cook, Shannon Farrelly, Christie Ko, Adjovi Koene, Justin Lockenwitz, and Susan Young maintained both high output and high standards, and continued to work with all of our stakeholders.

Of these stakeholders, we are particularly grateful to the individuals, companies, and foundations that provide financial support to the IDE. They're too numerous to list (which is a good sign), but we deeply appreciate all of them. Accenture has been the IDE's largest supporter, and a great partner in helping us define and execute our research agenda. Accenture believes, as we do, that digitization is a major force reshaping the business world now and into the future, and it is a pleasure to work with and learn from its team.

While the writing was going on, Lisa McMullen, Joan Powell, Esther Simmons, and Sue Welch kept Andy sane and focused, Mandla Nkosi kept his body at least as sound as his mind, and his friends and family tolerated his tunnel vision and got him out once in a while. Shai Horowitz, Yael Marzan, and Atad Peled provided research assistance and both thought- and fact-checking over three successive academic years. And just as the pressure to complete the manuscript really started to build, serendipity intervened in the form of Jonathan Ruane, a Fulbright scholar and recent graduate of MIT's Sloan Fellows program who was looking for interesting projects to work on while he figured out his next career move. Jonathan had read *The Second Machine Age* and taken Erik's MBA course, and he wanted to know if we needed help with anything. Yes, yes, we did. Jonathan dug in and demonstrated doggedness, initiative, and a keen mind as he chased down statistics, found compelling illustrations of points we were trying to make, and pushed our thinking in several areas. This book is immeasurably better (and done on time) because of him.

Erik benefited immensely from the help of his students and research team, who not only provided solutions to many of the puzzles that emerged as we worked on this book, but more important, asked the questions that occur only to people who look at problems with fresh eyes, including especially: Sagit Bar-Gill, Andrey Fradkin, Avi Gannamaneni, Shan Huang, Meng Lui, JooHee Oh, Daniel Rock, Guillaume Saint-Jacques, George Westerman, and Erina Ytsma. A few hundred students in Erik's MBA classes served as lively test subjects for many of the nascent ideas that made it into the book, and many more that didn't. Professors Marshall Van Alstyne, Geoff Parker, and Jean Tirole were particularly helpful in thinking through some of the issues relating to platform economics, while Naomi Stephen provided superb administrative support. Erik drew inspiration from ShaoLan Hsueh's encouragement as the project neared completion. He is especially grateful to his family's support throughout this project, even as it kept him away from them too often.

When the manuscript was finished(-ish) we turned it over to Norton. Because we'd published *The Second Machine Age* with them, we knew what we were in for at this point, and we knew it would be good. Brendan Curry once again edited the manuscript with his deft combination of sure eye and light touch. Copy editor Stephanie Hiebert's remarkable attention to detail made the final version tight and clean (any errors you've encountered happened despite her involvement, and because of ours), and Nathaniel Dennett provided invaluable help in bringing all the pieces together into the for-real book you're now at the end of. Our literary agent and consigliere Raphael Sagalyn was around and involved at the start, middle, and completion of the process. His interest in our work has always been laughably out of proportion to his commission, and we remain gobsmacked that he called us out of the blue one day years ago and told us to become full-fledged book writers. We were just smart enough to listen.

Finally, we especially want to thank, once again, our friend and colleague David Verrill. He launched the IDE with us and keeps it humming and growing while we write books. He provides an ongoing demonstration of how to deal with academic peculiarities, sponsor demands, and human foibles while never losing either composure or good cheer. We have no idea how he does it and would be lost without him.

Many thanks to all of you.

INDEX